Models, Methods and Decision Support for Management

Professor Dr. Paul Stähly

Peter Kischka · Ulrike Leopold-Wildburger
Rolf H. Möhring · Franz-Josef Radermacher
(Editors)

Models, Methods and Decision Support for Management

Essays in Honor of Paul Stähly

With 57 Figures and 35 Tables

Springer-Verlag Berlin Heidelberg GmbH

Professor Dr. Peter Kischka
University of Jena
Lehrstuhl für Wirtschafts-
und Sozialstatistik
Carl-Zeiss-Straße 3
07743 Jena
Germany
p.kischka@wiwi.uni-jena.de

Professor Dr.
Ulrike Leopold-Wildburger
University of Graz
Institut für Statistik
und Operations Research
Universitätsstraße 15
8010 Graz
Austria
ulrike.leopold@kfunigraz.ac.at

Professor Dr. Rolf H. Möhring
Technical University of Berlin
Fachbereich Mathematik
Straße des 17. Juni 136
10623 Berlin
Germany
moehring@math.tu-berlin.de

Professor Dr. Dr.
Franz-Josef Radermacher
University of Ulm
Forschungsinstitut für
Anwendungsorientierte
Wissensverarbeitung
Helmholtzstraße 16
89081 Ulm
Germany
radermacher@faw.uni-ulm.de

ISBN 978-3-7908-1373-9 ISBN 978-3-642-57603-4 (eBook)
DOI 10.1007/ 978-3-642-57603-4

Cataloging-in-Publication Data applied for
Die Deutschen Bibliothek – CIP-Einheitsaufnahme
Models, methods and decision support for management: essays in honor of Paul Stähly; with 35 tables / Peter Kischka ... (ed.). – Heidelberg; New York: Physica-Verl., 2001
ISBN 978-3-7908-1373-9

Originally published by Physica-Verlag Heidelberg New York in 2001

Softcover design: Erich Kirchner, Heidelberg

SPIN 10792895 88/2202-5 4 3 2 1 0 – Printed on acid-free paper

Preface

This title represents an ambitious undertaking, namely a broad view on the nature of intelligent decision making, which is characterized by the use of models and methods in the framework of decision support for management. With this title we want to reflect the scope of our field, but, at the same time, honor our colleague Paul Stähly on the occasion of his 65th birthday. Paul Stähly has over decades invested his energy in developing the area of Operations Research from such a broad point of view. He has done this not only at his chairs at the HSG / University of St. Gallen and the University of Linz, but also on a broad international level as editor of ITOR and as influential member of all the Operations Research societies in the German speaking countries. He has, in particular, enriched our area by application-oriented research and industrial projects in fields such as logistics, emergency planning, finance, and others, and he was pivotal in strengthening the cooperation between the national and international OR societies, particular in the German speaking area.

Consequently, many colleagues who partly cooperated very closely with him, have contributed to this monograph. Some of these contributions have been presented at a colloquium in January 2001 in St. Gallen in honor of Paul Stähly. This colloquium was attended by many colleagues coming from Germany, Austria, Switzerland, Italy and even from the United States. The contributions at the colloquium and in this monograph reflect the research interests of Paul Stähly and cover a broad scope of topics. We have organized them into three sections on optimization, OR models, and decision support. The reader will benefit from the multitude of views and approaches and will certainly enjoy the many applications. We thank all the authors for their contributions and also Dr. Werner A. Müller from Springer Verlag for his support in publishing this volume in Physica Verlag's program.

We hope that this book will serve as an example for the huge potential of Operations Research, and as a visible sign of the broad communication between science and society. We would like to dedicate it to Paul Stähly as a recognition for his positive influence and all his achievements in the field. We wish him all the best for the future !

Peter KISCHKA
Ulrike LEOPOLD-WILDBURGER
Rolf H. MÖHRING
Franz-Josef RADERMACHER

Contents

Research and Applied Projects at Paul Stähly's Institute for Operations Research

Andreas Klose
Institute for Operations Research
University of St. Gallen, Switzerland

Abstract

This paper gives a short overview on the history of the Institute of Operations Research at the University St. Gallen and the research as well as applied projects initiated and supervised by Paul Stähly. Some selected projects are described in more detail.

1 Introduction

I started to work for Paul Stähly's Institute for Operations Research at the end of the year 1989. Since this time, I was primarily engaged in research and applied projects in the field of logistics. Talking only about this period and the projects I have been involved, however, means to neglect large parts of Paul Stähly's tremendous work. Although the only one who is able to tell the whole story is Paul Stähly itself, I will at least try to briefly depict the institute's history and the work which has been carried out in section 2 and to sketch out some selected projects in more detail in section 3. Finally, section 4 comments on some factors characterising our common work at the Institute for Operations Research.

2 Brief history of the institute

Paul Stähly founded the Institute for Operations Research (IfU-HSG) at the University of St. Gallen (HSG) at the beginning of the eighties. The institute started its work on January 1, 1981, with three scientific collaborators and one teaching assistent. Due to Paul Stähly's success in acquiring projects, however, the institute quickly grew up to a size of more than 20 collaborators.

The institute emerged from a research department for operational research, which was part of the Institute of Management at the University of St. Gallen. It has to be noted that the institutes at the University of St. Gallen have a special status. On one hand, the institutes are integral parts of the university and linked with the HSG conceptionally and on a personnel level, as they are managed by HSG professors. On the other hand, the institutes have far-reaching autonomy and entrepreneurial freedom. In order to finance an institute's research it is, therefore, necessary to acquire additional funding from public and private firms and to supply additional services; fundings from research or science foundations are usually not sufficient. Accordingly, the structure of the IfU-HSG resembles the structure of a private firm; organs of the institute are the advisory committee, the supervising board, and the board of directors. The advisory committee, whose members are Swiss personages from science, industry and government, advises and supports the institute; the supervising board defines strategic goals and guidelines for the activities of the institute; finally, the director is the responsible executive manager and plans, organises, directs and coordinates the work of the staff members (see IfU-HSG, 1980). The main tasks of the institute were derived from a common definition of operational research and comprise (see IfU-HSG, 1980)

- research on operational research models and methods for solving complex problems arising in the management of systems in industry, business and government;
- imparting acquired knowledge and insights to practice;
- teaching and training in the field of empirical research in economics and operational research.

The independence of the institutes at the University of St. Gallen allows considerable freedom in defining goals and major working fields. On one hand, an institute at the HSG may, therefore, offer consulting services and courses for managers to a large extend, or be primarily engaged in fundamental and applied research on the other hand; additional services are then supplied in order to finance the research activities. Paul Stähly has chosen the latter way; profits earned were used for further education of staff members and to build a reserve allowing staff members to finish a Phd thesis and guaranteeing that staff members can be further employed even in the case of bad years. The support of the staff members was a primary concern of Paul Stähly and stated as an explicit goal in a paper on the institute's guidelines (IfU-HSG, 1987); most former members of the institute are today successful in industry, business, government and universities (see the appendix).

Although Paul Stähly's main research interests are simulation models and methods, research at the institute never did focus solely on a single topic. He has a flair for interesting and promising new developments in operations research and their use in applications in order to support (better) decision making. Research and applied projects at the institute covered, therefore, a broad range of methods (linear programming, decomposition, nonlinear programming, simulation, combinatorial optimisation, inventory theory, statistical methods and econometrics, queueing theory, stochastic programming, techniques from artificial intelligence) and application areas (national economy, military, insurance, location planning, logistics in general, inventory management, finance, production planning and scheduling, health care and health economics). The following is a (incomplete) list of projects carried out at the institute (see Ifu-HSG, 1981–1999):

- development of a decision support system for the Swiss Federal Office of National Economic Supply (Kränzlin and Stähly, 1983; Stähly, 1983; Schmid and Stähly, 1987; Stähly, 1987b);
- integrated planning and development of decomposition algorithms for linear programs (Stähly, 1984; Frauendorfer, 1985; Stähly, 1985; Frauendorfer *et al.*, 1995);
- implementation of simulation tools for public administration;
- conception of a management, control and billing system for a food retailer;
- design of a tool for supporting decision making of a bank regarding credits and loans;
- construction of a simulation model for a services enterprise analysing the impacts of changes in demand, competition, cost factors, etc. on profits, solvency ratio and capital cover;
- development and implementation of heuristics for machine scheduling problems of a Swiss manufacturer;
- construction of a simulation model for an insurance company predicting car production and traffic volume and simulating traffic accidents as well as the volume and composition of damages;
- research on methods for determining internal interest rates for a large Swiss bank;
- development of a simulation system for hospitals (Sperry and Stähly, 1985, 1986; Stähly, 1988; Dunant and Stähly, 1992);
- research on ellipsoid algorithms for solving quadratic programming problems arising in marketing (Stähly, 1987a);
- research on expert systems and knowledge-based systems applied in the field of market research;

- extension of the hospital simulation model to a model system analysing a complete hospitalisation region with an emphasis on manageing disasters and mass accidents (Stähly, 1989, 1991; Scharplatz, 1993; Stähly, 1994);
- research by order of a large Swiss bank on instruments for risk measurement and risk analysis of fixed-interest securities as well as development of a tool determining partial risk-neutralising portfolios in dependence on estimated interest rate structures (Deppner and Kischka, 1992; Deppner, 1992);
- development of a financial decision support system for a multinational company (Häuser, 1991);
- implementation of a software system administrating and evaluating security stocks of a large Swiss bank;
- development of a risk management system for a large Swiss bank (Kopp, 1992a,b, 1993; Mayrhofer, 1992);
- design and implementation of a budgeting system for a multinational company;
- research on variance reduction methods and perturbation analysis in simulation (Geiselhart and Kischka, 1992; Geiselhart *et al.*, 1992; Geiselhart and Tüshaus, 1993; Geiselhart, 1993);
- applied research in the field of computer-integrated manufacturing (conception of PPS-systems for a small and medium enterprise as well as development of a simulation program for production planning and scheduling);
- research on multi-objective optimisation models and methods for production control and scheduling problems based on multi-attributive utility theory for eliciting preference structures (Königsperger, 1997);
- development of a decision support system, which determines a Swiss bank's strategies for re-financing mortgages by means of stochastic programming techniques;
- conception and development of tools for supporting the cash-management of a Swiss insurance company;
- development and implementation of heuristic and interactive solution approaches to multi-Weber problems and p-median problems (Bönchendorf *et al.*, 1992; Stähly, 1995);
- research on exact and heuristic solution methods for p-median problems and generalised uncapacitated facility location problems (Klose, 1993, 1995a, 1998a);

- development of improved decomposition approaches for capacitated facility location problems (Wentges, 1993, 1994a,b, 1996, 1997);
- research on methods for estimating delivery costs in problems of combined location and routeing (Klose and Tüshaus, 1995; Klose and Wittmann, 1995; Tüshaus, 1995; Klose, 1996);
- development of heuristic solution approaches to combined location-routeing problems arising in two-stage distributions systems (Bruns and Klose, 1995, 1996; Bruns, 1998);
- research on solutions methods for two-stage capacitated facility location problems (Klose, 1995b, 1998b, 1999, 2000);
- location and distribution planning for a large Swiss brewery;
- location and distribution planning for a large Swiss food producer (Tüshaus and Wittmann, 1997, 1998; Klose and Stähly, 1997, 1998);
- planning the locations of transshipment points of a Swiss distributor of kiosk products;
- planning the locations of training centers for the Office of Civil Protection;
- location and distribution planning for a Swiss producer of dairy products (Engeler *et al.*, 1999a,b);
- location and transportation planning for the public Swiss parcel delivery services (Bruns *et al.*, 2000);
- research on methods for performance analysis and optimisation of safety stocks in multi-stage inventory systems with decentralised control (Tüshaus and Wahl, 1997b,a; Tüshaus and Wahl, 1998; Wahl, 1999);
- inventory and distribution planning for a Swiss company dealing at the travel retail business;
- development of a platform-independent and internet-based data base and simulation system for the Swiss Disaster Relief Authority.

Unfortunately, it is not possible to comment on all the projects above. The next section gives some more details on selected families of projects. The first two ones are the most ambitious and largest projects conducted at the institute, and different teams were working on them for years. The next two ones were chosen, since they cover logistics topics.

3 Selected research and applied projects

3.1 National economic supply

In a working market-based economic system sufficient supply of energy, raw and intermediate materials, food, clothing, and medicine is readily available. The system of free competion may be, however, seriously disrupted in cases such as the event of flood, drought, boycott, embargo or armed conflict in countries rich in raw materials. In case of such an event, special steps have to be undertaken in order to guarantee sufficient supply of vitally necessary goods and services. In Switzerland this is the task of the Federal Office for National Economic Supply. Depending on the type of a crises, the government may intervene in the supply of essential goods and, for example, encourage imports, release compulsary stocks or redirect such stocks in order to increase home production. Such measures must be used in an effective way in order to guarantee sufficient supply and to keep prices at a reasonable level. Since the foundation of the institute, Paul Stähly and his staff were working on management systems supporting the planning of adequate measures as well as decision-making required to deal with crises situations. The development of a decision support system appropriate for this purpose is a very challenging task, since it requires not only to model a national economy's key sectors and their interrelationsships but also to consider international trade and relations in detail. The developed model focusses on energy supply and considers key sectors as engery markets and energy production, transport markets, labor markets, and manufacturing of important industrial products. Input-output analysis is used for the purpose of modelling product/material flows and interdependence structures; optimised and coordinated plans are derived by means of decomposition methods for large linear programs; finally, simulation methods are employed in order to analyse the impacts of certain decisions and scenarios, for example energy bottlenecks, on total economic supply (Kränzlin and Stähly, 1983; Stähly, 1983; Schmid and Stähly, 1987; Stähly, 1987b).

3.2 Simulation systems for medical emergency care

Perhaps one of the most important achievements of Paul Stähly and his institute was the development of a large simulation-based decision support system for medical emergency care and crises management.

The system was developed in a series of research and applied projects starting in the early eighties with a research project on simulation models and tools for a single hospital (Sperry and Stähly, 1985, 1986; Stähly, 1988; Dunant and Stähly, 1992). The hospital model addresses the activities and processes in a hospital related to patients and medical attendance. The system considers different types of patients and injuries calling for different treatment functions. For a patient with an established diagnosis, however, several treatments are possible depending on the type of hospital, a temporary overload of the hospital and the patient's condition. The applied treatment processes compete for available and possibly scarce resources as hospital staff, materials, beds, mobile installations, internal transport facilities, etc. The availability of resources determines the duration of treatment and, depending on the type of injury, the survival probability. The model is suited for analysing extreme situations as disasters with mass casualties when far too many patients will arrive at once; the model aims at finding ways to improve hospital organisation, operational processes and a hospital's infrastructure for better coping with such situations.

In the early nineties the hospital model was further extended to a simulation tool analysing medical care functions in case of disasters and catastrophes (Stähly, 1989, 1991; Scharplatz, 1993; Stähly, 1994). This is accomplished by also considering external transport infrastructures and transport resources as well as different transport strategies and the assignment of patients to hospitals. The model was tested and validated in close corporation with several hospitals from the canton of St. Gallen. The development of the "catastrophe simulation system" was also accompanied by further research on topics as the improve of random number generators (Härtel, 1994), techniques for obtaining reliable results based on manageable sample sizes (Geiselhart, 1993; Koch, 1994), strategies for designing simulation experiments (Rachlitz, 1993), and concepts for developing problem and customer-oriented designed OR-based software systems (Reiff, 1994).

In the last years, the internet has dramatically changed communication and information capabilities. In the last two years, the simulation system was, therefore, extended to a decision support system which applies internet technology and features full access from different computer platforms and different geographical locations. The system does not only provide full access to information about resources needed in disaster situations, but also incorporates further OR methods available in real time for the purpose of providing solutions to decision problems as the routeing of ambulances or the scheduling of actions.

3.3 Location planning

From the end of the eighties until present a number of projects concerned with location planning and methods for solving different location problems were carried out at the institute.

The research in the field of location planning started with a project on heuristics and interactive solution approaches to multi-Weber problems, discrete p-median problems and uncapacitated facility location problems (Bönchendorf *et al.*, 1992; Stähly, 1995; Klose, 1993). For the latter problems, a game theoretic interpretation of the dual problem and visualisations of dual solutions in form of a graph were used for this purpose. The graph representing dual solutions is well suited for illustrating complementary slackness conditions as well as the steps and subproblems arising in primal-dual heuristics for p-median problems and uncapacitated facility location problems. Later on, exact branch-and-bound algorithms for families of uncapacitated and aggregate-capacitated facility location problems were developed and implemented. These methods are based on combining dual ascent approaches and subgradient optimisation for lower bounding and employing intensive Lagrangian probing techniques for the purpose of reducing problem size. This way even larger problems of this type are usually solved exactly in relatively small computation times (Klose, 1993, 1995a, 1998a).

In a following research project, decomposition techniques for solving capacitated facility location problems were investigated. The results obtained are methods for deriving stronger Benders' cuts and methods for improving the convergence of cross decomposition and Dantzig-Wolfe decomposition approaches for the capacitated facility location problem (Wentges, 1993, 1994a,b, 1996). These methods are also applicable to other mixed-integer programs if column generation is employed in order to solve the Lagrangian dual associated with a given Lagrangian relaxation (Wentges, 1997).

A first practical application of the developed methods was a location-allocation problem of a large Swiss brewery. A redesign of the brewery's distribution system was necessary because overcapacities resulted from the merger with another company. In the course of this project we had to learn that data gathering, data consilidation, data validation and the estimation of required cost coefficients are the most difficult and time-consuming tasks arising in practical applications of location planning methods. These experiences induced further research on parametric analysis for location problems (Klose and Stähly, 1997, 1998) as well as on methods for combined location-routeing problems. With high personal efforts, Paul Stähly succeeded in finding industrial partners and setting up a large project concerned with combined location-routeing problems in two-stage distribution problems and supported by the Swiss Commission of Technology and Innovation. In the course of this project, we conducted research on methods for estimating delivery costs in location-routeing problems (Klose and Tüshaus, 1995; Klose and Wittmann, 1995; Tüshaus, 1995; Klose, 1996), on heuristics for solving integrated location-routeing models (Bruns and Klose, 1995, 1996; Bruns, 1998) and on methods for obtaining sharp lower and upper bounds for two-stage capacitated facility location problems with single-source requirements (Klose, 1995b, 1998b, 1999, 2000). Furthermore, the methods developed were applied to a number of practial distribution and location planning problems (Tüshaus and Wittmann, 1997, 1998; Engeler *et al.*, 1999a,b; Bruns *et al.*, 2000).

3.4 Inventory management

Further research in the field of logistics was concerned with strategic inventory positioning in supply chains and inventory control in divergent inventory systems with decentralised control. The difficulty is to derive analytical approximations of effective lead and waiting times and to approximate the distribution of internal demand processes resulting from stochastic consumer demands and the ordering processes at the lower echelons of the system. In a research project funded by the Swiss National Research foundation, numerically attractive expressions for important performance measures as stock on hand, backlog, waiting times, service levels and inventory costs were derived and used for analysing and optimising ordering policies (Tüshaus and Wahl, 1997b,a; Tüshaus and Wahl, 1998; Wahl, 1999).

4 Final comments

When asking former staff members of Paul Stähly's institute what they did appreciate most during their work, they all remember the great experience of an extremely good working atmosphere and deep collegiality. Our cooperation was characterised by open-minded communication and always encouraged by Paul Stähly. Everybody was willing to help each other in any situation and we had a leader we could rely on in any case. The prerequisites for our good collaboration were created by Paul Stähly. Nobody was preferentially treated; administration, teaching and project related tasks were equally distributed among the staff members.

Colleagues leaving the institute were prepared to manage a wide spectrum of highbrow and challenging jobs.

References

Bönchendorf, K., Klose, A., Mayrhofer, H. H., and Stähly, P. (1992). Mensch-Maschine-Kommunikation in der Standortoptimierung. In J. Biethahn, editor, *Simulation als betriebliche Entscheidungshilfe*, volume 3 of *Fortschritte in der Simulationstechnik*, pages 17–35. Springer-Verlag, Berlin, Heidelberg, New York.

Bruns, A., Klose, A., and Stähly, P. (2000). Restructuring of Swiss parcel delivery services. *OR-Spektrum*, **22**, 285–302.

Bruns, A. D. (1998). *Zweistufige Standortplanung unter Berücksichtigung von*

Tourenplanungsaspekten – Primale Heuristiken und lokale Suchverfahren. Dissertation, Universität St. Gallen, Dufourstrasse 50, CH-9000 St. Gallen.

Bruns, A. D. and Klose, A. (1995). An iterative heuristic for location-routing problems based on clustering. Proceedings of the Second International Workshop on Distribution Logistics (IWDL-2).

Bruns, A. D. and Klose, A. (1996). A locate first – route second heuristic for a combined location-routeing problem. In *Operations Reseach Proceedings 1996*, chapter 3, pages 49–54. Springer-Verlag, Berlin, Heidelberg, New York.

Deppner, C. (1992). *Die Schätzung der Zinsstruktur und deren Bedeutung in der Kapitalmarkttheorie: eine empirische Untersuchung auf Basis von multiplen Regressions- und linearen Optimierungsmodellen mit Daten des schweizerischen Rentenmarktes.* Dissertation Nr. 1365, Hochschule St. Gallen, Dufourstrasse 50, CH-9000 St. Gallen.

Deppner, C. and Kischka, P. (1992). Schätzung der Zinsstruktur. In W. R. Heilmann, editor, *Geld, Banken und Versicherungen*, pages 349–457. VVW Karlsruhe.

Derigs, U., Bachem, A., and Drexl, A., editors (1995). *Operations Research Proceedings 1994*, Berlin, Heidelberg, New York. Deutsche Gesellschaft für Operations Research e.V. (DGOR), Springer-Verlag. Selected Papers of the International Conference on Operations Research Berlin, August 30 – September 2, 1994.

Dunant, J. H. and Stähly, P. (1992). Simulation models for the analysis of hospitals with regard to their emergency infrastructure. *Schweiz. Z. Milit. Med.*, **69**, 79–82.

Engeler, K., Klose, A., and Stähly, P. (1999a). A depot location-allocation problem of a food producer with an outsourcing option. In M. G. Speranza and P. Stähly, editors, *New Trends in Distribution Logistics*, volume 480 of *Lecture Notes in Economics and Mathematical Systems*, chapter 1, pages 95–109. Springer-Verlag, Berlin, Heidelberg, New York.

Engeler, K., Klose, A., and Stähly, P. (1999b). Optimierung der Distributionsstruktur eines Schweizer Nahrungsmittelherstellers. In P. Kall and H.-J. Lüthi, editors, *Operations Research Proceedings 1998*, pages 522–531. Springer, Berlin Heidelberg New York.

Fleischmann, B., van Nunen, J. A. E. E., Speranza, M. G., and Stähly, P., editors (1998). *Advances in Distribution Logistics*, volume 460 of *Lecture Notes in Economics and Mathematical Systems.* Springer-Verlag, Berlin, Heidelberg, New York.

Frauendorfer, K. (1985). An applicable decomposition principle. In Ohse *et al.* (1985).

Frauendorfer, K., Koch, B., and Stähly, P. (1995). On the degree of decentralization in large-scale linear programming. In Derigs *et al.* (1995), pages 1–6.

Geiselhart, W. (1993). *Effizientes Simulieren in stochastischen Systemen – Reduktion des Simulationsumfangs mit Methoden der Perturbationsanalyse.* Dissertation Nr. 1432, Hochschule St. Gallen, Dufourstrasse 50, CH-9000 St. Gallen.

Geiselhart, W. and Kischka, P. (1992). Sensitivitätsanalyse in ökonomischen Modellen mit der Perturbationsanalyse. In W. Bühler, G. Feichtinger, R. Hartl, F.-J. Radermacher, and P. Stähly, editors, *Operations Research '90*, pages 181–190, Berlin, Heidelberg, New York. Springer-Verlag.

Geiselhart, W. and Tüshaus, U. (1993). On a new finite perturbation analysis algorithm. In A. Karmann, K. Mosler, M. Schader, and G. Uebe, editors, *Operations Research '92*, 17. Symposium on Operations Research of the Gesellschaft für Mathematik, Ökonomie und Operations Research, Universität der Bundeswehr Hamburg, August 25–28, 1992, pages 223–225. Physica-Verlag, Heidelberg.

Geiselhart, W., Kischka, P., and Tüshaus, U. (1992). Perturbation analysis: Basics for deriving higher order propagation rules. In P. Gritzmann, R. Hettich, R. Horst, and E. Sachs, editors, *Operations Research '91*, 16. Symposium on Operations Research of the Gesellschaft für Mathematik, Ökonomie und Operations Research, Universität Trier, September 9–11, 1991, pages 254–258. Physica-Verlag, Heidelberg.

Härtel, F. (1994). *Zufallszahlen für Simulationsmodelle – Vergleich und Bewertung verschiedener Zufallszahlengeneratoren.* Dissertation nr. 1600, Hochschule St. Gallen, Dufourstrasse 50, CH-9000 St. Gallen.

Häuser, H. (1991). *Konzeption eines OR-gestützten Decision Support Systems für die Finanzplanung einer multinationalen Unternehmung.* Dissertation Nr. 1241, Hochschule St. Gallen, Dufourstrasse 50, CH-9000 St. Gallen.

IfU-HSG (1980). Satzung des Instituts für Unternehmensforschung. published in *Gesetzessammlung des Kantons St. Gallen.*

IfU-HSG (1981–1999). Jahresbericht.

IfU-HSG (1987). Organisationshandmappe.

Klose, A. (1993). *Das kombinatorische p-Median-Modell und Erweiterungen zur Bestimmung optimaler Standorte.* Dissertation Nr. 1464, Hochschule St. Gallen, Dufourstrasse 50, CH-9000 St. Gallen.

Klose, A. (1995a). A comparison between the Erlenkotter algorithm and a branch and bound algorithm based on subgradient optimization to solve the uncapacitated facility location problem. In Derigs *et al.* (1995), pages 335–339.

Klose, A. (1995b). A Lagrangean heuristic to solve the two-stage capacitated facility location problem. Proceedings of the Second International Workshop on Distribution Logistics (IWDL-2).

Klose, A. (1996). Using clustering methods in problems of combined location and routing. In P. Kleinschmidt, A. Bachem, U. Derigs, D. Fischer, U. Leopold-Wildburger, and R. Möhring, editors, *Operations Research Proceedings 1995*, pages 411–416, Berlin, Heidelberg, New York. Deutsche Gesellschaft für Operations Research e.V. (DGOR), Springer-Verlag.

Klose, A. (1998a). A branch and bound algorithm for an uncapacitated facility location problem with a side constraint. *International Transactions in Operational Research*, **5**, 155–168.

Klose, A. (1998b). Obtaining sharp lower and upper bounds for two-stage capacitated facility location problems. In Fleischmann *et al.* (1998), pages 185–214.

Klose, A. (1999). An LP-based heuristic for two-stage capacitated facility location problems. *The Journal of the Operational Research Society*, **50**(2), 157–166.

Klose, A. (2000). A Lagrangean relax-and-cut approach for the two-stage capacitated facility location problem. *European Journal of Operational Research*, **126**(2), 185–198.

Klose, A. and Stähly, P. (1997). Sensitivity analysis in facility location applied to a depot location problem of a food producer. In Zimmermann *et al.* (1997).

Klose, A. and Stähly, P. (1998). Parametric analysis of fixed costs in uncapacitated facility location. In Fleischmann *et al.* (1998), chapter 2, pages 215–240.

Klose, A. and Tüshaus, U. (1995). Abstimmung zwischen strategischer und operationeller Stufe hinsichtlich der Konzipierung der logistischen Infrastruktur und Distributionsabwicklung. Arbeitsbericht, Institut für Unternehmensforschung (Operations Research), Hochschule St. Gallen, Bodanstrasse 6, CH–9000 St. Gallen.

Klose, A. and Wittmann, S. (1995). Facility location based on clustering. Proceedings of the Second International Workshop on Distribution Logistics (IWDL-2).

Koch, B. (1994). *Effiziente Simulation in komplexen stochastischen Modellen – Dimensionierung des Simulationsumfangs unter taktischen Aspekten.* Dissertation nr. 1571, Hochschule St. Gallen, Dufourstrasse 50, CH-9000 St. Gallen.

Königsperger, E. (1997). *Entscheidungsunterstützung bei mehrkriteriellen Problemstellungen und partieller Information.* Dissertation Nr. 2061, Hochschule St. Gallen, Dufourstrasse 50, CH-9000 St. Gallen.

Kopp, U.-C. (1992a). *Quantitatives Risikomanagement in Banken: ein Entscheidungsmodell zum Management der Geschäftsrisiken.* Dissertation Nr. 1374, Hochschule St. Gallen, Dufourstrasse 50, CH-9000 St. Gallen.

Kopp, U.-C. (1992b). Risk management in banks. In P. Gritzmann, R. Hettich, R. Horst, and E. Sachs, editors, *Operations Research '91*, pages 500–504, Heidelberg. Physica-Verlag.

Kopp, U.-C. (1993). Risk management in banks – a stochastic approach. In A. Karmann, K. Mosler, M. Schader, and G. Uebe, editors, *Operations Research '92*, Heidelberg. Physica-Verlag.

Kränzlin, R. and Stähly, P. (1983). Modellkonzepte zur gegenseitigen Abstimmung der verschiedenen Bereiche und Entscheidungsstufen in der wirtschaftlichen Landesvorsorge. In P. Stähly, editor, *Wirtschaftliche Landesvorsorge im Rahmen der Sicherheitspolitik*, pages 201–215. Paul Haupt, Bern Stuttgart.

Mayrhofer, H. H. (1992). *Methodenorientiertes Währungsrisikomanagement.* Dissertation Nr. 1308, Hochschule St. Gallen, Dufourstrasse 50, CH-9000 St. Gallen.

Ohse, D., Esprester, A. C., Küpper, H.-U., Stähly, P., and Steckhan, H., editors (1985). *Operations Research Proceedings 1984*, Berlin, Heidelberg, New York. Deutsche Gesellschaft für Operations Research e.V. (DGOR), Springer-Verlag. Papers of the 13th Annual Meeting.

Rachlitz, B. (1993). *Die Planung von Simulationsexperimenten – Entwicklung und Überprüfung eines Planungsrahmens unter Berücksichtigung von Modell-, Daten- und Rechengenauigkeit.* Dissertation nr. 1480, Hochschule St. Gallen, Dufourstrasse 50, CH-9000 St. Gallen.

Reiff, M. F. (1994). *Entwicklung OR-basierter Softwaresysteme : Konzepte zur problem- und benutzergerechten Gestaltung.* Dissertation nr. 1530, Hochschule St. Gallen, Dufourstrasse 50, CH-9000 St. Gallen.

Scharplatz, D. (1993). Simulationsprogramm zur Analyse der Leistungsfähigkeit von Spitälern und Regionen in Notfallsituationen. *Helv. chir. Acta*, **28**, 807–812.

Schmid, B. and Stähly, P. (1987). Ein Netzwerk von Expertensystemen für die wirtschaftliche Landesversorgung. Arbeitspapiere 87/75, Institut für Wirtschaftsforschung, ETH Zürich.

Sperry, J. and Stähly, P. (1985). Computergestützte Analyse von Spitälern hinsichtlich der Bewältigung von Katastrophen. *Schweizer Spital*, **9**, 11–17.

Sperry, J. and Stähly, P. (1986). Analyse der Infrastruktur von Krankenhäusern hinsichtlich ihres Patienten-Throughputs unter Extrembelastung mit Hilfe der Simulation. In L. Streitferdt, H. Hauptmann, A. W. Marusev, D. Ohse, and U. Pape, editors, *Operations Research Proceedings 1985*, pages 178–183, Berlin, Heidelberg, New York. Deutsche Gesellschaft für Operations Research e.V. (DGOR), Springer-Verlag.

Stähly, P. (1983). Wirtschaftliche Krisenvorsorge. Oberösterreich 2000, Trauner-Verlag Linz.

Stähly, P. (1984). Optimale Koordination in der integrierten Planung. In H. Beran and F. Pichler, editors, *Beiträge zur Systemforschung*. Springer-Verlag, Berlin, Heidelberg, New York.

Stähly, P. (1985). Dekompositionsverfahren und integrierte Planung. In Ohse *et al.* (1985).

Stähly, P. (1987a). Marketing-Mix-Modellierung gestern und heute. *Thexis*, **3**, 12–22.

Stähly, P. (1987b). Zur Versorgung der politischen Entscheidungsträger mit aussagefähigen Informationen für veränderte Entscheidungssituationen. In R. Henn, editor, *Technologie, Wachstum und Beschäftigung (Festschrift für Lothar Späth)*. Springer-Verlag, Berlin, Heidelberg, New York.

Stähly, P. (1988). Simulation models for the analysis of hospitals with regard to their emergency infrastructure. In G. Fandel, editor, *Management Problems in Health Care*, pages 263–296. Springer-Verlag, Berlin, Heidelberg, New York.

Stähly, P. (1989). Simulationsmodelle im Hinblick auf die Bewältigung von medizinischen Notfallsituationen. *Output*, **18**, 17–23.

Stähly, P. (1991). Einsatzplanung für Katastrophenfälle mittels Simulationsmodellen auf der Basis von Simula. In J. Biethahn, editor, *Simulation als betriebliche Entscheidungshilfe*, volume 2 of *Fortschritte in der Simulationstechnik*, pages 81–94. Springer-Verlag, Berlin, Heidelberg, New York.

Stähly, P. (1994). Erste Erfahrungen beim Einsatz eines rechnergestützten St. Galler Modellsystems zur Analyse der Notfallversorgung bei Grossschadenereignissen. In J. Biethahn, editor, *Simulation als betriebliche Entscheidungshilfe*, volume 8 of *Fortschritte in der Simulationstechnik*, pages 34–45. Springer-Verlag, Berlin, Heidelberg, New York.

Stähly, P. (1995). Ein Überblick über einige Modelle der Standortplanung und ihre Implementierung. In Derigs *et al.* (1995), pages 340–345.

Tüshaus, U. (1995). Cost estimation in locational analysis. Proceedings of the Second International Workshop on Distribution Logistics (IWDL-2).

Tüshaus, U. and Wahl, C. (1997a). Cost-efficient control of common distribution system with non-identical warehouses. In P. Kischka, H.-W. Lorenz, U. Derigs, W. Domschke, P. Kleinschmidt, and R. Möhring, editors, *Operations Research Proceedings 1997*, pages 503–508, Berlin, Heidelberg, New York. Deutsche Gesellschaft für Operations Research e.V. (DGOR), Springer-Verlag.

Tüshaus, U. and Wahl, C. (1997b). Holding costs minimization with service level constraints in an arborescent distribution network. In Zimmermann *et al.* (1997), pages 271–276.

Tüshaus, U. and Wahl, C. (1998). Inventory positioning in a two-stage distribution network with service level constraints. In Fleischmann *et al.* (1998), pages 501–532.

Tüshaus, U. and Wittmann, S. (1997). Locating depots for a food producer by solving uncapacitated facility location problems. In Zimmermann *et al.* (1997), pages 508–513.

Tüshaus, U. and Wittmann, S. (1998). Strategic logistic planning by means of simple plant location: A case study. In Fleischmann *et al.* (1998), chapter 2, pages 241–263.

Wahl, C. (1999). *Bestandsmanagement in Distributionssystemen mit dezentraler Disposition.* Dissertation, Universität St. Gallen, Dufourstrasse 50, CH-9000 St. Gallen.

Wentges, P. (1993). On Bender's decomposition for the capacitated facility location problem. In A. Karmann, K. Mosler, M. Schader, and G. Uebe, editors, *Operational Research '92*, Heidelberg. Gesellschaft für Mathematik, Ökonomie und Operations Research (GMÖOR), Physica-Verlag.

Wentges, P. (1994a). Dually weighted cross decomposition for the capacitated facility location problem. In A. Bachem, U. Derigs, M. Jünger, and R. Schrader, editors, *Operational Research '93*, Heidelberg. Physica-Verlag.

Wentges, P. (1994b). *Standortprobleme mit Berücksichtigung von Kapazitätsrestriktionen: Modellierung und Lösungsverfahren.* Dissertation Nr. 1620, Hochschule St. Gallen, Dufourstrasse 50, CH-9000 St. Gallen.

Wentges, P. (1996). Accelerating Benders' decomposition for the capacitated facility location problem. *Mathematical Methods of Operations Research*, **44**, 267–290.

Wentges, P. (1997). Weighted Dantzig-Wolfe decomposition for linear mixed-integer programming. *International Transactions in Operational Research*, 4, 151–162.

Zimmermann, U., Derigs, U., Gaul, W., Möhring, R. H., and Schuster, K.-P., editors (1997). *Operations Research Proceedings 1996*, Berlin, Heidelberg, New York. Deutsche Gesellschaft für Operations Research e.V. (DGOR), Springer-Verlag. Selected Papers of the Symposium on Operations Research (SOR '96) Braunschweig, September 3 – 6, 1996.

Appendix. Former and current staff members of the Institute for Operations Research

The following is a list of former and current staff members (scientific collaborators and student employees). As far as I know it, I have also included where they are working today.

Kim Allemand, 1995–1996, EPFL Lausanne

Thomas Bauer, 1991–1993

Thomas Bergen, 1990–1992, getAbstract.com AG, CEO

Markus Biedermann, 1994–1996

Markus Bisig, 1986–1988, Health-Resort Center Rheinfelden, member of management team

Konrad Bönchendorf, 1988–1992

Christophe Bonvin, 1991–1995, SportAccess Kudelski, F&A Manager

Marco Boscardin, 1984–1987, department for urban development, municipality of Zürich, team leader

Sieglinde Breinbauer, 1987–1988

Arno Diego Bruns, 1994–1998, SAP AG

Christoph Deppner, 1989–1992, Bayrische Handelsbank AG, head of controlling department

Elisabeth Disch, 2000, IfU-HSG

Christian Eggenberger, 1987–1989, IBM Switzerland, Consulting Group

Rainer Eggers, 1997–1999

Andreas Ehrsam, 1991–1992, UBS AG, IT, project manager

Katja Engeler, 1994–1999, IBM Switzerland, Global Services

Heinrich Flückiger, 1995–1997, State Street Bank & Trust Company, Performance & Analytics, assistant of the vice president

Karl Frauendorfer, 1993, professor of Operations Research, University of St. Gallen

Markus Freiburghaus, 1986–1988, Fachhochschule Solothurn, lecturer

Ralf Gaese, 1996–1999

Wolfgang Geiselhart, 1989–1992, Credit Suisse, Luxembourg

Manfred Grollmann, 1997, IfU-HSG

Jens Güssow, 1998, IfU-HSG

Gido Haarbrücker, 1996, IfU-HSG

Veronika Halder, 1999, IfU-HSG

Jürgen Hansohm, 1987–1988, professor of Business Administration, University of the Federal Armed Forces Munich

Frank Härtel, 1991–1995, UBS Warburg, Private Clients-Investment Solutions, financial analyst

Robert Hartl, 1996–1997, Research Institute for Empirical Economics and Economic Policy, University of St. Gallen

Richard Hauser, 1987–1988

Hermann Häuser, 1985–1992, Philips Communication Systems, head financial controlling

Raoul-Thomas Herborg, 1997, IfU-HSG

Markus Herzog, 1993–1994, Swiss Federal Office for Statistics

Bodo Hinz, 1982–1984

Kay Holte, 1996, IfU-HSG

Mark Ineichen, 1994–1995, Otto's Warenposten AG, head of marketing department

Ulrich Jacoby, 2000, IfU-HSG

Alexander Jenny, 1994–1996

Axel Jeromin, 1998, IfU-HSG

Thomas Jürgensen, 1986–1989, KPMG Fides, vice-director

Panagiotis Kakarakis, 1985–1986

Christophe Kipfer, 1988–1988

Thomas Kirchhofer, 1987–1989, Health-Resort Center Rheinfelden, CEO

Peter Kischka, 1988–1990, profesor of Statistics in Economics and Social Sciences , University of Jena

Andreas Klose, 1989, IfU-HSG

Bernd Koch, 1991–1994, Bayrische Hypo- und Vereinsbank, head of asset & liability controlling group

Robert L. Koch, 1981–1985, UBS AG, vice-director

Karl Kohel, 1987–1987

Jerome Koller, 1997, IfU-HSG

Emil Könisperger, 1993–1996, SwissCom

Ulla-Christiane Kopp, 1989–1992, University Witten/Herdecke, member of the management team

Rene Kränzlin, 1981–1983, The Witan Group, managing director

Wilfried M. Kuhn, 1986–1987

Roland Küll, 1995–1997, Cantrade Privatbank AG, project manager

Karl Linowski, 2000, IfU-HSG

Hugo Lucca, 1988–1992, Lucca R&D

Franz R. Ludwig, 1986–1987

Christina Marohn, 1995–1998, CSC Ploenzke AG, Switzerland

Hans Helmut Mayrhofer, 1989–1992, Daimler Chrysler AG, IEV, project manager

Jens Meyer, 1993–1994

Pierre-Yves Moix, 1996–1999, RMF Investment Group, head quantitative analysis

Andea Nist, 1990–1990

Georg Ostermaier, 1998, IfU-HSG

Stefan Ott, 1996–1997

Andreas Pleninger, 1987–1989, 3E Handels- und Dienstleistungs AG, head central services

Bernd Rachlitz, 1990–1993, Macon Bau GmbH, head controlling department

Michael Falko Reiff, 1990–1995, COMIT Financial Systems AG, consultant

Markus Renfer, 1991–1991, Ernst & Young AG, chartered accountant

Reto Renz, 1984–1987, Horvath & Partner AG, CEO

Jean Saccet, 1988–1990

Dominique Salamin, 1986–1989

Maria-Christina Scharf, 1998–1999, Institute for Public Services and Tourism, University of St. Gallen

Robert Schaus, 1988–1989, Bain & Company, Switzerland, vice president & partner

Maria-Lore Scherrer, 1987–1988, Alaxa Consulting Group, authorised representative and project manager

Ivo Schillig, 1988–1990, Schindler Elevators Luzern, CEO

Beat F. Schmid, 1984–1987, professor of Information Management, University of St. Gallen

Olivier Schmid, 1996, IfU-HSG

Christian Schmidt, 1988–1988

Stefan Scholz, 1997–1999

Michael Schürle, 1994–1999, Investment Consulting Group AG, project manager

Stefan Schweickardt, 1996–1997

Heiko Siede, 1996, IfU-HSG

Dirk Solte, 1998, IfU-HSG and FAW-Ulm

Jürg Sperry, 1981–1987, University of St. Gallen, head of organisation department

Adrian Stäger, 1984–1987, owner of a consulting firm

Christian Stäuble, 1995–1996, Medien-Tech & Consulting GmbH, CEO

Detlef Steiner, 1998, IfU-HSG

Stephen Strauss, 1996–1996

Rudolf Suter, 1988–1988, Swiss Life, head of corporate finance/treasury, vice president

Ulrich Tüshaus, 1990–1996, professor of Operations Research, University of the Federal Armed Forces Hamburg

Christian van Gessel, 1988–1991

Peter Vrhovec, 1998, IfU-HSG

Christoph Wahl, 1995–1999, McKinsey & Company, consultant

Michael Wanner, 1996–1996, UBS AG, IC9T, project manager

Patrick Waser, 1995–1999

Paul Wentges, 1991–1994, University of Ulm, Department of Business Administration

Marc Wildi, 1988–1989, Research Institute for Empirical Economics and Economic Policy, University of St. Gallen

Günter Winkler, 1989–1990, Universal-Versand Salzburg, software engineer

Martin Wirth, 1995–1996

Stefan Wittmann, 1994–1997, Investment Consulting Group AG, project manager

Hans-Jürgen Wolter, 1986–1987, Swiss Re Investors, divisional operating officer

Hans Wulkop, 1982–1984, Credit Suisse, product manager, member of the board of directors

David Zumsteg, 1989–1990, Sefar AG, Corporate Marketing, head of corporate marketing and business development

Part 1:

Optimization

Environmental Policy Design and the Economics of Crime: Some Analogies in Intertemporal Optimization

Gustav Feichtinger

Institute for Econometrics, Operations Research and Systems Theory

Vienna University of Technology, Austria

Abstract

Environmental planning and cost-benefit modeling in crime control shows some striking analogies. The purpose of this note is to exploit this fact in an intertemporal framework. In particular, the optimal mix of '*prevention*' and '*treatment*' in pollution control and illicit drug consumption is illustrated by several optimal control and dynamic game models.

Acknowledgement. Thanks are due to Christian Almeder, Doris Behrens, Richard F. Hartl, Peter M. Kort and Franz Wirl for critical comments and valuable suggestions.

1 Introduction

Operational Research methods have been applied to many fields of decision-making and planning. Among those applications are models of environmental planning and the control of criminal behaviour (law enforcement). Although unrelated at the first look, both fields exhibit certain surprising similarities.

We will show that the analogies are particularly strong in an intertemporal context. It is well-known that environmental pollution control represents application of optimal control theory «par excellence». To illustrate that fact we refer to Forster (1977), Dockner and Long (1993), Tahvonen and Withagen (1996), Wirl (1998)[1].

More recently, optimal law enforcement policies have been based on dynamic optimization methods too. Although Becker's seminal approach to the economics of crime was essentially static, it has become clear that a more realistic approach to crime and punishment must include intertemporal aspects too. An optimal control approach for dynamic cost-benefit analysis in illicit drug control has been proposed by Caulkins (1993); compare also Kort et al. (1998), Borisov et al. (1998) as well as Tragler et al. (1997) and Behrens et al. (1997) for more realistic approaches to drug control modeling. A general extension of Becker's approach to a dynamic supply of offenders has been recently given by Feichtinger et al. (1997).

Let us briefly sketch the announced similarity between environment and crime. The state variable is the accumulated stock of pollution on the one hand, and the number of offenders (or offences) on the other hand. Among other instruments influencing the development of the state variable over time there are '*prevention*' and '*treatment*'. In a recent paper, Barrett and Segerson (1997) consider the damage from waste disposal. Preventive measures can be undertaken before contamination occurs, while 'treatment' may be an ex post response. Although these authors restrict themselves to a static decision situation, they are able to study how much an environmental agency should invest in prevention of events that can cause damages (flow abatement) versus investment in treatment to reduce damages if they have already occured (clean-up measures).

About the same time, Behrens et al. (1997) studied the optimal mix of prevention and treatment in a dynamic drug control model. The authors derived very interesting results on the intertemporal trade-off between expenditures for those control instruments and the damage, i.e. social cost, resulting from drug consumption. Among other dynamic cost-benefit properties they showed how the allocation between prevention and treatment should be optimally balanced.

The models we are going to discuss in this note are as simple as possible, since it is not our aim to study realistic situations in optimal law enforcement or environmental planning. The purpose of this paper is rather to stress certain striking analogies in both fields of intertemporal decision making. To illustrate this parallelism we focus on 'cartoons' instead of considering concrete planning situations. However, we are convinced that our preliminary approach may be extended to more concrete policy design and intertemporal decision making.

---

[1] Since environmental quality can be conceived as renewable resource, the intertemporal optimization literature of resource exploitation may also referred to in the present context, i.e. Dasgupta and Heal (1979) and Clark (1976, 1985).

The paper is organized as follows. After this introductory section we present three simple models in sections 2-4. In section 5 a dynamic game between an offender and a preventing agency is briefly analyzed. In Section 6 a two-state optimal control model to design efficient prevention and treatment policies is formulated. Finally, in section 7 we draw some conclusions and refer to several extension.

2 Model 1: Optimal law enforcement or cleaning-up

In one of his seminal papers, Becker (1968) suggested an economic approach to crime and punishment. Essentially, he asked how many resources and how much punishment should be used to enforce different kinds of legislation. The decision instruments are the expenditures on police and courts influencing the probability that an offender is convicted, and the type and size of punishment for those convicted. The goal is to find those expenditures and punishments that minimize the total social loss. This loss is the sum of damages from offences, costs of apprehension and conviction, and costs of carrying out the punishment imposed.

Extending Becker's static approach to a dynamic supply function of offenders, Feichtinger et al. (1997) consider an optimal control model to determine the optimal law enforcement expenditures over time (compare also Feichtinger, 1998). The system dynamics used by the authors (see also Caulkins, 1993) is comparable in some sense to the replicator dynamics described the evolutions of the frequencies on strategies in a population. The solutions are path-dependent optimal policies which are economically meaningful but generally not easy to analyze. Thus, we consider a simpler version (actually the simplest) of the dynamic extension of Becker's economics of crime scenario.

Formulation

Denote by P(t) the number of offenders at time t. By assuming that a representative offender commits a fixed amount of offences per time unit, we may identify the number of offences per time unit with the number of offenders. Let v(t) be the law enforcement rate at that time[2].

---

[2] The enforcement rate transforms the input of manpower, material and capital to a rate of police and court activities (see Becker, 1968).

The damage created by the offenders[3] is denoted by D(P), and C(v) are the law enforcement expenditures. As described in Feichtinger et al. (1997) there are good reasons to specify those functions as quadratic ones, i.e.

$$D(P) = \frac{1}{2}P^2, \quad C(v) = \frac{1}{2}v^2.$$

Note that here and in what follows the time argument is mostly omitted. As already announced, the system dynamics is kept very simple:

$$\dot{P} = \rho - \gamma v. \tag{1}$$

Here we assume a constant initiation rate, $\rho > 0$, of offenders. This input is simply reduced by convictions $\gamma v(t)$ at time t.

An explanation for (1) might be given as follows. Write the system dynamics (1) as

$$\dot{P} = \rho - \gamma\left(\frac{v}{P}\right)P,$$

where $\gamma(.)$ measures the rate by which the offenders are arrested or convicted. It makes sense to assume that this rates depends on the law enforcement outlays per offender, v/P. Although a realistic dependency would assume marginal decreasing efficiency, i.e. $\gamma' > 0$, $\gamma'' < 0$, we get the state equation (1) by assuming $\gamma'' = 0$, i.e. a conviction rate being linear in v/P.

Now the law enforcement agency is faced with the following dynamic optimization problem:

$$\max_{E \geq 0} \left\{ -\int_0^\infty e^{-rt} \frac{1}{2}(P^2 + v^2)dt \right\} \tag{2}$$

s.t. (1) and an initial condition

$$P(0) = P_0 \geq 0. \tag{3}$$

Due to the quadratic shape of the enforcement costs the optimal control trajectory v(t) is automatically non-negative for all t. Moreover, the state variable P(t) must

---

[3] This might include also the harm general by criminal activities as well as precautionary costs.

be non-negative. Since this is not guaranteed by (1) we have to impose a pure state constraint $P(t) \geq 0$ for all t. However, it will turn out that for the optimal stationary state $\hat{P} > 0$ holds, and we are able to restrict our analysis to a neighbourhood of this equilibrium.

Clearly, this is one of the simplest optimal control models which can be formulated. Before its analysis let us mention its environmental interpretation. Here ρ refers to a constant rate of emissions that accumulate over time to a stock of pollution P(.). While some environmental models take a constant natural cleaning rate (compare, e.g. Forster, 1977), here it is assumed that the state of pollution is reduced by clean-up efforts denoted by v. Again the damage is assumed to be convex, while the quadratic costs refer to the decreasing marginal efficiency of the abatement activities.

After all, it is quite easy to get the optimal solution of this planning problem by using Pontryagin's maximum principle; compare Kamien and Schwartz (1981), Feichtinger and Hartl (1986), or Leonard and Long (1992) for those optimization techniques.

Analysis

To state the necessary optimality conditions we define the current-value Hamiltonian as follows:

$$H = -\frac{1}{2}P^2 - \frac{1}{2}v^2 + \lambda(\rho - \gamma v),$$

where the adjoint variable $\lambda(t)$ measures the shadow price of an additional offender. Since offenders generate damages, λ is negative. The Hamilton maximizing condition $H_v = 0$ yields

$$v = -\gamma\lambda. \tag{4}$$

This shows that the optimal enforcement/abatement rate is proportional to the shadow costs of an offender, λ, as well as to the efficiency of the control.

The variable λ has to satisfy the following adjoint equation:

$$\dot{\lambda} = r\lambda - H_P = r\lambda + P. \tag{5}$$

Thus, we get three equations, (1), (4), and (5) for the three unknown variables, P, v, and λ.

There exists a unique equilibrium defined by $\dot{P} = \dot{\lambda} = \dot{v} = 0$, i.e. $(\hat{P}, \hat{v}, \hat{\lambda}) = (r\rho\gamma^{-2}, \rho\gamma^{-1}, -\rho\gamma^{-2}) = \rho\gamma^{-2}(r, \gamma, -1)$.

By substituting (4) into (1) we get

$$\dot{P} = \rho + \gamma^2\lambda. \tag{6}$$

Since the canonical system (6), (5) is linear, both branches of the stable manifold are straight lines as well as the isoclines.

The Hamiltonian is jointly concave in P and v. Since the limiting transversality condition

$$\lim_{t\to e} e^{-rt}\lambda(t)P(t) = 0,$$

is satisfied for any feasible path P(t), the sufficiency of the first-order optimality conditions is guaranteed.

Since the determinant of the Jacobian is negative, i.e.

$$\begin{vmatrix} \dot{P}_P & \dot{P}_\lambda \\ \dot{\lambda}_P & \dot{\lambda}_\lambda \end{vmatrix} = \begin{vmatrix} 0 & \gamma^2 \\ 1 & r \end{vmatrix} = -\gamma^2,$$

the equilibria $(\hat{P}, \hat{\lambda}), (\hat{P}, \hat{v})$ represent saddle points.

Due to the linearity of (1), (5) and (6) the stable (and the instable) manifolds are linear.

Discussion

The phase portraits are depicted in Fig. 1.

The optimal solution depicted in Fig. 1 are the branches of the saddle point path. Their slope is shown in Fig. 1. The economic interpretation is straightforward: In an initially 'clean' society or environment, i.e. for $P(0) < \hat{P}$, the initial control is relatively low, $v(0) < \hat{v}$ since the corresponding (negative) shadow price $\lambda(0) > \hat{\lambda}$. Along the optimal path $\lambda(t)$ decreases gradually, while v(t) increases monotonically (linearly) to $\hat{v}$. For many offenders (a highly polluted enforcement) both the (negative) shadow price and the optimal enforcement/ abatement rates are high but decrease monotonically.

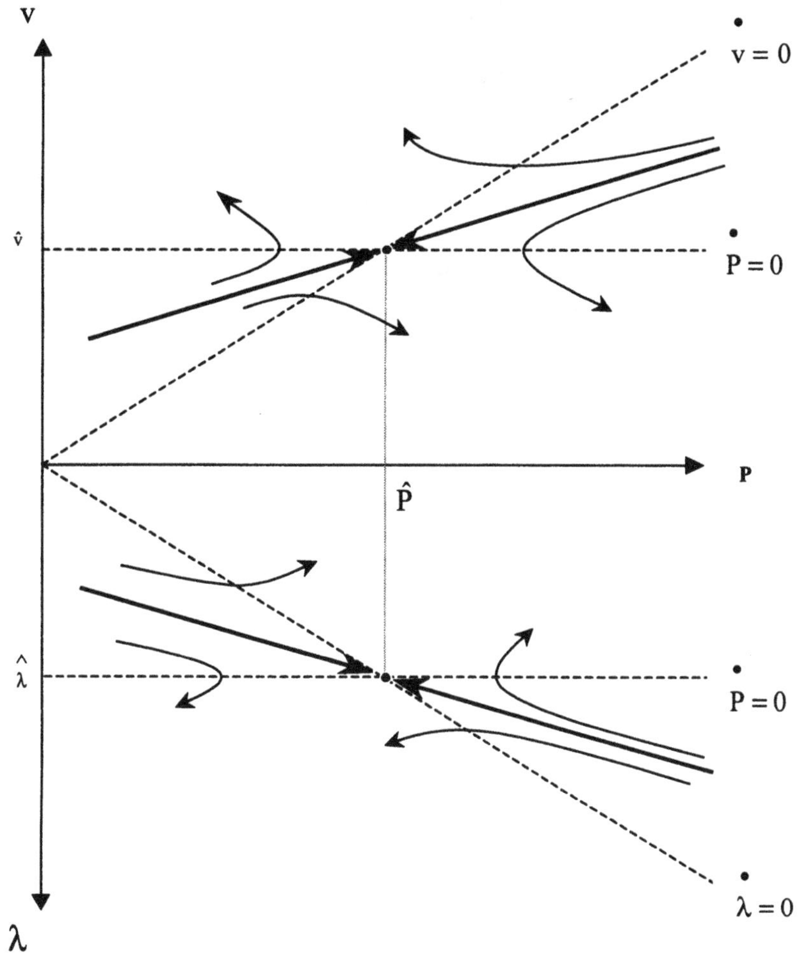

Fig. 1: Phase portraits of the (P,v)-space and the (P,λ)-space, respectively.

3 Model 2: Prevention and treatment

Many economic activities can lead to unintended side effects.

In the literature some attention has been devoted to prevention policies designed to reduce those damages (see Shavell, 1983). Barrett and Segerson (1997) assume that damages resulting from externality-generating activities can be reduced not only by prevention but also by treatment. As one example, they consider the contamination of groundwater or soils as a result of agricultural production. In contrast to prevention, which is undertaken prior to contamination, treatment is an ex post instrument. Other examples are unintended releases of toxic substances or illnesses from the consumption of hazardous products.

The following model provides a dynamic extension of the static analysis given by Barrett and Segerson (1997). It admits, however, a second interesting interpretation. To describe that we refer to the fact that illicit drug consumption can be controlled by various instruments. According to Rydell and Everingham (1994, p. 44) during 1992 $ 0.9 billion were spent on source country control, $ 1.7 billion on interdiction and $ 9.5 billion on domestic enforcement. Treatment programs received "only" $ 0.928 billion in 1992, and this sum includes private as well as government expenditures. Rydell et al. (1996) show that treatment emerges as the most cost-effective program compared to different enforcement strategies and Rydell (1997, p. 21) argues that prevention may be even more cost effective.

By interpreting the state variable as number of addicts, and assuming for simplicity a homogeneous population of (representative) offenders[4], the following model might yield the basis for a cost-benefit analysis of the optimal mix of prevention and treatment of drug addiction.

Formulation

As in section 1 the state P(t) denotes either the number of offenders (here: of addicts) or the stock of pollution. In contrast to model 1, there are two control instruments available for the decision-making agency, i.e.

- the prevention rate w(t), and
- the rate of treatment, u(t) at time t.

At any time period, there are three types of social costs, the damages implied by P, D(P), a well as the costs for prevention $C_{pr}(w)$, and those of treatment, $C_{tr}(u)$. It makes sense to assume all three of them convex, and for simplicity they are specified as quadratic functions:

$$D(P) = \frac{1}{2}P^2, \quad C_{pr}(w) = \frac{1}{2}w^2, \quad C_{tr}(u) = \frac{1}{2}u^2.$$

---

[4] A first step to extend this approach to light and heavy consumers of illicit drugs has been recently considered by Behrens et al. (1997).

Now the crucial issue is how the instruments, w and u, interfere with the dynamics of P. We assume that

$$\dot{P} = k\psi\left(\frac{w}{k}\right) - P\beta\left(\frac{u}{P}\right) \tag{8}$$

where k denotes the constant input stream per time unit, ψ measures the impact of the per capita prevention rate on k, and β is the per capita treatment rate.

The prevention from getting contaminated (or addicted) clearly depends on the prevention efforts, w, as well as on the number of cases, k, to which those efforts are to be applied. We assume that the quotient w/k is a good proxy to measure the joint influence of w and k. Note that this might be not true in particular for small values of k. In addition to that, for $k \to 0$ we get a singularity. A similar argument applies for the impact of u and P on the dynamics of P.

The following assumption on ψ and β, respectively, make sense

$$0 \le \psi \le 1, \;\; \psi(0) = 1, \;\; \psi' < 0, \;\; \psi'' \ge 0$$

$$\beta' < 0, \;\; \beta'' \le 0.$$

To simplify the analysis, we assume both functions as linear, i.e.

$$\psi\left(\frac{w}{k}\right) = 1 - \alpha\frac{w}{k} \tag{9}$$

$$\beta\left(\frac{u}{P}\right) = \beta\frac{u}{P}, \tag{10}$$

with α, β both positive. Note that by (9) $\psi\left(\frac{w}{k}\right)$ becomes negative for $w/k > 1/\alpha$ which is infeasible. However, the economically relevant behaviour around the long-run steady state occurs within the feasible region of w/k.

The optimal control problem is stated as follows:

$$\max_{w\ge0,u\ge0}\left\{-\int_0^\infty \frac{1}{2}(P^2 + w^2 + u^2)dt\right\} \tag{11}$$

s.t.

$$\dot{P} = k - \alpha w - \beta u \tag{12}$$

and a given initial state (3).

Analysis

Using the Hamiltonian

$$H = -\frac{1}{2}(P^2 + w^2 + u^2) + \lambda(k - \alpha w - \beta u)$$

with the adjoint variable λ we get the following necessary optimality conditions

$$H_w = 0 \Rightarrow w = -\alpha\lambda \tag{13}$$

$$H_u = 0 \Rightarrow u = -\beta\lambda \tag{14}$$

$$\dot{\lambda} = r\lambda + P. \tag{15}$$

Substituting (13) and (14) into equation (12) yields

$$\dot{P} = k + \lambda(\alpha^2 + \beta^2). \tag{16}$$

Thus, the canonical system (15) and (16) consists on two quite simple linear differential equations.

There exists a unique equilibrium

$$(\hat{P}, \hat{\lambda}, \hat{w}, \hat{u}) = \frac{k}{\alpha^2 + \beta^2}(r, -1, \alpha, \beta).$$

It is easily shown that $(\hat{P}, \hat{\lambda})$ is a saddle point, and also $(\hat{P}, \hat{w})$ and $(\hat{P}, \hat{u})$ have this property. The phase portraits are shown in Fig. 2. Note that the optimal solution is such that w and u influence the state variable P in the *same* direction. This property may be derived under more general conditions, see Feichtinger (1984), where it is called *'synergism'*. More formally, it means that along the optimal path it holds that

$$\frac{dw}{du} > 0.$$

Since $w = (\alpha/\beta)u$, this is clearly satisfied.

Discussion

This situation is illustrated in Fig. 2.

The optimal solution of the infinite time horizon problem is provided by the stable branches of the saddle point path. Since the sufficient conditions are satisfied – the Hamiltonian is jointly concave in P, w and u, and the limiting transverality conditions are also satisfied – we have ascertained an optimal feedback solution, i.e. for every value of P the corresponding values of w and u determine the optimal rate of prevention and treatment, respectively.

Again the result of this straightforward analysis may be easily interpreted:

The optimal mix of instruments is such that there is a fixed percentage of each of them along the whole optimal path which is simply proportional to the efficiencies α and β for prevention and treatment, respectively.

Moreover, Fig. 2 illustrates the fact for a small initial stock, $P(0) < \hat{P}$ the initial instruments are applied with a relatively weak intensity, i.e. $w(0) < \hat{w}, u(0) < \hat{u}$. Their gradual increase along the stable eigenvector leads to a convergence of $P(t) \rightarrow \hat{P}$. For serious initial environmental pollution (or many addicts) the optimal initial mix is higher then in the long-run steady-state, and it is optimal to decrease both over time approaching the equilibrium $(\hat{P}, \hat{w}, \hat{u})$.

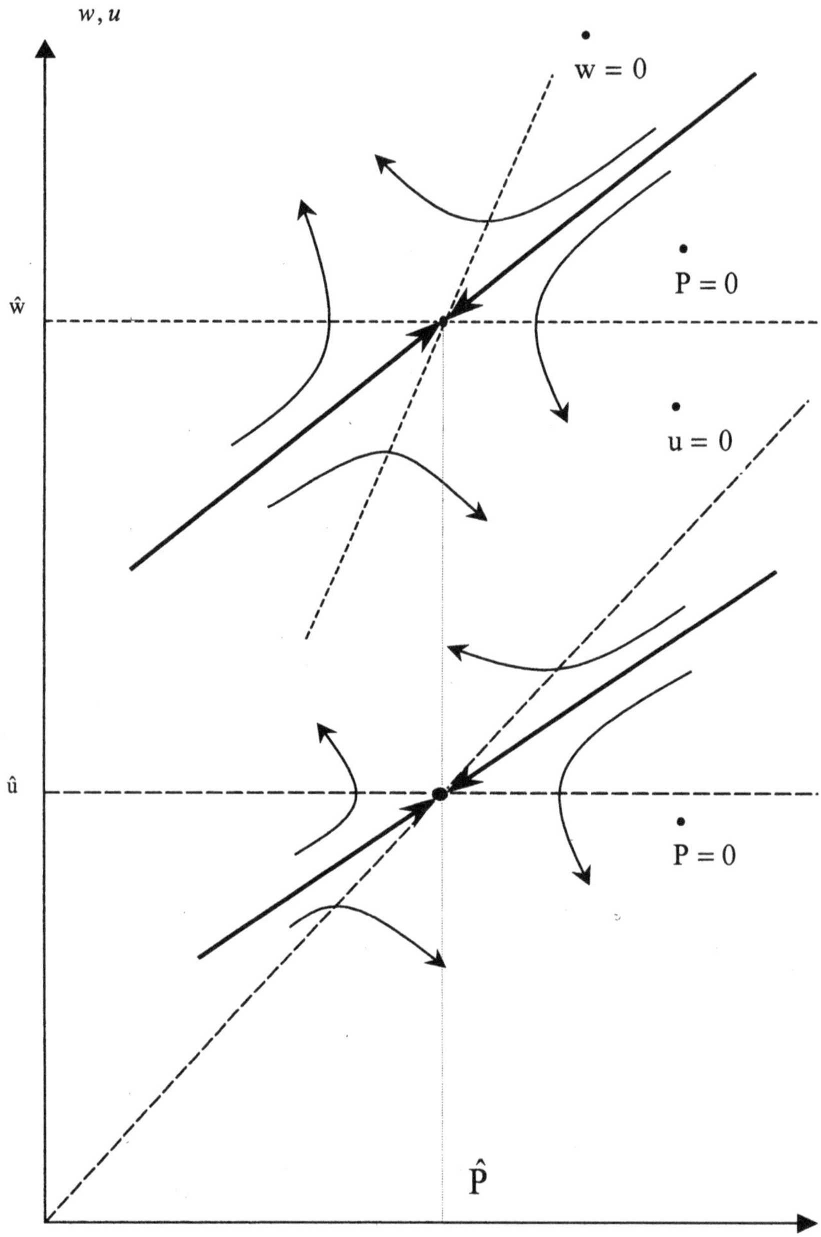

Fig. 2: (P,w)- and (P,u)-phase portraits. (The case $\alpha > \beta$ is illustrated, i.e. $\hat{w} > \hat{u}$.)

4 Model 3: Prevention to a pseudo-stochastic initiation

Barrett and Segerson (1997) stress the fact that contamination or catching an illness etc. is an uncertain event which should be described in stochastic terms.

By extending their static approach to a dynamic framework we apply an idea first proposed by Kamien and Schwartz (1971a,b), see also (1981). For a detailed discussion we refer to section 10.1. of Feichtinger and Hartl (1986).

In particular, Sethi (1979) has applied the KS approach to determine the optimal pilfering rate of a thief. In another earlier model of crime and punishment, Feichtinger (1983) extended the scenario to a dynamic game between an offender and the police.

Formulation

Consider a *non-recurrent* event, like contamination of clean water or initiation of illicit drug consumption. Denote by τ the time until this event (in the following denoted as initiation) occurs. The initial time measures the begin of the exposure to the initiation's risk.

The probability distribution of the random variable τ is denoted as

$$F(t) = \text{Prob}\{\tau \leq t\}.$$

F(t) measures the probability that the switch to initiation took place before time t. The KS idea mentioned above is to use F(t) as state variable of an optimal control model. The hazard rate h(t) at a certain time t may be reduced by prevention measures w(t) at that time, i.e. h = h(w(t)). According to the definition of the hazard rate, the density function $\dot{F}$ satisfies the following state equation:

$$\dot{F} = h(w)(1-F). \tag{17}$$

It seems reasonable to assume that:

$$h \geq 0, \;\; h' < 0, \;\; h'' \geq 0. \tag{18}$$

Note that the optimal control model we are just formulating is a deterministic one; since the governing differential equation is *not* stochastic. However, since a random variable occurs, we might denote it as 'pseudo-stochastic'.

The decision-maker takes the preventing measures to reduce the expected damage by taking into consideration the expected costs for prevention.

There are three possibilities for any time t:

(i) $\tau < t$, i.e. the initiation has already occurred before time t. The probability of this event is F(t). Then a (constant) damage D per time unit is assumed to occur;

(ii) $\tau = t$, i.e. the initiation just occurs in t, more exactly in an infinitesimal interval of length dt around t. The probability of this event is given by $\dot{F}(t)dt$. We assume a corresponding one-shot disutility $\overline{D}$;

(iii) $\tau > t$, i.e. the initiation has not yet occurred. The probability of this event is 1-F(t), and the prevention costs, C(w), have to multiplied with that to get the expected costs.

To summarize, the task of the preventing agent is to minimize its total expected social costs, i.e.

$$\max_{w \geq 0} \left\{ -\int_0^T e^{-rt} \left[DF + \overline{D}h(w)(1-F) + C(w)(1-F) \right] dt + e^{-rT} S(T)[1-F(T)] \right\} \tag{19}$$

s.t. to the state equation (17) and the initial condition

$$F(0) = 0. \tag{20}$$

The function S(T) measures the utility that the initiation has not yet occurred at the end of a given planning period of length T.

To get simpler analytic solutions we specify the hazard rate as linear, i.e.

$$h(w) = \overline{h} - hw \quad \text{for} \quad 0 \leq w \leq \overline{w} = \overline{h}/h \tag{21}$$

with $\overline{h}$, $h > 0$. The parameter $\overline{h}$ measures the 'natural' hazard rate, i.e. the intensity for initiation without any prevention efforts w. Moreover, h denotes the marginal efficiency of prevention which is assumed to be constant in that case. Clearly the second inequality in (21) has to be imposed to guarantee the non-negativity of the hazard rate.

As before, the decreasing marginal efficiency of prevention is modeled by convex, i.e. in our case quadratic, prevention costs,

$$C(w) = \frac{1}{2} w^2. \tag{22}$$

Analysis

Consider the Hamiltonian

$$H = -DF - \frac{1}{2}w^2(1-F) + (\lambda - \overline{D})(\overline{h} - hw)(1-F)$$

with the adjoint variable λ. The Hamilton maximizing condition yields

$$w = -(\lambda - \overline{D})h \tag{23}$$

for $F \neq 1$. Note that (23) admits an obvious economic interpretation.

The adjoint equation is

$$\dot{\lambda} = (r + \overline{h})\lambda + D - \overline{D}\overline{h} + \frac{1}{2}(\lambda - \overline{D})^2 h^2. \tag{24}$$

To get the canonical system we substitute (23) and (21) into (17) and (24). This yields

$$\dot{F} = (\overline{h} + (\lambda - \overline{D})h^2)(1-F) \tag{25}$$

$$\dot{\lambda} = \frac{1}{2}h^2\lambda^2 + (r + \overline{h} - \overline{D}h^2)\lambda + D - \overline{D}\overline{h} + \frac{1}{2}\overline{D}^2 h^2. \tag{26}$$

Note that the r.h.s. of (25) depends only on λ. This is due to the state-separability of the model (see Dockner et al., 1985). Thus, the saddle-point path is horizontal.

The r.h.s. of (25) is a quadratic polynomial Q(λ) in λ. To get the stationary state λ we solve Q(λ) = 0 and obtain

$$\lambda_{1,2} = \frac{-(r + \overline{h} - \overline{D}h^2) \pm \sqrt{(r + \overline{h} - \overline{D}h^2)^2 - 2Dh^2 + \overline{D}h^2(\overline{h} + \overline{D}h^2)}}{h^2}.$$

Setting $\overline{D} = 0$ for simplicity, we get

$$\lambda_{1,2} = \frac{-(r + \overline{h}) \pm \sqrt{(r + \overline{h})^2 - 2Dh^2}}{h^2} \tag{27}$$

To exclude complex solutions we have to assume that the discriminant in (27) is non-negative, i.e. that

$$D \le \frac{1}{2}\left(\frac{r+\bar{h}}{h}\right)^2. \tag{28}$$

Under this condition only λ_1 yields a feasible stationary state, since

$$\lambda_2 < -\frac{r+\bar{h}}{h^2} < -\frac{\bar{h}}{h^2}$$

implies $-\lambda_2 > \bar{h}/h^2$ which is a contradiction to (21) and (23):

$$w \le \bar{h}/h \;\Rightarrow\; -(\lambda-\bar{D})h \le \bar{h}/h \;\Rightarrow\; -\lambda \le \bar{h}/h^2$$

(since $\bar{D}=0$).

This situation is illustrated in Fig. 3.

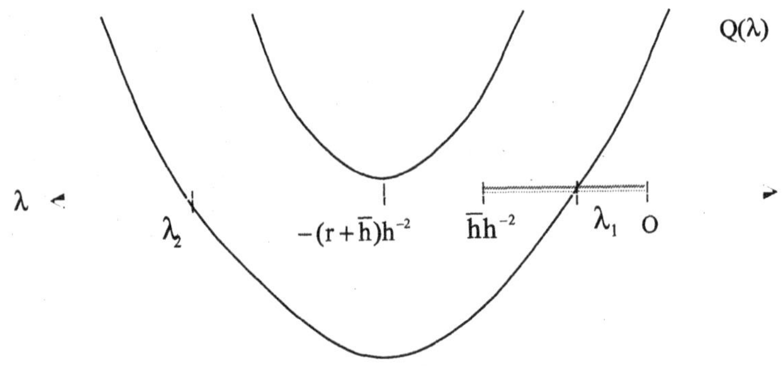

Fig. 3: Stationary state of λ, i.e. Q(λ) = 0.

Note that the negativity of λ(t) makes economic sense: It measures the marginal value that the initiation has not yet occurred at time t. The transversality condition yields

$$\lambda(T) = -S(T). \tag{29}$$

The phase portrait of the (F,λ)-plane and the (F,w)-diagram are depicted in Fig. 4.

The stationary values are is given by

$$\hat{\lambda} = \lambda_1 \quad \text{(see (27))}, \quad \hat{w} = -\hat{\lambda}h \quad \text{(see (23) for } \overline{D} = 0\text{)}.$$

The orientation of the trajectories is obtained by calculating of the signs of pertinent partial derivatives from (25) and (26) as follows:

$$\frac{\partial \dot{F}}{\partial F} < 0, \quad \frac{\partial \dot{\lambda}}{\partial \lambda} > 0.$$

The horizontal saddle-point path represent the optimal solution for an *infinite* planning horizon. Note that the long-run optimal prevention rate $\hat{w}$ increases with increasing damage making economic sense. On the other hand, $\hat{w}$ decreases with increasing marginal efficiency of prevention h.

The thick trajectories depicted in Fig. 4 illustrate the case of a given *finite* time interval, T, a given initial state (20) and a terminal condition (29) for S(T) = 0. The qualitative structure of the optimal prevention rate, $\hat{w}$, shows a monotonous decreasing behaviour with a corresponding increasing (negative) shadow price. This makes economic sense.

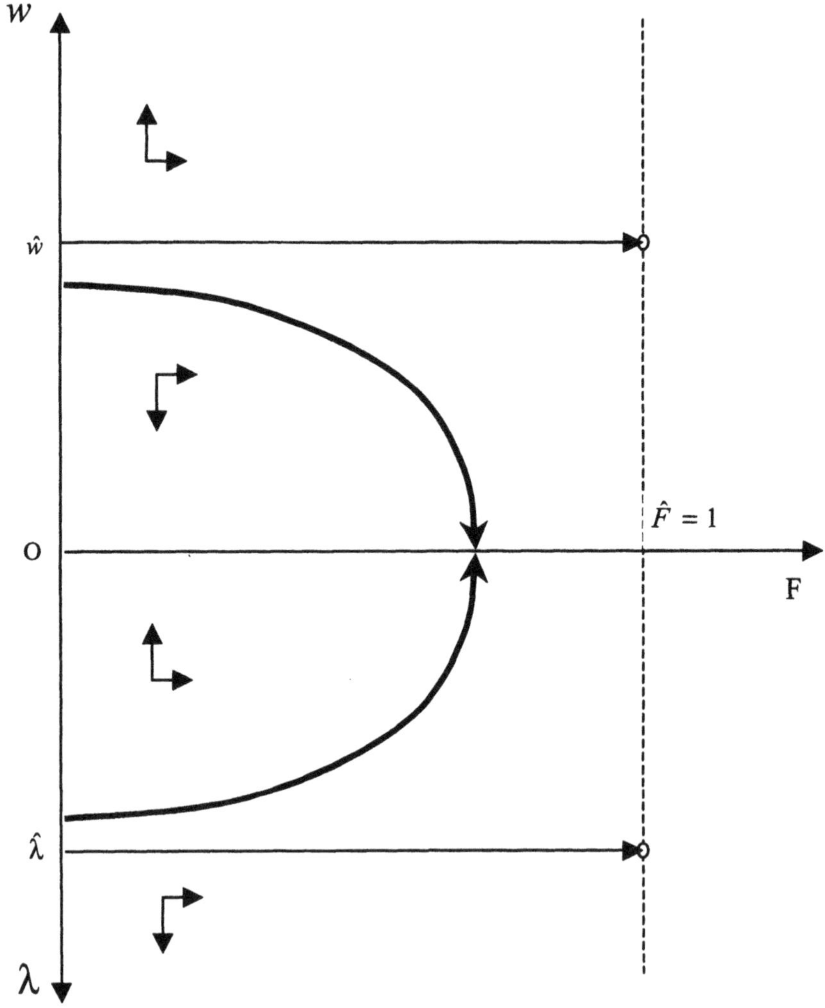

Fig. 4: Phase portrait of the (F,w)-diagram (above) and the (F,λ)-plane (below).

5 Model 4: A dynamic game of offending and prevention

Model 3 presented in the previous section can be extended to a bilateral competitive decision situation. The model we are going on to formulate is a slight variant of the thief-police differential game (see Feichtinger, 1983). While in this game the police tries to arrest the offender, the law enforcement agency's task is now that of prevention.

Denoting the offender as player 1, v being its offending rate, and the agency as player 2 whose instrument is the prevention rate w, the systems dynamics may now be written as

$$\dot{F} = h(v,w)(1-F), \tag{30}$$

where F is explained in Section 5, and with

$$h_v > 0, h_{vv} \leq 0; \quad h_w < 0, h_{ww} \geq 0; \quad \operatorname{sgn} h_{vw} = ? \tag{31}$$

The objective functional of player 1 is:

$$J_1 = \int_0^{\infty} e^{-rt_1} \left[U(v)(1-F) - \overline{D}_1\dot{F} - D_1F\right]dt, \quad + S(T)(1-F(T)),$$

where U(v) measures the instantaneous utility of player 1 offending with rate v, $\overline{D}_1$ is the one-shot penalty of the thief at the instant he/she is arrested (or convicted) and D_1 denotes the disutility from being convicted (or at least from being out of business)[5].

Player 2, i.e. the drug or environmental agency, tries to minimize its expected social costs created by prevention and damage caused by the 'deviant' behaviour (addiction or contamination in our example)[6]:

$$J_2 = -\int_0^{\infty} e^{-r_2t}\left[C(w)(1-F) + \overline{D}_2\dot{F} + D_2F\right]dt = -\int_0^{\infty} e^{-r_2t}\left[DF + \overline{D}\dot{F} + C(w)(1-F)\right]dt.$$

The analysis of this dynamic game may be carried out in a similar manner to the thief-police game analyzed in Feichtinger (1983).

---

[5] Compare Sethi (1979) for a more detailed explanation.

[6] See section 4 for details $(D_2 = D, \overline{D}_2 = \overline{D})$.

6 Model 5: Prevention and treatment: a two-state optimal control model

Finally, we consider the case that a stationary sequence of cohorts is exposed to a time-invariant but age-dependent risk of getting addicted, whereby this transition can be prevented. The initiations of drug consumption generate a population of addicts which may be diminished by mortality and treatment.

Let us denote by N(t,x) the number of non-users aged x years at time t. Neglecting for simplicity mortality and 'out of observation' as decrement causes the dynamics of non-users is described by the following linear partial differential equation[7]

$$\frac{\partial N(t,x)}{\partial t}+\frac{\partial N(t,x)}{\partial x}=-h(t,x,w(t,x))N(t,x), \tag{32}$$

where h(t,x) measures the intensity of initiation for illicit drug consumption of an individual aged x at time t. The actual initiation rate depends not only on age-and time-specific characteristics but also on the age-specific and time-dependent prevention measures w(t,x), i.e. the efforts at time to prevent age group x from illicit drug consumption.

Assuming a constant cohort size, i.e.

$$N(t,0)=k, \tag{33}$$

and time-independent natural initiation rates and prevention efficiencies, w(x), the partial differential equation reduces to an ordinary one[8]:

$$\frac{dN(x)}{dx}=-h(x,w(x))N(x), \quad N(0)=k. \tag{34}$$

Note that this state dynamics has the form of the differential equation (17) if we set

$$1-F=G, \ \ Gk=N.$$

The total number of initiations at any time t is given by

---

[7] In the literature this equation is denoted as McKendrick-von Foerster equation.

[8] To put it in other words, equation (34) describes the steady state of the PDE (32).

$$I = k\int_0^{\omega} [1 - F(x)]h(x, w(x))dx = k\int_0^{\omega} \dot{F}(x)dx = kF(\omega), \tag{35}$$

where ω denotes the maximal age, and (17) is used again.

The second state variable is the number of addicts at time t, P(t). Its dynamics is given by

$$\dot{P}(t) = I - \beta\left(\frac{u(t)}{P(t)}\right)P(t), \quad P(0) = 0 \tag{36}$$

where the coupling happens via the input rate I.

The objective of the two-state optimal control model is the following cost functional

$$J = -\int_0^{\infty} e^{-rt}\left\{\int_0^{\omega} [\kappa N(t,x)h(t,x,w(t,x))dx + w(t,x)]dx + D(P(t)) + u(t)\right\}dt, \tag{37}$$

where κ measures the social costs per initiation (and time unit), and D(P) denotes the damage of the drug consumption[9] as assessed by the decision-maker. Here we assume again a constant time preference rate r and an infinite planning horizon. Due to the stationary structure of the model, (37) may be written as

$$J = -\frac{1}{r}\left[kF(\omega) + \int_0^{\omega} w(x)dx\right] - \int_0^{\infty} e^{-rt}[D(P(t)) + u(t)]dt. \tag{38}$$

Clearly, $F(\omega)$ depends on the prevention efforts w(x) made in all age groups.

Since the initiation is constant, the two state control model may be *decoupled*, i.e. each of the two problems can be solved for its own. To put it in other words, we first determine the optimal prevention policy in a similar manner as in model 3 (section 4). Secondly, the optimal treatment pattern is calculated by selecting the initiation as (35). As mentioned before, $F(\omega)$ depends on the prevention policy. To determine the optimal treatment policy we may proceed analogously to model 2 (section 3).

---

[9] For simplicity, we assume a homogeneous population of addicts, i.e. each illicit drug consumer uses the same amount per time unit, and the consumption rate does not depend on the duration since initiation.

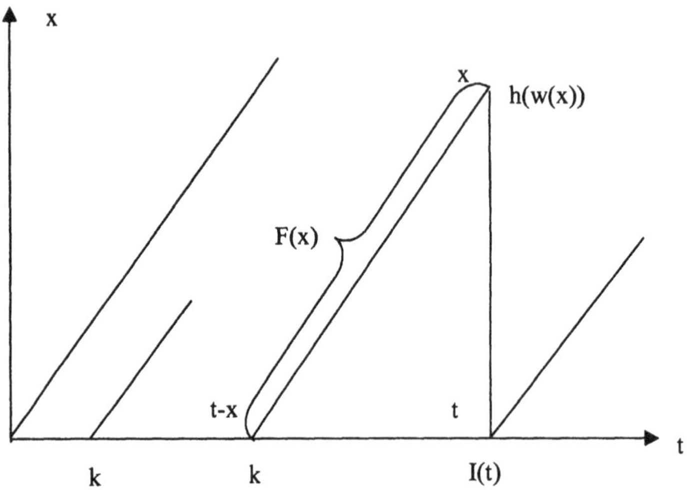

Fig. 5: Lexis diagram for model 5.

7 Conclusions and extensions

The purpose of this paper was to draw attention to the fact that environmental pollution modeling exhibits certain analogies to crime control. The main message is that exploitation of those similarities might be mutually advantageous for both disciplines. We hope that our stylized examples are able so illustrate this interdependence.

Quite a few extensions are possible.

First, the impact of the control instruments on the systems dynamics which we modeled in an (over-) simplified way could be formulated in a more realistic manner. For hints how this can be done we refer to Tragler et al. (1997) and Behrens et al. (1997).

Second, additional instruments may be included. In illicit drug control, the following instruments have been considered: source-country control, border control prevention, treatment, domestic law enforcement, street level enforcement ('crackdowns').

It would be an interesting task to model the *interaction* between the various control instruments. A similar problem arises, e.g., in marketing modeling. In this case, the sales are influenced by price, advertising, and the quality of the product, to mention the most important marketing instruments. It has been empirically proved that there are substantial intertemporal interaction effects with respect to the various control instruments (see, e.g. Lilien and Kotler, 1983, Feichtinger and Hartl, 1986, Chap. 11).

Third, as been illustrated in Model 4, dynamic games are the adequate methodological framework in which pertinent decision processes are to be modeled. To put it shortly: the strategic interactions of offenders or polluting firms and a law enforcement or environmental agency are essential for the design of realistic cost-benefit analyses.

References

Borisov, V., Feichtinger, G. Kryazhimskii, A. (1998): Optimal enforcement on a pure seller's market of illicit drugs. Forschungsbericht 224 des Instituts für Ökonometrie, OR und Systemtheorie, TU Wien

Barrett, J., Segerson, K. (1997): Prevention and treatment in environmental policy design. Journal of Environmental Economics and Management 33, 196-213

Becker, G.S. (1968): Crime and punishment: an economic approach. Journal of Political Economy 76, 169-217

Behrens, D., Caulkins, J.P., Tragler, G., Feichtinger G. (1997): Controlling the US cocaine epidemic: Finding the optimal mix of drug prevention and treatment. Forschungsbericht 214 des Instituts für Ökonometrie, OR und Systemtheorie, TU Wien

Clark, C.W. (1976): Mathematical Bioeconomics. The Optimal Management of Renewable Resources. Wiley, New York

Clark, C.W. (1985): Bioeconomic Modelling and Fisheries Management. Wiley, New York

Caulkins, J.P. (1993), Local drug markets' response to focused police enforcement. Operations Research 41, 848-863

Caulkins, J.P., Tragler, G., Feichtinger G. (1998): Addiction is like a switch. Working Draft, Vienna University of Technology

Dasgupta, P.S., Heal, G.M. (1979): Economic Theory and Exhaustible Resources. J. Nisbett, Welwyn, Cambridge, Univ. Press

Dockner, E.J., Feichtinger G., Jorgensen, S. (1985): Tractable classes of nonzero-sum open-loop Nash differential games: theory and examples. Journal of Optimization Theory and Applications 45, 179-197

Dockner, E.J., Long, Ngo Van (1993): International pollution control: cooperative versus non-cooperative strategies. Journal of Environmental Economics and Management 25, 13-29

Feichtinger, G. (1983): A differential games solution to a model of competition between a thief and the police. Management Science 29, 686-699

Feichtinger, G. (1984): On the synergistic influence of two control variables on the state of nonlinear optimal control models. Journal of Operational Research Society 35, 907-914

Feichtinger, G., Hartl, R.F. (1986): Optimale Kontrolle ökonomischer Prozesse: Anwendungen des Maximumprinzips in den Wirtschaftswissenschaften. de Gruyter, Berlin

Feichtinger, G., Grienauer, W., Tragler, G. (1997): Optimal dynamic law enforcement. Forschungsbericht 197 des Instituts für Ökonometrie, OR und Systemtheorie, TU Wien

Feichtinger, G. (1998): Dynamic economic models of optimal law enforcement. Forschungsbericht 200 des Instituts für Ökonometrie, OR und Systemtheorie, TU Wien

Forster, B.A. (1977), One a state variable optimal control problem: consumption-pollution trade-offs. In: Pitchford, J.D., Turnovsky, S.J. (Eds.): *Applications of Control Theory to Economic Analysis*. North-Holland, Amsterdam, 35-56

Hofbauer, J. and K. Sigmund, 1998, *Evolutionary Games and Population Dynamics*, Cambridge University Press, Cambridge

Kamien, M.I., Schwartz, N.L. (1971a): Optimal maintenance and sale age for a machine subject to failure. Management Science 17, B495-B504

Kamien, M.I., Schwartz, N.L. (1971b): Limit pricing and uncertain entry. Econometrica 39, 441-454

Kamien, M.I., Schwartz, N.L. (1981): Dynamic Optimization: The Calculus of Variations and Optimal Control in Economics and Management. North-Holland, New York

Kort, P., Feichtinger, G., Hartl, R.F., Haunschmied J.L. (1998): Optimal enforcement policies (crackdowns) on a illicit drug market. Optimal Control Applications and Methods 19, 169-184

Lilien, G.L., Kotler, P. (1983): Marketing Decision Making: A Model-Building Approach. Harper & Row, New York

Leonard, D., Long, N.V. (1992): Optimal control theory and static optimization in economics. Cambridge University Press, Cambridge

Rydell, C.P. (1997): The dynamics of cocaine control policy analysis based on exploratory modeling. Working paper

Rydell, C.P., Caulkins, J.P., Everingham, S.S. (1996): Enforcement or treatment? Modeling the relative efficacy of alternatives for controlling cocaine. Operations Research 44, 1-9

Rydell, C.P., and Everingham, S.S. (1994): Controlling cocaine. Supply versus demand programs. MR-331-ONDCP/A/DPRC, Santa Monica, Rand, CA

Sethi, S.P. (1979): Optimal pilfering policies for dynamic continuous thieves. Management Science 25, 535-542

Shavell, S. (1983): Torts in which victim and injurer act sequentially. Journal of Law Economics 26, 598-612

Tahvonen, O., Withagen, C. (1996): Optimality of irreversible pollution accumulation. Journal of Economic Dynamics and Control 20, 1775-1795

Tragler, G., Caulkins, J.P., Feichtinger, G. (1997): Optimal dynamic allocation of treatment and enforcement in illicit drug control. Forschungsbericht 212 des Instituts für Ökonometrie, OR und Systemtheorie, TU Wien

Wirl, F. (1998): Complex dynamic environmental policies. Forthcoming in Resource and Energy Economics

On Cross Decomposition for Mixed-Integer Programming

Paul Wentges
University of Ulm, Dep. of Business Administration, D-89069 Ulm

1 Introduction

Primal and dual decomposition procedures can lead – dependent on the structure of the problem – to efficient procedures for solving mixed–integer programming problems. Benders' decomposition takes advantage of the primal structure of a problem by temporarily fixing the aggravating integer variables, while dual structures can be exploited by relaxing the complicating constraints in Lagrangian fashion and solving the Lagrangian dual with subgradient optimization, multiplier adjustment methods, or Dantzig-Wolfe decomposition.

The cross decomposition algorithm was developed by Van Roy (see [Van Roy (1980] and [Van Roy (1983]) to solve linear mixed-integer programming problems which have both an exploitable primal structure *and* exploitable dual structure. Combining Benders' decomposition and Dantzig-Wolfe decomposition in one solution procedure, the cross decomposition algorithm tries to use both structures simultaneously.

In [Van Roy (1986], cross decomposition was applied to solve the capacitated facility location problem $(CFLP)$. Other applications of cross decomposition include the solution of stochastic transportation problems ([Holmberg and Jörnsten (1984]) and multiple right hand choice linear programming ([Kim et al. (1989]). [Holmberg (1990] and [Holmberg (1992a] generalize the cross decomposition procedure to solve non-linear (mixed-) integer problems as well.

While e.g. [Beasley (1988] stresses the efficiency of the cross decomposition procedure to solve the $(CFLP)$, [Cornuejols et al. (1991] report worse results for harder problem instances with large duality gaps. In the following, therefore, a modification of the cross decomposition algorithm to accelerate its convergence behaviour, the so-called *dually-weighted cross decomposition*, is proposed.

In section 2, the main elements of the cross decomposition algorithm are presented. The dually-weighted version of the cross decomposition algorithm is introduced in section 3. Finally, computational results for the capacitated facility location problem are provided in section 4.

Throughout the paper, the following notation is used: The feasible set of an optimization problem (P) is denoted $F(P)$, its optimal value $v(P)$.

2 Cross Decomposition

Let the following linear mixed–integer programming problem (MIP)

$$(MIP) \quad \begin{cases} \min\ c'x + d'y, & \\ A_1x + B_1y \geq b_1, & (1) \\ A_2x + B_2y \geq b_2, & (2) \\ x \geq 0,\ y \in P & (3) \end{cases}$$

with $c \in I\!R^m$, $d \in I\!R^n$, $A_1 \in \mathbb{Q}^{l\times m}$, $B_1 \in \mathbb{Q}^{l\times n}$, $b_1 \in \mathbb{Q}^l$, $b_2 \in \mathbb{Q}^e$, $A_2 \in \mathbb{Q}^{e\times m}$, $B_2 \in \mathbb{Q}^{e\times n}$, $x \in I\!R^m$ and $P \subset \mathbb{Z}^n$ be given. For ease of description, the following notation will also be used:

$$A = \begin{pmatrix} A_1 \\ A_2 \end{pmatrix}, \quad B = \begin{pmatrix} B_1 \\ B_2 \end{pmatrix}, \quad b = \begin{pmatrix} b_1 \\ b_2 \end{pmatrix}.$$

Benders' decomposition exploits the primal structure of MIP by separating the continuous from the integer variables and solving successively so-called Benders' subproblems and master problems: Temporarily fixing the complicating integer variables $y \in P$ leads to the following easier to solve primal or Benders' subproblems (SP_y)

$$(SP_y) \quad \begin{cases} \min\ c'x + d'y, \\ Ax \geq b - By, \\ x \geq 0, \end{cases}$$

and the Benders' master problems (MP_{T_P}) are given by

$$(MP_{T_P}) \quad \begin{cases} \min\ \rho, \\ b'\mu^t + (d - B'\mu^t)' \cdot y \leq \rho \quad \forall\, t \in T_P, \\ y \in P,\ \rho \in I\!R \end{cases}$$

for $T_P \subset T_{PA}$. T_{PA} denotes the set of all extreme points of the feasible set $F(DSP_y)$ of (DSP_y), where (DSP_y)

$$(DSP_y) \begin{cases} \max\ (b - By)' \cdot \mu + d'y, \\ A'\mu \leq c, \\ \mu \geq 0 \end{cases}$$

is the dual of (SP_y) (note that $F(DSP_y)$ is independent of y).
The following holds true (see e.g. [Minoux (1986, section 8.4]):

$$(v(SP_{\bar{y}}) \geq)\ v(MIP) = \min_{y \in P} v(SP_y) = v(MP_{T_{PA}})\ \ (\geq v(MP_{T_P})).$$

On the other hand, let the e restrictions (2) be the complicating constraints, i.e. (MIP) without restrictions (2) is relatively easy to solve compared to (MIP). This dual structure of (MIP) can be exploited by relaxing the complicating constraints in a Lagrangian fashion. Applying Dantzig-Wolfe decomposition to solve the Lagrangian Dual (LD) the following dual subproblems (SD_{μ_2})

$$(SD_{\mu_2}) \begin{cases} \min\ c'x + d'y + \mu_2' \cdot (b_2 - A_2x - B_2y), \\ A_1x + B_1y \geq b_1, \\ x \geq 0,\ y \in P, \end{cases}$$

and dual master problems (MD_{T_D})

$$(MD_{T_D}) \begin{cases} \max\ \delta, \\ c'x^t + d'y^t + (b_2 - A_2x^t - B_2y^t)' \cdot \mu_2 \geq \delta \quad \forall\, t \in T_D, \\ \mu_2 \geq 0,\ \delta \in \mathbb{R} \end{cases}$$

are obtained for $T_D \subset T_{DA}$. Here, $\{(x^t, y^t) : t \in T_{DA}\}$ is the set of all extreme points of the convex hull of $F(SD_{\mu_2})$ (independent of μ_2).
It follows: $v(LD) = \max_{\mu_2 \geq 0} v(SD_{\mu_2}) = v(MD_{T_{DA}}) \leq v(MIP)$.

The cross decomposition algorithm relies on the observation that the dual subproblems (SD_{μ_2}) are equivalent to special Benders' master problems and, vice versa, the primal subproblems (SP_y) are equivalent to particular Dantzig-Wolfe master problems (see [Van Roy (1983]). The main idea of the cross decomposition algorithm, therefore, is to use the dual and primal subproblems – instead of the harder to solve Benders' and Dantzig-Wolfe master problems – to generate new variables y and Lagrangian multipliers μ_2. To prevent the cross decomposition algorithm from cycling, though, primal and dual convergence tests have to be added (see [Holmberg (1990]).

In total, the main steps of the cross decomposition algorithm can be sketched as follows (for more details see the description of the dually-weighted version in section 4):

Algorithm 2.1: Cross decomposition

Step 1: Initialize (e.g. $k := 1$) and choose $y^1 \in P$.

Step 2: Solve the primal subproblem (SP_{y^k}). Add the Benders' cut belonging to the optimal dual solution $\mu^k = (\mu_1^k, \mu_2^k)$ to the Benders' master problem. If (LD) is solved τ-optimally, go to step 4. Otherwise perform a dual convergence test: If not fulfilled, go to step 5.

Step 3: Solve the dual subproblem $(SD_{\mu_2^k})$. Add the dual cut belonging to the optimal solution (x^{k+1}, y^{k+1}) to the Dantzig-Wolfe master problem. Perform a primal convergence test. If fulfilled, set $k := k + 1$ and go to step 2.

Step 4: Solve the Benders' master problem $(MP_{T_P^k})$. Let (ρ^k, y^{k+1}) be an optimal solution. If (MIP) is solved ϵ-optimally, terminate, otherwise set $k := k + 1$ and go to step 2.

Step 5: Solve the Dantzig-Wolfe master problem. Let (δ^k, μ_2^{k+1}) be an optimal solution. Set $k := k + 1$ and go to step 3.

Under reasonable assumptions (the sets P, $F(SP_{\tilde{y}})$ $\forall \tilde{y} \in P$ and $F(SD_{\mu_2})$ are all nonempty and bounded)[1], algorithm 2.1 terminates in a finite number of steps with an ϵ-optimal solution of (MIP) for all $\epsilon \geq 0$. For, finally, the algorithm amounts to Benders' decomposition – which is known to be finite (see e.g. [Minoux (1986, section 8.4]) – since the convergence tests prevent the algorithm from cycling, and the Dantzig-Wolfe decomposition procedure solves the Lagrangian Dual in finitely many steps as well.

There exist a lot of possible variations of the cross decomposition procedure. If no primal master problem is solved at all (and a dual master problem is solved in case of a failed primal convergence test), one gets a modified Dantzig-Wolfe decomposition algorithm to solve (LD) with an additional heuristic solution of (MIP). To solve (MIP) optimally, this procedure would have to be integrated in a branch-and-bound solution scheme. Avoiding to solve the dual master problem likewise, a modification of Benders' decomposition is obtained. Therefore, [Holmberg (1990] suggests that Benders' and Dantzig-Wolfe decomposition could also be seen as

[1] Otherwise, additional measures (different cut generation and convergence tests) have to be taken to take care of the extreme rays of $F(DSP_y)$ and $F(SD_{\mu_2})$ (see [Holmberg (1990, pp. 278] or [Wentges (1994, pp. 177] for more details).

modifications of the more general cross decomposition procedure.

Further note that – used as a heuristic – cross decomposition has the advantage of yielding good lower and upper bounds at the same time.
For a more detailed discussion of the cross decomposition algorithm see [Van Roy (1983], [Holmberg (1990], [Holmberg (1994] or [Wentges (1994, pp. 161].

3 Dually-Weighted Cross Decomposition

Summing up, the characteristic feature of the cross decomposition procedure is the explicit utilization of primal information (generated by solving the primal subproblems) for dual decomposition and vice versa. However, like Benders' or Dantzig-Wolfe decomposition, cross decomposition often shows a rather slow convergence behaviour. In particular, the occurrence of high jumps in the optimal values $v(SD_{\mu_2})$ (and $v(SP_y)$) of the dual (primal) subproblems is striking. There are grounds for the assumption that the information gathered so far in former iterations is insufficiently utilized. Therefore, the following modification of the cross decomposition algorithm based on [Wentges (1997] is proposed (cp. [Wentges (1994, pp.194]): Instead of taking the dual solutions of the primal subproblems or the solutions of the dual master problems as Lagrangian multipliers in the next iteration step, a specially weighted average of a subset of all Lagrangian multipliers generated so far is used. More precisely, to avoid the great variation of values $v(SD_{\mu_2})$ the Lagrangian multiplier μ_2^k used in iteration k is defined as the weighted average of the best Lagrangian multiplier $\mu_2^{\text{best},k-1}$ found so far (corresponding to the best lower bound $v(SD_{\mu_2^{\text{best},k-1}})$ after $k-1$ iterations) and the solution $\tilde{\mu}_2^k$ of the primal subproblem, if the dual convergence test was passed, or the dual master problem otherwise:

$$\mu_2^k = (\mu_{2j}^k)_{j=1}^e \text{ and } \mu_{2j}^k := \frac{\tilde{\mu}_{2j}^k + (w_k - 1) \cdot \mu_{2j}^{\text{best},k-1}}{w_k} \quad \forall j = 1, \ldots, e$$

with weight w_k ($\bar{c}$ is any constant ≥ 2)

$$w_k := \lfloor \min \{\bar{c}, (k + \text{ number of improvements of the lower bound})/2\} \rfloor .$$

Hence, starting from the best Lagrangian multiplier found so far only a small move (dependent on the weights w_k) into the direction of the newly constructed multiplier is performed. The dually-weighted cross decomposition procedure, therefore, looks for good multipliers in the vicinity of the best multipliers, and only those multipliers used in previous iterations are (implicitly) taken into account in the weighting process which contributed to the improvement of the lower bound. The weights w_k were chosen in the above manner in order to acknowledge the fact that the information contained in the best Lagrangian multiplier found so far increases with the number of iterations. Like in the weighted Dantzig-Wolfe decomposition procedure, the choice of the constant $\bar{c}$ is always a compromise between considering enough new information (through $\tilde{\mu}_2^k$) on one side and avoiding poor lower bounds $v(SP_{\mu_2^k})$ on the other side.

Proceeding with the primal variables y^k in exactly the same way is impossible, since the variables y are assumed to be integer variables. Nevertheless, the primal part of the cross decomposition algorithm could be accelerated by strengthening the Benders' cuts depending on the problem structure.

Apart from these alterations algorithm 2.1 remains unchanged so that the so-called dually-weighted cross decomposition procedure can be formally described in more detail as follows:

Algorithm 3.1: Dually-weighted cross decomposition

Notation: Let v_P (and v_D, respectively) be the value of the best upper (lower) bound and $(x^{\text{best},k}, y^{\text{best},k})$ $(u^{\text{best},k})$ the corresponding fixed integer variables (Lagrangian multipliers) after k iterations. N denotes the number of improvements of the lower bound v_D, and T_P^k (T_D^k) is the index set of the primal (dual) cuts generated after k iterations.

Step 1: *Initialization*
Set $k := 1$, $v_D := -\infty$, $v_P := \infty$, N:=0 and $\mu_2^{\text{best},0} :\equiv 0$. Determine suitable index sets[2] T_P^0 and T_D^0. Choose $y^1 \in P$. Go to step 2.

Step 2: *Solving the primal subproblem*

(i) Solve the primal subproblem (SP_{y^k}): Let x^k be an optimal primal and $\tilde{\mu}^k$ an optimal dual solution.

(ii) Add the primal cut belonging to $\tilde{\mu}^k$ to $(MP_{T_P^{k-1}})$: Set $T_P^k := T_P^{k-1} \cup \{k\}$.

(iii) If $v_P > v(SP_{y^k})$, set $v_P := v(SP_{y^k})$, $(x^{\text{best}}, y^{\text{best}}) := (x^k, y^k)$. Perform an optimality test: If $v_D \geq (1-\epsilon) \cdot v_P$ or $v(MP_{T_P^{k-1}}) \geq (1-\epsilon) \cdot v_P$, stop the procedure.

(iv) If (LD) is solved τ-optimal, go to step 4, otherwise set $w_k := \lfloor \min\{\bar{c}, (k+N)/2\} \rfloor$ and

$$\mu_{2j}^k := \frac{\tilde{\mu}_{2j}^k + (w_k - 1) \cdot \mu_{2j}^{\text{best},k-1}}{w_k} \quad \forall\, j = 1, \ldots, e.$$

[2]The index sets T_P^0 and T_D^0 should guarantee that the feasible sets of $(MP_{T_P^k})$ and $(MD_{T_D^k})$ are bounded.

(v) Carry out the dual convergence test (CTD): If

$$c'x^t + d'y^t + (b_2 - A_2x^t - B_2y^t)' \cdot \mu_2^k > v_D \;\; \forall\, t \in T_D^{k-1},$$

go to step 3, otherwise go to step 5.

Step 3: *Solving the dual subproblem*

(i) Solve the dual subproblem $(SD_{\mu_2^k})$: Let (x^{k+1}, y^{k+1}) be an optimal solution.

(ii) Add the dual cut belonging to (x^{k+1}, y^{k+1}) to $(MD_{T_D^{k-1}})$ (i.e. set $T_D^k := T_D^{k-1} \cup \{k+1\}$), if the cut is not contained in $(MD_{T_D^{k-1}})$.

(iii) If $v_D \geq v(SD_{\mu_2^k})$, set $\mu_2^{\text{best},k} := \mu_2^{\text{best},k-1}$. Otherwise set $v_D := v(SD_{\mu_2^k})$, $\mu_2^{\text{best},k} := \mu_2^k$, $N := N+1$, and check for optimality: If $v_D \cdot (1+\tau) \geq v(MD_{T_D^{k-1}})$, (LD) is solved τ-optimal. If $v_D \geq (1-\epsilon) \cdot v_P$, stop.

(iv) Perform the primal convergence test (CTP): If

$$b'\mu^t + (d - B'\mu^t)' \cdot y^{k+1} < v_P \;\; \forall\, t \in T_P^k,$$

set $k := k+1$ and go to step 2, otherwise go to step 4.

Step 4: *Solving the primal master problem*

(i) Solve the primal master problem $(MP_{T_P^k})$: Let (ρ^k, y^{k+1}) be an optimal solution.

(ii) If $v(MP_{T_P^k}) \geq (1-\epsilon) \cdot v_P$, stop, otherwise set $k := k+1$ and go to step 2.

Step 5: *Solving the dual master problem*
Solve the dual master problem $(MD_{T_D^k})$: Let $(\delta^k, \tilde{\mu}_2^k)$ be an optimal solution. Set

$$\mu_{2j}^k := \frac{\tilde{\mu}_{2j}^k + (w_k - 1) \cdot \mu_{2j}^{\text{best},k-1}}{w_k} \;\; \forall\, j = 1, \ldots, e,$$

$\mu_2^{\text{best},k} := \mu_2^{\text{best},k-1}$ and $k := k+1$. Go to step 3.

It can be shown analogously to [Wentges (1997] for the weighted Dantzig-Wolfe decomposition procedure that the lower bound v_D will be increased by at least $\frac{1}{w_k}(v(MD_{T_D^k}) - v_D)$, if a dual cut already contained in $(MD_{T_D^k})$ is duplicated in iteration $k+1$. Likewise it can be shown that if taking $\tilde{\mu}_2^k$ as Lagrangian multiplier leads to an improvement of the lower bound v_D, the same will hold true for μ_2^k (cp. [Wentges (1997, Theorem 4.1]).

Concerning the primal and dual convergence tests the following holds (cp. [Van Roy (1983, Lemma 5.2], [Holmberg (1990, Theorem 2.1] and [Wentges (1994, p. 198]):

Lemma 3.1:

a) For $y^{k+1} \in P$, passing the primal convergence test (CTP) in step 3 (iv) is a necessary condition for the improvement of the upper bound v_P (to $v(SP_{y^{k+1}})$) in the next iteration and a sufficient condition that either the upper bound v_P is decreased or a new primal (Benders') cut is generated.

b) For $\mu_2^k \geq 0$, passing the dual convergence test (CTD) in step 2 (v) is a necessary condition for the improvement of the lower bound v_D (to $v(SD_{\mu_2^k})$) and a sufficient condition for either a bound improvement or a dual cut improvement (generation of a new dual cut).

Proof:

a) (i) *"necessary"-part*
Assumption: y^{k+1} does not pass the primal convergence test (CTP), i.e. it exists a $\bar{t} \in T_P^k$ with:

$$b'\mu^{\bar{t}} + (d - B'\mu^{\bar{t}})' \cdot y^{k+1} \geq v_P.$$

It follows:

$$v(SP_{y^{k+1}}) = v(DSP_{y^{k+1}}) \geq b'\mu^{\bar{t}} + (d - B'\mu^{\bar{t}})' \cdot y^{k+1} \geq v_P.$$

An improvement of the upper bound, therefore, is impossible.

(ii) *"sufficient"-part*
If y^{k+1} does not lead to a bound improvement, for every optimal dual solution $\bar{\mu}$ of $(DSP_{y^{k+1}})$ the following holds:

$$\begin{aligned} b'\bar{\mu} + (d - B'\bar{\mu})' \cdot y^{k+1} &= v(SP_{y^{k+1}}) \geq v_P \\ &> b'\mu^t + (d - B'\mu^t)' \cdot y^{k+1} \quad \forall\, t \in T_P^k, \end{aligned}$$

i.e. a new primal cut will be generated.

b) Analogously to part a).

□

Under reasonable assumptions (see the comment in section 2), the finiteness of algorithm 3.1 can be shown with lemma 3.1:

Theorem 3.1:
Let the sets P, $F(SP_{\tilde{y}})$ $\forall \tilde{y} \in P$ and $F(SD_{\mu_2})$ be all nonempty and bounded. Then the following holds: The dually-weighted cross decomposition procedure terminates for all $\epsilon \geq 0$ after finitely many steps with an ϵ-optimal solution of (MIP).

Proof:
Because of the assumptions stated, all optimal dual solutions of the primal subproblems determined in step 2 (i) of algorithm 3.1 are extreme points of $F(DSP_{y^k})$ and all optimal solutions of the dual subproblems determined in step 3 (i) are extreme points of the convex hull of $F(SD_{\mu_2^k})$ (note that $F(DSP_{y^k})$ $(F(SD_{\mu_2^k}))$ is independent of y^k (μ_2^k)).

Since the number of extreme points of $F(DSP)$ and $F(SD)$ is finite, only a finite number of cut improvements and bound improvements is possible. With lemma 3.1, therefore, the primal convergence test (CTP) will be passed only a finite number of times. The assertion follows with the properties of the Benders' decomposition algorithm. □

Based on [Kornai and Liptak (1965], a somewhat similar approach, the so-called mean value cross decomposition algorithm, was proposed by Holmberg for linear programming problems to avoid solving the master problems at all, since solving the master problems is very time consuming compared to solving the subproblems (see [Holmberg (1992b], [Holmberg (1997] or [Holmberg (1999]). Instead of using the optimal dual solution of the primal subproblem as Lagrangian multiplier and the optimal solution of the dual subproblem as fixed integer combination for the primal subproblem, Holmberg suggests to take in both cases the average of *all* previously constructed solutions and to skip steps 4 and 5 completely. [Holmberg (1992b] shows for the non-integer case that this procedure converges to the optimal solution and leads to good computational results for a well-structured "purchase-or-produce"-problem.

4 Computational Results for the Capacitated Facility Location Problem

Both the original and the weighted cross decomposition algorithm were tested on instances of the capacitated facility location problem $(CFLP)$. The $(CFLP)$ is an attractive candidate for cross decomposition, since it inhabits an efficiently exploitable primal and dual structure. At the same time, $(CFLP)$ is one of the most important discrete location problems and can be formulated as the following mixed-integer programming problem:

$$
(CFLP) \quad \begin{cases}
\min \sum_{j=1}^{n} f_j y_j + \sum_{i=1}^{m} \sum_{j=1}^{n} c_{ij} x_{ij}, & \\
\sum_{j=1}^{n} x_{ij} = d_i \quad \forall\, i = 1, \ldots, m, & (D) \\
x_{ij} \leq d_i y_j \quad \forall\, i = 1, \ldots, m,\ j = 1, \ldots, n, & (B) \\
\sum_{i=1}^{m} x_{ij} \leq s_j y_j \quad \forall\, j = 1, \ldots, n, & (C) \\
x_{ij} \geq 0,\ y_j \in \{0,1\} \quad \forall\, i = 1, \ldots, m,\ j = 1, \ldots, n, & (G)
\end{cases}
$$

where n represents the number of potential facility locations and m the number of customers. s_j is the capacity of facility j, d_i the demand of customer i, c_{ij} are the costs of transporting one unit of the commodity from facility j to customer i, and f_j are the fixed costs of maintaining/building facility j. The variable y_j indicates whether facility j is open ($y_j = 1$) or not, and x_{ij} represents the amount shipped from facility j to customer i. The aim, therefore, is to locate a number of facilities (or warehouses etc.) for supplying customers with a certain commodity in such a way that the total distribution costs are minimized while the demand of all customers is met and all capacity restrictions are satisfied.

The capacitated facility location problem is strongly NP-hard (see [Cornuejols et al. (1991, p. 289]). The most efficient algorithms to solve $(CFLP)$ include the cross decomposition algorithm of [Van Roy (1986], a branch and bound procedure of [Beasley (1988] and a Lagrangian heuristic based on relaxing the customer constraints (D) of [Cornuejols et al. (1991]. In [Wentges (1996], an efficient modification of the Benders' decomposition algorithm for solving $(CFLP)$ is described.

Applying cross decomposition for solving $(CFLP)$, the primal subproblems obtained by fixing the integer variables y are relative easy to solve transportation problems. The best lower bounds for $(CFLP)$ using Lagrangian relaxation can be achieved by adding the valid inequality (T) "$\sum_{j=1}^{n} s_j y_j \geq \sum_{i=1}^{m} d_i$" to $(CFLP)$ and subsequently performing a Lagrangian relaxation with respect to the constraints (C) (see [Cornuejols et al. (1991, theorem 1]). Furthermore, adding inequality (T) guarantees that the feasible set of the primal subproblem corresponding to the optimal solutions y^k of the dual subproblems is nonempty and bounded, and with

$$
P = \{y = (y_j)_{j=1}^{n} : y_j \in \{0,1\} \ \forall\, j = 1, \ldots, n \text{ and } \sum_{j=1}^{n} s_j y_j \geq \sum_{i=1}^{m} d_i\}
$$

all assumptions of theorem 3.1 are fulfilled.

The (dually-weighted) cross decomposition algorithm was tested on 25 test problems with 19–108 facilities and 65–174 customers on the road network of Switzerland (see [Wentges (1994, p. 34f.]). The starting index set T_0 was constructed as described in [Van Roy (1986, p. 150f.]. In order to improve the primal convergence tests and the bounds derived from solving the primal master problems, the Benders' cuts were strengthened as described in [Wentges (1996]. Furthermore, the two Benders' cuts belonging to the solutions of the AddHi and DropHi heuristics (see [Jacobsen (1983]) were added to the primal master problem in order to enhance the convergence behaviour. Since the exact solution of the zero-one primal master problems is very time consuming, the primal master problems were solved only heuristically with the Balas-Martin algorithm (this explains the values "$v(MP_{T_P}) = 118530 > 117980 = v_P$" in example 1d or "$v(MP_{T_P}) = 88820 > 88790 = v_P$" in example 1i).[3] The algorithms were stopped if (i) the value of the Balas-Martin heuristic for $(MP_{T_P^k})$ coincided exactly with the upper bound v_P of the best primal solution found so far, and additionally $v(SP_{y^k}) = v_P$ held for the heuristic solution y^k of $(MP_{T_P^k})$, (ii) the value $v(MP_{T_P^k})$ determined by the Balas-Martin heuristic was in 6 iterations greater than v_P, or (iii) the maximum number of iterations (=50) was reached. The maximal value $\bar{c}$ for the weights w_k was set to 10, $\tau = 0,005$, and $\epsilon = 0$. Furthermore, as described in [Van Roy (1986], primal master problems were solved only when the Lagrangian dual (LD) was solved τ-optimal (in case the primal convergence test (CTP) in step 3 (iv) fails, one continues with step 5 i.e. another dual master problem is being solved). Proceeding in this manner, with the original cross decomposition procedure ten of the 25 examples could be solved "optimally"[4] (see table 1). In ten cases the Lagrangian dual was solved τ-optimal in less than 30 iterations and in another five cases within the maximal number of iterations.

Like already mentioned, the cross decomposition algorithm – though seen as one of the most efficient algorithms for solving $(CFLP)$ – yields worse results for harder problem instances, especially it the duality gap of the Lagrangian relaxation with respect to the capacity constraints is comparably high (see e.g. problem instances 3a-4a, 5a-5c). Van Roy himself points out that cross decomposition cannot be regarded as a panacea for solving the $(CFLP)$, since it is a NP-hard optimization problem. Nevertheless, cross decomposition can be improved substantially with the modifications described in section 3 as can

---

[3][Geoffrion and Graves (1974] point out that the exact solution of the Benders' master problems is not necessary at the start since they contain too little information at the beginning.

[4]Optimal was set in quotation marks, since the primal master problems were solved only heuristically. The optimality of the solutions found, however, could be verified in all cases with the ϵ-method as described in [Geoffrion and Graves (1974].

be seen from table 2. Now, the Lagrangian dual could be solved τ-optimally in 21 examples within 30 iterations. In the other four examples (3a,3c,5c,6c), the lower bounds were increased considerably.

Some further remarks are due. Without strengthening the Benders' cuts as described in [Wentges (1996] worse results were obtained. Also compared to the weighted Dantzig-Wolfe decomposition and especially compared to the original Dantzig-Wolfe decomposition the results were improved substantially with the dually-weighted cross decomposition algorithm (moreover, one obtains at the same time a feasible primal solution). Furthermore, proceeding as in the mean value cross decomposition algorithm proposed by Holmberg and taking the average mean of *all* previously constructed Lagrangian multipliers yielded poor results, since in this case the information of the quality of the lower bounds generated so far is not used at all.

References

[Beasley (1988] Beasley, J. E. (1988). An Algorithm for Solving Large Scale Capacitated Warehouse Location Problems. *European Journal of Operational Research*, 33:314–325.

[Cornuejols et al. (1991] Cornuejols, G., Sridharan, R. and Thizy, J. M. (1991). A Comparison of Heuristics and Relaxations for the Capacitated Plant Location Problem. *European Journal of Operational Research*, 50:280–297.

[Geoffrion and Graves (1974] Geoffrion, A. M. and Graves, G. W. (1974). Multicommodity Distribution System Design by Benders Decomposition. *Management Science*, 20(5):822–844.

[Holmberg (1990] Holmberg, K. (1990). On the Convergence of Cross Decomposition. *Mathematical Programming*, 47:269–296.

[Holmberg (1992a] Holmberg, K. (1992a). Generalized Cross Decomposition Applied to Nonlinear Integer Programming Problems: Duality Gaps and Convexification in Parts. *Optimization*, 23:341–356.

[Holmberg (1992b] Holmberg, K. (1992b). Linear Mean Value Cross Decomposition: A Generalization of the Kornai-Liptak Method. *European Journal of Operational Research*, 62:55–73.

[Holmberg (1994] Holmberg, K. (1994). Cross Decomposition Applied to Integer Programming Problems: Duality Gaps and Convexification in Parts. *Operations Research*, 42(4):657–668.

[Holmberg (1997] Holmberg, K. (1997). Mean Value Cross Decomposition Applied to Integer Programming Problems. *European Journal of Operational Research*, 97:124–138.

[Holmberg (1999] Holmberg, K. (1999). Mean Value Cross Decomposition Based Branch-and-Bound for Mixed-Integer Integer Programming Problems. In: Kall, P. and Lüthi, H.-J., editors, *Operations Research Proceedings 1998*, pages 200–209. Springer, Berlin.

[Holmberg and Jörnsten (1984] Holmberg, K. and Jörnsten, K. O. (1984). Cross Decomposition Applied to the Stochastic Transportation Problem. *European Journal of Operational Research*, 17:361–368.

[Jacobsen (1983] Jacobsen, S. K. (1983). Heuristics for the Capacitated Plant Location Model. *European Journal of Operational Research*, 12:253–261.

[Kim et al. (1989] Kim, S., Cho, S.-C. and Um, B.-S. (1989). A Simplified Cross Decomposition Algorithm for Multiple Right Hand Choice Linear Programming. *Journal of the Operational Research Society of Japan*, 32(4):441–449.

[Kornai and Liptak (1965] Kornai, J. and Liptak, T. (1965). Two-Level Planning. *Econometrica*, 33(1):141–169.

[Minoux (1986] Minoux, M. (1986). *Mathematical Programming - Theory and Algorithms*. John Wiley & Sons, Chichester et al.

[Van Roy (1980] Van Roy, T. J. (1980). *Cross Decomposition for Large-Scale, Mixed Integer Linear Programming with Application to Facility Location on Distribution Networks*. PhD thesis, Katholieke Universiteit Leuven.

[Van Roy (1983] Van Roy, T. J. (1983). Cross Decomposition for Mixed Integer Programming. *Mathematical Programming*, 25:46–63.

[Van Roy (1986] Van Roy, T. J. (1986). A Cross Decomposition Algorithm for Capacitated Facility Location. *Operations Research*, 34(1):145–163.

[Wentges (1994] Wentges, P. (1994). *Standortprobleme mit Berücksichtigung von Kapazitätsrestriktionen: Modellierung und Lösungsverfahren*. PhD thesis, University of St. Gallen.

[Wentges (1996] Wentges, P. (1996). Accelerating Benders' Decomposition for the Capacitated Facility Location Problem. *Mathematical Methods of Operations Research*, 44(2):267–290.

[Wentges (1997] Wentges, P. (1997). Weighted Dantzig-Wolfe Decomposition for Linear Mixed-Integer Programming. *International Transactions in Operational Research*, 4(2):151–162.

Notation: $v(MD_{T_D}), v_D, v(MP_{T_P})$ *and* v_P *denote the same values as described in algorithm 3.1 after termination of the cross decomposition algorithm after "it" iterations (*v_D^{30} *is the value of the best lower bound after 30 iterations). D-it denotes the number of iterations until the Lagrangian Dual (LD) is solved* τ*-optimally.*

Prob.	$v(MD_{T_D})$	v_D^{30}	v_D	D-It.	$v(MP_{T_P})$	v_P	It.
Ex1a	135980.00	135242.75	135772.22	34	135980.00	135980.00	45
Ex1b	144926.29	142262.16	143203.72	50		146710.00	50
Ex1c	163845.10	162944.47	163078.55	32	164040.00	164040.00	37
Ex1d	118061.47	117269.53	117712.68	42	118300.00	117980.00	50
Ex1e	99980.00		99593.50	19	99980.00	99980.00	39
Ex1f	104835.29	102693.37	103167.00	50		106650.00	50
Ex1g	111776.73	111161.26	111310.50	38	112040.00	112040.00	42
Ex1h	90930.10	90574.23	90574.23	31	90520.00	90950.00	50
Ex1i	80790.00		80408.33	10	80820.00	80790.00	50
Ex1j	69185.00		69090.00	5	69190.00	69190.00	15
Ex2a	168502.38		167707.47	27	170270.00	170270.00	39
Ex2b	164149.48		163772.91	12	164700.00	164700.00	25
Ex2c	226082.70		224971.19	17	229590.00	229590.00	30
Ex3a	142800.82	134880.00	134880.00	50		143450.00	50
Ex3b	102715.09	99449.86	102242.53	50		105110.00	50
Ex3c	123573.44	109600.00	109600.00	50		130640.00	50
Ex4a	529997.34	512100.00	516985.13	50		527560.00	50
Ex4b	304570.00		303750.00	2	304570.00	304570.00	44
Ex4c	356070.00		354570.00	15	355620.00	356070.00	50
Ex5a	141855.39	136490.00	138329.98	50		141910.00	50
Ex5b	101600.25	98601.55	100364.42	50		103320.00	50
Ex5c	554480.01	534330.00	534330.00	50		550120.00	50
Ex6a	43312.20		43107.10	5	43275.00	43480.00	50
Ex6b	59307.00		59197.00	18	57126.00	59307.00	50
Ex6c	69700.29	61081.00	61238.00	50		67207.00	50

Table 1: Cross decomposition algorithm to compute $v(CFLP)$

Notation: As in table 1.

Prob.	$v(MD_{T_D})$	v_D^{30}	v_D	D-It.	$v(MP_{T_P})$	v_P	It.
Ex1a	135980.00		135326.97	15	135980.00	135980.00	32
Ex1b	144408.78	143752.98	143752.98	30	145460.00	146710.00	50
Ex1c	164137.64		163322.89	16	164040.00	164040.00	27
Ex1d	117980.00		117444.86	17	117980.00	117980.00	30
Ex1e	99980.00		99518.44	17	99980.00	99980.00	39
Ex1f	104310.72		103877.91	27	104820.00	104820.00	49
Ex1g	111747.67		111291.16	16	112040.00	112040.00	26
Ex1h	90980.00		90532.32	15	90950.00	90950.00	46
Ex1i	80790.00		80573.80	8	80790.00	80790.00	49
Ex1j	69185.00		69120.00	5	69190.00	69190.00	6
Ex2a	168529.69		167897.97	22	170270.00	170270.00	34
Ex2b	164134.00		163915.13	21	164700.00	164700.00	31
Ex2c	226493.46		225449.38	14	229590.00	229590.00	25
Ex3a	139131.10	137755.13	138149.47	50		140840.00	50
Ex3b	101733.33		101232.41	20	101550.00	102680.00	50
Ex3c	118563.73	112939.45	113627.34	50		123450.00	50
Ex4a	523738.00		521244.28	23	516740.00	522720.00	50
Ex4b	304570.00		304165.00	2	304570.00	304570.00	44
Ex4c	356210.00		355763.28	4	355600.00	355880.00	50
Ex5a	138900.00		138218.94	27	138900.00	138900.00	31
Ex5b	101414.36		101062.39	20	102109.99	102600.00	50
Ex5c	546519.23	542162.00	543480.63	50		547630.00	50
Ex6a	43321.28		43243.67	3	43026.00	43480.00	50
Ex6b	59307.00		59216.51	21	57725.00	59307.00	50
Ex6c	67090.12	64163.67	64317.70	50		66641.00	50

Table 2: Dually-weighted cross decomposition to compute $v(CFLP)$

Optimal and Neuro–Dynamic Programming Solutions for a Stochastic Inventory Transportation Problem

L. Bertazzi[1], D.P. Bertsekas[2] and M.G. Speranza[1]

1 Dept. Quantitative Methods - University of Brescia, Italy

2 Laboratory for Information and Decision Systems - M.I.T., U.S.A.

Abstract

We study the problem of shipping a set of products from a supplier to a customer in the supply chain. Each product is made available at the supplier at a given constant rate and absorbed by the customer on the basis of a given probability distribution of the customer demand. An inventory cost is charged at the supplier and at the customer if the level of the inventory is positive and a penalty cost is charged at the customer if the demand exceeds the inventory on hand. Shipments from the supplier to the customer are performed by vehicles of given capacity which generate a fixed cost per journey. The aim is to find a shipping strategy that minimizes the total expected discounted cost over an infinite horizon. This problem is a sequential decision making problem under uncertainty which belongs to the class of problems that can be solved by dynamic programming techniques. We implement the well known Policy iteration algorithm in order to obtain the optimal solution of the problem. Then, we propose two heuristic algorithms based on Neuro–dynamic programming techniques and show their effectiveness on a set of randomly generated problem instances.

Keywords

Inventory, Transportation, Supply Chain, Neuro–dynamic Programming.

1 Introduction

The supply chain management has been recently recognized as a critical issue for the efficient and effective management of a company. The coordination of decisions among different stages of the supply chain and the consideration of various cost components in the decisions have been accepted as important principles in the supply chain management. In this paper we focus on the coordination of decisions between two stages of the supply chain, where a supplier serves a customer with a set of products. In the coordination of decisions a key role is played by the inventory levels at the supplier and the customer and by the transportation strategy between the two stages. We neither take the point of view of the supplier nor the point of view of the customer, but look at the system constituted by the two stages and aim at taking decisions which are good for the system and not for a part of the system only. The interaction between the two stages exists because flows of products physically go from the supplier to the customer. The transportation of these products is the physical operation which realizes the interaction. This operation lowers the inventory level at the supplier and rises the inventory level of the customer. We focus the analysis in this paper on the transportation costs and on the costs directly influenced by the transportation costs, namely the inventory costs at the supplier and at the customer and the stock-out costs. Our goal is to determine a shipping strategy which minimizes the sum of all the cost components.

The problem has been deeply studied in a deterministic setting, in which the products are made available at the supplier and consumed by the customer at a given constant rate. A classical approach to this problem can be found in Blumenfeld *et al.* (1985), where an EOQ–based model is presented. In this case shipments from the supplier to the customer are performed on the basis of a single frequency and the corresponding time between every two consecutive shipments can take any positive real value. Thanks to these assumptions, the problem can be easily solved and the optimal solution is in closed formula. Unfortunately, the optimal solution can be infeasible from a practical point of view, since the time between shipments can take any positive real value and a solution of the type "ship every $\sqrt{\pi}$ time instants" can be the optimal one. In order to go beyond this drawback of the EOQ approach, Hall (1985), Maxwell and Muckstadt (1985), Jackson *et al.* (1988) and Muckstadt and Roundy (1993) suggest that a more realistic assumption is to impose that the time between every two consecutive shipments is a multiple of a given feasible minimum time. For example, if the minimum time is equal to one day, a shipment, possibly with several vehicles, can be performed every day. A first approach based on this more realistic assumption can be found in Speranza and Ukovich (1994), where shipments are performed on the basis of a set of given "discrete" frequencies, and a second approach can be found in Bertazzi and Speranza (1997), where a shipment can be performed in each discrete time instant over a finite time horizon. In Bertazzi, Speranza and Ukovich (2000) it is shown that the former model can be efficiently solved.

All the above contributions consider two stages of the supply chain and assume a deterministic setting. While exact knowledge of the replenishment strategy can be reasonably assumed, realism can be certainly added to the model through the relaxation of the assumption of exact knowledge on the customer demand. Clearly, a stochastic assumption on the demand adds realism to the model, but makes it much more complicated to solve. While the stochastic assumption on the customer demand is typical in inventory theory, no paper is known for the situation analyzed here.

In this paper we consider a problem in which shipments can be performed in discrete time. Each product is made available at the supplier at a given constant rate and absorbed by the customer on the basis of a given probability distribution. Shipments from the supplier to the customer are performed by a fleet of vehicles with given transportation capacity and fixed cost per journey. The aim is to determine a shipping strategy that minimizes the expected discounted sum of inventory cost at the supplier and at the customer, penalty cost for the stock-outs and transportation cost over an infinite time horizon. The problem is an infinite horizon–sequential decision making problem under uncertainty in which each decision implies an immediate cost and has an influence on future decisions and thus on future costs. In other words, each decision has to take into account the trade–off existing between immediate cost and future costs. A natural way to approach this kind of problems is through stochastic dynamic programming (see Bertsekas, 1995). This technique gives a powerful framework for studying the problem and offers algorithms for computing the optimal solution. Unfortunately, dynamic programming algorithms can be applied only on small instances, given the well known Bellman's "curse of dimensionality". Therefore, a heuristic approach is required on problems of medium/large size. Recently, a new and promising heuristic approach has been introduced with the name of Neuro–dynamic programming (see Bertsekas, 1995 and Bertsekas and Tsitsiklis, 1996). This approach generates approximate dynamic programming solutions by using approximations of the optimal cost functions and possibly simulation and neural networks. An example of application of some of these techniques to logistic networks with one supplier and several customers can be found in Van Roy *et al.* (1997).

In this paper our aim is to use exact and Neuro–dynamic programming algorithms for the solution of the problem described above. In particular, we will implement the well known Policy iteration algorithm (see Bertsekas, 1995) in order to obtain the optimal solution of the problem and then we evaluate the performance of two Neuro–dynamic programming algorithms by comparing their solutions with the optimal one on randomly generated problem instances.

The paper is organized as follows. In Section 2 the problem is described and in Section 3 a dynamic programming formulation is given. In Sections 4 and 5 the exact and heuristic algorithms are presented, respectively. Finally, in Section 6 the computational results are shown.

2 Problem description

We consider the situation in which a set I of n products has to be shipped from a supplier A to a customer B. Each product $i \in I$ is made available at the supplier at a given constant rate q_i and is absorbed by the customer on the basis of a discrete random variable D_i with probability distribution P_i and mean q_i. The random variables D_i, $i \in I$, are independent and identically distributed. For each product $i \in I$ an inventory cost h_i is charged at the supplier and at the customer if the level of the inventory is positive. A penalty cost d_i is charged at the customer if the level of the inventory is negative. We denote with a_i and b_i the level of the inventory of product i at the supplier and at the customer, respectively. The level of the inventory of each product must satisfy the following constraints. At the supplier, a_i must be not lower than 0 and not greater than $\bar{a}_i$, being $\bar{a}_i$ the maximum quantity of product i that can be stored in A. At the customer, b_i must be not lower than $\underline{b}_i$, where $\underline{b}_i \leq 0$, and not greater than a maximum quantity $\bar{b}_i$. The quantity $\underline{b}_i$ represents the maximum backlog. In other words, when the level of the inventory b_i takes negative values, the excess demand is backlogged for the part that does not exceed $\underline{b}_i$, while the remaining part is lost. Shipments from the supplier to the customer are performed by an infinite fleet of vehicles. Each vehicle has a given transportation capacity r and cost c. The transportation cost is charged for each journey, independently of the quantity loaded on the vehicle. The transportation time is supposed to be constant and therefore equal to zero, without loss of generality. A shipment, possibly with several vehicles, can be performed in each discrete time instant.

The problem is to determine how to ship the products from the supplier to the customer in order to minimize the expected discounted total cost over an infinite time horizon. In particular, our aim is to find a stationary policy that, for each discrete time instant, gives the quantity of each product to ship from the supplier to the customer and the number of vehicles to use. The policy is a function of the level of the inventory at the supplier and at the customer and not also a function of the time instant in which the decision is taken.

3 Dynamic programming formulation

In this section we present a dynamic programming formulation of the problem described in the previous section.

State space

The state x is composed of the level of the inventory of each product $i \in I$ at the supplier and at the customer

$$x = (a_1^x, b_1^x, \ldots, a_n^x, b_n^x).$$

A	supplier
B	customer
i	index of the products
I	set of the products
n	number of products ($n = \|I\|$)
q_i	production rate of product i at the supplier and average demand of the customer
v_i	volume of product i
h_i	inventory cost of product i at the supplier and at the customer
d_i	penalty cost of product i at the customer
w_i	demand of product i by the customer
D_i	random variable representing the demand of product i by the customer
P_i	probability distribution of the discrete random variable D_i
$\bar{a}_i$	maximum quantity of product i that can be stored at the supplier A
$\bar{b}_i$	maximum quantity of product i that can be stored at the customer B
$\underline{b}_i$	maximum backlog of product i at the customer B
c	transportation cost per journey (independent of the volume loaded on the vehicle)
r	transportation capacity (volume)
α	discount factor
s_i	quantity of product i to ship from the supplier to the customer (variable)
y	number of vehicles to use (variable)

Table I: Table of Notation

Therefore, the state space is the set

$$S = \{x = (a_1^x, b_1^x, \dots, a_n^x, b_n^x) : 0 \le a_i^x \le \bar{a}_i, \quad \underline{b}_i \le b_i^x \le \bar{b}_i, \quad i \in I\},$$

and has the following cardinality:

$$|S| = \prod_{i=1}^{n} (\bar{a}_i + 1)(\bar{b}_i - \underline{b}_i + 1). \tag{1}$$

The cardinality of S can make the problem intractable even on instances with few products and with low capacity of the supplier and of the customer. For example, an instance in which only 5 products have to be shipped from the supplier to the customer, with maximum quantity $\bar{a}_i$ and $\bar{b}_i$ of each product that can be stored in A and in B, respectively, equal to 9 and maximum backlog $\underline{b}_i$ at the customer equal to 0, $\forall i \in I$, has a state space of cardinality equal to 10^{10}.

Control space

The control is composed of the quantity s_i of each product $i \in I$ to ship from the supplier to the customer and the number y of vehicles to use when the system is in state x.

The quantity s_i of each product $i \in I$ is supposed to be an integer number not lower than 0 and not greater than $\min\{a_i^x, \bar{b}_i - b_i^x\}$ when the system is in the state x. The first element on which the minimum is taken guarantees that the quantity of product i shipped from the supplier to the customer is available at the supplier when the shipment takes place. The second element guarantees that the quantity shipped can be stored at the customer.

The number of vehicles y can be optimally determined once the quantities s_i, $i \in I$, are known. In fact, given that the total cost increases with the number of vehicles, y is obviously equal to the minimum number of vehicles needed to ship the total volume, that is:

$$y^* = \left\lceil \frac{\sum_{i \in I} v_i s_i}{r} \right\rceil .$$

Therefore, the set $U(x)$ of feasible controls u associated to state $x \in S$ is given by the quantities s_i of each product $i \in I$ such that $0 \leq s_i \leq \min\{a_i^x, \bar{b}_i - b_i^x\}$, where the set $U(x)$ has the following cardinality:

$$|U(x)| = \prod_{i=1}^{n} \left(\min\{a_i^x, \bar{b}_i - b_i^x\} + 1\right) .$$

We can now define in a formal way the concept of stationary policy. A stationary policy μ is a stationary function (i.e., it does not depend on the time instant) that maps each state $x \in S$ into the control $u = \mu(x)$ such that $\mu(x) \in U(x)$.

Transition equation

Let $X_t = \left(A_t^1, B_t^1, \ldots, A_t^n, B_t^n\right)$ be the state of the system in the time instant t, where A_t^i is the level of the inventory of product i at the supplier A in the time instant t and B_t^i the corresponding level of the inventory at the customer B. Moreover, let $C_t = \left(C_t^1, \ldots, C_t^n\right)$ be the control applied in the time instant t, where C_t^i is the control applied for product i in the time instant t.

Suppose that in the time instant t the system is in the state $X_t = x$ and the control $C_t = u$ is applied. Then, in the time instant $t+1$ the system will be in the state $X_{t+1} = z$, where

$$a_i^z = \min\{a_i^x + q_i - s_i, \bar{a}_i\}$$

and

$$b_i^z = \max\{b_i^x + s_i - w_i, \underline{b}_i\}$$

for each product $i \in I$.
At the supplier $a_i^z = a_i^x + q_i - s_i$ if $a_i^x + q_i - s_i \leq \bar{a}_i$, while $a_i^z = \bar{a}_i$ otherwise. This means that a quantity q_i of product i is made available at the supplier

in the time instant t only if the inventory on hand in $t+1$ is not greater than the maximum quantity $\bar{a}_i$ that can be stored.

At the customer, $b_i^z = b_i^x + s_i - w_i$ if the demand w_i of product i is such that $b_i^x + s_i - w_i \geq \underline{b}_i$, while $b_i^z = \underline{b}_i$ otherwise. This means that the part of the demand that causes $b_i^x + s_i - w_i$ to be below $\underline{b}_i$ is lost.

Transition probabilities

The transition from state $X_t = x$ to state $X_{t+1} = z$ by using the control $C_t = u$ happens with probability

$$p(x,u,z) = \prod_{i=1}^{n} p\left(A_{t+1}^i = a_i^z | A_t^i = a_i^x, C_t^i = s_i\right) p\left(B_{t+1}^i = b_i^z | B_t^i = b_i^x, C_t^i = s_i\right)$$

where the first element is the probability that in the time instant $t+1$ the level of the inventory at the supplier A of product i is a_i^z, given that the level of the inventory in the time instant t is a_i^x and that the control s_i is used, while the second element is the probability that in the time instant $t+1$ the level of the inventory at the customer B of product i is b_i^z given that the level of the inventory in the time instant t is b_i^x and that the control s_i is used. The first probability can be expressed as follows:

$$p\left(A_{t+1}^i = a_i^z | A_t^i = a_i^x, C_t^i = s_i\right) = \begin{cases} 1 & \text{if } \min\{a_i^x + q_i - s_i, \bar{a}_i\} = a_i^z \\ 0 & \text{otherwise} \end{cases}$$

Recalling that the demand of product i is represented by a random variable D_i, then

$$p\left(B_{t+1}^i = b_i^z | B_t^i = b_i^x, C_t^i = s_i\right) = \begin{cases} p(D_i = b_i^x + s_i - b_i^z) & \text{if } b_i^z > \underline{b}_i \\ \sum_{w_i : b_i^x + s_i - w_i \leq \underline{b}_i} p(D_i = w_i) & \text{otherwise.} \end{cases}$$

Costs

The immediate cost $g(x,u,z)$ associated to the transition from state $X_t = x$ to state $X_{t+1} = z$ by using the control $C_t = u$ includes the inventory cost both at the supplier and at the customer if the level of the inventory is positive, the penalty cost at the customer for the stock-outs and the transportation cost:

$$g(x,u,z) = \sum_{i \in I} h_i[a_i^z + \max(0, b_i^z)] + \sum_{i \in I} d_i \max(0, -b_i^z) + c\left\lceil \frac{\sum_{i \in I} v_i s_i}{r} \right\rceil.$$

Therefore, the expected cost per stage can be expressed as follows:

$$\bar{g}(x,u) = \sum_{z \in S} p(x,u,z) g(x,u,z)$$

and the total expected discounted cost over an infinite time horizon when the system starts with the state x and the policy adopted is μ is:

$$J_\mu(x) = \lim_{N\to\infty} E\{\sum_{t=0}^{N} \alpha^t \bar{g}(x_t, \mu(x_t))|X_0 = x\}, \tag{2}$$

where α is a given discount factor ($0 < \alpha < 1$) and x_t is the state at time t. The problem is to find a policy μ that minimizes the expected discounted cost (2). In particular, if we denote with Π the set of feasible policies, the optimal cost is

$$J^*(x) = \min_{\mu\in\Pi} J_\mu(x) \qquad x \in S.$$

4 An exact algorithm

The problem formalized in the previous section can be optimally solved by using the well known *Value iteration* and *Policy iteration* algorithms (see Bertsekas, 1995). We implemented the Policy iteration algorithm.

Given any arbitrary starting policy μ_0, we generate a sequence of policies μ_1, μ_2, ... by iterating the following two steps. In the first one, referred to as *Policy evaluation step*, the current policy μ_k is evaluated by solving a linear system. The output of this step is the cost–to–go $J_{\mu_k}(x)$ of each state $x \in S$ associated to policy μ_k. In the second step, referred to as *Policy improvement step*, a new policy, not worse than the previous one, is generated on the basis of the cost–to–go $J_{\mu_k}(x)$ obtained in the previous step. These two steps are iterated until the new policy is equal to the previous one. More formally, the algorithm can be described as follows.

1. *Initialization step*: Set $k = 0$ and generate a starting policy μ_0 (in our implementation of the algorithm, μ_0 is generated in random way).

2. *Policy evaluation step*: Compute the costs $J_{\mu_k}(x)$, $\forall x \in S$, corresponding to the policy μ_k, by solving the following system of linear equations:

$$J_{\mu_k}(x) = \bar{g}(x, \mu_k(x)) + \alpha \sum_{z\in S} p(x, \mu_k(x), z) J_{\mu_k}(z) \qquad x \in S. \tag{3}$$

3. *Policy improvement step*: Generate a new policy μ_{k+1} greedy with respect to the cost-to-go $J_{\mu_k}(x)$ obtained in the previous step, that is:

$$\mu_{k+1}(x) = \arg\min_{u\in U(x)} [\bar{g}(x, u) + \alpha \sum_{z\in S} p(x, u, z) J_{\mu_k}(z)] \qquad x \in S. \tag{4}$$

4. If $\mu_{k+1}(x) = \mu_k(x)$, $\forall x \in S$, then stop. Otherwise, $k := k + 1$ and go to step 2.

This algorithm finds the optimal policy in a finite number of iterations. Unfortunately, the problem described in the previous section is such that even instances with a small number of products cannot be solved by any exact algorithm within a reasonable amount of time. The Policy evaluation step requires the solution of a linear system with dimension equal to the cardinality of the state space (1) and in the Policy improvement step a new policy is determined by enumerating all feasible controls $u \in U(x)$ for each state $x \in S$. Obviously, when the sets $U(x)$, $x \in S$, and the state space S are large, solving these steps can be very cumbersome or practically impossible. For that reason, in the next section we present heuristic algorithms for the solution of the problem.

5 Neuro–dynamic programming algorithms

In this section we present two heuristic algorithms based on the approximation of the cost–to–go function. In particular, we consider two approximate policy iteration algorithms (see Bertsekas and Tsitsiklis, 1996) in which the Policy evaluation step is solved heuristically by using simulation. In fact, instead of solving the linear system (3) exactly to obtain $J_\mu(x)$, $\forall x \in S$, we compute only an approximate cost–to–go function $\tilde{J}_\mu(x,\beta)$ that depends on the state x and on a vector of parameters β. Then, these approximate costs are used in the Policy improvement step in order to obtain a new policy. This new policy is not guaranteed to be better than the previous one. Therefore, the Approximate policy evaluation and the Policy improvement steps are iterated a fixed number of times T.

Let us describe in more detail the *Approximate policy evaluation step.* This step can be implemented in different ways depending on how the approximate cost–to–go function is chosen and on how the vector of parameters is updated. The cost architecture $\tilde{J}_\mu(x,\beta)$ we use is a linear function in the parameter vector $\beta = (\beta_0, \beta_1, \beta_2, \dots, \beta_m)$, that is

$$\tilde{J}_\mu(x,\beta) = \sum_{j=0}^{m} \beta_j \hat{w}_j(x), \tag{5}$$

where $\hat{w}_j(x)$ are given scalars referred to as basis functions. In particular, we use two different sets of polynomial basis functions, obtaining in this way two different heuristic algorithms. For the sake of simplicity, we will now show the basis functions we use only for the case with one product. The extension to several products is straightforward. In the first heuristic algorithm, referred to as *Linear*, the set of basis functions is the following

$$\hat{w}_0(x) = 1 \qquad \hat{w}_1(x) = a_1^x \qquad \hat{w}_2(x) = b_1^x,$$

while in the second one, referred to as *Quadratic*, it is

$$\hat{w}_0(x) = 1 \qquad \hat{w}_1(x) = a_1^x \qquad \hat{w}_2(x) = b_1^x$$

$$\hat{w}_3(x) = (a_1^x)^2 \quad \hat{w}_4(x) = \hat{w}_5(x) = a_1^x b_1^x \quad \hat{w}_6(x) = (b_1^x)^2.$$

Let us now consider how the parameter vector is updated during the algorithm. At each iteration k, a given number of states is generated in random way. Let $\tilde{S}$ be the set of all the generated states, $N(x)$ be the number of times the state x is in the set $\tilde{S}$ and $M = |\tilde{S}|$ the cardinality of $\tilde{S}$. Then, for each state $x \in \tilde{\tilde{S}}$, where $\tilde{\tilde{S}}$ is the set of the different states in $\tilde{S}$, we generate by simulation $N(x)$ trajectories of given length L and compute the corresponding total discounted cost $c_{\mu_k}(x,l)$, $l = 1, 2, \dots, N(x)$. Then, the parameter vector β is obtained by solving exactly the following least–squares optimization problem

$$\min_{\beta} \sum_{x \in \tilde{\tilde{S}}} \sum_{l=1}^{N(x)} (\tilde{J}_{\mu_k}(x,\beta) - c_{\mu_k}(x,l))^2.$$

Once the optimal parameter vector β^* is obtained, then the cost–to–go $J_{\mu_k}(x)$ is approximated by $\tilde{J}^+_{\mu_k}(x,\beta^*) = \max\{\tilde{J}_{\mu_k}(x,\beta^*), 0\}$, $\forall x \in S$.
The *Policy improvement step* is solved as in the exact Policy iteration algorithm. The only difference is that the approximate cost $\tilde{J}^+_{\mu_k}(x,\beta^*)$ is used instead of $J_{\mu_k}(x)$, $\forall x \in S$. Therefore, this step becomes:
Generate a new policy μ_{k+1} greedy with respect to $\tilde{J}^+_{\mu_k}(x,\beta^*)$, that is:

$$\mu_{k+1}(x) = \arg \min_{u \in U(x)} [\bar{g}(x,u) + \alpha \sum_{z \in S} p(x,u,z) \tilde{J}^+_{\mu_k}(z,\beta^*)] \qquad x \in S. \quad (6)$$

6 Computational results

The exact and heuristic algorithms presented in the previous sections have been implemented in C and compared on the basis of a set of randomly generated problem instances. The computations have been carried out on a personal computer with a Pentium II Intel Processor.

The instances have been generated according to the following data:

- Number of products: 1;
- Volume v_i: Randomly generated between 0.1 and 1 from a uniform distribution;
- Inventory cost h_i: Randomly generated between 1 and 5 from a uniform distribution;
- Penalty cost d_i: Randomly generated between 80 and 100 from a uniform distribution;

- Three different values of the maximum level of inventory at the supplier and at the customer $\bar{a}_i = \bar{b}_i$: 5, 10, 20;
- Maximum backlog at the customer $\underline{b}_i$: -5;
- Demand w_i: Randomly generated between 0 and $\bar{b}_i$ from a truncated Poisson distribution with mean q_i (randomly generated between 1 and $\bar{b}_i$);
- Transportation capacity r: 1
- Transportation cost c: 80;
- Discount factor α: 0.99;
- Length of the trajectories L: 1500;
- Total number of cost samples M: 50, 100, 1000;
- Number of iterations of Approximate policy iteration algorithm T: 100.

Let us briefly discuss the data chosen for the computational experiment. All the instances have been generated with a single product by implicitly assuming that a unit of the product represents either a transportation unit (for instance a pallet or a container) or a unit of a composite product (a proportional mixture of several products having volume, inventory cost and penalty cost equal to the corresponding weighted average values – see for instance Blumenfeld *et al.*, 1987). Given that the transportation capacity is normalized to 1, one vehicle can load from 1 to at most 10 of these units. By taking as time unit one day and as monetary unit 1\$ and by assuming that the yearly inventory cost is 10% of the value of the products, the value of one of these units ranges from \$3,650 to \$18,250.

The penalty cost ranges from \$80 to \$100, given that the transportation cost is 80\$.
Finally, the length of the trajectories generated in the neuro–dynamic programming algorithms is 1500 time units in order to guarantee a low truncation error with a discount factor of 0.99.

For each combination of the parameters, 5 instances have been randomly generated.

The performance of the heuristic algorithms has been evaluated as follows. For each instance, the optimal and heuristic policies have been evaluated by using the exact Policy evaluation step described in Section 4. Let $J^*(x)$ and $J^H(x)$ be the cost–to–go of state x generated by the optimal algorithm and

$\bar{a}_i = \bar{b}_i$	M	$\bar{\rho}_m^L$	$\bar{\rho}_m^Q$	$\bar{\rho}_a^L$	$\bar{\rho}_a^Q$	$\bar{\rho}_M^L$	$\bar{\rho}_M^Q$
5	50	1.9492	11.4912	2.3977	13.6956	3.1392	15.6721
5	100	2.5113	4.5659	3.1023	6.0760	3.6142	7.3707
5	1,000	0.6110	2.2991	0.7265	2.7999	1.0786	3.8432
10	50	2.5605	4.9847	3.2268	7.2108	4.9000	10.1740
10	100	0.9374	2.7316	1.1291	3.2901	1.6986	3.8477
10	1,000	0.6252	1.6370	0.7479	1.8662	1.1505	2.3006
20	50	5.4414	8.1689	7.2136	9.8166	12.2240	13.8701
20	100	2.8073	2.8890	3.9286	3.6228	6.3905	4.3021
20	1,000	0.0871	0.0254	0.1047	0.0294	0.2112	0.0532

Table II: Average percent increase errors on 5 instances

by the heuristic algorithm H, respectively. Then, for each state $x \in S$ we computed the average increase error between $J^H(x)$ and $J^*(x)$ as follows:

$$\rho^H(x) = \frac{J^H(x) - J^*(x)}{J^*(x)} * 100.$$

Then, we computed the maximum error ρ_M^H, the average error ρ_a^H and the minimum error ρ_m^H of heuristic H over all states $x \in S$. Finally, we computed the average values $\bar{\rho}_m^H$, $\bar{\rho}_a^H$ and $\bar{\rho}_M^H$ on the 5 instances.

The computational results are shown in Table II. In this table the first two columns contain the maximum level $\bar{a}_i$ and $\bar{b}_i$ of the inventory of each product i at the supplier and at the customer, respectively, and the number M of sample costs generated in the Approximate policy evaluation step. Columns 3 and 4 show the minimum errors $\bar{\rho}_m^L$ and $\bar{\rho}_m^Q$ of heuristics *Linear* and *Quadratic*, respectively; columns 5 and 6 the average errors $\bar{\rho}_a^L$ and $\bar{\rho}_a^Q$ and columns 7 and 8 the maximum errors $\bar{\rho}_M^L$ and $\bar{\rho}_M^Q$.

The following conclusions can be drawn from these computational results:

- The average error on all instances of the heuristic *Linear* is about 2.51% and the average error of the heuristic *Quadratic* is about 5.38%; moreover, when the number M of sample costs is $1,000$ the average error is about 0.53% for the heuristic *Linear* and about 1.57% for the heuristic *Quadratic*.

- the error tends to decrease when the total number M of sample costs increases;

- for the heuristic *Linear* the error tends to increase with the maximum quantity $\bar{a}_i$ and $\bar{b}_i$ of each product i that can be stored at the supplier and at the customer, respectively, while for the heuristic *Quadratic* tends to decrease;

- the heuristic *Linear* outperformes the heuristic *Quadratic*, with few exceptions in the situations with maximum level of inventory $\bar{a}_i$ and $\bar{b}_i$ equal to 20.

Conclusions

One of the critical issues in the supply chain management is the global view of the chain and, thus, in the quantitative modelling of the chain, the coordination among different stages and the optimization of a cost function which includes as many different cost components as possible. In this paper we have studied the problem of shipping products from a supplier to a customer with the objective of minimizing the sum of the different cost components related to this operation, namely the transportation cost, the inventory cost both at the supplier and at the customer and a penalty cost for the stock-out situations at the customer. Various contributions appear in the literature for deterministic settings and deterministic discrete time versions of the problem are known to be NP-hard. On the contrary, a stochastic version of the discrete time problem has never been studied. We assume here that the demand at the customer is stochastic and the discrete time problem we consider becomes very interesting and very complicated to solve. We show that neuro-dynamic programming techniques can be successfully applied for the solution of this problem, since the average error generated by a heuristic, based on a linear approximation of the cost-to-go function, with respect to the optimum is 0.53%, when implemented with 1000 sample costs.

References

Bertazzi, L. / Speranza, M.G. (1997): Optimal Periodic Shipping Strategies for the Single Link Problem. in: Technical Report n. 132, Department Quantitative Methods, University of Brescia, Italy (submitted)

Bertazzi, L. / Speranza M.G. / Ukovich, W. (2000): Exact and Heuristic Solutions for a Shipment Problem with Given Frequencies. in: Management Science 46, 973–988

Bertsekas, D.P. (1995): Dynamic Programming and Optimal Control, 2 Vols., Athena Scientific, Belmont

Bertsekas, D.P. / Tsitsiklis, J. N. (1996): Neuro–dynamic Programming, Athena Scientific, Belmont

Blumenfeld, D.E. / Burns, L.D. / Diltz, J.D. / Daganzo, C.F. (1985): Analyzing Trade-offs between Transportation, Inventory and Production Costs on Freight Networks. in: Transportation Research 19B, 361–380

Blumenfeld, D.E. / Burns, L.D. / Daganzo, C.F. / Frick, M.C. / Hall, R.W. (1987): Reducing Logistics Costs at General Motors. in: Interfaces 17, 26–47

Hall, R.W. (1985): Determining Vehicle Dispatch Frequency when Shipping Frequency Differs among Suppliers. in: Transportation Research 19B, 421–431

Jackson, P.L. / Maxwell, W.L. / Muckstadt, J.A. (1988): Determining Optimal Reorder Intervals in Capacitated Production–Distribution Systems. in: Management Science 34, 938–958

Maxwell, W.L. / Muckstadt, J.A. (1985): Establishing Consistent and Realistic Reorder Intervals in Production–Distribution Systems. in: Operations Research 33, 1316–1341

Muckstadt, J.A. / Roundy, R.O. (1993): Analysis of Multistage Production Systems. in: Graves, S.C., Rinnooy Kan, A.H.G. and Zipkin, P.H. (eds.), Handbooks in Operations Research and Management Science, Vol. 4: Logistics of Production and Inventory, North–Holland, 59–131

Speranza, M.G. / Ukovich, W. (1994): Minimizing Transportation and Inventory Costs for Several Products on a Single Link. in: Operations Research 42, 879-894

Van Roy, B. / Bertsekas, D.P. / Lee, Y. / Tsitsiklis, J.N. (1997): A Neuro–Dynamic Programming Approach to Retailer Inventory Management. in: Technical Report, Laboratory for Information and Decision Systems, Massachusetts Institute of Technology, Cambridge, MA

Modeling Approaches for Median Relations

Ulrich Tüshaus

Institute for Operations Research
University der Bundeswehr Hamburg, Germany

Abstract

In the recent past, different tools have been developed for a more problem-oriented approach to modeling which, in turn, might shorten the problem-solving process itself. For a problem example from qualitative data analysis—determining a median relation—it is illustrated how different modeling / optimizing environments (AMPL, OPL, LPL) as well as a developer environment (ECL^{i}PS^e) support a more natural problem formulation. In this context, a brief outline of the programming paradigm of constraint logic programming is given.

Keywords

Modeling, Modeling languages, Constraint logic programming, Data analysis, Median relations

1 Introduction

For the analysis of qualitative data, one possible approach suggests to transform the information—as described by the qualitative object characteristics—into one or more corresponding binary relations on the set of objects. As the result of the analysis, a single relation (usually with certain properties) has then to be determined which approximates best the input data as a whole. (Barthélemy and Monjardet (1981, 1988) give a detailed overview on this area; Schader (1981) proposes different ways how binary relations can be used to describe and evaluate qualitative data.)

Thus, the analysis is based on two sets of relations: the set $\mathcal{D}$ of data relations (describing the qualitative data of an application) and the set $\mathcal{M}$ of model relations (describing the objective, i.e., the desired result in an application). For the data of the problem instance, i.e., the set of relations $(R_m)_{m \in M} \subset \mathcal{D}$, an adequate approximation has to be determined: that is, (at least) one element $R^* \in \mathcal{M}$ with minimal distance to $(R_m)_{m \in M}$. Depending on the problem objective "classification" or "ordering", resp., the set $\mathcal{M}$ can be defined as the set of equivalence relations, the set of total preorders or the set of total orders on the set of objects.

To develop a method which can be used to determine the best classification or ordering, as a first step it is necessary to define a distance measure between $(R_m)_{m\in M} \subset \mathcal{D}$ and $R^* \in \mathcal{M}$—the distance between a set of relations and a single relation. Within the approximation it has to be assured that the result has the desired structural properties (classification or ordering, resp.)

2 Median relations

Let $\mathcal{R}$ be the set of binary relations on a (finite) set X, and R and S again two relations from $\mathcal{R}$. The *symmetric difference* of two relations R and S on X, i.e, two subsets $R \subset X \times X$ and $S \subset X \times X$, is defined as

$$\begin{aligned} R\Delta S &= (R \setminus S) \cup (S \setminus R) = \\ &\quad \big\{(x,y) : \big((x,y) \in R \wedge (x,y) \notin S\big) \vee \big((x,y) \notin R \wedge (x,y) \in S\big)\big\}\,. \end{aligned} \tag{1}$$

($R \setminus S$ is the set of elements of R not being elements of S.)

With the *cardinality* of the symmetric difference of R and S, i.e., $|R\Delta S|$, a distance on the set of binary relations on X is defined:

$$\delta(R,S) = |R\Delta S| = |R \setminus S| + |S \setminus R| = |R \cup S| - |R \cap S|\,. \tag{2}$$

This term counts the "differences" between the relations R and S, or more precisely: the binary relations between (with respect to the lattice order) R and $\inf\{R,S\}$ resp. $\inf\{R,S\}$ and S; here, $\inf\{R,S\} = \{(x,y) : x,y \in X,\, x\,R\,y \wedge x\,S\,y\}$. Barthélemy and Monjardet (1981, 1988) give an extensive discussion of the axiomatic properties of $\delta(R,S) = |R\Delta S|$.

The following definitions are based on Barthélemy and Monjardet (1981). For an arbitrary set $(R_m)_{m\in M}$ of relations and an arbitrary relation R Barthélemy and Monjardet denote as *remoteness* the expression

$$\Delta\big((R_m)_{m\in M}, R\big) = \sum_{m\in M} \delta(R_m, R), \tag{3}$$

where the distance $\delta(R_m, R)$ is defined as $|R_m \Delta R|$ (see (2)).
A relation R^* is a *median relation* of a set $(R_m)_{m\in M}$, if and only if

$$\Delta\big((R_m)_{m\in M}, R^*\big) = \min_{R\in\mathcal{R}} \Delta\big((R_m)_{m\in M}, R\big)\,. \tag{4}$$

Thus, the median relations have *minimal remoteness* with respect to the set $(R_m)_{m\in M}$.

Let $\mathcal{D}$ and $\mathcal{M}$ be two sets of relations on X and the set $(R_m)_{m\in M}$ a subset of $\mathcal{D}$. A relation R^* is a $\mathcal{M}$*-median*, if and only if

$$\Delta\big((R_m)_{m\in M}, R^*\big) = \min_{R\in\mathcal{M}} \Delta\big((R_m)_{m\in M}, R\big)\,. \tag{5}$$

Here, the set $\mathcal{M}$ defines the properties which the $\mathcal{M}$-median must possess.

The procedure which determines for an arbitrary set $(R_m)_{m\in M} \subset \mathcal{D}$ the set of $\mathcal{M}$-medians is the *median procedure.*

Several well-known problems can be formulated in this (relational) form: the minimal sum of distances to a given set (Fermat), the medians of an ordered sequence (Laplace), the medians of a set of total orders (Kemeny, 1959) or the medians of a set of equivalence relations (Régnier, 1965).

A first algebraic formulation of this problem is due to Barbut (1961); it shows that an appropriate solution procedure is a generalization of the well-known "majority rule" in voting theory by de Condorcet (1785).

In the following, the classification of objects, i.e., determining an equivalence relation as $\mathcal{E}$-median of a set of data relations, will be used as an example for discussion; here, the set $\mathcal{M}$ of model relations is the set $\mathcal{E}$ of equivalence relations.

The classification of objects may now be reformulated as searching for an $\mathcal{E}$-*median* relation R^*:

$$\Delta\left((R_m)_{m\in M}, R^*\right) = \min_{R\in\mathcal{E}} \sum_{m\in M} \delta\left(R_m, R\right), \tag{6}$$

i.e, R^* is equivalence relation, thus *reflexive, transitive* and *symmetric.*

With I as the set of objects, the following more detailed *optimization problem* in *algebraic form* results:

$$\left.\begin{array}{lll}
 & \multicolumn{2}{l}{\min\limits_{R} \sum\limits_{m\in M} \delta\left(R_m, R\right)} \\
\text{subject to} & & \\
\text{Reflexivity} & \text{for all } i \in I: & iRi \\
\text{Symmetry} & \text{for all } i,j \in I: & iRj \Rightarrow jRi \\
\text{Transitivity} & \text{for all } i,j,k \in I: & iRj \text{ and } jRk \Rightarrow iRk
\end{array}\right\} \tag{7}$$

3 Modeling

With

$$r_{mij} = \begin{cases} 1, & i\,R_m\,j \\ 0, & \text{otherwise} \end{cases} \qquad \text{and} \qquad x_{ij} = \begin{cases} 1, & i\,R\,j \\ 0, & \text{otherwise} \end{cases}$$

as the characteristic vector of R_m and R, resp., the term $\delta(R_m, R)$ can be expressed as

$$\begin{aligned}
\delta(R_m, R) = |R_m \Delta R| &= \sum_{i,j\in I} r_{mij}(1 - x_{ij}) + \sum_{i,j\in I} (1 - r_{mij})x_{ij} \\
&= \sum_{i,j\in I} \left(r_{mij} - 2r_{mij}x_{ij} + x_{ij}\right) \\
&= \sum_{i,j\in I} (1 - 2r_{mij})x_{ij} + \sum_{i,j\in I} r_{mij} \, . \qquad (8)
\end{aligned}$$

Determining a $\mathcal{M}$-median R^*

$$\Delta\left((R_m)_{m\in M}, R^*\right) = \min_{R\in\mathcal{M}} \Delta\left((R_m)_{m\in M}, R\right) = \min_{R\in\mathcal{M}} \sum_{m\in M} \delta(R_m, R)$$

can now be rewritten with (8) as

$$\min_{R\in\mathcal{M}} \sum_{m\in M} \delta(R_m, R) =$$

$$\min_{R\in\mathcal{M}} \left(\sum_{i,j\in I} \left(|M| - 2 \sum_{m\in M} r_{mij} \right) x_{ij} + \sum_{i,j\in I} \sum_{m\in M} r_{mij} \right) . \qquad (9)$$

For an arbitrary but fixed family $(R_m)_{m\in M}$ of data relations the last term $\sum_{i,j\in I} \sum_{m\in M} r_{mij}$ is constant; thus, $\Delta\left((R_m)_{m\in M}, R\right)$ is a linear function of the characteristic vector of R.

The requirement "R^* is equivalence relation", i.e., R^* is reflexive, symmetric and transitive, can be written with

Reflexivity:	$x_{ii} = 1$	for all $i \in I$
Symmetry:	$x_{ji} = x_{ij}$	for all $i, j \in I$
Transitivity:	$x_{ij} + x_{jk} - x_{ik} \leq 1$	for all $i, j, k \in I$

as linear constraints on R^*. Using

$$a_{ij} := \left(|M| - 2 \sum_{m\in M} r_{mij} \right) ,$$

a median relation is a solution of a binary linear optimization problem:

$$\left.\begin{aligned} &\text{Minimize} \sum_{i,j\in I} a_{ij}x_{ij} \\ &\text{subject to} \\ &\text{Reflexivity} \quad \text{for all } i \in I: \quad x_{ii} = 1 \\ &\text{Symmetry} \quad \text{for all } i,j \in I: \quad x_{ji} = x_{ij} \\ &\text{Transitivity} \quad \text{for all } i,j,k \in I: \quad x_{ij} + x_{jk} - x_{ik} \le 1 \\ &\qquad\qquad \text{for all } i,j \in I: \quad x_{ij} \in \{0,1\}\,. \end{aligned}\right\} \tag{10}$$

For this problem instance—the aggregation of equivalence relations to a single equivalence relation R^*—, Régnier (1965) already had written the requirement "R^* is reflexive, transitive, and symmetric" as constraints in the x_{ij}; in his approach, however, the transitivity constraints (written as $x_{ik} \ge x_{ij}x_{jk}$) are nonlinear in the variables x_{ij}.

A linear form of these restrictions has been developed by de Cani (1969); thus, he is able to define and solve his problem instance—the fitting of a total order to paired comparison data—as a linear optimization problem (linear objective function and linear constraints).

From this point of view, determining a median relation is a special instance of a classic optimization problem for which several solution methods have been developed: for example, linear programming (Régnier (1965), de Cani (1969), Marcotorchino and Michaud (1979)), *branch and bound* (Tüshaus (1983)), special cutting plane methods (Grötschel *et al.* (1982), Wakabayashi (1986), Grötschel and Wakabayashi (1987)), subgradient methods (Arditti (1982), Schader and Tüshaus (1986)), *simulated annealing* and *tabu search* (de Amorim *et al.* (1992)).

At this stage, we have two different forms of the problem: an algebraic form (7) and a linear model (10). In the following, several approaches will be introduced which are based on these model forms.

4 Modeling approaches

A classic approach for determining a median relation can be explained by developing and solving the corresponding binary linear optimization problem. First, the problem is described in algebraic form; next, human consideration leads to a specific model which, in most cases, is chosen with respect to appropriate solutions methods being at hand.

In our case, with the restrictions having a special form—for an arbitrary but fixed number of objects, the matrix of coefficients for the restrictions of problem (10) is constant—it is possible to develop a matrix generator for these coefficients. This generator can be used to provide a standard solver with these structural restrictions in an adequate input format (for example, the MPS format for linear programming). The other problem specific data are contained in the coefficients of the objective function.

This optimization problem can now be treated by one of the classic methods of the optimizers, e.g., ***branch and bound*** combined with the simplex method. The general problem solving process can be summarized as:

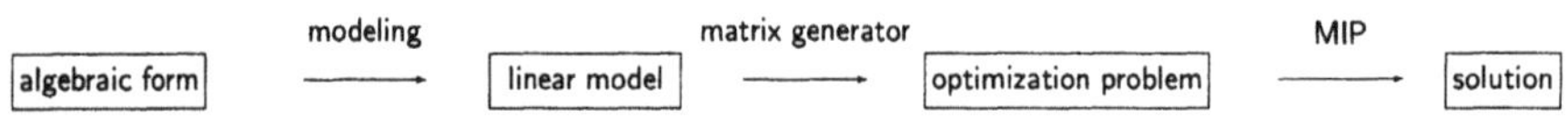

Guided by the concrete problem this approach naturally leads to optimal solutions; however, well-founded knowledge of the structure and the characteristics of the problem as well as a deep understanding of model forms and model alternatives together with suitable solutions methods are required.

While human problem understanding can hardly be replaced, recent optimizers offer some opportunities to support the problem solving process at least with some aspects of modeling and solving.

4.1 AMPL: A Mathematical Programming Language

The language AMPL (*A Mathematical Programming Language*) (Fourer *et al.* (1993), `http://www.ampl.com`) is a comprehensive and powerful algebraic modeling language for linear and nonlinear optimization problems in discrete and continuous variables.

It was developed at *Bell Laboratories* and allows to use the common notation and the familiar concepts for formulating optimization models and analyzing solutions without having to manage the data exchange with an appropriate solver.

The flexibility of the language makes it well-suited for the design of prototypes as well as for model development. Because of its speed and options for control it may also be used for repeated production runs. For many optimizers the corresponding interface is provided.

The modeling language offers broad support for sets and set operators as well as a general and natural syntax for arithmetic, logical, and conditional expressions; for summations and other iterated operators the usual notations are used. Alternative formulations are available for specific applications as, for example, network problems or piecewise-linear functions.

A central feature of this modeling language is the separation of model and data: the models remain concise even with growing problem size.

Here, the steps of the problem solving process can be described as:

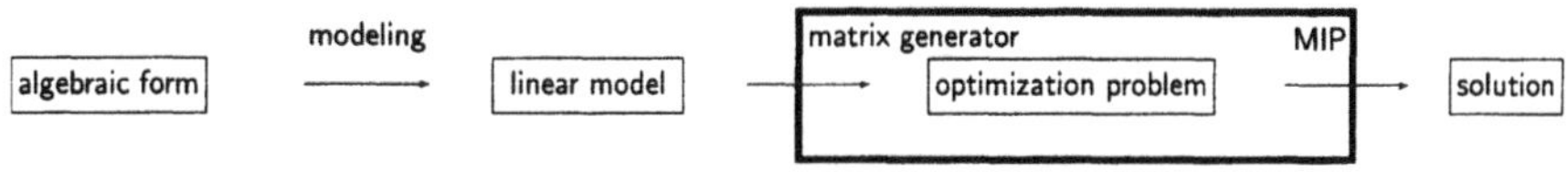

In Fig. 1, the linear model and its implementation in AMPL are compared. The distinction between parameters, variables, objective function and constraints emphasizes the model structure. The flexibility of modeling is supported by the clear separation of model and data: As neither dimensions nor values have to be supplied at this stage, the same model instance can be used for a whole problem class. Furthermore, it is easy to choose from alternative objective functions or to change restrictions: in our case, the symmetry constraint could be replaced by an antisymmetry constraint to determine an order (instead of an equivalence) as median relation.

Being similar to the algebraic formulation and notation, the language facilitates the implementation as well as the readability and intelligibility of a model.

As knowledge on certain (linear, nonlinear etc.) model structures is embedded, the choice of the appropriate type of solution approach (integer programming in our example) is supported. The necessary input data are then internally handed over to the optimizer, solved and presented externally in an uniform syntax.

4.2 LPL: Logical Programming Language

The language LPL (*Linear / Logical Programming Language*) (Hürlimann (1998), `http://www2-iiuf.unifr.ch/tcs/lpl/`) is also a modeling language for the design, development and documentation of large-scale mathematical models; for linear and mixed integer optimization problems the corresponding input data for optimizers are generated as well as reports of the results.

A compiler transforms the LPL model into the input format of the chosen optimizer, calls the optimizer and presents the results in an standardized internal format. Based on this, user-defined tables can be generated.

linear model

$$\text{Minimize} \sum_{i,j \in I} a_{ij} x_{ij}$$

subject to

$$\begin{array}{rrl} \text{Reflexivity} & \text{for all } i \in I: & x_{ii} = 1 \\ \text{Symmetry} & \text{for all } i, j \in I: & x_{ji} = x_{ij} \\ \text{Transitivity} & \text{for all } i, j, k \in I: & x_{ij} + x_{jk} - x_{ik} \leq 1 \\ & \text{for all } i, j \in I: & x_{ij} \in \{0, 1\} \end{array}$$

linear model: AMPL

□

Figure 1: Linear model and AMPL

In addition, LPL is a language for modeling logical restrictions: symbolically formulated logical constraints are internally transformed into corresponding linear constraints (modeled with binary variables).

A documentation feature, i.e., the automatic generation of a textual model description in a form suitable as input for a text processor (here TEX), is under development.

Thus, the problem solving process for determining a median relation with LPL can be described as:

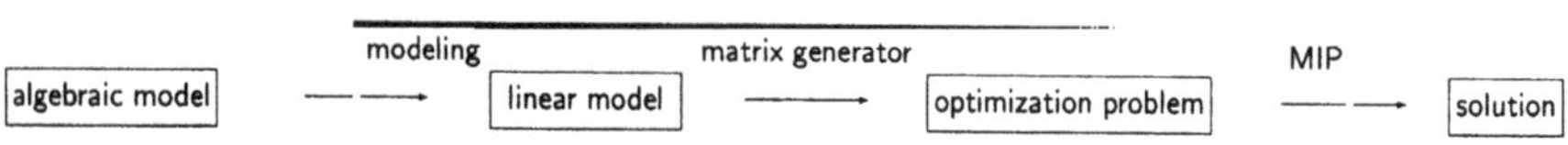

In Fig. 2, the algebraic form of the model and its implementation in LPL are compared.

As AMPL, the language LPL, too, is based on the algebraic notation of a model. Both languages (intentionally) share many common features, both with emphasis on clear model structure and flexible modeling.

An important difference becomes evident in the formulation of the restrictions for the problem example at hand. With LPL, the constraints for reflexivity, algebraic form

$$\min_R \sum_{m \in M} \delta(R, R_i)$$

subject to

$$\begin{array}{rll} \text{Reflexivity} & \text{for all } i \in I: & iRi \\ \text{Symmetry} & \text{for all } i,j \in I: & iRj \Rightarrow jRi \\ \text{Transitivity} & \text{for all } i,j,k \in I: & iRj \text{ and } jRk \Rightarrow iRk \end{array}$$

algebraic model: LPL

□

Figure 2: Algebraic form and LPL

symmetry and transitivity can be taken more or less directly from the algebraic form (Fig. 2). The transformation into a form suitable for the optimizer (linear constraints with binary variables, for instance) is done internally by the compiler of the modeling language.

In our example, the user is supported in an earlier step of the problem solving process and more specialized modeling knowledge is implicitly provided. The remaining steps are similar to those when using AMPL.

The main application areas for LPL are linear and mixed integer programming.

4.3 OPL: Optimization Programming Language

The third language, OPL (*Optimization Programming Language*) (Van Hentenryck (1999), `http://www.ilog.com`), is a modeling language for combinatorial optimization problems. As the other two languages, OPL, too, supports modeling of linear and integer optimization problems and their solution by an optimizer.

In addition, OPL offers *constraint programming.* Because the constraint component as well as the programming component of this approach are supported, the user can improve the solution procedure by providing problem-specific search methods.

For certain applications, such as scheduling or resource allocation problems, specific modeling and solution procedures are implemented.

More recent concepts as, for example, the logical combination of constraints enlarge the usual expressive possibilities of modeling languages.

These extensions for determining a median relation with OPL can now be summarized as:

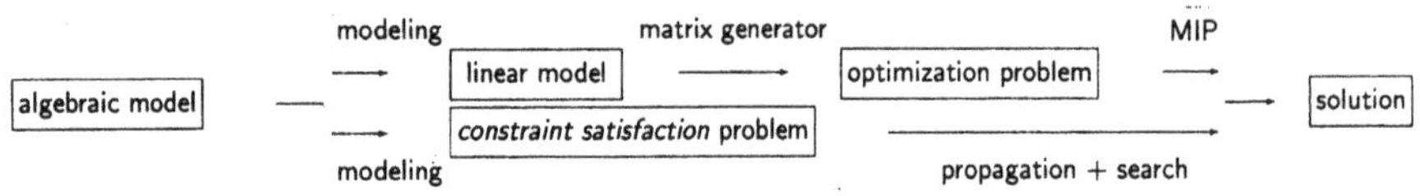

In Fig. 3, the algebraic form and its implementation in OPL are compared. As before, the reference to the usual algebraic notation of mathematical models enables clear model structures and flexible modeling.

A special feature of OPL can be found in how the model structure—expressed in the constraints—is evaluated to choose a problem-specific solution approach. In case of a linear model, a linear optimizer is used; if a constraint satisfaction problem is detected, a constraint-based method is chosen.

The solution of constraint satisfaction problems is based on a general solution procedure which for a given problem instance can be enhanced by special heuristic search strategies.

The simple method in Fig. 3 indicates how, on the one hand, OPL provides a general search method, and how, on the other hand, problem-specific knowledge can be used to improve the search strategy.

The constraint logic programming which provides techniques for modeling and solving constraint satisfaction problems will be discussed in more detail in the next section.

5 Constraint logic programming and median relations

At first, the development of constraint logic programming as an extension of logic programming will be sketched (Sec. 5.1). In particular, the integration of constraint systems in logic programming languages for solving special problem classes will be discussed. In Sec. 5.2 the constraint system $\mathcal{FD}$ (*Finite Domain*) will be described which has been used quite successfully to treat constraint satisfaction problems. Finally, a median relation is determined by a short declarative constraint logic program using a constraint system $\mathcal{FD}$ (Sec. 5.3).

algebraic form

$$\min_R \sum_{m \in M} \delta(R, R_m)$$

subject to

Reflexivity	for all $i \in I$:	iRi
Symmetry	for all $i, j \in I$:	$iRj \Rightarrow jRi$
Transitivity	for all $i, j, k \in I$:	iRj and $jRk \Rightarrow iRk$

algebraic model: OPL

□

Figure 3: Algebraic form and OPL

5.1 Background

In the seventies based on research in the area of artificial intelligence the programming paradigm of logic programming has been developed.

Using logic as a foundation to define a programming language seems natural with regard to two aspects: first of all, it is easy to represent a multitude of problems by logic; furthermore, with logic calculus, a formalism is available to describe the operational semantics of a programming language. Thus, by purely syntactical operations on strings, new expressions can be deduced from existing knowledge.

When compared to the classic programming paradigm, the main novelty in formulating and solving problems using a logic programming language is the strict separation of the knowledge component (describing the problem knowledge) and the control component (defining how to apply the knowledge to solving the problem) (Kowalski, 1979).

The probably best-known representative of such a logic programming language is Prolog (Programming in Logic) (Sterling and Shapiro, 1994). Developed in 1972 at Marseille by the "Groupe d'Intelligence Artificielle de Luminy" lead by A. Colmerauer, it was first used as an automatic theorem prover.

In Prolog, the knowledge component of a problem is described by a subset of first order predicate logic, the Horn clause logic. This defines the type of logic formula which might be used to specify problem knowledge as well as the logic calculus, the latter being used by the control component to evaluate the declared logic formulas.

Prolog's control component is based on an embedded evaluation mechanism. When the knowledge component of a problem has been specified by its logic description, the user can query the system by entering a logic formula. The system then tries by unification—a form of equating of logic expressions—and by resolution—a form of determining the satisfiability of logic formulas by logical deduction—to derive the user's query from the knowledge component of the problem (Rautenberg, 1996).

During the deduction process a state might be reached where alternative resolutions are possible; the system then stores this state, chooses one of the alternatives and continues with the calculation. If the deduction sequence fails because of a contradiction, the last state where an alternative resolution has been possible is restored and one of the remaining alternatives is analyzed next.

This nondeterministic evaluation strategy denoted as *backtracking* (Bitner and Reingold, 1975) represents a significant advantage of Prolog (compared to classic programming languages) when treating combinatorial problems with search. On the one hand, this is due to fact that the search process within the decision tree is provided by the programming language, and on the other, that backtracking has been implemented therein very efficiently.

To increase the flexibility in modeling and the efficiency of use for different applications of logic programming, in the mid eighties *constraint systems* were integrated within some logic programming languages.

Using a constraint system, the user is able to define a certain problem class very concisely in an adequate language. Here, the constraint system defines the feasible domain of a variable, a set of feasible algebraic operations and a set of possible relations between expressions. Logic formulas build from function and relation symbols of a constraint system are denoted as *constraints*. Examples for constraint systems are systems of linear equations for real numbers, the Boolean algebra or the calculus with finite domains, the latter often denoted as the constraint system $\mathcal{FD}$ (*Finite Domain*).

For defining the (typically quite complex) relations within a problem class, in logic programming *global constraints* are available. Such constraints define the relations between objects at a high level of abstraction; with an appropriate specification they can be adapted for a multitude of modeling situations.

To process constraints in a constraint logic program the unification algorithm from logic programming—deciding on the equality of two logic terms—was generalized to a decision procedure deciding on the satisfiability of a constraint or a set of constraints within a constraint system.

Furthermore, the concept of *constraint propagation* was introduced to treat constraint sets. By constraint propagation, new information which is implicitly contained in a constraint set is deduced; it is then added as new constraints to the existing problem knowledge. This leads to a more specific description of the problem solution and helps further to restrict the solution space.

This evaluation of the constraint sets is implemented in the *constraint solver*. However, the constraint propagation starting from the constraint solver is usually not sufficient to determine the problem solution directly: this is either because too few information is available or because the necessary deduction rules are unknown at this stage.

Therefore, the constraint propagation is followed by a phase in which search strategies are applied. By generating additional assumptions (expressed as constraints) based on the search strategy, the problem is divided into several subproblems and the evaluation process then continues.

In this way, constraint propagation alternates with search, thus steadily reducing the solution space. The problem solving process ends if the solution space consists of only one possible answer (the solution) or is empty (the problem being unsolvable).

Based on the synthesis of "processing constraints" and "programming in logic" the paradigm of "constraint logic programming" evolved. The introductory literature on constraint logic programming is still somewhat restricted; for readers with a background in predicate calculus and in logic programming a theoretical introduction is given in Frühwirth and Abdennadher (1997), while Marriott and Stuckey (1998) demonstrate practical applications. A comprehensive overview on constraint logic programming provide Jaffar and Maher (1987).

5.2 Constraint satisfaction problems and the constraint system $\mathcal{FD}$

A combinatorial problem with variables restricted to certain values from a finite domain is denoted as a constraint satisfaction problem (CSP). A CSP consists of a constraint set C on variables $X_1, \ldots, X_n$ and a function D which assigns to each variable X_i a finite set of values $D(X_i)$. The CSP can be characterized by the constraint

$$C \wedge X_1 \in D(X_1) \wedge \ldots \wedge X_n \in D(X_n) .$$

Problems like this are of major interest in operations research and in artificial intelligence as well as other areas of computer science. On the one hand, this is due to the natural way of describing decision alternatives by constraint satisfaction problems, for example, by relating the different values a variable can take with different decision alternatives. On the other hand, the generality of this concept contributed to the development of new search techniques for decision trees; together with the evaluation by a constraint solver, inconsistent variable assignments can be detected earlier. In many cases, it is then possible to exclude significant parts of the solution space from further analysis. Denoted as "local consistency techniques" (Kanal and Kumar, 1988) these techniques helped to successfully treat several problem classes known as NP-hard even for practically relevant problem sizes, e.g., scheduling problems, set covering problems, packing problems or graph coloring problems.

To model and solve constraint satisfaction problems, the constraint system $\mathcal{FD}$ was developed at the end of the eighties; since then, it has made significant contributions to the solution of problems from this class. Its integration within a logic programming language was done first in the programming language CHIP (Van Hentenryck, 1989).

The signature (as in logic theory) of a constraint system $\mathcal{FD}$ can vary with the actual constraint logic programming language. Mostly, it contains the usual function symbols "+" to add $\mathcal{FD}$ variables, together with ".." to define intervals on integer numbers, the binary constraint symbols $=_{FD}$, $\leq_{FD}$, $<_{FD}$, $>_{FD}$, $\geq_{FD}$, $\neq_{FD}$, and the symbol "::" for assigning a domain to a $\mathcal{FD}$ variable.
The feasible constraints of a (exemplary) constraint system $\mathcal{FD}$ could be defined as follows:

$$C ::= \mathit{true} \mid \mathit{false} \mid X :: n..m \mid X :: [k_1, ..., k_l] \mid X \odot Y \mid X + Y =_{FD} Z \mid C \wedge C \ ,$$

where n, m, $k_1, \ldots, k_l$ $(0 \leq l)$ are integer numbers from the variable domains, the symbol $\odot$ is one of the constraint symbols $=_{FD}$, $\leq_{FD}$, $<_{FD}$, $>_{FD}$, $\geq_{FD}$ or $\neq_{FD}$, and X, Y and Z are variables or integer numbers. In addition, some of the global constraints already mentioned might also be used.

The (operational) semantics of the constraint operators and symbols introduced above depend on the implementation of the constraint solver, in particular the consistency technique used. In general, the solver will be implemented such that those variables assignments will be removed which lead to an inconsistency.

Example The CSP

$$X \neq Z \wedge Z \neq Y \wedge W + X = Y + 1 \wedge D(X) = \{0, 1, 2\} \wedge$$

$$D(Y) = D(Z) = \{0,1\} \wedge D(W) = \{0,2\}$$

can be formulated—after having introduced an auxiliary variable $V1$—using the simple constraint system $\mathcal{FD}$ (from above) as follows:

$$X \neq_{FD} Z \wedge Z \neq_{FD} Y \wedge W + X =_{FD} V1 \wedge Y + 1 =_{FD} V1 \wedge \\ X :: [0,1,2] \wedge Y :: [0,1] \wedge Z :: [0,1] \wedge W :: [0,2] \wedge V1 :: [1,2] \, .$$

The unique solution of this CSP is

$$X = 2 \wedge Y = 1 \wedge Z = 0 \wedge W = 0 \wedge V1 = 2 \, .$$

In the meantime, the constraint system $\mathcal{FD}$ has shown to be useful for modeling numerous applications. Particularly for solving problems of industrial scheduling (Breitinger and Lock, 1995), crew scheduling (Guerinik and van Caneghem, 1995) and timetabling (Goltz and Matzke, 1999), the constraint system $\mathcal{FD}$ is well suited. A up-to-date overview on constraint satisfaction problems and their constraint-based solution together with applications can be found in Brailsford *et al.* (1999).

5.3 Determining a median relation by constraint logic programming

Using the constraint system $\mathcal{FD}$, a concise constraint logic program can be formulated that redefines the model for determining an equivalence relation R^*, i.e.,

$$\min_R \sum_{m \in M} \delta(R, R_m)$$

subject to

$$\begin{array}{rll} \text{Reflexivity} & \text{for all } i \in I: & iRi \\ \text{Symmetry} & \text{for all } i,j \in I: & iRj \Rightarrow jRi \\ \text{Transitivity} & \text{for all } i,j,k \in I: & iRj \text{ and } jRk \Rightarrow iRk \, , \end{array}$$

in a declarative form.

The program (including a simple greedy search) is here implemented in the programming language ECL^{i}PS^e (*ECL^{i}PS^e Common Logic Programming System*) (Aggoun *et al.* (1999), `http://www.icparc.ic.ac.uk/eclipse`). The programming environment ECL^{i}PS^e is a Prolog-based system integrating some extensions of logic programming, particularly constraint logic programming.

To represent the reflexivity and the symmetry property, a $|I| \times |I|$ matrix is generated: with a binary variable for every pair of objects, the value "one" is assigned if the pair belongs to the same equivalence class (and "zero" otherwise). Defining the diagonal elements as "one" and forcing variables of "opposite" pairs to equal values, the reflexivity and symmetry properties are satisfied. The following constraint implements this matrix:

```
bin_re_sym_matrix(Matrix,I) :-
   integer(I), I > 0,
   dim(Matrix,[I,I]),
   ( for(J,1,I),
     param(Matrix,N)
     do
       ( for(K,J,I),
         param(Matrix,J,N)
         do
           subscript(Matrix,[J,K],X),
           ( J = K
             -> X = 1
             ; subscript(Matrix,[K,J],X),
             X::0..1 ) ) ).
```

For implementing the transitivity restrictions within the constraint system $\mathcal{FD}$, the domain of a variable can be used to model alternative decisions. In our example, the following relation holds for each triple of elements of the set of objects: either the three objects belong to different equivalence classes, just two belong to the same class or all three objects are elements of the same class. Thus:

$$\forall \{i,j,k\} \in \{N \mid N \subset I \wedge |N| = 3 \wedge i < j < k\} : x_{ij} + x_{jk} + x_{ik} \in \{0,1,3\}\,.$$

The constraint

```
transitive(I,Matrix):-
   ( for(J,1,I), param(N,Matrix)
     do
       ( for(K,(J+1),I), param(J,I,Matrix)
         do
           ( for(L,(K+1),I), param(J,K,Matrix)
             do
               Domain::[0,1,3],
               subscript(Matrix,[J,L],X),
               subscript(Matrix,[J,K],Y),
               subscript(Matrix,[K,L],Z),
               X+Y+Z #= Domain              ) ) ).
```

ensures that the equation above holds for all triples of the set of objects.

Together, the two constraints define all necessary restrictions for the relation R^*.

As a starting point for a suitable search strategy, it seems reasonable—with respect to the objective function—to assign a value of "one" (same class) preferably to variables with a coefficient less than zero (high similarity of objects) in the objective function and a value of "zero" to all others. Furthermore, it makes sense to make these assignments in increasing order of the objective function coefficients. This heuristic tries to arrange first the pairs of objects with stronger similarity into the same equivalence class.

The resulting algorithm can then be formulated as follows:

1. Generate a list `SortList` with elements $[i, j]$ sorted by increasing objective function coefficients a_{ij}.
2. Take the first element $[i, j]$ from the list `SortList`.

   If $a_{ij} < 0$, then
   Try $x_{ij} := 1$, else Try $x_{ij} := 0$;
   else
   Try $x_{ij} := 0$, else Try $x_{ij} := 1$.

3. Remove $[i, j]$ from the list, continue with step 2.

Here, the nondeterministic behavior of the algorithm becomes evident. In a first try, those variables are tentatively assigned a value of "one" whose objective function coefficients can decrease the objective function value; the other variables are assigned a value of "zero". If such an assignment fails at one point of the search—because of violating one or more constraints generated so far—backtracking immediately starts and the variable concerned is assigned an alternative value.

The following ECL^{i}PS^e code implements this search:

```
heuristic(Matrix):-
gen_sort_list(SortList),
   labeling(SortList,Matrix).

gen_sort_list(SortList) :- !,
   bagof(ObjCoeff-[J,K],data(J,K,ObjCoeff),List),
   keysort(List,SortList).

labeling([],_,_).
labeling([X|RestList],Matrix):-
   ObjCoeff-[J,K] = X,
```

```
    ( ObjCoeff < 0
       -> labeling1([J,K],Matrix)
       ;   labeling2([J,K],Matrix)
    ),
labeling(RestList,Matrix).

labeling1([J,K],Matrix):-
   1 is Matrix[J,K].

labeling1([J,K],Matrix):-
   0 is Matrix[J,K].

labeling2([J,K],Matrix):-
   0 is Matrix[J,K].

labeling2([J,K],Matrix):-
   1 is Matrix[J,K].
```

Modifications of this model, for example, a restriction on the number of classes or on the number of elements of a class, can be easily implemented by additional constraints.

6 Concluding remarks

The structure of many combinatorial optimization problems requires time and broad expertise not only with respect to the problem domain (modeling), but also with respect to algorithmic development (solving). As often the gap between the mathematical model and the computer model might be considerable, a significant investment in algorithmic implementation and in problem solving is necessary.

With modeling languages, the separation of model and data allows for the development of model libraries and the easy application of few well-tested models for many problem instances.

Modeling systems offer a uniform interface to different, often specialized optimizers and thus simplify a problem-adequate choice of the solution method.

They enable a simpler, more natural implementation of the original problem. Different models (from "more concrete" to "more abstract" formulations) provide different options to incorporate knowledge on structure (and properties) of the problem and its solutions.

For the problem at hand—determining a median relation—, the different modeling approaches possible within the optimizing systems are summarized once again in Fig. 4.

These advantages (the separation of data and model, the declarative form of modeling, the embedding of problem-specific knowledge into the solution procedure) can also be found within ECL^{i}PS^e.

It becomes evident that such systems represent a development environment for models and algorithms in which alternative model formulations and different solution strategies can be realized and tested in a flexible and simple way.

References

Aggoun, A., Chan, D., Dufresne, P., Falvey, E., Grant, H., Herold, A., Macartney, G., Meier, M., Miller, D., Mudambi, S., Novello, S., Perez, B., van Rossum, E., Schimpf, J., Shen, K., Tsahageas, P. A., and de Villeneuve, D. H. (1999). ECL^{i}PS^e user manual release 4.2. Technical report, IC-Parc, Centre for Planning and Resource Control, Imperial College of Science, Technology and Medicine, London SW7 2AZ.

Arditti, D. (1982). Un nouvel algorithme de recherche d'un ordre induit par des comparaisons par paires. Note technique NT/PAA/TIM/MTI/ 811, Centre National d'Études des Télécommunications, Issy-les-Moulineaux, France.

Barbut, M. (1961). Médiane, distributivité, éloignements. Publications du Centre de Mathématique Sociale, E. P. H. E., 6e section, Paris. (*Mathématiques et Sciences humaines*, vol. 18 (1980), no. 70 (Été), pp. 5–31).

Barthélemy, J. P. and Monjardet, B. (1981). The median procedure in cluster analysis and social choice theory. *Mathematical Social Sciences*, **1**(3), 235–267.

Barthélemy, J. P. and Monjardet, B. (1988). The median procedure in data analysis: New results and open problems. In Bock (1988), pages 309–316.

Bitner, J. R. and Reingold, E. (1975). Backtrack programming techniques. *Communications of the ACM*, **18**, 651–656.

Bock, H. H., editor (1988). *Classification and Related Methods of Data Analysis.* First Conference of the International Federation of Classification Societies, Rheinisch-Westfälische Technische Hochschule Aachen, June 29 – July 1, 1987. North-Holland, Amsterdam.

Brailsford, S. C., Potts, C. N., and Smith, B. M. (1999). Constraint satisfaction problems: Algorithms and applications. *European Journal of Operational Research*, **119**, 557–581.

Breitinger, S. and Lock, H. C. R. (1995). Using constraint logic programming for industrial scheduling problems. In C. Beierle and L. Plümer, editors, *Logic Programming: Formal Methods and Practical Applications*, pages 273–299. Elsevier, Amsterdam.

de Amorim, S. G., Barthélemy, J.-P., and Ribeiro, C. C. (1992). Clustering and clique partitioning: Simulated annealing and tabu search approaches. *Journal of Classification*, **9**(1), 17–41.

de Cani, J. S. (1969). Maximum likelihood paired comparison ranking by linear programming. *Biometrika*, **56**(3), 537–545.

de Condorcet, M. J. A. N. C. (1785). *Essai sur l'Application de l'Analyse à la Probabilité des Décisions Rendues à la Pluralité des Voix.* Paris. (Reprint Chelsea Publ. 6, New York, 1974).

Fourer, R., Gay, D. M., and Kernighan, B. W. (1993). *AMPL: A Modeling Language for Mathematical Programming.* Duxbury Press / Wadsworth Publishing Company, Belmont, CA.

Frühwirth, T. and Abdennadher, S. (1997). *Constraint-Programmierung: Grundlagen und Anwendungen.* Springer-Lehrbuch. Springer-Verlag, Berlin Heidelberg New York.

Goltz, H.-J. and Matzke, D. (1999). University timetabling using constraint logic programming. In G. Gupta, editor, *Practical Aspects of Declarative Languages*, volume 1551 of *Lecture Notes in Computer Science*, pages 320–334. Springer-Verlag, Berlin Heidelberg New York.

Grötschel, M. and Wakabayashi, Y. (1987). A cutting plane algorithm for a clustering problem. Report 9, Institut für Mathematik, Universität Augsburg, Memminger Straße 6, D–8900 Augsburg.

Grötschel, M., Jünger, M., and Reinelt, G. (1982). A cutting plane algorithm for the linear ordering problem. WP 82219-OR, Institut für Operations Research, Universität Bonn.

Guerinik, N. and van Caneghem, M. (1995). Solving crew scheduling problems by constraint programming. In Montanari and Rossi (1995), pages 481–498.

Hürlimann, T. (1998). Reference manual for the LPL modeling language (version 4.30). Working paper, Institute of Informatics, University of Fribourg, site Regina Mundi, rue de Faucigny 2, CH-1700 Fribourg.

Jaffar, J. and Maher, M. J. (1987). Constraint logic programming: A survey. *Journal of Logic Programming*, (19, 20), 503–573.

Kanal, L. and Kumar, V. (1988). *Search in Artificial Intelligence.* Springer-Verlag, New York, Berlin, Heidelberg.

Kemeny, J. G. (1959). Mathematics without numbers. *Daedalus*, **88**, 577–591.

Kowalski, R. (1979). Algorithm = logic + control. *Communications of the ACM*, **22**(7), 424–436.

Marcotorchino, J. F. and Michaud, P. (1979). *Optimisation en analyse ordinale des données*, volume 4 of *Statistiques et décisions économiques.* Masson, Paris.

Marriott, K. and Stuckey, P. J. (1998). *Programming with constraints: An introduction.* MIT Press, Cambridge, MA.

Montanari, U. and Rossi, F., editors (1995). *Principles and Practice of Constraint Programming – CP'95*, volume 976 of *Lecture Notes in Computer Science.* Springer-Verlag, Berling-Heidelberg-New York.

Rautenberg, W. (1996). *Einführung in die mathematische Logik.* Vieweg, Braunschweig.

Régnier, S. (1965). Sur quelques aspects mathématiques des problèmes de classification automatique. *International Computer Centre Bulletin*, **4**, 175–191. Reprint in *Mathématiques et Sciences humaines*, vol. 21 (1983), no. 82, pp. 13–29.

Schader, M. (1981). *Scharfe und unscharfe Klassifikation qualitativer Daten*, volume 65 of *Mathematical systems in economics.* Verlagsgruppe Athenäum Hain Scriptor Hanstein, Königsteim/Ts.

Schader, M. and Tüshaus, U. (1986). Subgradient methods for analyzing qualitative data. In W. Gaul and M. Schader, editors, *Classification as a Tool of Research*, Karlsruhe, pages 397–403. North-Holland, Amsterdam.

Sterling, L. and Shapiro, E. (1994). *The Art of PROLOG: Advanced Programming Techniques.* MIT Press series in logic programming. MIT Press, Cambridge, MA, 2. edition.

Tüshaus, U. (1983). *Aggregation binärer Relationen in der qualitativen Datenanalyse*, volume 82 of *Mathematical Systems in Economics.* Athenäum Hain Hanstein, Königstein/Ts.

Van Hentenryck, P. (1989). *Constraint Satisfaction in Logic Programming.* Logic Programming Series. MIT Press, Cambridge, MA.

Van Hentenryck, P. (1999). *The OPL Optimization Programming Language.* MIT Press, Cambridge, MA.

Wakabayashi, Y. (1986). *Aggregation of Binary Relations: Algorithmic and Polyhedric Investigations.* Dissertation, Universität Augsburg.

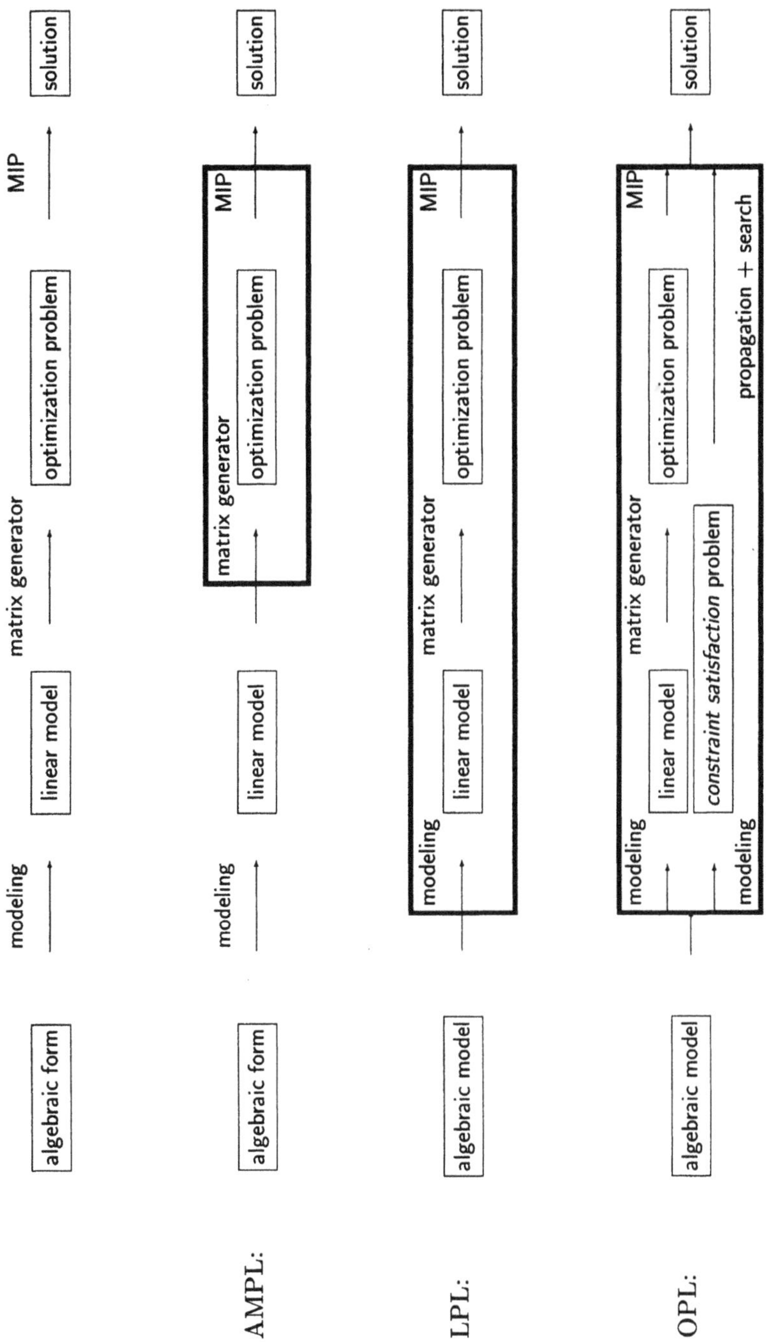

Figure 4: Median relations and optimizer systems

A Note on the "More-for-Less" Paradox

Mikulas Luptacik

Department of Economics,

Vienna University of Economics and Business Administration, Austria

Abstract

The more-for-less paradox, arising in some linear programming models is connected with a rather unexpected result: by increasing all or some output requirements (without reducing other outputs) we can obtain lower total cost (under ceteris paribus assumption). Using the notion of "technological" optimal structure and its analytical expression an economic interpretation of this paradox is discussed.

1 Introduction

In two independent papers, first by CHOBOT - TURNOVEC (1974) and then by CHARNES - DUFFUAA - RYAN (1987) the so called more-for-less paradox was explored and the necessary and sufficient conditions for its existence were derived. In CHOBOT - TURNOVEC (1974) an economic interpretation of the paradox using the notion of "technological" optimal output structure is discussed.

In this paper the "technological" optimal structure is characterized analytically which leads to a deeper economic interpretation of the "more-for-less" paradox. In Section 2 the paradox is illustrated by a numerical example. In Section 3 the "more-for-less" paradox is described generally and "technological" optimal output structure is defined. In Section 4 the "technological" optimal structure is characterized analytically and an economic interpretation of the paradox is discussed.

2 Numerical example

Suppose the firm using 6 different technologies T_1, T_2 ... T_6 has to produce the given amounts of two products. The technology $T_j\,(j = 1, 2, \dots 6)$ is described by the output coefficients a_{ij} giving the amount of good $P_i\,(i = 1, 2)$ produced by the technology T_j with unit intensity. In our example the matrix A of the output coefficients is

$$A = \begin{pmatrix} 3 & 2 & 3 & 2 & 2 & 4 \\ 1 & 1 & 2 & 2 & 3 & 5 \end{pmatrix}$$

The output requirements are denoted by the vector $\underline{b}' = (30, 40)$. The unit costs (expressed in Euro) are described by the vector $\underline{c}' = (2, 1, 4, 2, 6, 8)$. The decision problem of the firm is: how to combine the different technologies and at which intensities in order to produce the given amounts $\underline{b}'$ of the products P_1 and P_2 at the minimal cost?

The corresponding linear programming problem can be formulated as

$$\text{minimize } \textit{to} \quad f_0(\underline{x}) = 2x_1 + x_2 + 4x_3 + 2x_4 + 6x_5 + 8x_6$$

$$\text{subject to} \qquad \begin{aligned} 3x_1 + 2x_2 + 3x_3 + 2x_4 + 2x_5 + 4x_6 &= 30 \\ x_1 + x_2 + 2x_3 + 2x_4 + 3x_5 + 5x_6 &= 40 \\ x_1, x_2, x_3, x_4, x_5, x_6 &\geq 0 \end{aligned} \tag{1}$$

The optimal solution to problem (1) is $\underline{x}^0 = (0, 0, 0, 0, 5, 5)$ with the objective function value $f_0(\underline{x}^0) = 70$ Euro.

Suppose we increase the output requirements in the production problem (1) from (30, 40) to (50, 60). The optimal solution for this new problem (with the new right handside in (1)) is now $\underline{x}^* = (0, 10, 0, 20, 0, 0)$ with the objective function value $f(\underline{x}^*) = 50$ Euro. The firm produces more of both products (100 % more of the product P_1 and 25 % more of the product P_2) for less total costs (71,4 % of the previous cost). Hence we have the more-for-less paradox in this situation.

Looking carefully at the example (1), the interpretation of this result is straightforward. Because of the equality constraints in (1) the output requirements

(30, 40) forces the firm to choose a combination of technologies T_5 and T_6 which are in the structure similar or more closed to this required output structure. Change in the level but primarily in structure of the outputs (the proportion of the product P_1 is higher than of the product P_2) allows to switch from technologies T_5 and T_6 to the technologies T_2 and T_4 which are cheaper (the unit cost is lower) and their combination corresponds to the structure of the new output vector $\underline{b}' = (60, 50)$. In this way – despite of the increasing production of both goods – the total cost decreases.

3 "More-for-less" and "technological" optimal output structure

After the numerical illustration we define the more-for-less paradox generally. Let us consider the following problem of linear programming with all $c_j\,(j = 1, 2, ..., n)$ and $b_i\,(j = 1, 2, ..., m)$ assumed positive:

$$\text{minimize} \qquad f_0(\underline{x}) = \underline{c}'\underline{x}$$

$$\text{subject to} \qquad \begin{array}{l} A\underline{x} = \underline{b} \\ \underline{x} \geq \underline{0} \end{array} \tag{2}$$

where A is an $m \times n$ matrix $(m < n)$ and of full rank, $\underline{b}$ is an $m \times 1$ vector, $\underline{x}$ is an $n \times 1$ vector and $\underline{c}$ is an $n \times 1$ vector.

The problem (2) has the property more-for-less if we can increase all or some components of $\underline{b}$ and reduce the value of the objective function $f_0(x)$ without reducing other components of $\underline{b}$, and keeping all c_j fixed. The following theorem (CHOBOT - TURNOVEC (1974), p. 379) or (CHARNES - DUFFUAA - RYAN (1987), p. 195) provides the necessary and sufficient condition for the more-for-less paradox.

Theorem 1: The linear programming problem (2) has the property more-for-less if and only if every optimal solution of corresponding dual problem

$$\text{maximize} \qquad g(\underline{u}) = \underline{b}'\underline{u}$$

$$\text{subject to} \qquad A'\underline{u} \leq \underline{c}$$

has at least one negative dual variable u_i^0.

Returning to our numerical example (1), the reader may verify that the corresponding dual problem yields the unique optimal solution $\underline{y}^0 = (-3, 4)$. Thereupon an increase of the production of good P_1 by one unit (under ceteris paribus assumption) reduces the total cost by 3 Euro. In this way the sources for the reduction of total cost and for the situation more more-for-less can be revealed. In the example (1) we have increased more substantially the production of good P_1 and the production of good P_2 (its shadow price y_2^0 is positive) only moderate.

As shown in the example (1) from the economic interpretation point of view the explanation for the more-for-less paradox can be find in the deviation of the given output structure described by the vector $\underline{b}$ from the structure of the technologies used by the firm. This leads to the notion of "technological" optimal structure.

For the given unit cost $c_j (j = 1, 2, ..., n)$ and the output coefficients a_{ij} there exist a "technological" optimal structure of production described by $\underline{s}^0 = (s_1^0, s_2^0, ..., s_m^0)$

which can be found by solving the following linear programing problem (CHOBOT - TURNOVEC (1974), p. 348):

$$\text{minimize} \quad f_0(\underline{x}) = \sum_{j=1}^{n} c_j x_j \tag{3}$$

subject to

$$\sum_{j=1}^{n} a_{ij} x_j - s_i = 0 \qquad (i = 1, 2, ..., m) \tag{4}$$

$$\sum_{i=1}^{m} s_i = 1 \tag{5}$$

$$\begin{aligned} x_j &\geq 0 \qquad (j = 1, 2, ..., n) \\ s_i &\geq 0 \qquad (i = 1, 2, ..., m) \end{aligned} \tag{6}$$

The "technological" optimal structure can deviate considerably from the given output structure, described by the coefficients b_i:

$$\underline{s} = (s_1, s_2, ..., s_n),$$

$$\text{where} \qquad s_i = \frac{b_i}{\sum_{i=1}^{n} b_i}.$$

Because of the equalities constraints in the problem (2) it is not always possible to realize the "technological" optimal structure $\underline{s}^0$. If the value of the structures $\underline{s}^0$, described by the optimal value of the objective function (3) deviates considerably from the value of the required production structure s, the increasing production in the problem (2) accompanied by changing the production structure towards the "technological" optimal structure $\underline{s}^0$ will lead to decreasing production cost.

4 Analytical characterization of the "technological" optimal structure

The numerical illustration given by example (1) (and numerical examples in CHOBOT - TURNOVEC (1974) and then by CHARNES - DUFFUAA - RYAN (1987) may lead to the interpretation that the cost reduction can be achieved by the switch to the technologies with lower unit cost c_j only.

Let us consider another example with five technologies, two products and the following matrix of output coefficients:

$$A = \begin{pmatrix} 3 & 2 & 1 & 2 & 4 \\ 1 & 1 & 2 & 2 & 5 \end{pmatrix}$$

The output requirements are given by vector $\underline{b}' = (15, 5)$ and the unit cost by vector $\underline{c}' = (5, 3, 3, 4, 6)$.

The optimal solution of problem (2) yields $\underline{x}^0 = (5, 0, 0, 0, 0)$ with the objective function value $f(\underline{x}^0) = 25$ Euro. The optimal solution of the dual problem is not unique but for every optimal solution the dual variable y_2^0 is negative. One of the optimal solutions is e.g. $\underline{y}^0 = (2, -1)$. Due to Theorem 1 the necessary and sufficient condition for the more-for-less paradox is fulfilled.

Suppose the output requirements increase from (15, 5) to (16, 20). To meet these new requirements, it is optimal for the firm to switch from the technology T_1 to the most expensive technology T_5 $(c_5 = \max c_j)$ because the output structure of this technology coincides with the structure of the new output vector $\underline{b}$. Despite of the increasing production of good P_2 four times, the total cost decreases from 25 to 24 Euro. The deeper explanation of this result may be find in the analytical characterization of the "technological" optimal structure of production.

For this purpose we consider the dual problem corresponding to the problem (3) – (6):

$$\text{maximize} \quad g(\underline{u}) = u_{m+1} \tag{7}$$

$$\text{subject to} \quad \sum_{i=1}^{m} a_{ij} u_i \le c_j \qquad (j = 1, 2, \ldots, n) \tag{8}$$

$$-u_i + u_{m+1} \le 0 \qquad (i = 1, 2, \ldots, m) \tag{9}$$

Assuming $s_i > 0$ the complementary slackness theorem yields:

$$u_{m+1} = u_i \qquad (i = 1, 2, \ldots, m).$$

The dual constrains (8) can be then rewritten as:

$$\sum_{i=1}^{m} a_{ij} u_{m+1} \le c_j \qquad (j = 1, 2, \ldots, n)$$

or

$$u_{m+1} \le \frac{c_j}{\sum_{i=1}^{m} a_{ij}} \qquad (j = 1, 2, \ldots, n).$$

The optimal solution of the dual problem (7) – (9) is given by

$$u_{m+1}^0 = \min \frac{c_j}{\sum_i a_{ij}} \qquad (j = 1, 2, \ldots, n). \tag{10}$$

Using the complementary slackness theorem the "technological" optimal structure can be easily obtained according to the relation (10).

In our example “technological” optimal structure is described by the structure of the technology T_5, which coincides with the output requirements. The minimum in (10) is unique, only the technology T_5 will be chosen.

References

Charnes, A., Duffuaa, S. , Ryan, M. (1987): The more for less paradox in linear programming,. European Journal of Operational Research 31, 194 – 197

Chobot, M., Turnovec, F., (1974): O jednom ekonomickom paradoxe v modeloch linearneho programovania (One economic paradox in linear programming models, Ekonomicko-matematický obzor 4, 374-386

Project Experiences and Some Principal Considerations Concerning Operations Research as an Interesting Branch of Science

T. Kämpke and F. J. Radermacher

Forschungsinstitut für anwendungsorientierte Wissensverarbeitung, Ulm, Germany

Introduction

This paper first gives some considerations concerning major fields of Operations Research and addresses experiences, potential and philosophy of the field. In the second part, some hints are given to project work done at the FAW (Forschungsinstitut für anwendungsorientierte Wissensverarbeitung in Ulm, Germany). The topics concern practical applications in fields such as optimization, decision theory and knowledge management. The approaches taken are of an interdisciplinary nature and combine different levels of expertise. We demonstrate the availability of a variety of choices and applications and the interaction of methodological and managerial aspects. The paper concludes with some remarks on the Institut für Unternehmensforschung, Operations Research of the Hochschule St. Gallen and some indications to contributions of Prof. Paul Stähly, whose 65 birthday is celebrated with this paper.

1 Optimization, decision support and knowledge management. Some trends in Operations Research

Operations Research in the past 50 years has been a vital academic discipline. This area of science contributes to decision making and efficient resource allocation by applying optimization tools in a wide sense. Operations Research today is applied in almost all areas of society, even in robotics. It is typical for Operations Research that the work is based on a broad range of models including a broad range of optimization aims and that, at least in part, quite elaborate analytical approaches are used. The methodological spectrum is flexibly adapted to application needs rather than cultivated in a narrow or exclusively mathematical fashion. It is essential to combine heuristics with mathematics and to combine modelling in the large with modelling in the small.

The field has gained enormously by the development of modern information and communication technologies. The availability of huge data bases or data warehouses, the World Wide Web with direct access to many sources of knowledge, the automatic acquisition of data etc. are of great importance. All this has totally changed the picture, has broadened the scope of applications and always gives new stimulations. Of particular interest are e. g. business support systems such as by SAP, which, based on access to many data resources, addresses issues like human resource management, logistic, etc. They involve ever more elaborated tools from optimization which may or may not be hidden from the user. In other areas, such as autonomous agents, we see the use of tools that intend to capture preferences of users and make them directly available for internal computation and decision making.

As a whole, the effort needed to translate the needs of users into information system frameworks that can use OR tools is constantly reduced, while the integration of different aspects of an application problem is always becoming easier. Of course, this development is driven by many academic disciplines. We mention here, in particular, computer science with its many branches, but also many areas of engineering. There is a fruitful interaction between Operation Research and fields such as artificial intelligence, neural networks, fuzzy systems and knowledge management.

To summarize, Operations Research is a very interesting field which, with its emphasis on optimization, decision support and knowledge management is placed at the heart of where intelligent technology is going to improve processes of various nature. Also, via an integration with other areas such as artificial intelligence, simulation, virtual reality and e-commerce new interesting opportunities emerge that are also attractive from a commercial point of view. In the following Part 2 we will give hints to a few applications. In Part 3 a few remarks to Prof. Stähly and his contributions will conclude the paper.

2 Optimization, decision support and knowledge management

In this chapter we illustrate project work at the FAW that addresses the fields of optimization, decision support and knowledge management. Concerning one topic there is a close co-operation with Prof. Stähly himself and with Dr. Solte, FAW Ulm, Dozent Hochschule St. Gallen.

2.1 Use of optimization methods

2.1.1 Integrated electronic traffic information: the projects DELFI and EU Spirit

Modern information systems provide access to detailed traffic information like optimal connections between two train stations. This may concern optimization aims such as minimization of transition time, number of train changes, cost etc. By now there are information systems on the national and even on the European level that deal with optimal train connections. The optimization methods used to find the best connections are essentially of a graph theoretic nature. In effect, most problems in this field can be translated into a suitable shortest path problem. The nature of the optimization aim determines the particular kind of graph optimization problem. Within the project DELFI, FAW and a branch of the Deutsche Bahn collaborated with the major information system suppliers for regional traffic information systems in Germany to cover all public transport. The project was funded by the Federal Ministry of Transportation in Germany.

While in principle that could have been done with the presently available algorithms by applying them to a pool of data of all operators of public transportation, this approach did not work because of practical concerns and probably hidden agendas and commercial interest of the different economic actors involved.

FAW helped to overcome these obstacles by bringing in the idea of a distributed algorithmic solution. It lies in the nature of this problem and of the graph optimization problems occurring that it is possible to solve a nationwide optimization problem of that type by doing quite a number of optimization steps on the regional level and then combining these partial solutions on an abstracted level for a solution for Germany. Again, this is a classical approach from graph theory, but here it opens the way to overcome an organisational problem, comp. (Radermacher, Schaal, Schnittger (1998)), (Radermacher and Schaal (1997)), (Möhring (1999)), (Kämpke and Radermacher (1999)).

Interesting enough it turned out that a distributed approach is also a key to extend the approach further into areas where data pooling would never have been possible. This concerns European-wide information systems as well as even more integrated traffic systems, combining the public side with individual traffic but also with other kinds of travel related information such as traffic agencies. DELFI lead to activities in both directions. On the European scale the project EU-Spirit was started and is by now essentially implemented. It provides a European version of DELFI ranging from Scandinavia via Germany and Austria to Italy and proves the validity of the approach also in this context (Schnittger (1999)), (Henninger Schnittger, Haug (1999)).

To summarize, a quite involved issue of providing information with huge effect on the quality of traffic information has been solved by combining organisational and institutional arrangements to bypass specific legal and economic constellations. The essential step was the use of a graph theoretic optimization approach which allowed a distributed solution to finding optimal travel connection. As so often it is "mathematics inside" that opens the door while an enormous amount of organisational requirements concerning the nature of data structures, naming issues, quality assurance, interfacing, communication protocols and so on is then the real tough practical issue to do the implementation.

2.1.2 Scheduling in the field of wafer handling

Scheduling is a very important field of operations research. A great part of real life is about the question when to start a certain activity and when not. It is therefore not surprising that scheduling applications are found everywhere. Scheduling offers a broad range of algorithmic challenges by varying the parameters of a problem. In the following, we report on one example that FAW has recently been involved with, namely the processing of quite involved wafers, that need special handling machines including a robot. The scheduling task is about the movements and activities of that robot.

Reduction of clean room cost in wafer fabrication calls for the use of so-called machine clusters. Typically, these clusters are layed out as hexagons with work stations on the perimeter and a manipulator (robot arm) for loading and unloading the work stations placed in the center. The essential work stations are ovens which heat the wafers according to a prescribed temperature profile up to 600°C - 1100°C. By pouring gas, the wafers are built up layer by layer each layer requiring a separate heating cycle. Optimization of wafer handling consists of path planning (generation of trajectories) for the manipulator, sequencing operations and assignment to work stations (scheduling), and design of placement of the work stations (layout).

Scheduling problems for wafer handling basically are flow shop problems with the manipulator being an additional resource. Scarcity of this resource plays a dominant role. In case the wafers pass the work stations in prescribed sequences, the problem amounts to a job shop problem with an additional resource. In case of optional use of work stations the problem becomes an open shop with one additional resource. Wafer scheduling is always non-preemptive meaning that operations may not be interrupted; this applies to the thermal process in particular. An appropriate objective function of scheduling is the completion time of the last wafer (make span) of a batch. A practically important issue is dead lock avoidance of the robot operations.

In the most simple case, machine clusters are operated locally meaning that there is no central control. This renders working with due dates infeasible and entails that all scheduling strategies must be computable locally on the cluster processor. The cluster processor must also run the cluster control which severely limits time for schedule computation.

Local, easily modifiable, and efficient scheduling strategies are formed by index policies known from deterministic (Baker (1974)), (Shararay (1989)) as well as from stochastic (Gittins (1979)) problem settings. At any decision moment, the greedy heuristics obtained for wafer handling select an operation which is ready for service according to an index like LRTPT (longest remaining total processing time first). At least to some extent, the crux lies in an appropriate definition of the total processing time.

The optional use of work stations in wafer fabrication may require to deviate from the index in certain situations. Moreover, the requirement to exactly meet oven times may also require the scheduling strategy to deviate from the greedy character by inserting deliberate idle time. This means to stall current robot operations in favour of waiting for a wafer to complete its heating cycle and then to immediately unload it from an oven.

Such index policies were developed for steag AST company (Advanced Semiconductor Technologies, Dornstadt), a manufacturer of machines for wafer production (Kämpke (1999a)). Before porting the strategies into the target environment, all procedures were evaluated in a simulation environment built in SIMPLE++. Dead locks could be ruled out and performance in terms of make span as well as throughput was considered satisfactory and did not admit any obvious improvement.

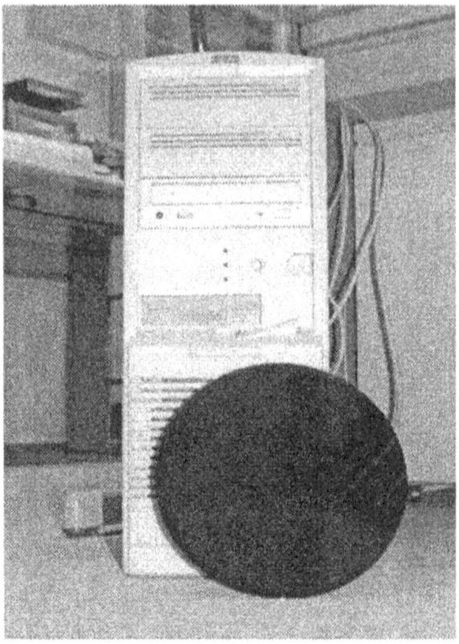

Figure 1: *Wafer in front of personal computer*

2.1.3 An application of non-linear optimization in image segmentation

In general, non-linear optimization is a tough issue resulting from the possibility of many local optima that requires quite involved and time-consuming screening and enumeration approaches. Still, many applications are of this nature. In the following, an application of non-linear optimization in image segmentation is given.

A pivotal function in image processing is segmentation which is the partitioning of an image into (its) meaningful components (Gonzalez and Wintz (1987)). To this end, extremality principles are being developed such as the Mumford Shah-functional (Mumford and Shah (1989)) which however is difficult to handle. A desirable feature of such approaches is to make procedures free of parameters meaning that they should be free of threshold values, window sizes etc. If that appears to be unobtainable, algorithms should use as few parameters as possible. This should provide for "robustness" of the analysis of images from one class though a formal class description may practically be out of reach. In the scope of this robustness, a two step scheme was proposed which first approximates a discrete function and then uses the approximations either within a recursion (Kämpke and Kober (1998)) or within a discrete scale space approach (Kämpke and Kober (1999)).

In the first step, the histogram of the gray values of the image is considered to be a discrete function (step function) over a finite interval. This function is approximated in the sense of minimum squared distance by a step function with fewer levels. These approximations amount to shortest paths in the break point graph with fixed number of vertices between the interval boundaries. Edges in this graph are labeled by the approximation error (quantization error) resulting from replacing the original step function by a single level between the break points denoted by an edge. The best approximation of a discrete function with N levels by a discrete function with n levels, $n < N$, can be computed in $O(n N^2)$ by dynamic optimization as well as by a variant of Dijkstra's algorithm.

In the second step, the approximations are used to "smooth" the histogram until so many so-called deep minima are generated which are required for segmenting the image into a given number of region types. A sketch for two types of regions used for a typical foreground-background segmentation is given in figure 2 where the histogram is drawn continuously. An application to spot detection in images of biochips is given in figures 3 and 4 (Kämpke, Kaifel, Schieckel (2000)). Distortions in the second, binary image can be removed by standard filters.

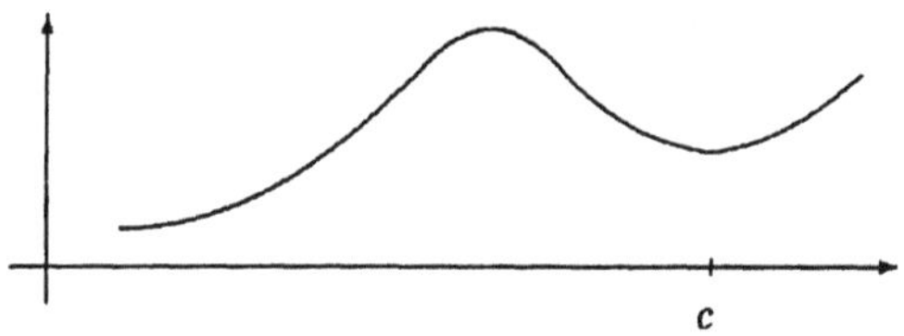

Figure 2: *Smoothed (continuous) histogram with segmentation according to threshold value c.*

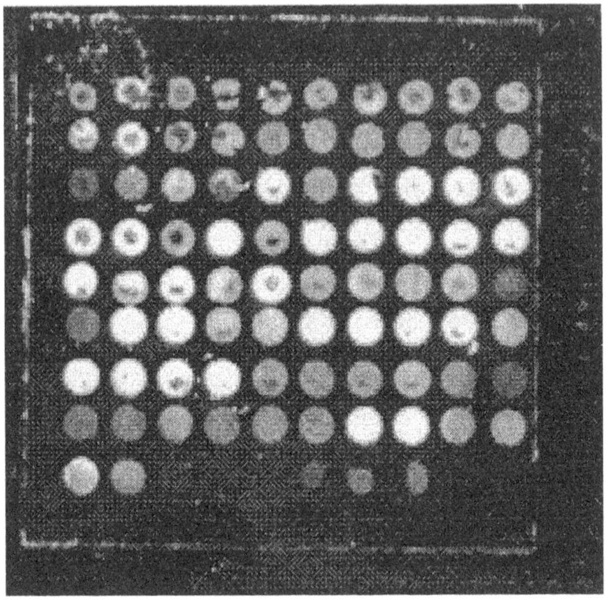

Figure 3: *Gray value image of a biochip*

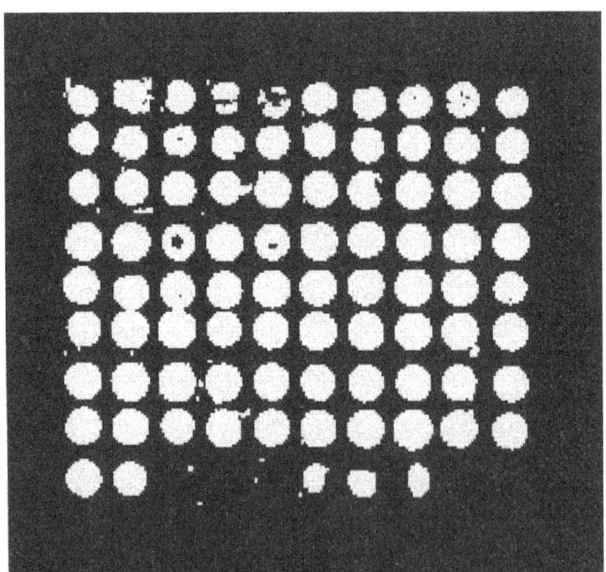

Figure 4: *Segmented spots.*

The binarized image provides a so-called mask for the spots. This allows automatic or semi-automatic intensity measuring which leads to a set of in-vitro measurements of parameters in biological experiments and medical tests.

2.2 Decision theory

Decision making is one of the most basic and frequent human activities. Competence of humans often is a competence to make good decisions. Decision making is hard, particularly if the problem is not completely posed, if there are stochastic or game like elements involved and if complex objective functions have to be dealt with. One of the most amazing mathematical insights into the nature of such problems is the basic theorem of von Neumann and Morgenstern in the context of multi-attributive decision making (von Neumann and Morgenstern (1976)). Essentially, if the attributes and scales are known, if some quite natural axioms of rationality are fulfilled, and if the problem is extended in a natural way to be broad enough (all finite lotteries of alternatives admitted), then there is a complete formalization of the decision behaviour. Essentially, it leads to maximising the expected utility with respect to subjective probabilities and the subjective utility or objective function.

The fundamental theorem reduces the question of making decisions between alternatives to computing the respective attributed expected utility so that a quite standard formalization is available. This does not imply that decisions are actually made like that, but it offers a complete framework in case of any "consistent" decision behaviour. I.e. any deviation from the framework indicates a conflict with the axioms of rationality or that the available space of alternatives is in effect smaller than assumed.

It belongs to the most wonderful results of the field that under certain normalisation conditions the determination of such a subjective utility function can be broken down to determining all the one-dimensional conditional utility functions and combining them in a suitable way (Keeney and Raiffa (1976)). The criteria that allow such decompositions can be verified in a natural, holistic way without knowing the function itself. That has direct practical consequences and makes the determination of a utility function much easier. In effect, finding the one-dimensional utilities means to look for certain trade-offs. The same is true for combining the one-dimensional functions to the n-dimensional overall utility function.

By elaborating this approach, science has uncovered a way to assist humans to make decisions without directly doing comparisons between alternatives. Instead, by certain trade-off decisions, an n-dimensional utility function is determined.

Based on this function, the expected utility values of alternatives then can be determined, which eventually leads to decisions.

It is one of the most amazing observations, that while this is a new way to come to decisions without considering alternatives directly, once the mathematical framework was developed, a new way was found to approximate a utility function. The approximation is based on holistic decisions between alternatives from a small set rather than on trade-offs over mere criteria. That is because the overall utility function can often be assumed to be a parameterised linear function. Making decisions on a small number of alternatives suffices to yield a system of linear inequalities that restrict the set of all utility functions so that any of the remaining functions can be used to make decisions on a large set alternatives.

In the following chapter 2.2.1 we give a number of hints to how this approach works. In the subsequent chapter 2.2.2 we give an application of managing a groundwater monitoring network.

2.2.1 Preference assessment

Preference relations provide that component of decision processes which admit the explicit formulation of favour and trade-offs. A preference relation over a set of alternatives is represented by a real-valued preference function f that is order preserving which means that $A <_P B$ amounts to $f(A) < f(B)$ with $<$ being the strict order over the real numbers. Preference relations $<_P$ are typically assumed to be asymmetric and negative transitive meaning that "$\neg (A <_P A)$" and "$\neg (A <_P B)$ and $\neg (B <_P C)$ implies $\neg (A <_P C)$", comp. (Fishburn (1979)). The degree to which preference relations resp. –functions are actually revealed varies considerably.

Numerous methods for assessing preference functions have been developed. *Extrapolation* methods appear to be the most general. Trade-offs between certain alternatives are investigated for their implications to the whole set of alternatives. This is achieved for example by linear programming, where preferences between alternatives are expressed as linear constraints. Further constraints result from normalization and monotonicity requirements. The variables of the linear program comprise values of the preference functions at particular points of support. In order to avoid inconsistent input to the linear program, the transitive hull of expressed preferences is computed (by the triple algorithm). An alternative being implicitly preferred to itself can thus be detected and be prompted to be revised.

The extrapolation technique is suitable for assessing single criteria as well as multi criteria preference functions as long as the latter are additive meaning that $f(x_1,...,x_n) = f_1(x_1) + ... + f_n(x_n)$. This approach going back to (Jacquet-Lagrèze et al. (1987)) has been extended to other types of preference functions as well as to so-called cardinal preference articulations (Wolf (1992)), (Kämpke, Radermacher, Wolf (1993)). The latter intends to render preference functions unique up to positive affine transformations.

2.2.2 Application of utility function determination via linear optimization to a problem in water management

It is well known that humans, and in particular groups of humans, have a very hard time if they are required to order a huge set of alternatives that have to be judged in several dimensions, where the preference structure is not generally clear. A typical case is decision making concerning proposals for research projects. A group of say ten referees has to assess say 250 proposals out of which 30 have to be chosen to get into a more detailed funding analysis. If the case with the 250 alternatives is already difficult, how much more difficult is a situation with thousands of alternatives.

FAW had been involved in such a problem in water management, where thousands of sites of possible pollutants had to be ranked according to their potentially hazardous impact on drinking water. 20 experts tried over one day to get anywhere, but with thousands of alternatives the task appeared to be unmanageable.

The method described in chapter 2.2.1 offered a way to go forward. The group was able to make holistic decisions on the ranking of 20 sites, which were artificially composed to cover extreme cases. This information turned out to be enough to compute a utility function, which was used to generate a first proposal for the ranking of all potential pollution sites. This ranking was fine tuned later.

The method of holistic preference assessment was applied to the ground water hazards such as paint shops, gas stations, and dry cleaners in order to establish a monitoring plan (Kämpke, Mund, Schulz (1993)). Missing data resp. the complete lack of damage data were replaced by so-called expert judgements, which were formulated as preference relations. The assessment was based on six criteria. The first three were continuous and the last three were discrete: storage amount of hazardous liquids according to particular classes WGK 1, WGK 2, and WGK 3, demand for clean-up, safety of storage device, and existence of an operational plant sewage system.

The extrapolation technique for preference assessment has been extended to non-linear problems (Kämpke (1995)) as well as to cases with situative variables similar to game theory (Rosenmüller (1997)). Situative variables turn up in autonomous decision support for technical systems (Kämpke (1999b)).

2.3 Knowledge management

FAW has a long history of work in knowledge management. The approach is holistic and biologically inspired. Complex systems are considered as superorganisms. The location of knowledge and its ways of being handled are identified. This involves a differentiation between e. g. symbolic and non-symbolic knowledge as well as specific considerations concerning issues such as learning, creativity, and making decisions on limited resources. A detailed description can be found in (Radermacher (1999a)), (Radermacher (1999b)).

We just mention that FAW, for the time being, is working on a study for the BMBF (German federal ministry of education and research) on a possible new research programme on the issue of handling non-explicit knowledge, integrating contributions from more than 10 academic disciplines. In particular, the distinguished levels of representation of knowledge are as follows:

1. Signal level

At the lowest level we observe a direct interaction of a physical nature between systems and their surrounding world. Signals in particular are part of this. Signals are picked up or identified by sensor systems, inducing, on one hand, direct effects and, on the other, serving as a source of features, which are an initial form of *information-compression.* Certain sensors are directed (primarily) to *the world outside* the system, others primarily to the system's *inner life.*

2. Feature level

Features are the input-information on the second level of information processing under consideration. Here, on one hand, begins a functional transformation of such features, for example, into motor response or actuation, perhaps in the form of trained (artificial) neural networks. On the other hand, *objects or concepts* are identified by classifiers on the basis of features.

3. Symbol level

The symbol level is concerned with *objects or concepts* and deals with them by means of various mechanisms of symbol processing (the processing of rules, logic, relational systems, etc.). This is the classic domain of *Artificial Intelligence (AI)* as a scientific discipline.

4. Theory level

From the third level one can, in certain domains, proceed to the fourth level of *theories and models*. This allows, for example with the aid of mathematical methods from the fields of optimization, statistics, decision theory and numerical analysis, to make assertions and to come to conclusions on the model level, which can be re-translated into concrete behaviour via the other levels involved.

The work on knowledge management for superorganizations done at FAW concerns at least three application areas, for which a common meta approach is pursued, namely autonomous systems, companies as "bodies", and humankind as a complex system. These fields are subsequently considered in more detail. In addition, some hints to extract knowledge from data are given for a particular situation.

2.3.1 Architectures for robots

The FAW has a 10 year long history of work on the architecture of information processing for human decision making and in the challenging field of service robots. First contributions were made in relation to the AMOS system (Knick and Radermacher (1992)), (Knick and Schlegel (1994)) followed by more detailed work within the SFB 527 as well as broad projects funded by the BMBF and by the state of Baden-Württemberg. The following is a short overview of the major architectural structure of the system, now used at FAW, namely the SMART approach developed by Christian Schlegel (Schlegel et al. (1999)).

The main focus of the FAW within the SFB 527 was on the interplay of symbolic and subsymbolic information processing. To this end, a concrete sensomotoric system was instantiated on the basis of the mobile platform B21/RWI-ISI, called the demonstrator. This system shall autonomously execute a large variety of different tasks in a scenario environment over a longer period of time. To this end, a demonstrator has to use independently both deliberative symbolic approaches and sensor related reactive mechanisms.

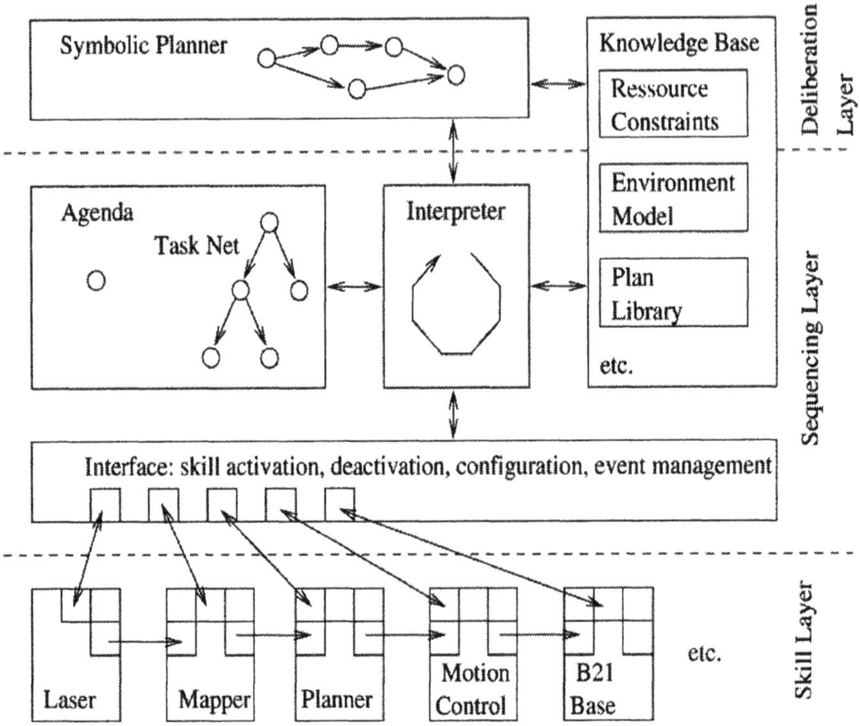

Figure 5: *The multilayer architecture*

As starting point a technical system architecture (fig. 5) was first designed (Schlegel et al. (1999)), which is construed as a multilayer architecture and oriented at a general 4-layer-architecture (Radermacher (1996)). The lowest level is called the "skill layer". It comprises mainly continuously working algorithms for sensor data processing and actor control. The "sequencing layer" is responsible for coordinating the overall activities. It also provides context-dependent and resource-compliant configurations for the skill layer. In contrast to the skill layer the sequencing layer works on discrete events. The deliberation layer finally includes the action planning.

The skill layer works mostly reactive within the boundaries of the current configuration. It mainly ensures the reactivity of the system. The sequencing layer is based on task networks which support the representation of standard operations by compact symbolic descriptions. On the one hand situation dependent versions of task steps can be formulated, on the other hand knowledge about proven procedures can be integrated. The sequencing layer forms the link between the sensor and actor related basic skills of the skill layer and the abstract symbolic descriptions used on the deliberative layer by considering the task execution context within the task nets.

Finally, the deliberative layer also considers future states. By stating order relations between single task, it coordinates the achievement of overall goals. Complex task nets, which comprise context dependent execution threads, are accessed as single operators by the deliberative layer. In this manner, details of a complex task net structure are hidden from the symbolic task planning. This is a prerequisite to enable the task planner to generate complex plans within reasonable time.

A prominent role is performed by the sequencing layer and its task agenda. The agenda represents tasks which are currently being executed as well as tasks which still have to be executed. The task execution is coordinated by the sequencing layer using the deliberative layer. Tasks are executed in a real-world environment by choosing an appropriate activation of the skill layer (Schlegel et al. (1999)), (Schlegel et al. (2000)).

2.3.2 Data analysis

The ever increasing variety and availability of data bases requires resp. favours the development and application of methods for data analysis. Formal objectives of data analysis may be mutually dependent. For example, a time series may be partitioned into sections such that distinct regression curves are fitted over the sections with partitioning and fitting being interrelated (Hamerle (1989)). In case the data neither adhere to time nor to any other order relation, partitioning may still be meaningful for regression. This has lead to the development of regression trees (Breiman et al. (1984)). The difficulty of these constructions stems from the partitioning strategies. Though the "generalization feature" of partitioning strategies is intuitive, it is formally difficult to establish and appears to be missing in many strategies.

Partitioning can be made neighborhood stable for numerical data (Kämpke and Urban (2000)). Each vector of data is therefore related to its nearest neighbor with this relation being expressed by a directed edge. The data together with these edges form the nearest neighbor graph. The edge relation is generally unsymmetric but it partitions the data base (vertex set of the nearest neighbor graph) into so-called nearest neighbor chains by taking weak connect components. Two vectors belong to the same chain if they eventually lead to a common vector following sequences of consecutive arcs.

Nearest neighbor chains will never be cut when forming the regression tree i.e. when partitioning the data base so that each class of the partition receives an own regression surface. More precisely, the procedure works as follows: a (sub)set of data with its regression surface which is to be (further) partitioned is tentatively split into the two sets of data which lie above and below the regression surface. Nearest neighbor chains which were cut hereby, are assigned completely to one of the two sets so that the overall regression error is minimal. The two resulting regression surfaces may penetrate each other.

This as well as other classification methods have been applied to evaluate radio traffic data of a cellular phone network of e-plus company (Mobilfunk Düsseldorf) (Urban (1999)). The aim was to forecast the amount of radio traffic within candidate regions for new radio cells. Neighborhood stabilization, which had a mean chain length of about eight here, lead - besides more plausibility - to a reduction of the regression error by about 10% compared to mere regressions resp. regressions based on partitions of pure classification algorithms.

2.3.3 Companies as superorganisms

Knowledge management in companies is a particularly challenging topic these days. Here, intranets may be seen as nervous systems of such organisms. The approach chosen by FAW goes far beyond document management, thesauri etc. It rather combines questions of organization, human resources management and IT infrastructures to one coherent approach. In particular, trying to capture desirable states not only for the individual but also for the company as a body itself is a major issue.

The FAW has done consulting work for large enterprises and administrations as well as for SMEs, comp. (Richter and Rose (2000)), (Richter et al. (2000)). With regard to the integration into enterprise information systems, the use of simulation tools and application in emergency services has been an issue investigated by the Hochschule St. Gallen.

2.3.4 Issues of global sustainability

FAW has a long-term involvement in consulting with politics on the German and European level and also for the EXPO 2000 concerning the issues of globalization, information society and sustainable development. Humankind is seen as an organism and the issue at stake is long-term survival. Work here addresses societal questions and analysis on the level of world models. A main reference point is the so-called European Way approach (van Dijk et al. (2000)).

Better ways into the future and towards sustainability are now being broadly discussed within Europe. Here, sustainability is understood as an adequate balance between society's economic, social, cultural and environmental concerns from a long-term perspective. This topic is also central to the Information Society Forum (ISF) which is the key advisory body to the European Commission concerning all questions of Europe's participation in a transition into a world-wide Information and Knowledge Society.

In this context, the Information Society Forum has analysed the central - perhaps predominant - role of information and communication technology (ICT) in eventually reaching sustainability and improvements in the quality of life. The Forum takes the position that reachability of a sustainable state depends on the way the Information Society will be shaped in the future. That is because, on one hand, these technologies are major driving factors of economic globalization in a world that will eventually reach a population of 10 billion people or more, and because of this - in an indirect way - are now causing additional social, cultural and environmental burdens world-wide. This is a typical so-called rebound effect of technological progress. On the other hand, these technologies offer, in principle, huge opportunities for overcoming social exclusion, for supporting cultural diversity, for stimulating the economy and for reducing environmental burdens by increasing material productivity. While this so-called dematerialization is a typical, promising feature of most technological progress, ICT has by far the highest potential in this regard.

Whether information and communication technologies will, in the end, lead to more sustainability or not, essentially depends on the further development of global economic and societal frameworks and corresponding attitudes and values. Building such frameworks is the single most important challenge to politics and societies when entering the 21st century. In this respect, better global instruments are needed in the social and ecological fields in particular, to commit the industrialized countries to support and co-fund social and ecological developments and standards in countries in transition and in developing countries. This aims in the long run at something like a global civil society and a global citizenship. Caring for and trading of ever-scarcer environmental resources - such as an atmosphere with a sufficiently low concentration of greenhouse gases – in the form of pollution rights is seen as an instrument to justify and organize such co-funding. In this context, the Kyoto protocol and its international instruments (Tradable Permits, Clean Development Mechanism, Joint Implementation) offer promising starting points for further agreements and international partnerships.

The rationale behind the European Way results from world modelling, taking into account aggregated quantities such as world population, gross national product, environmental burden, resource consumption, dematerialization and equity. The specific consideration of equity is a distinguishing feature. It is this issue which distinguishes the European view from the US perspective most. Equity slows down economic growth and innovation, but also leads to a reduction of the reproduction/birth rate and tougher control of the environment. Modeling and analysis strengthen the position that long-term sustainability needs equity, see also the graphs for two futures in figure 6, one sustainable and the other not, comp. (Fritz, Pestel, Radermacher, Schauer (2000)). Therefore, Europe has to bring this aspect stronger into the world-wide debates for developing further WTO, Global Environmental Agreements and others. Here, the recent decisions at the G8 summits in Cologne (debt relief) and Okinawa (fighting the global digital divide) point in the right direction.

Figure 6: *Sustainable vs. non sustainable development*

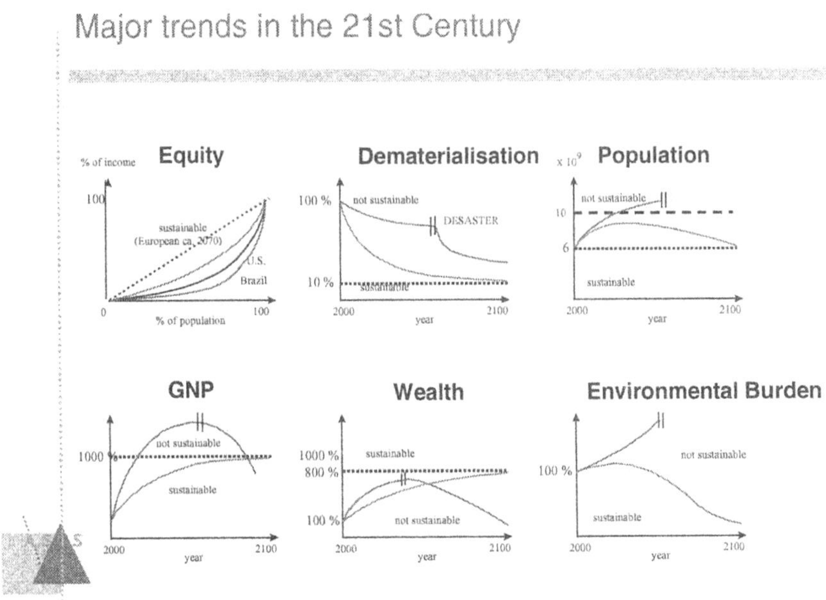

3 The *Institut für Unternehmensforschung (Operations Research)* at the University of St. Gallen

Operations Research as an academic discipline was first established in St. Gallen in 1955 when the *Forschungsstelle für Ökonometrie und Operations Research* at the HSG (Hochschule St. Gallen) was founded by W. Krelle. Other famous names followed, namely R. Henn and E. Soom.

In 1981, Paul Stähly succeeded in establishing the *Institut für Unternehmensforschung (Operations Research)*. St. Gallen is an important place for management studies on the Europaen map, maybe because of or inspite of a not too thorough quantitative orientation of the studies in St. Gallen in general. Paul Stähly's institute constitutes perhaps the most advanced quantitative element concerning management science in this environment.

Over the years, his institute was involved in application-oriented work of notable economic impact (Stähly (1984), (1987), (1992)). This is particularly demonstrated by the fact that the institute is essentially funded via contracts that have to be formed with government, industry, banks, insurance companies, and research foundations. With a strong orientation to quantitative models, a broad emphasis on simulation and on dealing with linear and stochastic optimization frameworks, Paul Stähly and his team have succeeded in building applications for the health sector, public administration, the military, the financial sector, etc. In recent years, all this was broadened by integrating new approaches to intelligent decision making, such as coming from Artificial Intelligence (AI). Here, cooperation with FAW, in particular with PD Dr. D. Solte should be mentioned.

Achieving this in an academic environment where the own staff essentially needs to be "imported from outside" has not been easy. Paul Stähly, however, has turned this additional burden into an advantage, seeing this as a chance to create synergy effects by the interacting of staff coming from many different universities. This point demonstrates his great openness and is rooted in the close contact he has with many colleagues. In this process, he has always been personally engaged in identifying and supporting promising young scientists, often helping them in making the first steps in their professional careers.

Particularly due to his many contacts and to his close personal relationships with many of the Operations Researchers in Switzerland, Germany, Austria, and other countries, he also had played a crucial and successful role in keeping together different schools of Operations Research. He did so even in times of high tension between the groups. Thus, the whole Operations Research community is obliged to Paul Stähly for his permanent, fruitful contributions to the community, the field and the people in it. The GOR intends to make this obvious by appointing Paul Stähly an honorary member.

The intention of this paper is to thank Paul Stähly for all the contributions and achievements he has made over a long period of time. Also this is to thank for his support in the professional development of the second author, starting from the time of his diploma thesis at the RWTH Aachen in 1973 and including almost 20 years of involvement in St. Gallen as a lecturer and cooperating scientist. We wish Paul Stähly all the best for his personal and professional activities in the years ahead.

References

Applegate, L.M., Konsynski, B.R., Nunamaker, J.F. (1986): Model Management Systems, Design for Decision Support. Decision Support Systems 2, 81-91

Baker, K.R. (1974): Introduction to sequencing and scheduling. John Wiley, New York

Bonczek, R.H., Holsapple, C.W., Whinston, A.B. (1980): Future Directions for Developing Decision Support Systems. In: Decision Sciences 11

Breiman, L. et al. (1984): Classification and regression trees. Wadsworth, Belmont

Fischhoff, B., Slovic, P., Lichtenstein, S. (1980): Knowing What You Want, Measuring Labile Values. In: Wallstein, T. (ed.): Cognitive Processes in Choice and Decision Behaviour. Erlbaum, Hillsdales, N.J.

Fishburn, P.C. (1979): Utility theory for decision making. Krieger, Huntington

Fritz, M., Pestel, R., Radermacher, F.J., Schauer, T. (2000): A European way to a world wide sustainable information society. submitted.

Gittins, J.C. (1979): Bandit processes and dynamic allocation indices. Journal of the Royal Statistical Society B 14, 148-177

Gonzalez, R.C., Wintz, P. (1987): Digital image processing. Addison-Wesley, Reading

Günther, O., Müller, R., Weigend, A.S. (1995): The Design of MMM: A Model ManageMent System for the Time Series Analysis. In: Ford J., Makedon, F., Rebelsky S.A. (eds.): Electronic Publishing and the Information Superhighway (DAGS95). Birkhäuser, Boston, Basel, Berlin, 223-233

Günther, O., Radermacher, F.J. (1992): Systemunterstützte Unternehmensführung. Contribution to „EIS (Executive Information Systems)" Conference, Zürich

Hamerle, A. (1989): Multiple spell regression models for duration data. Applied Statistics 38, 127-138

Henninger, T., Schnittger, S., Haug, A. (1999): Recommendations for Harmonisation of Data Bases and Specification for Implementing of Travel Planning API. EU-SPIRIT Deliverable MD 4.6/4.7

Jacquet-Lagrèze, E., Meziani, R., Slowinski, R. (1987): MOLP with an interactive assessment of a piecewise linear utility function. European Journal of Operational Research 31 350-357

Jarke, M., Radermacher F.J. (1988): The AI Potential of Model Management and its Central Role in Decision Support. Decision Support Systems 4, 387-404

Kämpke, T. (1995): Nonadditive preference assessment by nonlinear programming. Foundations of Computing and Decision Sciences 20, 187-204

Kämpke, T. (1999a): Handlingoptimierung in Ofenclustern. FAW report B-99006, Ulm

Kämpke, T. (1999b): Functional arbitration for multi purpose senso-motory systems. Robotics and Autonomous Systems 27, 129-150

Kämpke, T., Kaifel, T., Schiekel, C. (2000): Spotting approaches for biochip arrays. In: Proceedings 15th International Conference on Pattern Recognition ICPR, vol 4, Barcelona, 356-359

Kämpke, T., Kober, R. (1998): Nonparametric image segmentation. Pattern Analysis and Applications 1, 145-154

Kämpke, T., Kober, R. (1999): Discrete signal quantization. Pattern Recognition 32, 619-634

Kämpke, T., Mund, J., Schulz, K.-P. (1993): Erhebung und mehrkriterielle Bewertung von Grundwassergefährdungspotentialen. Wasserwirtschaft 83, 82-86

Kämpke, T., Radermacher, F.J. (1999): Deutschlandweite Verbindungsauskunft im ÖPNV: verteilte Wegesuche in Graphen. In: Horster, P. (Ed.): Angewandte Mathematik, insbesondere Informatik, Vieweg, Braunschweig, 144-161

Kämpke, T., Radermacher, F.J., Wolf. P. (1993): Supporting preference elicitation - The FAW preference elicitation tool. Decision Support Systems 9, 381-391

Kämpke, Th., Schaal, M. (1998): Distributed Generation of Fastest Paths. Proceedings of 10th IASTED International Conference on Parallel and Distributed Computing and Systems, Las Vegas, 172-177

Kämpke, T., Urban, T. (2000): Stabilization of regression trees. In: Ebecken, N., Brebbia, C.A. (Eds.): Data Mining II. WIT Press, Southampton, UK, 535-544

Keen, P.G.W., Scott Morton, M.S. (1978): Decision Support Systems: An Organisational Perspective. Addison Wesley, New York

Keen, P.G.W. (1987): Decision Support Systems: The Next Decade. Decision Support Systems 3, 253-265

Keeney, R.L. (1992): Value-Focussed Thinking: A Path to Creative Decisionmaking. Harvard University Press

Keeney, R.L., Raiffa, H. (1976): Decisions with multiple objectives. Wiley, New York

Knick, M., Radermacher, F.J. (1992): Integration of sub-symbolic and symbolic information processing in robot control. In: Proceedings IEEE Annual Conference on AI, Simulation and Planning in High Autonomy Systems, Perth, 238-243

Knick, M., Schlegel, C. (1994): AMOS: active perception of an autonomous system. In: Proceedings International Conference on Intelligent Robots and Systems IROS, Munich, 281-289

Krishnan, R., Müller, R., Schmidt, P. (1995): Accessing Computable Information over the WWW: The MMM Project. In: T. X Bui (ed.): Third ISDSS Proceedings, Vol.1, International Society for Decision Support Systems, 137-146

Krishnan, R., Piela, P., and Westerberg, A. (1991): Reusing Mathematical Models in ASCEND. In: Proceedings of NATO ASI on Decision Support Systems

Möhring, R.H. (1999): Verteilte Verbindungssuche – Algorithmische Möglichkeiten und Grenzen. In: DELFI-2 Projektbericht, FAW/DELFI-Konsortium

Möhring, R.H., Müller, R., Radermacher, F.J. (1994): Advanced DSS for Scheduling: Software Engineering Aspects and the Role of Eigenmodels. In: Proceedings of 27th Annual Hawaii International Conference on Systems Sciences, Maui, Hawaii, USA

Mumford, D., Shah, J. (1989): Optimal approximations by piecewise smooth functions and associated variational problems. Communications on Pure and Applied Mathematics 42, 577-685

Radermacher, F.J. (1990a): Model Management: The Core of Intelligent Decision Support. In: Schader, M., Gaul, W. (eds.): NATO ASI Series Knowledge, Data and Computer-Assisted Decisions, Springer, Berlin-Heidelberg, 393-406

Radermacher, F.J. (1990b): Neuere Entwicklungen in der Verbindung von Operations Research und Informatik. In: Feichtinger, G. et al. (Eds.): Österreichische Gesellschaft für Operations Research, ÖGOR-News

Radermacher, F.J. (1991): Modeling and Artificial Intelligence. Applied Artificial Intelligence 5, 131-151

Radermacher, F.J. (1994): Decision Support Systems: Scope and Potential. Decision Support Systems 12, 257-265

Radermacher, F.J. (1996): Cognition in Systems. Cybernetics and Systems 27, No. 1, 1-41

Radermacher, F.J. (1999a): Wissensmanagement: Herausforderung für Unternehmen.Beitrag für die Jubliäumsbroschüre zu den 20. Salemer Gesprächen

Radermacher, F.J. (1999b): Komplexe Systeme und lernende Unternehmen. In: Mainzer, K. (Ed.), Komplexe Systeme und Nichtlineare Dynamik in Natur und Gesellschaft. Springer-Verlag, Berlin, 423-445

Radermacher, F.J., Schaal, M., Schnittger, S. (1997): Durchgängige Elektronische Fahrplaninformation – DELFI. Proceedings IST world congress, Berlin

Radermacher, F. J., Schaal, M., Schnittger, S. (1998): DELFI-Durchgängige Elektronische Fahrplaninformation. In: Nahverkehrsforschung 97, Statusseminar XXII, Ed.: Projektträger Bodengebundene Verkehrstechnologien (PT-BVT), TÜV Rheinland, contracted by BMV and BMBF, Cologne

Raiffa, H. (1982): The art and science of negotiation. Harvard University Press, Cambridge

Richter, T., Rose, T. (2000): KMTools – Wissensmanagement und Organisation von Unternehmen. FAW survey, Ulm

Richter, T. et al. (2000): Wissensmanagement für kleine und mittelständische Unternehmen. FAW study, Ulm

Rosenmüller, J. (1997): Bargaining with incomplete information – an axiomatic approach. Theory and Decision 42, 105-146

Schlegel, C., Illmann, J, Jaberg, H., Schuster, M., Wörz, R. (2000): Integrating vision-based behaviors with an autonomous robot. VIDERE Journal of Computer Vision Research 4, MIT Press

Schlegel, C. Wörz, R. (1999): Interfacing different layers of a multilayer architecture for sensorimotor systems using the object-oriented framework SmartSoft. In: Eurobot, Zürich, Schweiz

Schnittger, S. (1999): The EU-Spirit Approach. Passenger Information Conference, London

Shararay, M.S. (1989): Dynamic sequencing rule applied to job shop scheduling. Technical report, Siemens Research and Technology Laboratory Princeton

Sol, H.G. (1985): DSS: Buzz Word or OR Challenge. European Journal of Operational Research 22, 1-8

Sol, H.G. (1987): Conflicting Experiences with DSS. Decision Support Systems 3, 203-211

Sprague, R.H. (1987): DSS in Context. Decision Support Systems 3, 197-202

Stähly, P. (1985): Dekompositionsverfahren und Integrierte Planung. In: Operations Research Proceedings, Springer, Berlin, 80-92

Stähly, P. (1987): Marketing-Mix-Modellierung, gestern und heute. Thexis 3, 12-19

Stähly, P. (1992): Einsatzpläne für Katastrophenfälle mittels Simulationsmodellen auf der Basis von Simula. In: Biethahn, J., Hummeltenberg, W., Schmidt, B. (Eds.): Simualtion als betriebswirtschaftliche Entscheidungshilfe, Berlin, Springer, Band 2, 81-94

Turban, E. (1990): Decision Support and Expert Systems: Managerial Perspectives. MacMillan, New York

Urban, T. (1999): Untersuchung von KI Methoden sowie verwandten formalen Methoden zur Analyse und Prognose der Verkehrslast in Mobilfunkzellen. FAW report, Ulm

van Dijk, A.G.M., Pestel, R., Radermacher, F.J. (2000): Sustainability in Times of a Global Information Society: the Promise of a European Way. In: Germany - Global Visions, MVV Medien Vertriebs- und Verlagsgesellschaft mbH, Düsseldorf, 164-170

von Neumann, J., Morgenstern, O. (1976): Theory of Games and Economic Behaviour. Princeton University Press, Princeton, N.J.

Wolf, P. (1992): Rechnerunterstützte Elizitierung mehrattributiver Präferenz Strukturen. Dissertation, University of Ulm

Part 2:

Operations Research Models

Concepts, Aims, and Problems which Modelling in OR and OOP Have in Common

Jörg R. Mühlbacher

Institute for Information Processing and Microprocessor Technology (FIM),

University of Linz, Austria

Preface

This paper is dedicated to Paul Stähly on the occasion of his 65th birthday. It reflects many private discussions between us, in particular, on modelling and the use of an appropriate programming language. Paul Stähly has always been a dedicated user of SIMULA 67, already in those days when object oriented programming (OOP) was not invented yet. He has early noticed the power of object orientation in his research area (OR). The authors of SIMULA 67 introduced classes as templates which define data structures and algorithms to be included in a particular instance (of a model). In addition, classes may be defined in terms of each other.

Paul Stähly has also been and still is aware of the problem to which extent the results of a calculation process can be interpreted semantically correct, if the model is used for a different application area as it was designed for originally. In component oriented software development this is referred to as "domain dependency", and there is a demand for a "contract" which may be understood as additional semantic information for the user of a model and its implementation.

1 Aims of modelling

Let us briefly recall a couple of major reasons why modelling is essential. In this context we have in mind applied disciplines as operations research and software development. In order to focus on central aspects, we use examples which are well known and used in such areas.

Abstraction to master complexity

Talking about models we have to restrict to abstract ones in which physical situations or alike are described in symbolic form, and in this case we often make use of the language of mathematics (mathematical expressions, systems of equations, graphs, ...) or - with respect to computer science (CS) - we use notations and languages which have been developed for CS.

The most obvious purpose of models is: they are designed by an abstraction process in order to avoid too much complexity and to allow us to master the complexity which still remains after this process of abstraction. Using "complexity" we refer generally to both: time complexity as it is defined in the theory of algorithms, and complexity meaning interactions between components the model consists of.

A simple example is the calculation, whether a path from a source s_0 to destinations s_i ($i = 1, 2, ..., n-1$) exists. The abstraction process, step by step, starts at a map of the region in question (of course, the map already is a model of the landscape), omits geographical orientation and finally ends up in a sparse matrix A, where

if a connection between s_i, s_j exists *then* $A\,[i, j] = 1$ *else* $A\,[i, j] = 0$ *end*.

Whether, in terms of programming, the matrix A as model of the resulting digraph is represented as an array or as a list of lists of neighbours (adjacency list) is a question of convenient representation and depends on the programming language used for the implementation. At this stage the representation has no influence on what the model represents and which kind of information we can gather from it.

Reusability of models and their associated algorithms

Another purpose of abstract models is the aim to reuse them. We can apply identical algorithms whenever we have brought down a task to a model which is "isomorphic" to a model having been derived from another problem. With "isomorphic" we refer to the fact that sometimes a transformation might be necessary in addition.

At this point the important aspect is: we have omitted details during the abstraction process.

In our example the matrix A does not contain any information on the distances between nodes s_i, s_j and, consequently, we can not calculate shortest paths from s_0 to s_i ($i = 1, 2, ..., n$-1).

So the aim of "reusability" contains the danger of drawing wrong conclusions or deriving incorrect "results", because the required additional information has been filtered out in earlier stages of the modelling process. We are aware of this danger. In many cases, through abstraction, the resulting models become what is called domain specific and often one lacks the information which application domain the model has been derived from.

We regard a model as consisting of

(a) a data structure and

(b) a set of algorithms (see: methods in OOP) which are designed to operate on the data structure.

The interpretation of results delivered by these algorithms is a semantic problem and therefore is domain specific. Consequently, reusability is limited and depends on how far the abstraction went: the more abstract the model is, the less any domain dependency counts. But at the same time semantic information is lost.

One possibility however is to add to a model

(c) a description of the application domain.

We refer to this remark later on, when we make comparisons with component oriented programming.

Extending models: inheritance and the need for contracts

One benefit of an abstract model is the ability to extend the behaviour of the model. Instead of designing a new model M_2 from scratch, the previous model M_1 may be extended so that the resulting model M_2 inherits all the involved data structures and algorithms of M_1. In some cases we can add additional functionality just by adding new algorithms and/or data structures. However, often the original algorithms of M_1 have to be modified, too, they are subject of an overwriting process.

In our example concerning the calculation of paths between nodes in a graph we make use of inheritance. In order to calculate shortest paths as well we can expand the original adjacency matrix A by a matrix B which contains distances and other information, e.g. the quality or costs of a connection, so that speed and therefore time and path length costs may be calculated, if one has to travel from s_i to s_j. (At this point it is not relevant, whether A and B are kept separately or if they should be combined conveniently involving a side effect on the chosen algorithms.)

Extending an existing model usually is quite straight forward as long as the designer of the model remains within the original application area (domain) the model has been written for.

If we focus on graph based models, we see that such models are more or less domain independent due to the previous abstraction process f.

Consequently, the extension of a model could also imply a change from the original domain D_1 to D_2:

$$f_1: M_1 \rightarrow M_2 \Rightarrow f_2: (M_1 \times D_1) \rightarrow (M_2 \times D_2)$$

Let D_1 be an application domain concerning delivery of goods without unloading. The meaning of edge $e = (u,v)$ could be: the agent e delivers goods to both, u and v. So the problem ends up in the vertex cover problem:

A vertex cover of $X = (V, E)$ is a subset $S \subseteq V$ such that each edge of X is incident upon some vertex in S. Is there a vertex cover of size r?

This problem is formally equivalent to the clique problem:

A k-clique in a graph X is a complete subgraph of X with k nodes. Does X contain a k-clique?

Both problems are NP-complete. If we replace X by its complement graph X_c, then the following lemma holds:

A set $S \subseteq V$ is a clique in X_c if and only if $V - S$ is a vertex cover of X.

One is attempted to solve the first problem formulated in D_1 in another domain D_2 which reflects an application area e.g. in communication. As long as we design both models from scratch and have the mapping $X \rightarrow X_c$ carefully in mind, the approach would work.

But the idea of reusability includes the aim to reuse somebody else's model and implementation. We can only do so if we have access to a full semantic explanation of the model and the involved algorithms. What we need is a "contract" on the model which contains all the relevant semantic information in order to take advantage of reusability.

In our example the following could happen: because finding a clique is NP-complete, the designer of the model wants to reduce the underlying graph X by replacing it by Y, where certain paths (u,v), (v,w) are shrunk to (u,w) and expanded afterwards again. This makes sense, because in D_2 the (semantic) assumption is reasonable, that within a path of length 2 no information is lost on the way from u to w. But cliques contained in Y do not correspond to vertex covers in X_c. The solution achieved in D_2, although not "optimal", may have practical value in D_2, but presumably is pointless in D_1. We become victims of the missing contract.

Designer of models in OR are fully aware of this danger. But, as a forward reference: in component oriented programming it turns out that missing contracts on reusable software components currently cause a major problem.

2 Aims of object oriented programming

The availability of object oriented programming languages brought a major change in software design generally. The previous procedure oriented programming style has been replaced by a different paradigm. Such programming languages as Smalltalk, C++, Oberon-2 or JAVA also changed the way how a software system is designed.

A programming language is called object oriented if it supports objects as instances of classes and inheritance in particular.

Abstraction to master complexity

Classes can be understood as plans how instantiated objects look like and behave. Therefore classes are the result of an abstraction process and must be designed carefully. One specific aim, when designing classes, is to master complexity, because objects instantiated from such classes will communicate with other objects and this interaction reflects the complexity of the system built upon or by class libraries.

As we have pointed out earlier, this concept of classes had already been invented before OOP penetrated the software landscape. We find these ideas in SIMULA 67 and later on in languages as Modula-2 which allows the specification and implementation of abstract data structures and abstract data types.

An abstract data structure is a mechanism for encapsulating data together with access procedures which operate upon them.

Abstract data types (ADT) can manage any number of instances of abstract data structures. Clients of an object, constructed by an ADT do not need to know how the access procedures are actually implemented or will be implemented. During the design phase (i.e.: modelling) it is sufficient to know about the master plan (= definition/specification) behind the ADT. Exactly this helps to master complexity, because ADTs can be used as structuring mechanisms which help to partition a general model into smaller parts.

Reusability

One specific way of implementing ADTs is provided by classes. Reusability is provided as soon as we can use class libraries which are designed (usually by other people) to solve subproblems occurring frequently.

In the ideal case such libraries are domain independent, but in most cases they are dedicated to a specific application domain.

Examples are user interfaces for windowing systems, basic building blocks for file systems, and databases: scanning data, sorting, searching, inserting, and deletion of data etc.

This kind of reusability already was the design goal and aim of subroutine libraries of procedure oriented languages as FORTRAN or PASCAL.

But classes go one step ahead: they allow extension and modification.

Extending classes: inheritance and the need for contracts

In OOP inheritance is a special mechanism and concept. It allows that (classes of) objects can be defined as special cases of more general ones, automatically including the associated procedures (in OOP: methods) and the definition of the underlying data structure.

Special cases of classes are called subclasses and they inherit methods and data structure from their superclass but may define their own methods additionally and may also, to some extent, override any of the inherited characteristics.

If we want to inherit capabilities from a superclass in order to design a new subclass then we must have information about the master plan from which we want to inherit.

This information can be drawn from the implementation code (implementation inheritance) or by inspecting and using the available interface description (interface inheritance).

If we do not allow so called multiple inheritance we get a class hierarchy, because inheritance can be nested to any degree.

Apart from syntactic needs the mentioned interface serves as a contract or contractual interface. It provides semantics to the designer of the class hierarchy.

Exactly at this point we want to recall the potential danger of reusability. When we discussed the reuse of models we stated the demand for a contract which should provide information, in particular, if a model is used in a different application domain, possibly after some modifications and/or extensions have been applied.

In OOP basically we have two forms of changing a contract given by the interface and description in a metalanguage. If we change the interface then we do a (rather simple (?)) syntactic change. But if we change the description by changing its specification, then we commit a dangerous semantic break of a contract.

If one does so within the inner levels of a class hierarchy, the results for clients of the leafs of the hierarchy can be unpredictably unpleasant.

One could argue that a contract never must be broken. But as soon as one wants to reuse a class library, originally designed for a certain domain D_1, and tries to transfer it to another domain using inheritance, then a semantic break of the contract may occur easily or is unavoidable.

This is the major hindrance of making classes/objects domain independently deployable. It puts intrinsic limits for extensibility.

We are already familiar with this situation in the context of reusability of OR models.

3 Summary

Designing a model involves the design of class libraries if the model should be implemented under the OOP paradigm, and vice versa. Both are based on abstraction and the aim of reusability and extensibility in particular.

The latter concept contains the danger of changing underlying semantics coming from a remaining application domain dependence. Therefore there is an evident need to have contracts which must not be broken. But this in turn imposes limits to an arbitrary inheritance when at the same time there is a need to change the application domain, too.

We have seen that common problems exist in modelling for OR, too. On the one hand there is a demand for reusability and inheritance, on the other hand the domain dependency imposes restrictions. And we need contracts for such models, too.

On the Use and Misuse of Holding Cost Models

Bernhard Fleischmann

Department of Production and Logistics

University of Augsburg, Germany

Abstract

This paper considers the relationship between holding cost and discounted cash flow models. Rather than arguing for or against one of these types of models, their close relationship is underlined by interpreting the holding cost criterion as first order approximation of the discounted cash flow criterion. Various planning models, both for dynamic operations in a finite horizon and for cyclic operations in an infinite horizon are considered. It is shown that flow-oriented modelling of the holding costs avoids misinterpretations and problems with the evaluation of inventories.

1 Introduction

Inventory is a major issue in supply chain planning. Decision models for optimizing supply chain operations usually include *holding cost (HC)* for the inventory as a linear function of stock level and time in store. This cost may consist of two components: first, true out-of-pocket cost depending on the stock level, e.g. warehouse rent, cooling or heating cost and insurance, and second, capital asset cost. The latter is well known to be an opportunity cost for the capital tied up in the stock and approximates the impact of the operational decisions on the cash flow. More precise models consider the cash flow explicitly and use, as an objective function, the discounted cash flow (DCF) instead of costs and revenues. The discussion whether DCF or HC models should be preferred in operational decision making has been running throughout the literature for several decades (see e.g. Gurnani, 1983; Haase, 2000; Helber, 1998; Rieper, 1989; Teunter and Inderfurth, 1998). It is not the purpose of this paper to contribute new arguments to that debate. Anyhow, there are good reasons for using the approximating HC models for short and medium term planning: they allow to separate the optimization of operational decisions from the financial area, are easy to use and widely accepted in practice. For long term strategic decisions involving investments, however, cost models usually fail to include the financial impacts correctly.

The purpose of this paper is to point out dangers of misuse of HC models in non-standard situations and to give recommendations for correct HC modeling to those readers who like to work with HC models, as does the author. In particular, the case is considered where there are several sources of stock replenishment which differ in the procurement cost, but not in the physical utility of the items in stock. Examples of this situation are several suppliers with different prices and restricted capacity as well as procurement prices with quantity discounts. Recently, this case has become very important in the context of *reverse logistics*, when newly manufactured items and *recycled items* are mixed in one stock of spare parts or materials for production (see e.g. Richter, 1996; Teunter et al., 2000; Teunter and Inderfurth, 1998).

To make the right use of the HC models in non-standard situations, it is necessary to remember the derivation of the HC from the DCF. This is considered generally in Section 2, which leads to some postulates for correct HC models. Section 3 considers the integration of HCs into dynamic multi-period decision models with finite horizon. Section 4 does the same for cyclic decision models with continuous time and infinite horizon.

2 Impact of the DCF on HC models

Throughout this paper, holding costs only consist of cost of capital. Additional out-of-pocket holding costs, which are not concerned by the present investigation, could be added in the usual way to all HC models in the following.

In this section, a stock of a single item is considered and the following notations are used:

i	interest rate
v	procurement price per quantity unit (the *value* of the inflow)
w	sales price
$h = vi$	the holding cost rate.

Helber (1998) points out that v must only contain payments that are influenced by the short term decisions on the inflow. In case of production this usually concerns only expenses for materials and energy.

Now, consider a single inflow of quantity q to the stock at time t and a single outflow of the same quantity at time $t + \tau$, where $\tau \geq 0$. These flows of goods imply cash flows of $-vq$ at time t and $+wq$ at time $t + \tau$. The DCF or net present value (NPV) at time 0 is, for continuous discounting,

$$NPV_c = -vq\, e^{-it} + wq\, e^{-i(t+\tau)} \tag{2.1}$$

and for discrete discounting with integer τ

$$NPV_d = -vq\,(1+i)^{-t} + wq\,(1+i)^{-(t+\tau)} \tag{2.2}$$

Assuming $w = v$ and using the first order approximation of e^{-it} or of $(1+i)^{-t}$, which is in both cases $1-it$, leads to the approximate NPV

$$NPV_a = vq\,(-1 + it + 1 - i\,(t+\tau)) = -\,ivq\tau,$$

This defines the holding cost function

$$HC\,(q,\tau) = -\,NPV_a = h\,q\,\tau \tag{2.3}$$

which is proportional to the quantity q times the storage duration τ. Note that h is the HC rate per quantity unit and time unit. Thus, the HC approximates the DCF and can be interpreted as the interest to be paid, or, better, the lost interest for the capital tied in stock, neglecting the compound interest. The first order approximation is justified by the fact that in short and medium term planning the value *it* is very small: *t* is the length of a period in a dynamic model or of a cycle in a cyclic model and typically less than 3 months, *i* is seldom over 20% p.a., so that $it < 0.05$ can be assumed.

In general, the total inflow and outflow consist of a set of single discrete flows or continuous flow functions over the time. The DCF is then obtained as a sum or an integral of terms (2.1) or (2.2). This will be considered in more detail in Sections 3 and 4, respectively.

In many decision situations, only the inflow to the stock can be influenced, whereas the outflow, and hence the corresponding cash flow, is fixed. In this case the unrealistic assumption $w = v$ is not necessary: the holding cost (2.3) can be used even for $w \neq v$, where the resulting total HC differs from the 'right' holding cost by a constant, namely the fixed outflow, evaluated by $w - v$ and discounted.

The derivation of the holding cost as an approximation of the DCF (2.1) or (2.2) suggests the following postulates on the holding costs that are relevant in a decision model:

(P1) If the outflow is fixed, the relevant holding cost must not depend on time or value of the outflow.

(P2) The relevant holding cost must depend on the time and value of controllable inflows, in particular it must consider differences in the expenses for the inflows.

The interpretation of the holding cost based on (2.3) is somewhat dangerous, in so far as it involves the *duration in stock*. This may lead to a conflict between (P1) and (P2), if there are several inflows with different values: If the HC rate is different for the different inflows, according to (P2), the individual duration of the different classes of items (e.g. new and recycled items) has to be recorded so that the holding cost depends on the 'depletion strategy', (see Teunter et al., 2000), i.e. the sequence in which the items are taken from the stock. But this contradicts (P1). This dilemma has been recognized, but not resolved, by ter Haseborg (1990) for quantity discounts and by Teunter et al. (2000) for reverse logistics. A possible resolution consists in giving up HC models and returning to the DCF, as suggested by Haase (2000). However, in the following Sections, it will be shown that, in case of finite horizon, proper use of a HC model works as well, and that in some infinite horizon models even the DCF does not help.

3 Dynamic finite horizon models

The dynamic behavior of inventory in a finite planning horizon is usually modeled as follows: With the notations

T	planning horizon
$t =$	$1,\dots,T$ periods
x_t	inflow in period t
y_t	outflow in period t
I_t	inventory at the end of period t
I_0	starting inventory

the inventory is

$$I_t = I_{t-1} + x_t - y_t$$

or

$$I_t = I_0 + \sum_{s=1}^{t} (x_s - y_s). \tag{3.1}$$

Usual assumptions are:

- The periods have equal length of 1 time unit.
- The inflows and outflows (or at least the related cash flows) happen at the beginning of the period.
- Interest is paid with rate i per period
- $I_t \geq 0$ i.e. backorders are not allowed.

With v, w and h defined as in Section 2, the DCF objective is to maximize the NPV

$$\Sigma_t (1+i)^{-(t-1)} (wy_t - vx_t) = \max! \tag{3.2}$$

or, equivalently, the final value

$$\Sigma_t (1+i)^{(T-t+1)} (wy_t - vx_t) = \max! \tag{3.3}$$

The first order approximation of (3.3) is

$$\Sigma_t i (T\text{-}t\text{+}1) (wy_t - vx_t) + \Sigma_t (wy_t - vx_t) = \max! \tag{3.4}$$

A correct HC objective must be equivalent to (3.4). The usual cost oriented objective with HC

$$\Sigma_t h I_t + \Sigma_t vx_t - \Sigma_t wy_t = \min ! \tag{3.5}$$

is, for w = v, equivalent to (3.4), because (3.1) implies

$$\Sigma_t h I_t = \Sigma_t h (T\text{-}t\text{+}1) (x_t - y_t) + h T I_0 \tag{3.6}$$

where the last term is constant. Further costs and revenues, in particular fixed costs per inflow, can be added to (3.2) as discounted cash flows and to (3.5) without discounting. (3.5) can be interpreted as the payment or loss of interests for the capital tied in the inventory.

Some authors (see e.g. Haase, 2000; Helber, 1998; Rieper, 1989), suggest to discount the interest payments and to minimize the objective

$$\Sigma_t (1+i)^{-t} h I_t \tag{3.7}$$

which equals, due to (3.1), to

$$h I_0 + \Sigma_t (x_t - y_t) iv \sum_{s=t}^{T} (1+i)^{-s}$$

$$= h I_0 + \Sigma_t (x_t - y_t) v \left[(1+i)^{-(t-1)} - (1+i)^{-T} \right]$$

$$= h\, I_0 + \Sigma_t\, (1+i)^{-(t-1)}\, v\, (x_t - y_t) - (1+i)^{-T}\, v\, I_T$$

and is therefore, if the final stock level I_T is fixed, exactly equivalent to the DCF objective (3.2). When using (3.7) all further costs have to be discounted as well, except for the cost of the inflow. However, this mix of HC and DCF model appears little useful, as it requires the same involvement of cash flows as the pure DCF model (3.2).

The right hand side of (3.6) applies the HC rate to the inflow and outflow, rather than to the stock level, but multiplied with the *time factor* (T – t + 1). This *flow-oriented HC model* is more flexible than the usual stock-oriented model (3.5). It can be easily extended to more general cases.

Fixed outflow, w ≠ v

In this case, the standard HC model (3.5) is still valid, as the 'wrong' value v for the outflow is not relevant. But, using the flow-oriented form, the relevant costs can be separated as

$$\Sigma_t\, h\, (T\text{-}t\text{+}1)\, x_t + \Sigma_t\, v x_t = \min! \qquad (3.8)$$

Often the total inflow $\Sigma_t\, x_t$ in the planning horizon is also fixed (e.g. equal to the total outflow), i.e. only the distribution of the inflow over the time is to be planned. Then (3.4) is equivalent to

$$\Sigma_t\, c_t\, x_t = \min! \qquad (3.9)$$

where c_t = h (T-t+1). This form of holding costs is used in lotsizing models (see e.g. Fleischmann 1990). Note that the relevant part (3.9) of the holding cost does not depend on the storage duration nor on properties of the outflow and satisfies (P1). The only impact of the outflow is a restriction of the inflow, due to (3.1) and $I_t \geq 0$.

Different types of inflow, fixed outflow

As mentioned in the Introduction, several types of inflow r = 1,...,R with different cost may result from quantity discount prices, different suppliers or, in reverse logistics, from new and recycled materials. Let

v_r procurement price of inflow type r
$h_r = v_r i$ HC rate.

As long as the procurement policy has the *zero inventory (or Wagner/Whitin) property* – i.e. an inflow only occurs if the inventory is zero – the evaluation of the stocks I_t with the right HC rate h_r is obvious and unique. However, nonconcave inflow costs or capacity constraints may prevent this structure of an optimal solution. Then, any attempt to base the HC model on the physical inventory

$$I_t = I_{t-1} + \Sigma_r x_{rt} - y_t$$

leads to a violation of either postulate (P1) or (P2) as explained in Section 2 and misleads the operational decisions. But the objective (3.8) allows an easy extension to

$$\Sigma_{r,t} h_r (T-t+1) x_{rt} + \Sigma_{r,t} v_r x_{rt} = \min! \quad (3.10)$$

which is a correct first order approximation of the DCF criterion. It might be criticized that this model does not provide a figure for the real holding cost. However, the right evaluation of present inventories is a (sometimes difficult) question for accountants and controllers, but does not affect decision making. If wanted, some key figures on inventory cost can be derived from the optimal solution of the decision model, using and evaluation principle *ex post*.

Controllable outflow, multi-echelon inventory

If the outflow y_t is itself a decision variable and $w \neq v$, the standard HC model (3.5) differs from (3.4) by the term Σ_t i (w-v) y_t which has to be subtracted from the objective function (3.4). However, if the outflow is again an inflow into a subsequent stock, the stock-oriented HC model can be used in a multi-echelon form.

As an example, consider a product that is assembled from components j = 1,...,J and let

a_j input coefficient of component j for the product

I^1_{jt} stock of component j

$h^1_j = iv_j$ HC rate of component j

x_{jt} inflow of component j

I^2_t stock of the product

$h^2 = iw$ HC rate of the product

y_t production quantity (inflow in the product stock)

z_t outflow from the product stock (non-controllable)

The relationship between the stock-oriented and the flow-oriented model is as follows:

$$\Sigma_{j,t} h^1_j I^1_{jt} + \Sigma_t h^2 I^2_t = \Sigma_t (T\text{-}t\text{+}1) [\Sigma_j h^1_j (x_{jt} - a_j y_t) + h^2 (y_t - z_t)] =$$

$$\Sigma_t i (T\text{-}t\text{+}1) [\Sigma_j v_j x_{jt} + (w - \Sigma_j a_j v_j) y_t] - C$$

with the constant $C = \Sigma_t h^2 (T\text{-}t\text{+}1) z_t$. Thus, both the stock-oriented and the flow-oriented HC model are equivalent to the first order DCF approximation, if the HC rate is based, in the former, on the *cumulated value* up to the corresponding echelon, and in the latter, on the *value added* by the corresponding flow, i.e. $w - \Sigma_j a_j v_j$ for the production flow. More precisely, the value added must include only the expenses of the corresponding operation. The 'right holding costs' of Teunter and Inderfurth (1998) for a two-stage inventory system in reverse logistics are of this form.

Payment deadline

A potential misuse of HC models concerns the case, when there is a positive time δ between an inflow x_t and the deadline for the payment vx_t. Sometimes it is argued, based on (2.3), that as long as the storage duration $\tau \leq \delta$, the holding cost is zero. First, this argument links the holding cost with the storage duration and hence with the outflow, in contradiction to (P1). Looking to the flow-oriented HC-model, the effect of the payment deadline only consists in a shift of the cash flow against the inflow x_t by the time δ, i.e. into $v\, x_{t+\delta}$. Thus, the time factor (T-t+1) has to be modified to (T-t-δ+1) and the objective function, as far as it depends on the inflow, becomes

$$\Sigma_t h (T\text{-}t\text{-}\delta\text{+}1) x_t + \Sigma_t vx_t = \Sigma_t h (T\text{-}t\text{+}1) x_t + \Sigma_t (v - h\,\delta) x_t.$$

This leads to the following conclusions:

- If the total inflow $\Sigma_t x_t$ is fixed, the payment deadline has *no effect* on the decisions.
- If the total inflow is controllable, a payment deadline of δ reduces the price v of the inflow to v-hδ, but has *no effect* neither on the HC rate nor on the relevant holding cost.

The modification of the HC rate $h = iv$ into $h(1+i)^{-\delta}$, as proposed by Silver et al. (1998), is a second order effect which should not be included in the HC concept of a first order approximation. Note that also payments after the planning horizon, at time $t+\delta > T$, but caused by inflows at time $t \leq T$, are relevant for the decision problem.

4 Cyclic infinite horizon models

Cyclic inventory control models are usually based on the following assumptions:

- Time is continuous (and therefore continuous discounting is appropriate).
- External demand is steady and constant. (Since only single-stage systems are considered in this Section, every outflow is steady).
- Inflows occur cyclically with a (variable) cycle time in t. There might be several inflows within one cycle.
- Demand must be met without backorders.
- The planning horizon is infinite.

The most popular model of this kind is the economic order quantity (EOQ) model for one product, one instantaneous inflow per cycle of size q, the data

d	demand per unit of time
F	fixed cost per inflow
$h = vi$	HC rate

and the variables t and $q = dt$.

It is important to note, that cyclic planning models are rough aggregated models for at least two reasons:

- The steady demand is always a simplification of reality.
- A cyclical model does not take into account a given initial state, e.g. initial stocks, but rather describes the ideal steady repetition of identical cycles.

Thus, the result of a cyclic planning model can only be used as a rough guideline. It is established in medium term planning and always needs to be refined by more detailed short-term planning, considering the actual initial situation. This character of a cyclic planning model suggests the following additional postulate:

(P3) The objective criterion of a cyclic planning model must not depend on a given initial state nor on a given starting point within the cycle.

There are again two different ways to define an *objective criterion* in an infinite horizon model: In a *DCF model*, all cash flows due to the inflows are discounted over the infinite horizon usually in the following way (see e.g. Grubbström, 1980; Rieper, 1989): Let C(t) be the cash flow of a single cycle of length t discounted to the beginning of the cycle; then the NPV of the infinite horizon is

$$\text{NPV} = C(t) \int_0^{\infty} e^{-i\tau}\, d\tau = C(t)\,(1-e^{-it})^{-1} \tag{4.1}$$

and the annuity, i.e. the cash flow per unit of time

$$A = C(t)\, i\,(1-e^{-it})^{-1}. \tag{4.2}$$

Note that this criterion is only based on the inflows and satisfies (P1).

The *HC model* uses, as a criterion, the *average cost* per unit of time, calculated as the total cost of one cycle, divided by t. The cost consists of the fixed and variable cost of the inflow and the holding cost. The latter is calculated as the *average inventory level*, resulting from inflows and outflows, multiplied by the HC rate. The variable cost of the inflows is only relevant, if there are different sources of inflow, because the total inflow per time must equal the demand.

Unfortunately, both types of models have deficiencies: The *HC model* violates (P1) because the average stock involves the outflow. The *DCF model* violates (P3), because for cycles with several inflows the objective value depends on the choice of the time when the cycle is started, as illustrated below. Moreover, if a stock is necessary at the starting time, it has to be included in the cash flow. Therefore, in case of cyclic models, the DCF model loses its role as "the right model" and as a benchmark for the approximating HC models. Nevertheless, it is possible to derive again the HC criterion from the DCF criterion (4.2), thus avoiding the involvement of the outflow. The attempt to try to overcome dependence on the cycle start does not succeed in all cases.

Using the first order approximation (see e.g. Grubbström, 1980)

$$it\,(1-e^{-it})^{-1} = 1 + \tfrac{1}{2}\, it + O\,(i^2t^2)$$

the annuity (4.2) becomes approximately

$$\tilde{A} = C(t)\,(1/t + \tfrac{1}{2}i). \tag{4.3}$$

This is the key formula for deriving HC criteria in the following. It is also used by Rieper (1989) in a modified form, based on discrete discounting. For the EOQ model, (4.3) and the usual HC model are equivalent, because then, $C(t) = F + vdt$ and

$$\tilde{A} = (F + vdt)\,(1/t + \tfrac{1}{2}i) = F/t + \tfrac{1}{2}i\,vdt + vd + \tfrac{1}{2}iF. \tag{4.4}$$

The first two terms represent exactly the average cost of the EOQ model. The last two terms do not depend on t and can be suppressed when optimizing t. They represent the variable cost of inflow per unit of time and the neglected interest for the fixed cost, respectively.

If the cycle starts at time $t_0 < t$ after the inflow, an initial inventory $I_0 = d(t - t_0)$ is necessary. Thus, vI_0 has to be added to the NPV or ivI_0 to the annuity. The DCF of one cycle is

$$C(t) = (F + vdt)\,e^{-i(t - t_0)}$$

and hence the annuity in the first order approximation is

$$\begin{aligned}\tilde{A}(t_0) &= ivd\,(t - t_0) + (F + vdt)[1 - i(t - t_0)]\;(1/t + \tfrac{1}{2}i)\\ &= F/t + vd + \tfrac{1}{2}ivdt + iF\,(t_0/t - \tfrac{1}{2}) + O(i^2)\end{aligned} \tag{4.5}$$

The annuity does not depend on the start time, except for the interest on the fixed cost. But the average of the latter term, over all start times t_0 ($0 \le t_0 < t$), is zero. Omitting this term results in an annuity which is independent of the start time and can be used as average cost per unit of time. This is true for a single inflow per cycle.

It follows from (4.5) that the interest on the fixed cost has no impact on the lotsizing decision, i.e. only the frequence of the fixed costs, but not their distribution over time, is relevant. This also justifies the suppression of interest payments on fixed costs in the discrete finite horizon models (see Section 3).

In the following, the use of (4.3) is considered for some extensions of the basic EOQ model.

Inflow with finite production speed

If the inflow and the corresponding cash flow are not instantaneous, but continuous during the time $u = q/p < t$, i.e. with production speed $p > d$, the DCF of the cycle is

$$C(t) = F + vp \int_0^u e^{-i\tau}\, d\tau = F + \frac{vq\,(1-e^{-iu})}{iu}$$

and (4.3) leads to the annuity

$$\begin{aligned}\tilde{A} &= [F + vq\,(iu - \tfrac{1}{2}i^2u^2)/iu]\,(1/t + \tfrac{1}{2}i) \\ &= F/t + vq/t + \tfrac{1}{2}ivq\,(1 - u/t) + \tfrac{1}{2}iF + O(i^2).\end{aligned}$$

Using $q = dt$ and $u/t = d/p$, the terms depending on t are

$$F/t + \tfrac{1}{2}hdt\,(1 - d/p)$$

which is the well-known cost per unit of time of the EOQ model for this case (see Silver et al. 1998, Chapter 5.8).

Payment deadline

If the payment for the inflow at time t is due at time $t + \delta$, the terms $\frac{1}{2}ivdt + vd$ in the annuity (4.4) are to be multiplied by the discounting factor $(1-i\delta)$. In the first order approximation, this has *no effect* on the relevant cost for the lotsize decision, like in the case of the finite horizon (see Section 3). Rieper (1989) and Silver et al. (1998, Chapter 5.9.2) include the second order effect of multiplying the HC rate h by the discounting factor. However, the first order approximation deviates from the optimal second order EOQ only by the factor $\alpha = \sqrt{e^{i\delta}}$ and hence from the minimal cost by the factor $\frac{1}{2}(\alpha + 1/\alpha)$ (see Silver et al., 1998, Chapter 5.3). Even for the extremely large value of $i\delta = 0.05$ (see Section 2), the deviation from EOQ is $\alpha = 1.025$ and from the minimal cost 1.0003. Thus, the first order approximation really provides a satisfying accuracy.

ELSP

The *Economic Lot Scheduling Problem* (ELSP) (see Silver et al., 1998, Chapter 11.6.1) comprises several products $k = 1,\ldots,K$ produced on a single machine in a cyclic sequence. The notations are used as before, with the subscript k if relevant. For a cycle with a single inflow of every product, the inflow of product k is $q_k = d_k\, t$ for the EOQ and its annuity is independent of the start time, as shown before. Therefore, the annuity of the total cycle is independent of the start time and on the position of the single inflows within the cycle. It is obtained by simply adding the EOQ terms per product

$$\tilde{A} = \Sigma_k (F_k / t + v_k d_k + \tfrac{1}{2} i v_k d_k t)$$

Several inflows of one product

Now consider inflows q_k ($k = 1,\dots,K$) within one cycle for the same steady demand d, but maybe different in the value v_k, as it is the case in reverse logistics or for variable prices. This situation also applies to the ELSP with more than one inflow per product and cycle, but then the v_k are equal. Now $q_k < dt$ is possible so that the annuity (4.3) becomes dependent on the start time for every single inflow. Let again t_o be the start time after the inflow q_k. At this time, at least the inventory

$$I_0 = \max(q_k - dt_0, 0)$$

is left and hence required for the cycle. In the following, the fixed cost is omitted, because it causes no problem w.r.t. the starting time, as shown above. The annuity is

$$\begin{aligned}\tilde{A}(t_0) &= i v_k I_0 + v_k q_k (1 - i(t - t_0))\,(1/t + \tfrac{1}{2} i) \\ &= v_k q_k / t + \tfrac{1}{2} i v_k q_k - B(t_0) + O(i^2)\end{aligned}$$

where

$$\begin{aligned}B(t_0) = {} & i v_k t_0 (d - q_k / t), \text{ if } t_0 < q_k / d \\ & i v_k q_k (1 - t_0 / t), \text{ if } t_0 \geq q_k / d.\end{aligned}$$

One possible criterion that overcomes the influence of the start time t_0 is the average over the entire cycle

$$\tilde{A}_k = \frac{1}{t}\int_0^t \tilde{A}(t_0)\,dt_0 = v_k q_k / t + \tfrac{1}{2} i v_k q_k - B$$

where

$$\begin{aligned}B &= \frac{1}{t}\int_0^t B(t_0)\,dt_0 = \frac{i v_k}{t}\left[(d - \frac{q_k}{t}) \frac{1}{2}\frac{q^2}{d^2} + q_k (t - \frac{q_k}{d} - \frac{1}{2}(t - \frac{q_k^2}{d^2 t})) \right] \\ &= \frac{1}{2} i v_k q_k (1 - \frac{q_k}{dt});\end{aligned}$$

hence

$$\tilde{A}_k = v_k q_k / t + \tfrac{1}{2} i v_k q_k r_k \tag{4.6}$$

where $r_k = q_k / dt$ is the fraction of the demand covered by inflow k. If the periods, in which the demand is covered by a certain inflow do not overlap, i.e. if the stock is zero at the beginning of every inflow (*zero inventory property*), the terms (4.6) can be added up to the total annuity of the cycle

$$\tilde{A} = \Sigma_k (v_k q_k / t + \tfrac{1}{2} i v_k q_k r_k). \tag{4.7}$$

It is obvious, that the zero inventory arrangements of several lots within the cycle are dominating w.r.t. both the DCF and the HC criterion, because the inflow and the corresponding cash flow are postponed to the last possible time. However, there might be restrictions in the production or procurement process or nonconcave costs which prevent a zero inventory cycle. In this case, there occur periods where the stocks from different inflows overlap. Unfortunately, the proposed method for deriving a DCF criterion that is independent of the start time, requires the evaluation of the initial inventory at every start time within the cycle. Thus, the attempt to avoid the violation of (P3) for the DCF criterion, leads just to the problem of evaluating mixed stocks. It appears that there is a fundamental conflict between the postulates (P1) and (P3) for the cyclic model.

Example

The case of different inflows for one product is illustrated using an example of Teunter and Inderfurth (1998): The demand of a material is covered at 20% by new manufactured items (inflow k = 1) and at 80% by (cheaper) recycled items (inflow k = 2).

The data are

$$i = 0.2, \quad d = 100$$
$$F_1 = 30, \quad v_1 = 10, \quad r_1 = 0.2$$
$$F_2 = 10, \quad v_2 = 5, \quad r_2 = 0.8$$

As the fractions r_1, r_2 are fixed, the cost of the inflow cannot be influenced, per unit of time it amounts to $C_0 = (r_1 v_1 + r_2 v_2)\, d = 600$.

A cycle of length t with a single inflow of both types has lot sizes $q_1 = 20$ t, $q_2 = 80$ t and holding costs, according to (4.7)

$$\tilde{A}=\tfrac{1}{2}(0.4q_1+0.8q_2)+C_0=\tfrac{1}{2}(8t+64t)+C_0=36t+600$$

and the fixed cost

$$(F_1+F_2)/t=40/t.$$

the optimal cycle length and lot sizes are

$$t^*=\sqrt{40/36}=1.054,\ q_1^*=21.1,\ q_2^*=84.3$$

and the minimal cost $C_{HC}=2\sqrt{40\cdot 30\cdot 36}=75.9$. Note that $it^*\approx 0.2$ is unrealistically high (either the interest rate too high or the cycle length too long), but this stresses the interesting effects.

The exact annuity based on the DCF depends on the start time. Starting with inflow 1 at time 0 and with inflow 2 at time $t_1 = 0.2\ t$ yields for $t = t^*$ the annuity according to (4.2)

$$A_1=[F_1+v_1q_1+(F_2+v_2q_2)e^{-it_1}]i(1-e^{-it})^{-1}=688.9$$

and starting with inflow 2 at time 0 and with inflow 1 at time $t_2 = 0.8t$:

$$A_2=[F_2+v_2q_2+(F_1+v_1q_1)e^{-it_2}]i(1-e^{-it})^{-1}=668.3$$

The HC evaluation $\tilde{A}+C_0=675.9$ which has been shown to be an average of the annuities over all starting times is between the values A_1 and A_2 which differ remarkably.

Now consider the case that the two inflows are restricted, by some external constraint, to have equal distance. We keep the values $q_k = q_k^*$ and $t = t^*$, though no longer optimal, since we are only interested in the evaluation.

The cycle can now start with inflow 2 and zero initial stock, but when it starts with inflow 1 of $q_1 = 0.2$ dt it needs the initial stock $I_0 = 0.3$ dt in order to bridge the time until the start of inflow 2 at time 0.5 t (see Figure 1). In this case, both the DCF and the HC criterion are ambiguous:

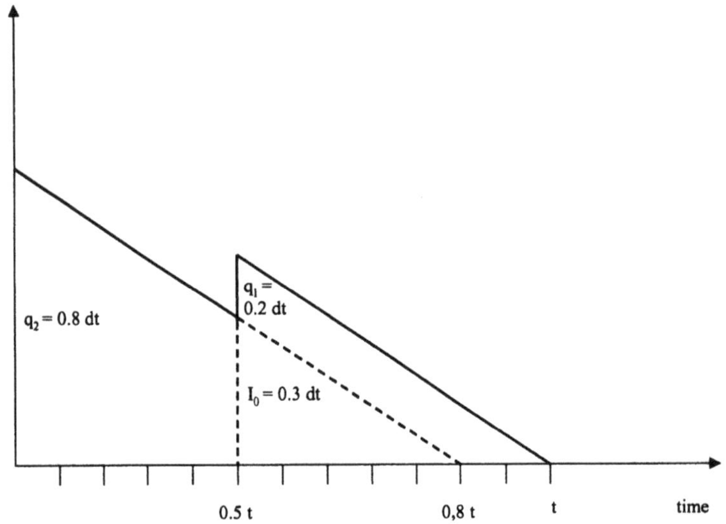

Figure 1.Two different inflows with overlapping

The conventional HC criterion depends on the depletion strategy between inflow 1 and inflow 2. The two extremes are the consumption of inflow 1 or inflow 2 first, respectively, which lead to the holding costs for that half cycle:

$$0.2\left(\tfrac{1}{2}h_1 q_1 + h_2 \cdot I_0\right) + 0.3\left(\tfrac{1}{2}h_2\, I_0\right) = 15.3$$

and

$$0.2\left(\tfrac{1}{2}h_1 q_1\right) + 0.3\left(h_1 q_1 + \tfrac{1}{2}h_2 I_0\right) = 21.6\,.$$

Together with the HC of the other half cycle $0.5\left(\tfrac{1}{2}v_2(q_2 + I_0)\right)$, the fixed cost 40/t and $C_0 = 600$, the two cost evaluations are

$$\tilde{A}_1 + C_0 = 682.2 \text{ and } \tilde{A}_2 + C_0 = 688.5$$

for the comparison with the DCF criterion.

The DCF annuities for the start with inflow 2

$$A_2 = [F_2 + v_2 q_2 + (F_1 + v_1 q_1) e^{-0.5i}]\, i (1 - e^{-it})^{-1} = 682.3$$

and for the start with inflow 1

$$A_1 = [F_1 + v_1 q_1 + (F_2 + v_2 q_2) e^{-0.5i}]\, i (1 - e^{-it})^{-1} + i v_2 I_0 = 693.8\,,$$

differ even more than the two HC evaluations.

5 Conclusion

The use of linear holding costs is widespread in operational planning models. HC objectives are first order approximations of DCF objectives for short and medium term decisions. An apparent difference between these objectives is that the HC is based on inventory, whereas the DCF is based on cash flow. But this difference is not fundamental: By strictly considering a HC objective as a DCF approximation, the HC rate can be linked with inflows and outflows of the inventory as well. This avoids misinterpretations and problems with the evaluation of inventory.

In dynamic finite horizon models, the usual inventory-oriented HC objectives can be transformed in an equivalent flow-oriented objective, where the HC rate is applied to the flows, multiplied with a time factor. The latter represents the time from the occurence of the flow until the end of the planning horizon. This way, even mixed inventories caused by different inflows can be modelled easily and correctly without ambiguity.

In cyclic infinite horizon models the usual HC objective represents the average cost per unit of time. The inventory-oriented HC objectives of the basic EOQ model and extensions can also be explained on the basis of the lot-wise inflow and can be derived as first order approximation of the DCF annuity. However, the DCF criterion may be ambiguous in this case, as it depends on the start time within the cycle. A unique criterion can be obtained by taking the average over all start times within the cycle. However, this fails exactly in the case of mixed inventories, when the HC criterion is ambiguous too. Arguments for the unique 'right' criterion in a decision model are still missing for that case.

References

Fleischmann, B. (1990): The discrete lotsizing and scheduling problem. European Journal of Operational Research 44, 337-348

Grubbström R.W. (1980): A principle for determining the correct capital costs of work-in-progress and inventory. International Journal of Production Research 18, 259-271

Gurnani C. (1983): Economic analysis of inventory systems. International Journal of Production Research 21, 261-277

Haase K. (2000): Kapitalwertorientierte Bestellmengenplanung bei Mengenrabatten und dynamischer Nachfrage. To appear in: Zeitschrift für Betriebswirtschaft

Haseborg F. ter (1990): Dynamische Materialdisposition im Beschaffungsbereich. Zeitschrift für Betriebswirtschaft 60, 705-730

Helber S. (1998): Cash-Flow Oriented Lot Sizing in MRP II Systems. In: Drexl, A., Kimms, A. (eds.), Beyond Manufacturing Resource Planning (MRP II). Springer, 147-183

Richter K. (1996): The EOQ repair and waste disposal model with variable setup numbers. European Journal of Operational Research 96, 313-324

Rieper B. (1989): Zahlungs- oder erfolgsorientierte Entscheidungsrechnungen? Zeitschrift für Betriebswirtschaft 59, 875-887

Silver E., Pyke D., Peterson R. (1998): Inventory Management and Production Planning and Scheduling, 3rd Edition, John Wiley & Sons

Teunter R., Inderfurth K. (1998): The 'right' holding cost rates in undiscounted cost inventory models with reverse logistics. Preprint No. 28, Faculty of Economics and Management, Otto-von-Guericke University of Magdeburg, Germany

Teunter R., van der Laan E., Inderfurth K. (2000): How to set the holding cost rates in average cost inventory models with reverse logistics? Omega 28, 409-415

From the Publisher to the Wholesalers Determination of the Number of Copies and Their Distribution among the Wholesalers

Roland Dillmann

Fachbereich Wirtschaftswissenschaft

Bergische Universität Gesamthochschule Wuppertal, Germany

Abstract

I report about a project in press distribution. Its target is to develop a tool which automatically proposes how many copies should be printed and how they should be distributed among the 91 wholesalers. The publisher intends to use the same tool for all his different journals. In a first introductory chapter some important specialities of the commerce with press products are described. The second chapter offers a detailed description of the problem. In a third chapter the underlying model is presented. The fourth chapter deals with the mathematical methods. In the fifth chapter some results are presented. The paper ends with a short conclusion. The main technique to validate the model and to recommend the use of the model in practice is ex – post – simulation of the forecasting procedure over a long period using only data available at the time forecasts in practice had to be done.

1 Introduction

Freedom of opinion, guaranteed by the fundamental law, influences very intensively the modalities of the commerce of journals and magazines in Germany. This can be demonstrated by the following facts:

- The publishers are legitimated by law to fix the prices of press products on the complete logistic chain.
- There are essentially three ways of distribution; the first channel serves the subscribers; furthermore the publishers directly deliver their products to the shops in the railway stations where customers can buy it; the chain

of interest for this article goes from the publishers over the 91 wholesalers with 112 territories handled as independent unities to the 120.000 retail outlets. Every wholesaler serves exclusively the retail outlets of his territories. Nearly 4.080.000.000 copies are sold during a year, the average price is 1.52 DM (2.04 DM for the retailers) for the wholesaler in Western Germany and 1.39 DM for a wholesaler in Eastern Germany (1.79 DM for the retailers. The market share of the wholesale is 54% (Informations dated to the 1.1.2000, Internet:http://www.presse-grosso.de.grossist/htm).

- Journals and magazines can be regarded as perishable goods. They have a fixed sales period. Nearly all goods are delivered to the retail outlets in the night before the beginning of the sales period. The resulting stockkeeping problem for every retailer is solved by disaggregating the complete delivery into a first part expected to be sold and a reserve to encounter unexpected demand. The quantities are calculated to assure that 80% of the retail stores are not sold out until the end of the sales period. Actually nearly 2 of 5 copies are planned as reserve (planned return remittance, Richtremission in German.

- Publishers have the right to determine the number of copies they deliver to the wholesalers, the wholesalers have the duty to adequately distribute the goods. Respecting neutrality towards the different political opinions the wholesalers determine the assortment of newspapers and journals for the retail outlets. On the one hand retailers are allowed to remit the unsold copies to the wholesalers who in turn can remit them to the publishers. The publishers have to bear nearly the complete sales risk the only censor is the customer as long as the publisher accepts some general rules. As a consequence of these legal rules the dispositional part of the distribution problem can be disaggregated into the following subproblems:

- Problems of the publishers:

    - Formulation of a sales forecast for every wholesaler or railway station

    - Determination of the volume of the planned return remittance for every wholesaler and railway station.

- Problems of the wholesalers:
  - Division of the total delivery in that part delivered directly to the retail outlets and a reserve for subsequent delivery
  - Determination of the retail outlets to which copies of a newspaper or journal are delivered (not every retail store sells the complete offer)
  - Formulation of a sales forecast for every of the included retail outlets with regard to the publisher‘s global forecast for his territory
  - Distribution of the planned return remittance on the retail outlets included in the distribution process.

This paper only deals with the problem to automatically forecast the sales of every newspaper or journal in every wholesaler's territory.

2 Description of the problem

Actually the publisher distributes nearly 50 journals. With respect to the forecasting problem the following differences between the journals are of importance:

- publication dates (weekly, 14 days, 3 weeks, 4 weeks, monthly, two months, others)
- duration of existence of a journal (longer than 10 years for the well established journals as the one and newly introduced journals as the other extreme position.
- To explain the importance of these differences it makes sense to introduce the groups of independent variables used in the model. These groups are
- calendar data (bank holidays, school holidays
- seasonal figures
- different variables to express trends of different durability

- dummy variables to describe changes of the assignment of parts of the territory from one wholesaler to another one, partitions or merger of territories.

The importance of different publication dates results from the influence of bank holidays ect. The shorter the sales period of a journal the more important are the calendar data and possible shifts of the sales period for the forecasts.

Publication dates and the duration of existence together determine the volume of data underlying the reconstruction of the past and the forecast of the future. This not only influences the quality of forecasts but also how forecasting should be done. Furthermore the school holidays of the different Länder in Germany differ; there are blocks of Länder where school holidays start and end at the same days, but these blocks are not stable.Therefore for journals with a long duration of existence the influence of the holidays of different Länder can be separated statistically, but for newer journals this may be impossible. To handle the problem of different publication days or different durations of existence we classified the journals with respect to the following categories:

- A first classification criteria is given by the use calendar data in the forecasting model. After a lot of tests we decided to forecast with the help of calendar data for journals with publication dates of a month or less.

- The second classification criteria is caused by different length of time series of the sales of different journals.

Combining both classification criteria we have to distinguish six cases, as seen in the following

Table 1

	model with calendar data	model without calendar data
no observations	Case 1	Case 2
some observations	Case 3	Case 4
many observations	Case 5	Case 6

The six cases are handled in the following manner:

- In cases 1 and 2 a new object has to be introduced into the market. There is no object – specific experience forecast can be based on. Therefore all forecasts have to be derived from the sales of other objects regarded to be similar to the new object. If we forecast the sales of all territories by first forecasting the sales in Germany and then forecasing the market share of of the 112 territories the first task was regarded to be decided politically. Methods of market research may give first hints to the market chances of a new product, not more. The forecast of the market shares of the territories have to be derived from the market shares of other objects in the same region regarded as similar by the responsable factor manager. For the tool the difference between case 1 and case 2 is that in case 1 (case 2) the market share of every region is derived from the market share of other objects whose forecasts are based on a model with (without) calendar data. Experience shows that the forecasts for the market shares are of a far better quality than the forecasts for the global sales. The question which journals may be regarded as similar to the new journal is decided by the responsable factor manager.

- Case 3 seems to be contradictory in itself. The use of calendar data is only possible if enough observations are available.

- Case 4 is tackled by elementary methods of time series; exponential smoothing is a technic well known to factor managers of the publishing houses and the wholesale trade. It serves as a first proposal to handle this case.

- Case 5 can be tackled successfully by a regression model. Here it is of interest that the frontiers between „only some observations available“ and „many observations available“ are fluid. The classification between cases 3 or 4 and cases 5 or 6 is arbitrary. We decided to choose a data volume of three years as demarcation line.

- Case 6 was regarded as practically irrelevant.

We should expect that the attempt to forecast all journals fulfilling the conditions of case 5 with the same model is suboptimal. The opinion that the photo on the journal's title page is of importance for the number of sold copies is widely accepted. Some arguments against the introduction of items to compare the the quality of different items of the same object are:

- Different analysts would propose different quality criteria. Which approach has to be regarded as adequate? How long is the phase of success keeping quality standards by repeating features of outfit? We have made the experience that success cannot be repeated by pure repetition. The reader prefers to be surprised.

- Comparing figures of delivery with sales figures leads to the impression that the very successful issues had not been anticipated by the factor managers of the journals and expectations to repeat earlier successes were not fulfilled. For example tattoos as an addition to a youth magazine were a very sales hit at the beginning, after some repetitions tattoos seemed to have lost their attractiveness. On the other hand the fact that an addition to a magazine is new does not guarantee that it is accepted.

- A good characterization of the successful features of an issue of a journal would not be of high value with respect to the forecasting because at the time print decisions have to be done these features are not known to the factor managers. The factor manager who proposed the project to the owner of the publishing house told me that the owner accepted the project because the underlying model only used variables which were regarded by him as objective. The owner explicitly refused to base the forecasts on subjective impressions of a sales manager about the attractiveness of the issue.

Forecasting different journals with the same model implies the problem that the number of observations could differ from journal to journal. This means that the rank of the part of the matrix of exogeneous variables corresponding to the calendar data is journal – dependent. We developed routines to reformulate automatically the model to fulfill the rank condition.

3 The model

Next we explain how we built the forecasting model. In a first step we propose a collection of variables which are available and which can be regarded as explaining variables for the sales by plausibility arguments.

These plausibility arguments behind the model may be explained by the following questions:

- In which region do people spend their time during the sales phase of the journal?

- How do seasonal aspects influence the sales of a journal?

- What are the actual trends for the sales of the journal?

- How are the sales influenced by the height of planned reserve globally and regionally?

- Which sales are expected for Germany?

- Were there changes of the assignment of regions to wholesalers?

- Were the sales in the past of anticipated or surprising height?

The first question explains the importance of calendar data. These data were modelized by 16*7 variables for the holidays and 15 variables for bank holidays.

For all 16 Länder of Germany we included the different holidays for Christmas, winter, Easter, Whitsun, summer and automn. Holidays are of importance because a lot of people go away during a part of this time. That means that they buy their journals in another region as usually. We used the following encoding rules for holidays: When more than the half of the sales of one issue of a journal is expected to be influenced by holiday makers then we encoded for this issue a 1 for the variable for the type of holidays and the "Bundesland" the territory of the wholesaler is a part of. We supposed typical rates of velocity of sales during the sales period and typical routines for the start and the end of the holiday trips. The typical day for the start of the summer trips is saturday, the last week of summer holidays is regarded as a normal week. The summer holidays were encoded by two variables, one for the complete weeks 1 – 5 of the holidays and one for the weeks 2 – 4. We encoded one variable for every other holidays in every "Land" following the explained rule.

Seasonal variables were described by two groups of figures of different length; in the first group we defined six time series with ones in specific consecutive weeks of every year and zeros else; the second group contained the same sequences of weeks of the year as the first group, but with different weights. The choice of fixed periods of the year regarded to be of a seasonal interest enabled us to formulate these variables for different lengths of the sales period. Furthermore we introduced some sinus – and cosinus – terms with a period of one year and half a year.

We constructed six trend variables for the sales by moving averages of different lengths. The basis for these averages is built by fixed relative parts of a year; we had trends for the sales of the youngest known sales over 1, 13, 26, 52 weeks. This explains 4 trend variables. Further we implemented a linear trend. For the construction of the seventh trend variable it is of interest that we have an information lag whose length depends on the publication dates, especially on the length of the sales period. We discuss the background of this information lag, then we construct the sixth trend variable.

The information lag is four numbers for objects published every week, three numbers for objects with a sales period of 2 weeks, 2 numbers for the rest. Newspapers are regarded as a collection of journals with a publishing date of one week, one journal for every day of the week. We explain the reason for the length of this information lag by the example of a journal published every week: the forecast has to be finished 10 days before the first sales day. This time is calculated for printing. For newpapers this time is 1 day. After the last sales day the unsold copies are recollected, the sales numbers have to be reported to the publisher. This makes 10 – 14 days. The information lag can be shortened by reorganizing the begin of printing. Daily collection of return remittance offers a second possibility to reduce the information lag. Using all chances the information lag theoretically can be reduced to two weeks for an object with a weekly appearence period and to one week for daily appearing newspapers. The sixth trend variable is a weighted short – trend – variable. Forecasting the issue n of a year using a short – trend – term of 8 weeks we have to construct this trend variable for weekly appearing objects with the help of the issues n-11 to n-4. Therefore we introduce a further trend of 8 weeks. It is constructed on the basis of the weeks n-7 til n of the year before. This trend is weighted by the quotient of the mean value of the weeks n-4 to n-55 and the mean value of the weeks n-56 to n-107. For journals with other publication dates the calculations of all trend variables are adjusted adequately to the length of the sales period.

The influence of the planned return remittance describes the policy of a publisher how to handle the risk of unexpected sales on some retail outlets. The number of sold copies can be enlarged by enlarging the planned return remittance. The degree to which this is possible is one of the most interesting questions for factor managers. How do purchasers react if a retail outlet is sold out? To which degree do they buy a substitute or change the retail outlet or finish their attempt to buy? We introduced the planned return remittance for Germany as a further explaining variable into the model.

Experiments with the data showed the importance of the most actual sales for high – quality sales forecasts. But they are not known as a consequence of the information - lag. Turning – points of the sales are detected late. Therefore differences between planned return remittance and realized return remittance typically are autocorrelated to a high degree. As a first reaction we introduced a lagged three – period – moving average of forecasting errors for every wholesaler as explaining variable.

Earlier we modelized quality differences between different issues of the same journal by the forecast for sales in Germany given by the responsable factor manager. Experience showed that the forecast of global sales is very important explaining for forecasting the sales of every wholesaler. To say it in other words: the problem of distributing the global forecast on the wholesalers seems to be easy compared with the task of a high quality global forecast. Therefore we introduced a global forecast as explaining variable into the model. Such a forecast could be constructed only by an indirect argument: the complete delivery is divided into the planned sales and the planned return remittance. As a first global forecast we choose

global forecast = delivered copies – copies for planned return remittance.

Elementary data checks showed that in average this value is too high, from 1% - 2% of the sales for the very big journals to 40% - 60% for the smallest journals. This degree of overestimation was regarded as significant, and for this judgment we found one plausible argument:

- We observed that publishers believe that higher rates of stores sold out lead to an important increase of lost sales. Factor managers can get problems with their publishers if the average of stores sold out is high for a long period. Further publishers wish that the average sales of the stores sold out are less than the average of all stores. From a statistical point of view this is a bad rule. It is far more plausible that the average sales of the stores sold out are higher than the average sales of all stores, because unexpected high demand is an important reason that a store is sold out. We presented to publishers results of simulation experiments obtained by systematically reducing delivery. We showed that a marginal reduction of 10 delivered copies implied a reduction of 1 sold copy on the assumption that demand unserved at one retailer was not served by another one. These estimates can further be reduced because a part of customers not served by the first store tries to buy at a second store.

Using global delivery - global planned return remittance as an estimator for global sales would overestimate global sales to an important degree. Replacing global delivery – planned return remittance by an estimator not overestimating systematically the global sales in the future would lead to underestimation of the sales of the wholesalers for the first issues. To avoid such problems it seemed adequate to construct by the instrument of ex - post - simulation an ex - post - forecast for the global sales for all issues used as input into the forecasts of the sales of the wholesalers. We construct this ex - post - forecast in two steps. In a first step we use lagged exponential smoothing for the global sales. In a second step we construct the time series for the global ex - post - forecast by ex - post - simulation using the sales model for Germany with the lagged exponential smoothing forecast as explaining variable.

Reassignments of regions to wholesalers are modelized by dummy variables separating the phases before and after the reassignment.

We separated sales of anticipated heigth from sales of surprising height by creating a reference standard using the method of exponential smoothing. We classified the observations by the difference between the smoothed sales and the observed sales, divided through the standard deviation of sales, and constructed some further 0 – 1 – variables grouping special issues within the categories extremely high sales, very high sales, high sales, normal sales and low sales. The responsable factor manager can introduce his sales expectations of the issue to be forecasted with the help of these grouping variables. The preselection is given by the category "normal sales".

Finally we have to discuss the problem of reallocation of the regions to the wholesalers. There are 2 evident reasons:

- Merger of wholesalers. This is done easily by adding the dates of the merging wholesalers and introducing a dummy variable separating the time before merger und the time after merger.

- Renewal of the depot buildings of a wholesaler and reallocation of parts of wholesaler's work to other places. This is done by including a dummy variable to separate the time of renewal from the other time.

The third reason depends on different sorts of depots and their role for the daily delivery process. We differ between three types of depots:

- Depots where all tours start and the return remittance is brought back to (main depots without further auxiliary depots);

- Depots where some tours start but the return remittance is not brought back to; these depots may be delivered daily with all objects or only a part of objects or only seasonnally with only a part of objects (auxiliary depot of a main depot);

- Depots where some tours start and where the return remittance is brought back also for those tours which start at another depot (main depot with auxiliary depot).

Bookkeeping is done in the following form:

Table 2

	main depot without auxiliary depot	auxiliary depot	main depot with auxiliary depot
delivery	booked for the depot	booked for the dependance	booked for the depot
Planned return remittance	booked for the depot	no booking	booked for the depot and the auxiliary depot
Return remittance	booked for the depot	no booking	booked for the depot and the auxiliary depot

The sales have to be determined with the following rules:

Main depot without auxiliary depot:

Sales of the wholesaler = delivery – return remittance

auxiliary depot:

Sales cannot be determined

Main depot with auxiliary depot:

Sales of the wholesaler = delivery to the main depot

\+ delivery to all auxiliary depots

– Return remittance to the main depot.

Time series had to be aggregated following these rules.

A statistically significant problem resulted when auxiliary depots became main depots. Normally there was a fixed day for that change. The part of the time series before that fixed day had to be recalculated by disaggregating planned return remittance and return remittance only known in aggregated form; This was done by extrapolating the relative situation observed during a phase after the fixed day to the past where no information about the relative situation was given. The responsability for the data was delegated to the publisher.

These modifications had a double influence for our forecasting model:

- They influenced the data underlying the forecasts.

- We introduced dummy variables for the time before and after the fixed days.

Totally we regarded as possibly significant 112 variables for holidays, 15 variables for bank holidays, 12 variables for seasonal aspects, 4 variables for periodicity, 6 variables for trends, 1 variables for the forecast of global sales, 5 variables for higher differences between global sales and their forecast based on exponential smoothing, 1 variable for the global planned return remittance, 1 variable for the weighted estimation error of the youngest past, 3 dummy variables to describe reallocations of regions to wholesalers. We had 160 possible variables of possible importance. All data are available or can be derived from available data.

The next step was to decide which of these variables had to be regarded as significant for the sales of different territories. For example it seems implausible that the summer holidays of Thüringen influence the sales of a region in the Ruhr – district to a remarkable degree. We assigned to every of the proposed explaining variable the wholesalers, whose sales might be influenced by it. These assignments are based on plausibility arguments, on publication dates, on the duration of existence, and on trial and error. We only take in consideration events that could be observed more often than three times. Simulation experiments showed that the influence of bank holidays on the sales is less important if the sales period grows.

These decisions were also done with respect to the full rank of the observation matrix. As a result we got for every wholesaler a specific part of the complete variable set, which was regarded as possibly important. In average 25 of the 160 variables were regarded as possibly relevant for a specific wholesaler for objects published weekly. This average reduced to 18 for objects published monthly.

Some variables were regarded as possibly relevant for every region; such a variable is the global forecast. Other variables, for example holiday variables, were proposed only for some regions.

In a third step we had to determine those explaining variables regarded as significant the forecast. That was done in the following manner: First we estimated a regression equation using all possibly relevant variables. Then we eliminated stepwise one or more variables judged as insignificant on the basis of the t – test. Here we were confronted with two problems:

- The status of insignificance may drastically change when several of the intercorrelating and therefore insignificant variables are eliminated in one step. We had to look for a cautious and quick strategy to eliminate insignificant variables.

- We observed that following some rules of elimination the set of finally remaining variables changed when we used different sets of observations for the same wholesaler and the same object. This means that the regression equation cannot be regarded as valid over a long period. The explanation is easy: The selected variables describe behaviour patterns of people, and people change their behaviour. This can be elucidated regarding the holidays. Today people plan more holiday trips of shorter length compared to the situation 10 years ago. For example the prolongation of autumn holidays from 7 to 14 days resulted in a new wave of voyages.

We handled both problems by automatization of the elimination procedure: Using the t – value and the proposed grouping of the explaining variables we eliminated parallely the most insignificant variable of every group. The selection procedure ended when all remaining variable passed the t – value. This elimination procedure is repeated every time a forecast has to be done. As a consequence the stable part of the model is given by fixing the possibly explaining variables. The variables regarded as significant for the forecasts may change. As a rule an average of 10 to 12 variables finally underlied the forecasts.

4 The estimation procedure

Analysing the results of earlier forecasting experiments of special journals of different publishers led to the following judgments:

- The very difficult task is to formulate a forecast for the sales in Germany, because the global forecast for Germany was central for the forecasts of all regions. A forecast of the relative market shares of the wholesalers normally had a sufficient quality. We interpret this in the following manner: the quality of the global forecast beyond the trends can only be enlarged by adequately characterizing the features of attractiveness of a special issue. But quality arguments are of less importance for the regional distribution of the sales.

- Calendar data seem to be of minor importance for the total sales but of high importance for the regional distribution of the sales.

- It was easier to estimate the influence of calendar data on the market share of a region than to estimate their influence on the absolute heigth of sales in that region.

- The sum of all regional sales forecasts often is a better forecast for the German sales than a forecast based on a model for Germany.

- The forecast of sales in Germany is important for most regional sales forecasts.

Therefore the following procedure was proposed as reasonable:

1. Get a forecast for the German sales with the help of exponential smoothing.

2. Propose a forecast for Germany on the basis of a sales model for Germany using the forecast of 1. as explaining variable.

3. Use the forecast for Germany to get a forecast for the territories of every wholesaler.

4. Take the sum of all regional forecasts as a forecast for Germany..

5. Forecast the relative market share of every wholesaler, make sure that the sum of all relative market shares is 1.

6. Get as forecast for the sales of the wholesaler the product of its relative market share and the forecast for Germany.

As estimation procedure we took weighted least squares. The weights stem from a geometric series with fixed values. This leads to a greater importance of the observations with higher actuality.

The proposed procedure produces for every wholesaler and every object some series of forecasts of a fixed lenth n. The nth element of every series is a forecast for the sales of the issue m to be forecasted, the other elements are ex – post – forecasts for the sold copies of issues m-n+1, ..., m-1. The sales for the issues m-n+1, ..., m-lag are known. That enables us to compare the ex – post – forecasts with the sales. We use the forecast of that series whose ex – post – forecasts are regarded to be the best. Using different methods of forecasting we can enrich the number of series and candidates for the final forecast. The trick and the danger is that we decide on the basis of the ex – post forecasts, whose quality can be quantified, which of the possible forecasting principle is used. We know that this choice is based only on plausibility and cannot be justified with statistical arguments. But experience shows that it is helpful in practice.

Exponential smoothing underlies the forecastings when time series are too short for model – based forecasts. Here we had to handle the lag – problem separately. The lag – problem is important when forecasting objects with a clear trend. If sales grow strictly, exponential smoothing with lagged information strictly underestimates the actual sales and vice versa. Therefore we modified the exponential - smoothing - based forecasts by introducing a weighted term for sales differences of two consecutive issues. With

k: length of moving average

lag: length of information lag (forecast x_t with the known information $x_{t\text{-}1\text{-}lag}$)

t: issue to be forecasted

the procedure can be formalized as follows:

$$SD_{t,lag} = sales_{t-lag} - sales_{t-1-lag}$$

$$MASD_{t,lag,k} = \frac{1}{k}\sum_{i=1}^{k} SD_{t-i-lag}$$

$$DMASD_{t,lag,k} = \frac{1}{k}\sum_{i=1}^{k} \left| SD_{t-i-lag} - MASD_{t,lag,k} \right|$$

$$PK_{t,lag,k} = \frac{MASD_{t,lag,k}}{DMASD_{t,lag,k}}$$

Let the exponential smooting forecast be given by

$$ESFCS_t = koeff * ESFCS_{t-1} + (1 - koeff) * Sales_{t-lag}$$

Then the forecast is given by

$$MFCS_t = ESFCS_t + Faktor_{t,lag,k} SD_{t,lag,k}$$

$$Faktor_{t,lag,k} = \begin{cases} lag + 1 & |PK_{t,lag,k}| \geq c \\ 0 & else \end{cases}$$

The symbols mean:

SD: Sales difference

MASD: Moving average of Sales differences

DMASD: Deviance of moving average of Sales differences

ESFCS: Exponential – smoothing based forecast for sales

MFCS: Modified forecast for sales

PK: Pearson - coefficient

There existed one object freshly introduced into the market showing a strong growth tendency. The modification reduced the sum of all global errors from 3.900.000 copies to 1.500.000 copies. The simulation phase was 25 periods, the object is a new television journal appearing all 14 days.

5 Results

In the context of this paper exact results are of less interest. We prefer to present some figures typically for the press distribution in practice and to compare them with figures typical for the model.

We describe some figures of the realized distribution. For statistical reasons we discuss only objects with an existence time of some years. Objects with a small number of observations can only be handled by elementary methods, here it is of more importance that tools work.

First we discuss consequences of underestimation and overestimation of sales. As a rule the planned return remittance is of the order

Planned return remittance = a *average sales$^{1/2}$ of all included stores * number of included retail stores

with $0.7 \leq a \leq 1$. This means that for objects with an average of sales of 40 copies for every shop we have a rate $^1/_7$ to $^1/_8$ for planned return remittance to total delivery. For an object with an average of sales of 1 copy for every shop the quote is near ½. These quotes seem to be adequate with respect to a politics that tries to realize a rate of 20% shops sold out in average and a similar probability for every store to be sold out. The calculations are supported theoretically by the assumption of a Poisson distribution of the sales for an average retail store.

With the background of a lot of simulation experiments with real sales data we propose to estimate the marginal rate of sales to delivery by $^1/_{10}$ .If global sales are underestimated by say 12.000 copies of 1000.000 copies and overestimated by 12.000 estimates the next week in the first week this leads to a loss of sales of 1500 copies in the first week and to a gain of sales of 1000 copies in the second week. The total effect of the estimation error averaging to zero is 500 copies, not more. We base this calculation on a very defensive assumption to loose one of 8 copies by underestimation of the sales and to win one of 12 copies by overestimation. The quotes become bader if the relative error grows, therefore the estimator should not be of a too bad quality.

In reality we observe a nearly permanent overestimation of the sales. Therefore overestimation has to be judged to be a very expensive marketing tool.

In practice an average overestimation of the sales of a journal can be found, small for objects with an average of nearly a million of sold copies, and far bigger for journals with 40000. Underestimation in average is observed scarcely. These figures seem to be typical. Partly they may be explained by another observation: the time series of sales show a long – run – estimation error between a small average of underestimation and a higher average of over-estimation when exponential smoothing in the form

$$forecast_t = 0.7*forecast_{t-1} + 0.3 *sales_{t-4}$$

$$error_t = sales_t - forecast_t$$

was tried. We observe a permanent increase of the number of published journals. But permanently increasing the number of journals must be paid by a permanent decline of the number of sold copies of the other journals. Over all journals we observe an average error of 5% for the global forecast. This has to be confronted with the variation of sales. As a first measure we take the average of the estimation errors based on exponential smoothing of the above form. The average error over all journals was 4.25%. The range of the average error of different journals measured in this form was between 1.6% for the journal with best stability and 15.6% for those with largest variability. The number of copies sold in average is only one indicator with the tendence that the relative variability of the journal grows if the number of copies sold in average declines. A second indicator is given by the relative importance of the journal photo or a photo series for example in a magazine for men or the quality of assets characteristic for different journals. A third indicator is given by the degree of competitive activities on the markets for the different objects. The given measure has the least values for some television magazines appearing weekly. Television magazines appearing weekly seem to be far more stable than the television magazines appearing all 14 days. This cannot be explained by the average of sold copies because these magazines appearing all 14 days are characterized by very high sales in average.

The sum of all absolute regional errors is larger than the absolute total error. Our data showed that the sum of all absolute regional errors was 55% larger than the sum of all absolute global errors. Therefore in practice the following thumb rule may be used: $^{2}/_{3}$ of the estimation errors are explained by global forecasting errors and only $^{1}/_{3}$ has to be regarded as additional distribution error.

The performance of the journals varies very intensively over time. Comparing the average forecasting errors for the same object over different years showed that these errors can vary for more than 100%. This may result from a temporary market activity of the object's publisher, from the start of a competitive journal or an aggressive price policy of publishers in competition. A part of the overestimation of the sales may be interpreted as a sign for competitive behaviour in the way that an established object does not retire deliberately. Therefore we proposed to split the total delivery into three parts:

Delivery = sales forecast + planned return remittance + planned return remittance for political manoevrability

Publishers explicitely give figures for sales forecasts and planned return remittance in absolute or relative values. Planned return remittance figures are more stable than total delivery because planned return remittance for political manoevrability is handled as expected sales. This leads to problems how to distribute them; should their distribution follow the relative market shares of the retailers or the relative part of their risk? A method – oriented marketing should prevent later misinterpretations of the delivery figures. Factor managers should be ready to change the delivery proposed by a model – based forecast, but ist should be possible to differ between a change for political reasons or for a lack of plausibility of the underlying forecast.

At a first view exponential smoothing appears to be more successful than the distribution of the factor managers. But we observed long phases where factor managers' forecasts are far better than exponential smoothing. We interpret this in the sense that during some periods delivery – planned return remittance was no adequate expression for the sales forecasts of the factor managers. The concept of planned return remittance for political manoevrability was introduced for more transparency in such situations. We prefer to compare our forecasting with exponential smoothing and not with the realized distribution which is regarded as a mixture of politics and forecasting. For comparison we select all objects (28), for which forecasting seems possible with the help of the regression model. For the other objects we recommend to use exponential smoothing. We compare ex – post – simulated model – based forecasts with ex – post – simulated exponential – smoothing – based forecasts. That means that we forecast always on the data base known at the time the editor had to forecast himself. Only the decision which variables are regarded as significant in the model is based on the whole data set. From a theory – of – science – view this is not completely correct; to be very correct we should also select the significant variables using the data known at the moment editor had to forecast; the reasons not to do it are:

- the enormeous amount of computer time;
- the experience that the variables regarded as significant vary over time but not quickly
- the experience that the best specification is done by using the data known at the time forecasts have to be done. That is due to the change of behaviour of people over time.

We describe the quality by three indicators:

- the sum of all absolute forecast errors for Germany during a given period SAGFE
- the sum of all forecast errors for Germany SGFE
- the sum of all absolute regional forecast errors SARFE.

In formulas:

$$SAGFE = \sum_{t=1}^{n} \left| forecast_{Germany,t} - sales_{Germany,t} \right|$$

$$SGFE = \sum_{t=1}^{n} forecast_{Germany,t} - sales_{Germany,t}$$

$$SARFE = \sum_{t=1}^{n} \sum_{i=1}^{m} \left| forecast_{region_i,t} - sales_{region_i,t} \right|$$

n: number of issues forecasted

m: number of regions included (112 for Germany and between 0 and 10 abroad).

Using the model for Germany it is possible to forecast the sales of other countries. Here we forecast the copies sold in some countries, especially in Austria and Swizzerland; both are counted as regions abroad. The forecast errors abroad are included in SARFE.

We forecast a period during which nearly 500.000.000 copies were sold. The sum of SARFE over all objects was 4% for exponential smoothing with information lag of 0 periods (sales of issue n were forecasted knowing the sales of issue n-1) to 5% for exponential smoothing with information lag of 3 periods (forecasting issue n knowing the sales of issue n-4). The sum of SAGFE over all objects was between 3% for an information lag of 0 issues to 4% for an information lag of 3 periods. Finally the sum SGFE over all objects was 0.7% higher than the sum of all sales using an information error of 0 periods and raised to 1.5% for an information lag of 3 periods. Forecasting on the basis of the model and adding up over all regions SARFE was 3.9%, SAGFE was 2.9% and SGFE was also 0.7%. The values for the realized distribution are: SARFE 5.6%, SAGFE 4%, SGFE 2%.

Next we disaggregate the objects with respect to their publication dates and their subject.

With respect to publication dates we include 15 objects appearing weekly, 4 objects appearing all 14 days and 9 objects appearing every month. We examine forecasts for 48, 22, 8 issues for the objects appearing weekly, all 2 weeks, monthly.

With respect to subjects we differ between television journals (5), yellow press (9), youth magazines (3), magazines for men (2), special issues magazines (8), journals for children (1). We are interested answering two questions:

1. Comparison of quality of model – based forecasts or exponential – smoothing based forecasts under both disaggregations (Tables 3, 4)

2. Comparison of the quality of the sales forecasts for Germany, based on a model for Germany and based on the sum of model – based forecasts for all German regions (Tables 5,6)

All errors are relative to 1000.000 sold copies. The last line rounds the number of sold copies.

Table 3 shows that model – based forecasts are of better quality than the forecasts underlying the distribution in reality. The aspect of the return remittance for political manoevrability has been discussed earlier. Insofar the better quality of SAGFE of the model, compared to reality, should not be overestimated. Here the difference of SARFE and SAGFE is of interest. This difference is significantly better for the model compared to reality. The model distributes better than the factor managers in reality. This is valid for all 3 publication dates.

The comparison of the model – based forecasts with the exponential – smoothing – based forecasts shows similar results; for information lags believed to be realizable the model – based forecasts are better. SARFE – SAGFE is nearly the same for both methods. But that does not mean that the better global forecast is the only source of quality: with growing value for SAGFE the value SARFE – SAGFE diminishes. The argument is that regional forecasts tend to overestimation when the global forecast overestimates. The value SARFE – SAGFE tends to grow when regional underestimation and regional overestimation tend to compensate each other. We observed the highest difference between SARFE and SAGFE when SAGFE had a value near 0. That means that the model distributes better than exponential smoothing. Comparing the values for SAGFE and SGFE it is easily recognized that the diminished quality of the forecast with higher information lag is mainly caused by the effect of overestimation in average.

Table 3

	appearing weekly	appearing all 14 days	appearing monthly
Model:SARFE	33881	64784	116132
Reality:SARFE	51605	75833	287275
Lag0: SARFE	34755	60974	141309
Lag1: SARFE	37572	71677	149544
Lag2: SARFE	40864	82393	155594
Lag3: SARFE	43157	91224	164227
Model: SAGFE	25886	47832	96213
Reality: SAGFE	33897	51011	252350
Lag0: SAGFE	26847	44640	123800
Lag1: SAGFE	28490	54067	128897
Lag2. SAGFE	31155	64083	133862
Lag3: SAGFE	32740	72816	145435
Model:SGFE	8428	-2003	14638
Reality: SGFE	14622	20369	228233
Lag0: SGFE	7501	3163	16863
Lag1: SGFE	9819	4882	26879
Lag2: SGFE	12180	7223	45262
Lag3: SGFE	14755	10377	57941
Reference point	1000000	1000000	1000000
totally sold copies	420.000.000	50.000.000	800.000

Obviously the quality of forecasts diminishes when sales periods are longer. Reasons are:

1. With increased appearence period the average of sales is reduced and the quotient of average sales and deviance of sales increases. In the case of objects appearing all 14 days there is one exception: a television journal with a very high number of sold copies. The market of the television journals appearing all 14 days is very competitive compared to the market for television journals appearing every week.

3. For the objects with shorter appearence periods the number of observations increases.

4. The influence of calendar data decreases when appearence periods increase.

5. The model tends to overestimate sales because sales numbers are decreasing. The only exception is caused by a television journal appearing all 14 days. For this journal we had observed a turning point which was detected late (information lag).

6. Comparing the quotients

$$\frac{SARFE_{Model}}{SARFE_{Lag}}$$

with lag = 3 for weakly appearing objects, lag = 2 for objects appearing all 14 days and lag = 1 for objects appearing monthly the model reduces the forecast error for all publication dates to a relative similar degree of 20% (see table 3). Totally $SARFE_{model}$ is 4.900.000 copies less than $SARFE_{lag}$. For $SGFE_{model}$ – $SGFE_{lag}$ we get the value 3.700.000 copies printed less. Assume a value of 1/3 for the quotient of marginal production costs of a copy and publisher's price of a copy and calculate that 10 copies delivered more lead to 1 copy sold more. We estimate the possible returns in the form 3.700.000 copies printed less * marginal production costs * part of marginal costs realizable as return. The third factor is 0.7 because the cost reduction of 10 copies printed less is compensated by 1 copy sold less. That means that the returns can be enlarged to a volume of the costs for printing 2.470.000 copies. These returns have to be reduced by the returns made by enlarging the issue without selling it. For these returns we have no estimate.

Table 4

	Television journals	Yellow Press	Magazines for men	Youth magazines	Special Issues Magazines	Journals for Children
Model: SARFE	21374	48199	44828	68236	122528	152151
Reality: SARFE	31325	72630	89920	82704	330904	707623
Lag0: SARFE	20325	48715	49956	73480	151007	213687
Lag1: SARFE	24116	51187	54516	81831	160221	222423
Lag2: SARFE	28536	53955	57887	90442	171894	203753
Lag3: SARFE	32131	55672	61176	96121	182064	215198
Model: SAGFE	15045	36740	33168	57336	103983	111816
Reality: SAGFE	22941	42714	63243	66765	298066	624239
Lag0: SAGFE	14892	38704	40209	52392	137162	170544
Lag1: SAGFE	17859	39610	44581	59037	145165	159717
Lag2: SAGFE	21863	41640	47203	66327	156515	132973
Lag3: SAGFE	25317	42453	48672	70623	167006	157723

Model: SGFE	2742	12234	16897	4500	16504	19965
Reality: SGFE	21153	9940	49264	4551	275322	624239
Lag0: SGFE	5972	6844	20042	10667	-4073	1341
Lag1: SGFE	7929	8942	25995	14546	-1112	11029
Lag2: SGFE	10104	10995	31550	18626	11756	31615
Lag3: SGFE	12441	13369	37938	23262	16604	66184
Reference point	1000000	1000000	1000000	1000000	1000000	1000000
totally sold copies	220000000	200.000.000	10000000	40.000.000	7.000.000	500.000

For the subject – oriented disaggregation the following points are of interest:

1. The importance of the information lag is especially high for television journals. The reduction of the information from 3 to 0 would increase the quality of the exponential smoothing to 1/3. For the childrens' journal the information lag is unimportant.

2. Very high overestimations of the sales can be observed for three of the six groups. The low overestimation for magazines for men seems to be astonishing: but it is explained very easily. These objects have very high planned return remittances. The sales of these objects decreased enormously during the last years, but the planned return remittance was kept on the same level.

3. The good performance of exponential smoothing forecast compared to the model based forecast is caused by the one journal appearing all 14 days. Here exponential smoothing with lag 0 was very successful, 25% better than the model based forecast. The reason was the existence of some important ups and downs and a turning point marking an important increase of sales. This turning point was detected directly by exponential smoothing with lag 0 and detected late by the model. Have in mind that we have an information lag of length 2 for this object.

4. It is difficult to forecast youth magazines. The reasons are:

   - dependence of the distribution on calendar data

   - high influence on sales by additions (tattoos, stickers and so on) and a quick change of what is actually in

   - permanent attempts to bring new products on the market (especially by disaggregating youth in younger youth and older youth)

5. Table 4 shows that no group of objects exists for which the model shows results of minor quality than realized in practice.

Table 5 and 6 show under which circumstances the forecast for Germany based on a regression equation was dominated by the sum of all German regions forecasts.

Table 5

	appearing weekly	appearing all 14 days	apperaring monthly
Number of objects	15	4	9
error1 total	26280	48091	121955
error2 total	22937	55692	99742
cases with error2 better than error1	8	1	6
error1 (error2 < error1)	22548	75610	137006
error2 (error2 < error1)	14954	58888	101618
error1 (error2 > error1)	31484	45696	86144
error2 (error2 > error1)	34069	55414	95277
reference	1000000	1000000	1000000
number of copies	420000000	50000000	8000000

We define:

Error1: Sum of all absolute forecast errors based on a regression model for Germany

Error2: Sum of all absolute forecast errors based on the sum of forecasts for all German regions

Error1 and error2 are set in relation to 1000000 sold copies.

In 15 from 28 cases the forecasts based on the regression equation for Germany was beaten by the sum of regional forecasts. In no of these 15 cases a second iteration with the corrected global forecast was successful.

Furthermore it is of interest that the global forecast derived as the sum of regional forecasts is significantly better in cases where it is better. The computational efforts necessary to get all regional forecasts can be justified.

Table 6

	television journals	Yellow press	Magazines for men	Youth magazines	Special issues magazines	Journals for children
Nr. of objects	5	9	2	3	8	1
error1 total	16104	36097	33990	56377	131622	115682
error2 total	16655	29031	35291	61430	108964	113563
Nr. of cases error2 better than error1	4	4	1	1	4	1
error1 (error2<error1)	12556	54693	40655	75610	150235	115682
error2 (error2<error1)	11498	25392	40605	58888	102201	113563
error1 (error2>error1)	33692	28411	29258	54354	110203	0
error2 (error2>error1)	42219	30535	31517	61697	116747	0
reference	1000000	1000000	1000000	1000000	1000000	1000000
Nr. of copies	22000000	20000000	10000000	40000000	7000000	500000

6 Conclusion

We described the construction of a forecasting model for publishers to determine the issue. We explained reasons why printed issue is (often far) larger than sold issue. We introduced the concept of planned return remittance for political manoevrability to separate special actions of the publisher from the all – days – business. Comparing the forecasting quality of the model with the forecasting quality done in practice is difficult because the planned return remittance for political manoevrability exists but cannot be reconstructed. Comparing the forecast quality with the classical assumption of a stable mean value is useless; therefore we compared it to the simple exponential smoothing alternative. We quantified the importance of the information lag by comparing exponential smoothing for different information lags. By disaggregating all journals with respect to publication dates and the subject we showed that the model runs for all subjects and all publishing periods. It can be an important support for the sales managers. Special actions of publishers for competitive reasons should be reported for reasons of data interpretation and data quality. The explaining variables are well known to the factor managers in publisher's houses, therefore the model found was accepted by people who tried to work with it. Reducing the average error of 5% in practice to 4% by model – based forecasting seems to be a minor success; the picture changes when we have in mind the enormeous number of copies of which we win 1%. Remember the lack of knowledge of important influences at the time forecastings have to be done. Statistics can be a valuable help for practice, but lack of knowledge about reality cannot be compensated by mathematical methods. The heart is the model and not the method.

Scheduling Scarce Resources in Chemical Engineering*

Rolf H. Möhring and Marc Uetz

Department of Mathematics
University of Technology, Berlin, Germany

Abstract

The efficient utilization of scarce resources, such as machines or manpower, is major challenge within production planning in the chemical industry. We describe solution methods for a resource-constrained scheduling problem which arises at a production facility at BASF AG in Ludwigshafen. We have developed and implemented two different algorithms to solve this problem, a novel approach which is based upon Lagrangian relaxation, as well as a branch-and-bound procedure. Since the Lagrangian approach is applicable for a whole variety of resource-constrained scheduling problems, it is of interest not only for the specific problem we describe, but is of interest also for many other industrial applications. In this paper, we describe both approaches, and also report on computational results, based upon practical problem instances as well as benchmark test sets.

1 Scheduling under Limited Resources

Facing the increasing international competition, there is a growing need for planning tools in chemical engineering that allow an efficient utilization of scarce resources. Within the cooperation with BASF AG, Ludwigshafen, we focus on a scheduling problem that is typical for a production process in the chemical industry, but also occurs in many other industrial applications.

The aim is to schedule the production process for several so-called *orders*, or *campaigns*. Each order represents the demand of a certain amount of a product, which must be produced on a suited machine. Due to limited machine

*This research has been supported by the Bundesministerium für Bildung und Forschung (bmb+f) under grant 03-MO7TU1-3 within the program "Mathematische Verfahren zur Lösung von Problemstellungen in Industrie und Wirtschaft". A collection of articles from this research program will be published in a volume on mathematical methods for solving problems in industry and business by the Springer Verlag in 2001. We thank the Springer Verlag for the permission to prepublish our contribution in this monograph.

capacities, an order is usually split up into several identical steps, so-called *jobs*. In other words, the production process for each order consists of a sequence of identical *jobs*, each of which must be scheduled on an assigned machine. The objective is to schedule all orders, or jobs, such that the overall production time is minimized. Due dates for individual orders are given, and there may also be *temporal constraints* between jobs of different orders in the form of *time lags*, for instance if an intermediate product of an order is needed within the production process of others.

Apart from temporal restriction, resource constraints are imposed by limited availability of machines and scarce personnel. The availability of personnel depends on the organization of shifts, breaks, etc. Any job itself consists of several consecutive steps, so-called *tasks*, and each of these tasks requires a specified amount of personnel. Hence, the required personnel to operate a job is varying in time, and given by a corresponding piecewise constant function like depicted in Fig. 1. In a less restrictive model, the tasks of a job are only linked by so-called *time-windows*, which means that there may be idle periods of restricted time between two consecutive tasks. This leads to a model with so-called *maximal time lags*, which will be discussed in Sect.6.

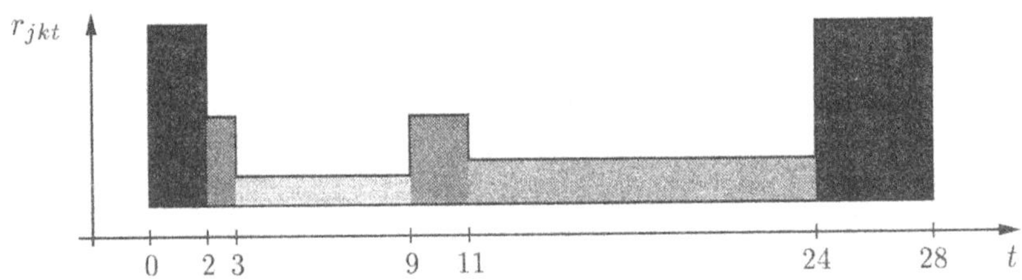

Figure 1: Resource requirement of a sample job which consists of 6 tasks. Each colored rectangle corresponds to a task. The higher (darker) the rectangle, the more resources are required during the execution of the corresponding task.

The objective is to find a production schedule such that temporal as well as resource constraints are satisfied, and the overall production time, the so-called *makespan*, is minimized. For a more detailed problem description, we refer to [KW].

1.1 Notation and Formulation of the Problem

The problem described above can be formulated as a *resource-constrained project scheduling problem*. In order to put up a mathematical formulation, we introduce some notation. Let us denote by $J = \{0, \ldots, n\}$ be the set of all *jobs* which have to be scheduled, where a job j has an integral processing time p_j. Except for Sect. 6, we assume that jobs must be processed with-

without interruption, and by $S = (S_0, \ldots, S_n)$ we denote a schedule, where S_j is the start time of job j. The entity of all jobs, together with their temporal constraints and resource requirements will be called a *project* in what follows. Jobs 0 and n are assumed to be dummy jobs with processing time 0, indicating the project start and the project completion, respectively. In other words, job n indicates when the production of all orders terminates. This can be easily modeled by introducing additional temporal constraints. In general, temporal constraints are given in the form of arbitrary minimal time lags between any pair of jobs, and by $d_{ij} \geq 0$ we denote the length of the required time lag (i, j) between two jobs $i, j \in J$. $L \subseteq J \times J$ is the set of all time lags, and by $m := |L|$ we denote the number of given time lags. We assume without loss of generality that the time lags always refer to the start times of jobs, thus every schedule S has to fulfill $S_j \geq S_i + d_{ij}$ for all $(i, j) \in L$. Ordinary *precedence constraints* can be represented by letting $d_{ij} = p_i$ if job i must precede job j. Additionally, we suppose that a time horizon T as an upper bound on the *project makespan* (the time to produce all orders) is given. It can be checked in polynomial time by longest path calculations if such a system of temporal constraints has a feasible solution.

As indicated before, jobs need resources while they are operated. We assume that we are given a finite set R of different, so-called *renewable resources*, and the availability of resource $k \in R$ at time t is denoted by R_{kt}. These resources can represent machines, manpower, or any other device which is required to operate a job. We assume that a job j requires an amount of r_{jkt} units of resource k, $k \in R$, during the t-th period of its execution. Note that a job may require several resources at the same time.

The objective is to find a schedule which respects all constraints, and has minimal total processing time, or in other words, which minimizes the project makespan S_n. It is well known that this problem is NP-hard. It is even NP-hard to approximate within any constant factor (see [Sch]). That means that there is virtually no hope to find an efficient, that is, polynomial time algorithm which computes an optimum or near-optimum solution for all problem instances.

1.2 Integer Programming Formulation

In order to model the problem mathematically as an integer linear program, so-called time-indexed formulations are quite common. Pritsker, Watters, and Wolfe [PWW] were presumably the first to give an integer programming formulation in time-indexed 0-1-variables of the type

$$x_{jt} = \begin{cases} 1 & \text{if job } j \text{ starts at time } t, \\ 0 & \text{otherwise,} \end{cases}$$

where $j \in J$, and $t \in \{0, ..., T\}$. we then obtain the following integer linear programming formulation, which is crucial for our subsequent approach

$$\text{minimize} \qquad \sum_t t\, x_{nt} \tag{1}$$

$$\text{subject to} \qquad \sum_t x_{jt} = 1, \quad j \in J, \tag{2}$$

$$\sum_{s=t}^{T} x_{is} + \sum_{s=0}^{t+d_{ij}-1} x_{js} \le 1, \quad (i,j) \in L,\ t = 0, \ldots, T, \tag{3}$$

$$\sum_j \sum_{s=t-p_j+1}^{t} r_{jk,t-s}\, x_{js} \le R_{kt}, \qquad k \in R,\ t = 0, ..., T, \tag{4}$$

$$x_{jt} \ge 0, \qquad j \in J,\ t = 0, \ldots, T, \tag{5}$$

$$x_{jt} \text{ integer}, \qquad j \in J,\ t = 0, \ldots, T. \tag{6}$$

Note that $S_j = \sum_t t\, x_{jt}$, thus the objective (1) is to minimize the project completion time S_n. Constraints (2) indicate that each job is started exactly once, and inequalities (3) represent the temporal constraints given by the time lags L. Inequalities (4) assure that the jobs simultaneously processed at time t do not consume more resources than available. Given the temporal constraints and the time horizon T, it is easy to compute *earliest* and *latest starting times* for each job $j \in J$. For convenience of notation, however, we simply assume (without stating explicitly) that variables with time indices outside these boundaries are fixed at values zero, such that no job is started before its earliest start or after its latest start, respectively.

2 Relaxations and Lower Bounds

Recall that we are dealing with a minimization problem which is even NP-hard to approximate within any constant factor. Hence, we cannot expect to find an efficient algorithm which computes a provably good solution for any given problem instance. Is such a situation, *heuristic* solutions are usually sought. However, in order to judge the quality of a given solution, *lower bounds* on the optimal objective value are crucial. In order to compute lower bounds, a variety of different methods are available. Usually, one tries to solve *relaxations* of the problem, preferably in such a way that the relaxed problem is solvable efficiently, that is, in polynomial time.

Based upon the above integer programming relaxation, we have shown in [MSSU1] that a *Lagrangian* relaxation of the problem can be reduced to a *minimum-cut* problem, and thus can be solved quite efficiently. In Sect. 3 we show how this can be seen. Let us first recall the principles of Lagrangian relaxation. The idea is to dualize the resource constraints (4), and introduce nonnegative Lagrangian multipliers $\lambda = (\lambda_{kt})$, $k \in R$, $t \in \{0, ..., T\}$. Doing this, one obtains the *Lagrangian subproblem*

$$\begin{array}{ll} \text{minimize} & \sum_t t\, x_{nt} + \sum_j \sum_t \Big(\sum_{k \in R} \sum_{s=t}^{t+p_j-1} r_{jk,s-t} \lambda_{ks} \Big) x_{jt} - \sum_t \sum_{k \in R} \lambda_{kt} R_{kt} \\ \text{subject to} & (2), (3), (5), \text{ and } (6). \end{array} \tag{7}$$

It is well known that for any set of nonnegative Lagrangian multipliers, the optimum solution of the Lagrangian subproblem is a lower bound on the optimum objective value of problem (1)– (6). Already Christofides, Alvarez-Valdes, and Tamarit [CAT] have proposed to use this Lagrangian relaxation, however, they solved the Lagrangian subproblems by branch-and-bound. If one omits the constant term $\sum_t \sum_{k \in R} \lambda_{kt} R_{kt}$ and introduces weights

$$w_{jt} = \begin{cases} \sum_{k \in R} \sum_{s=t}^{t+p_j-1} r_{jk,s-t} \lambda_{ks} & \text{if } j \neq n, \\ t & \text{if } j = n, \end{cases} \tag{8}$$

problem (7) can be rewritten as

$$\text{minimize} \quad c_\lambda(x) := \sum_j \sum_t w_{jt}\, x_{jt} \quad \text{subject to (2), (3), (5), and (6).} \tag{9}$$

Formulation (9) specifies the problem of finding a minimum-cost schedule for a set of jobs which must respect a set of temporal constraints, and where each job $j \in J$ incurs a cost of w_{jt} if it is started at time t. We refer to this problem as *project scheduling problem with start-time dependent costs*. It will be discussed in Sect. 3 below.

3 Scheduling with Start-Time Dependent Costs

Not only due the fact that is arises as Lagrangian subproblem for various resource-constrained scheduling problems, the scheduling problem with start-time dependent costs as formulated in (9) is of interest in its own. For instance, it generalizes the well-known net-present-value problem [Rus] to arbitrary costs w_{jt}. In the paper by Christofides et al. [CAT], this problem is solved by a branch-and-bound algorithm.

However, it is in fact solvable in polynomial time, which follows from results by Gröflin, Liebling, and Prodon [GLP], and has been observed independently also in [CWM] and [RMH+]. We have given an overview of the corresponding complexity results in [MSSU2]. We next describe a direct reduction of the scheduling problem with start-time dependent costs given in (9) to a

minimum-cut problem in a directed graph. This is a crucial result with respect to the efficiency of the Lagrangian approach, and we refer to [MSSU1] for more details.
Define a digraph D by introducing a vertex u_{jt} for every job $j \in J$ and every $t = 0, \ldots, T+1$. Now, define directed chains $(u_{j0}, u_{j1}), (u_{j1}, u_{j2}), \ldots,$ $(u_{jT}, u_{j,T+1})$ for any j. The corresponding arcs $(u_{jt}, u_{j,t+1})$ are called *assignment arcs*. Furthermore, define arcs between those chains which correspond to the given temporal constraints by $(u_{it}, u_{j,t+d_{ij}})$ for all temporal constraints $(i,j) \in L$. The cost coefficients w_{jt} are interpreted as the arc capacities of arc $(u_{jt}, u_{j,t+1})$, for all j and t. The capacity of the remaining arcs is set to infinity. Then, after the introduction of a dummy source a and sink b, a solution of the original scheduling problem can be computed as a minimum a-b-cut in that digraph. Fig. 2 gives an example for the construction of D.

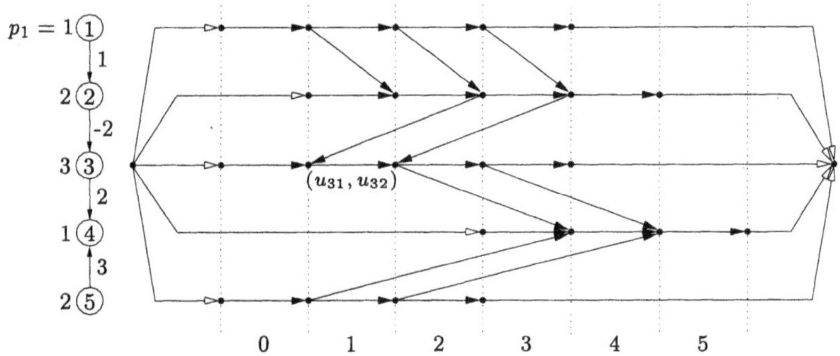

Figure 2: The left digraph represents the data of the sample instance: Each vertex represents an job, each arc represents a temporal constraint. The values for the time lags are $d_{12} = 1, d_{23} = -2, d_{34} = 2$, and $d_{54} = 3$. The job processing times are $p_1 = p_4 = 1$, $p_2 = p_5 = 2$, and $p_3 = 3$. $T = 6$ is a given upper bound on the project makespan. The right digraph D is obtained by the above transformation. Each assignment arc $(u_{jt}, u_{j,t+1})$ corresponds to a binary variable x_{jt} of formulation (9).

Theorem 1 ([MSSU1]) *A minimum a-b-cut $(X, \bar{X})$ of the digraph D described above corresponds to an optimal solution of the project scheduling problem with start time dependent costs* (9) *by virtue of*

$$x_{jt} = \begin{cases} 1 & \textit{if } (u_{jt}, u_{j,t+1}) \textit{ is a forward arc of the cut } (X, \bar{X}), \\ 0 & \textit{otherwise.} \end{cases} \tag{10}$$

Moreover, the value $c_\lambda(x)$ of that solution equals the capacity $c(X, \bar{X})$ of any minimum cut $(X, \bar{X})$ of D.

Using a push-relabel maximum-flow algorithm [GT], this results in an algorithm for solving the project scheduling problem with start-time dependent costs with running time $O(n\,m\,T^2 \log T)$. Note that this holds for arbitrary (also maximal) time lags.

4 Linear Programming or Lagrangian Relaxation?

Based on this insight, the computation of lower bounds via Lagrangian relaxation can be realized quite efficiently: Using a standard ***subgradient optimization*** procedure to compute a near-optimal set of Lagrangian multipliers, the computation of lower bounds reduces to a series of minimum-cut computations in the above defined digraph. In fact it is well known that, since the polytope defined by inequalities (2), (3), and (5) is integral, the optimum solution value of the *Lagrangian dual*

$$c_{\lambda^*} := \sup_{\lambda \geq 0} c_\lambda\,,$$

equals the value of an optimal solution of the linear programming relaxation (1) – (5). Here, c_λ denotes the value of an optimum solution of (9) for a fixed value of Lagrangian multipliers $\lambda = (\lambda_{kt})$, $k \in R$, $t = 0, \ldots, T$.
The benefit of the new insights described in the preceding section is perhaps best documented by the comparison of the corresponding computation times in Tab. 1. There, we compare the computation times when solving linear programming relaxation (1) – (5) to the computation times to solve the Lagrangian multiplier problem as described above. The figures in Tab. 1 are based upon the well-established ProGen benchmark instances for resource constrained project scheduling [KS]. We used 600 ProGen instances, each with 120 jobs. The instances are available under [Pro1]. The table shows computation times as well as the average quality of the lower bounds in terms of improvement over the so-called *critical path* lower bound, which is the length of a longest path in the project network.

Table 1: Comparison of computation times to solve the linear programming (LP) relaxation (1) – (5) and the multiplier problem for the Lagrangian relaxation (LR). Computation times were obtained on a Sun Ultra 2 with 200MHz, operating under Solaris. The linear programs have been solved with CPLEX version 6.5.3.

Algorithm	Average CPU		Above Crit. Path
LP	38 min.	(max. 23 h)	20.5%
LR	37 sec.	(max. 8 min.)	19.6%

Obviously, the computation times are drastically reduced when using the Lagrangian approach instead of solving the linear programming relaxation. The average computation times for the Lagrangian approach are based upon an average number of 70 iterations. The quality of the corresponding lower bounds deviate only marginally, due to the fact that the subgradient optimization is not exact, but rather converges to the optimum value c_{λ^*}.

5 From Minimum Cuts to Feasible Solutions

Let us now turn to the question of how to obtain feasible solutions for the scheduling problem at BASF AG. So far, we have computed a lower bound on the best possible solution as described before. In fact, we not only have computed a lower bound, but in every iteration of the above described subgradient procedure, we have computed a schedule which respects all temporal restrictions, but might be infeasible with respect to the resource constraints. The intuition behind our approach to obtain good feasible solutions is to exploit some of the information held in these resource-infeasible schedules. The simple idea is to use *list scheduling* algorithms which are based upon so-called *α-completion* times of the jobs.

Such *relaxation-based ordering heuristics*, combined with α-completion time variables, have been used previously to obtain worst case performance bounds for certain *machine scheduling* problems. The papers [PSW] and [HSW] are two of the early references in this direction. An application of *linear programming* based approaches to resource-constrained scheduling problems has been previously analyzed in [CDS$^+$] and [SUW].

Let us now briefly sketch the framework for a combined algorithm which computes both, lower bounds and feasible solutions. First, to obtain an initial valid upper bound to start with, we use list scheduling algorithms fed with some standard priority rules. (Remember that we use a time-indexed formulation and require a time horizon T.) Then, in each iteration of the subgradient optimization algorithm, a time-feasible (but likely resource-infeasible) schedule is computed by solving the Lagrangian subproblem (9) as described in Sect. 3. The cost of this time-feasible schedule, in terms of the w_{jt} defined in (8), is now a valid lower bound for the original problem (1)– (6). Using orderings according to α-completion times of jobs, we then compute feasible solutions by means of different list scheduling algorithms, schematically depicted in Fig. 3. In fact, we have developed new list scheduling algorithms which showed to be particularly suited for our approach. See [SU] and [MSSU3] for more details.

With this Lagrangian approach, we could solve a practical instance provided by BASF AG to optimality within a couple of seconds by computing matching lower and upper bounds. The instance originally consists of 21 orders which are split up into 2121 jobs, resulting in a total number of 4545 tasks. The resulting number of time lags is 2100. Although this is a very large

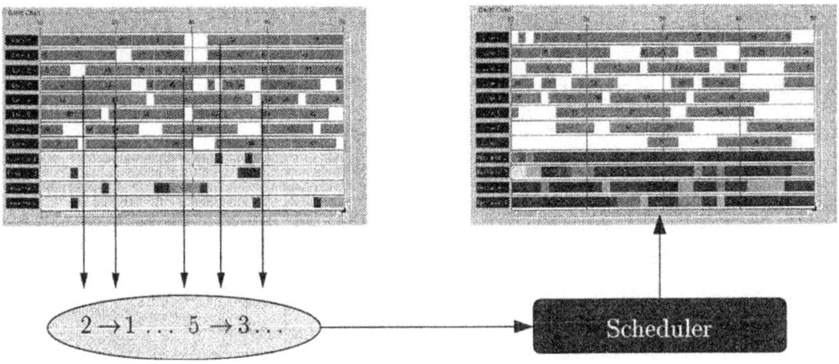

Figure 3: Computing feasible solutions by relaxation-based ordering heuristics. Information is extracted from the resource-infeasible solution of the Lagrangian relaxation (left picture), and used as input for List-Scheduling heuristics.

Table 2: Deviation of lower bounds and feasible solutions from best known lower and upper bounds. Computation times were obtained on a Sun Ultra 2 with 200MHz, operating under Solaris.

CPU	Average Deviations in % best known lower bound	best known solution
88 sec. (max. 11 min.)	2.7 (max. 23.0)	2.1 (max. 9.3)

problem instance, it turned out to be comparatively easy to solve, since a simple preprocessing reduces its size to 129 jobs and 557 tasks.

Also on the well established ProGen benchmark instances [KS], the performance of the Lagrangian approach was very encouraging. In fact, the solutions compare to results obtained with state-of-the-art local search algorithms. The figures in Tab. 2 are again averaged over 600 ProGen instances [KS], each with 120 jobs. The values for best known lower bounds and feasible solutions for these problem instances are maintained and available at [Prol]. As Tab. 2 suggests, the average deviations from both best known lower bounds and feasible solutions are below 3%, at an average computation time of 88 seconds per instance. Note that the best known solutions have been obtained by various researchers using different local-search, as well as branch-and-bound algorithms over the years, thus computation times cannot be given. The best known lower bounds are due to Brucker and Knust [BK]. They, however, require up to 72 h computation time per problem instance, whereas the Lagrangian approach only requires a maximum computation time of 11 minutes. In view of these figures, the Lagrangian approach seems to offer an excellent tradeoff between the quality of the bounds and the computational effort to get them.

Additionally, we have tested the algorithm using a benchmark set of 25 instances of the BASF-type which are available at [Cav]. These instances are known to be notoriously difficult. Tab. 3 shows the results obtained with four of these sample instances of different size. The Table shows the number of jobs and tasks as well as the critical path lower bound. T denotes the time horizon, and #it is the number of iterations in the subgradient optimization. The columns LB and UB show the lower and upper bounds obtained with the Lagrangian approach described above. Although the Lagrangian

Table 3: Results for sample instances of BASF-type with one resource type (manpower) and variable resource requirements of jobs (see Fig. 1). Computation times have been obtained on a Sun Ultra 10 with 330 MHz, operating under Solaris.

Instance	#jobs	#tasks	crit. path	T	LB	UB	CPU	#it
4o_24j_B_18	24	109	54	75	55	72	1 sec.	81
6o_44j_A_18	44	224	75	128	88	121	6 sec.	169
10o_87j_A_18	87	1001	194	633	412	595	8 min.	198
10o_106j_A_18	106	1653	383	1224	748	1126	33 min.	239

approach was not able to close the still existing gaps, are the results encouraging. Given that the computation time to solve linear programming relaxations is usually prohibitive for large instances, the computation times shown in Tab. 3 can still be ranked as moderate. (We refer to the comparison of computation times in Tab. 1, and also to [CDS+], who could solve only small problem instances due to enormous computation times.) Moreover, the feasible solutions given in Tab. 3 improve upon results obtained with constraint propagation by Heipcke [Hei], and compare to results with a tabu search algorithm by Cavalcante and de Souza [CD, CDS+]. It is worth to note, however, that in comparison to tabu search, the Lagrangian approach provides both a lower bound and a feasible solution at the same time.

6 Time-Critical Tasks and Maximal Time Lags

Until now, we have assumed that the temporal restrictions are given by arbitrary minimal time lags $d_{ij} \geq 0$ between any two jobs i and j, and the sequence of tasks of a job had to be processed without interruption. An additional feature which would be 'nice to have' in some practical applications is the possibility of modeling also *maximal time distances* between certain jobs or tasks. The motivation is that the execution of certain tasks may be postponed in time, but must not be postponed too much, for instance because the temperature must not fall below a certain threshold. Such constraints can be easily anticipated by introducing *negative* time lags between jobs, or tasks, where a time lag $d_{ji} < 0$ now implies a maximal time lag of S_j relative to S_i. Hence, so-called *time windows* of the form $S_i + d_{ij} \leq S_j \leq S_i - d_{ji}$ between any two jobs (or tasks) can be modeled.

Unfortunately, this has the effect that the problem of finding a feasible solution already is NP-complete (see, e.g., [BMR]). Although the computation of lower bounds via Lagrangian relaxation as described in Sections and remains valid also if maximal time lags are present, the approach described in Sect. to compute feasible solutions can no longer be applied. This is due to the fact that this approach is based upon list-scheduling algorithms which generally fail to find feasible solutions if maximal time lags exist. Hence, we have implemented a *branch-and-bound* algorithm for this problem (see [FMSU]). The underlying idea is that the problem is easy solvable via longest path calculations if resource-constraints are absent. Thus, the resource-constraints are relaxed, and within an enumeration tree so-called *resource conflicts* are *resolved* by introducing additional temporal restrictions. A resource conflict is a time interval where a schedule consumes more resources than available, thus violating inequalities (4). In contrast to previous approaches by Bartusch, Möhring, and Radermacher [BMR], de Reyck and Herroelen [dRH], or Schwindt [Sch2], we implemented a branch-and-bound algorithm which uses earliest start times (or *release dates*) to resolve a resource conflict. This has the effect that the necessary computations in every node of the enumeration tree can be realized very efficiently. We do not go into details here, but refer to [FMSU].

Also with this branch-and-bound algorithm, we could optimally solve the above described instance provided by BASF AG within less than a minute computation time. Applied to the notoriously difficult benchmark instances from [Cav], we could solve to optimality most of the smaller instances, however, for large instances the results with the Lagrangian approach were much better. (Note that these instances do not involve maximal time lags.)

Additionally, we tested this algorithm using a benchmark set of 1080 instances which involve also maximal time lags. The instances have been generated by Schwindt [Sch1], and consist of 100 jobs each. Tab. 4 compares the results of our implementation with previous branch-and-bound algorithms which also follow the paradigm to resolve resource conflicts. All algorithms have been run for a certain time limit (30 and 100 sec., respectively), for each of the

Table 4: Comparison of the performance of branch-and-bound algorithm [FMSU] with previous branch-and-bound algorithms, based upon 1059 ProGen/max instances [Sch1]. Computations for [FMSU] have been obtained on a Sun Ultra 2 with 200 MHz, operating under Solaris. Computations for [dRH] and [Sch2], however, have been conducted in a different environment.

Algorithm	Time limit	Optimized	Feasible	Av. Dev.
De Reyck, Herroelen [dRH]	30 s*	57.5%	93.6%	10.0%**
Schwindt [Sch2]	30 s	63.7%	100%	7.0%
	100 s	64.7%	100%	6.9%
Fest, Möhring,	30 s	70.6%	100%	7.8%
Stork, Uetz [FMSU]	100 s	72.8%	100%	6.8%

*Corresponds to 100s on a 60MHz personal computer.

**Average deviation based upon different lower bounds.

1080 instances. The figures refer to 1059 instances only, since the remaining 21 do not have a feasible solution. The table shows the number of instances that could be solved to optimality, as well as the number of instances where a feasible solution could be found within the given time limit. The last column shows the total average deviation from lower bounds, based upon a benchmark set of lower bounds obtained from [Pro2]. In terms of the average deviation, the results we obtained in [FMSU] could be further improved using constraint propagation by Dorndorf, Pesch, and Phan Huy in [DPP].

Concerning lower bounds for the ProGen/max instances, it is worth to mention that the Lagrangian approach could improve upon the best known lower bounds for 91 instances. We refer to [MSSU3] for more details.

7 Final Remarks and Outlook

We have implemented and tested two different approaches to solve resource-constrained scheduling problems which arise in a typical production process at BASG AG, Ludwigshafen. On the one hand, this is a Lagrangian approach which is suited for a whole variety of different resource-constrained scheduling problems, and hence is of practical interest not only within chemical engineering. On the other hand, this is a branch-and-bound algorithm which handles also arbitrary maximal time lags, or so-called *time windows* between jobs (or tasks). Computational experiments with practical instances from BASF AG as well as benchmark test sets were quite successful with both algorithms. In the remaining period, we intend to further improve the performance of these algorithms. Apart from the algorithmic side, we have also

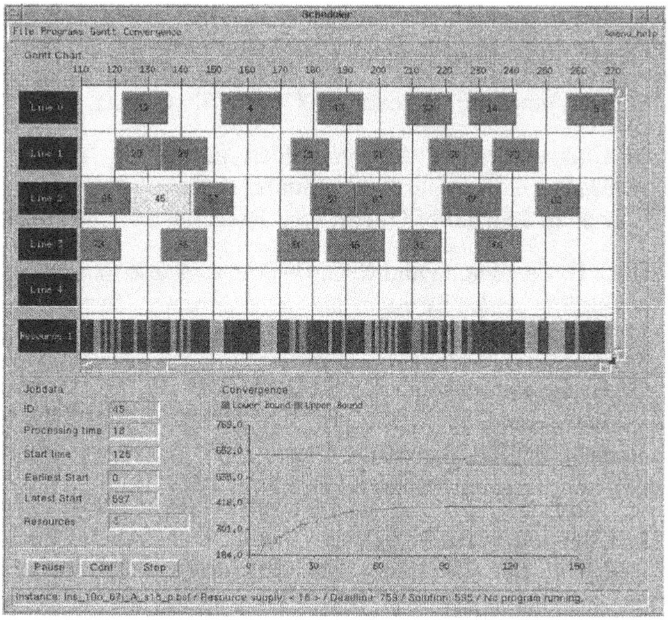

Figure 4: Screen-shot of the user interface (based on instance 10o_87j_A; see Tab. 3). Jobs are red rectangles on the time axis, and the blue bottom line visualizes resource utilization, where dark blue indicates heavy utilization. The two curves show the lower and upper bound improvements during the course of the algorithm.

implemented a user interface which allows to display both solutions as well as problem instances, and which enables the user to manipulate the problem instances on-line. Fig. 4 shows a screen-shot of the schedule visualization.

Due to its wide applicability, already several software companies indicated their interest to incorporate the Lagrangian-based algorithm into their software products.

References

[BK] P. Brucker and S. Knust, *A linear programming and constraint propagation-based lower bound for the RCPSP*, Tech. Report 204 (revised 1999), Department of Mathematics, University of Osnabrück, 1999.

[BMR] M. Bartusch, R. H. Möhring, and F. J. Radermacher, *Scheduling project networks with resource constraints and time windows*, Annals of Operations Research **16** (1988), 201–240.

[Cav] `http://www.dcc.unicamp.br/~cris/SPLC.html`, 1997.

[CAT] N. Christofides, R. Alvarez-Valdés, and J. M. Tamarit, *Project scheduling with resource constraints: A branch and bound approach*, European Journal of Operational Research **29** (1987), 262–273.

[CD] C. C. B. Cavalcante and C. C. De Souza, *A tabu search approach for scheduling problems under labour constraints*, Tech. Report IC-97-13, Instituto de Computação, UNICAMP, Campinas, Brazil, 1997.

[CDS+] C. C. B. Cavalcante, C. C. De Souza, M. W. P. Savelsbergh, Y. Wang, and L. A. Wolsey, *Scheduling projects with labor constraints*, CORE Discussion Paper 9859, Université Catholique de Louvain, Louvain-la-Neuve, Belgium, 1998.

[CWM] S. Chaudhuri, R. A. Walker, and J. E. Mitchell, *Analyzing and exploiting the structure of the constraints in the ILP approach to the scheduling problem*, IEEE Transactions on Very Large Scale Integration (VLSI) Systems **2** (1994), 456 - 471.

[dRH] B. de Reyck and W. Herroelen, *A branch and bound procedure for the resource-constrained project scheduling problem with generalized precedence relations*, European Journal of Operational Research **111** (1998), 152–174.

[DPP] U. Dorndorf, E. Pesch, and T. Phan Huy, *A time oriented branch-and-bound algorithm for resource-constrained project scheduling with generalized precedence constraints*, Tech. rep., University of Bonn, Germany, 1998.

[FMSU] A. Fest, R. H. Möhring, F. Stork, and M. Uetz, *Resource constrained project scheduling with time windows: A branching scheme based on dynamic release dates*, Tech. Report 596/1998 (revised 1999), Fachbereich Mathematik, Technische Universität Berlin, Germany, 1999. Submitted.

[GLP] H. Gröflin, T. M. Liebling, and A. Prodon, *Optimal subtrees and extensions*, Annals of Discrete Mathematics **16** (1982), 121–127.

[GT] Andrew V. Goldberg and Robert E. Tarjan, *A new approach to the maximum-flow problem*, Journal of the Association for Computing Machinery **35** (1988), 921–940.

[Hei] S. Heipcke, *Combined modelling and problem solving in mathematical programming and constraint programming*, Ph.D. thesis, School of Business, University of Buckingham, U.K., 1999.

[HSW] L. A. Hall, D. B. Shmoys, and J. Wein, *Scheduling to minimize average completion time: Off-line and on-line algorithms*, Proc. of the 7th ACM–SIAM Symposium on Discrete Algorithms, Atlanta, 1996, pp. 142–151.

[KS] R. Kolisch and A. Sprecher, *PSPLIB - A project scheduling problem library*, European Journal of Operational Research **96** (1996), 205–216.

[KW] J. Kallrath and J. M. Wilson, *Business optimisation using mathematical programming*, Macmillan Business, London, U.K., 1997.

[MSSU1] R. H. Möhring, A. S. Schulz, F. Stork, and M. Uetz, *Resource-constrained project scheduling: Computing lower bounds by solving minimum cut problems*, Algorithms – ESA'99 (J. Nešetřil, ed.), Lecture Notes in Computer Science, vol. 1643, Springer, 1999, Proc. of the 7th Annual European Symposium on Algorithms, Prague, Czech Republic, pp. 139–150.

[MSSU2] R. H. Möhring, A. S. Schulz, F. Stork, and M. Uetz, *A note on scheduling problems with irregular starting time costs*, Tech. Report 664, Technische Universität Berlin, Germany, February 2000, Submitted.

[MSSU3] R. H. Möhring, A. S. Schulz, F. Stork, and M. Uetz, *Solving Project Scheduling Problems by Minimum Cut Computations*, Tech. Report 680, Technische Universität Berlin, Germany, July 2000, Submitted.

[Pro1] `ftp://ftp.bwl.uni-kiel.de/pub/operations-research/psplib/HTML/data.html`, January 2000.

[Pro2] `ftp://ftp.wior.uni-karlsruhe.de/public/ProGen-max/pspMaxLib/RCPSPMax/benchmarkC+D.txt`, May 2000.

[PSW] C. A. Phillips, C. Stein, and J. Wein, *Scheduling jobs that arrive over time*, Algorithms and Data Structures (S. G. Akl, F. Dehne, J.-R. Sack, and N. Santoro, eds.), Lecture Notes in Computer Science, vol. 955, Springer, 1995, Proc. of the 4th International Workshop WADS'95, Kingston, Canada, pp. 86–97.

[PWW] A. A. B. Pritsker, L. J. Watters, and P. M. Wolfe, *Multi project scheduling with limited resources: A zero-one programming approach*, Management Science **16** (1969), 93–108.

[RMH+] R. O. Roundy, W. L. Maxwell, Y. T. Herer, S. R. Tayur, and A. W. Getzler, *A price-directed approach to real-time scheduling of product operations*, IIE Transactions **23** (1991), 149–160.

[Rus] A. H. Russel, *Cash flows in networks*, Management Science **16** (1970), 357–373.

[Sch] M. Schäffter, *Scheduling with respect to forbidden sets*, Discrete Applied Mathematics **72** (1997), 141–154.

[Sch1] C. Schwindt, *Generation of resource constrained project scheduling problems with minimal and maximal time lags*, Tech. Report 489, WIOR, University of Karlsruhe, Germany, 1996.

[Sch2] C. Schwindt, *A branch-and-bound algorithm for the resource-constrained project duration problem subject to temporal constraints*, Tech. Report 544, WIOR, University of Karlsruhe, Germany, 1998.

[SU] F. Stork and M. Uetz, *Resource-constrained project scheduling: From a Lagrangian relaxation to competitive solutions*, Proc. of the 7th International Workshop on Project Management and Scheduling, Osnabrück, Germany, 2000, pp. 254–257.

[SUW] M. W. P. Savelsbergh, R. N. Uma, and J. Wein, *An experimental study of LP-based approximation algorithms for scheduling problems*, Proc. of the Ninth Annual ACM-SIAM Symposium on Discrete Algorithms, San Francisco, California, 1998, pp. 453–462.

Short–Term Planning of Batch Plants in Process Industries

Klaus Neumann, Christoph Schwindt, Norbert Trautmann

Department of Economic Theory and Operations Research
University Karlsruhe, Germany

Abstract

The paper deals with short–term planning problems in process industries where final products are obtained by several successive chemical or physical transformations of raw materials using scarce multi–purpose equipment. In batch production mode, the total requirements for intermediate and final products are partitioned into batches. The production start of a batch at a given level requires the availability of all input products. We consider the problem of scheduling the production of given primary requirements for final products such that the makespan is minimized, where the batch sizes can be chosen within prescribed intervals. Further constraints arise from limited production and storage capacities as well as sequence–dependent cleaning times for processing units. We propose a new solution approach which is based on the decomposition of the short–term planning problem into computing appropriate batch sizes (batching) and the subsequent scheduling of batches on processing units (batch scheduling). The former problem is modelled and solved as a nonlinear mixed integer program, whereas the latter problem is addressed using models and methods of resource–constrained project scheduling. The solution procedure proposed (approximately) solves problems of industrial size within a reasonable amount of computing time.

Keywords:
Production planning, batch production, process industries, project scheduling

1 Introduction

In process industries, e.g. the chemical, pharmaceutical, food, or paper industry, the production of final products typically takes place through several successive chemical or physical transformation processes (also called *tasks*) such as heating, filtration, or packaging. We distinguish between continuous and batch (discontinuous) production mode (cf. Pinto and Grossmann 1998). Continuous production is characterized by a continuous flow of material, which, e.g., is typical of oil industry. In the following, we focus on process industries operating in batch production mode, where for simplicity we assume that the input of a task is consumed at its start and the output arises at its completion. Usually, the production is processed in batch mode if small amounts of a large number of products are required. The combination of a task and a corresponding production quantity is called a *batch*. The production of a batch is referred to as an *operation*. The peculiarity of batch production in process industries is that the processing times of operations are independent of the respective batch sizes.

The problem of short–term planning considered in this paper consists of allocating scarce resources over time to the production of given primary requirements such that all operations are completed within a minimum amount of time (*makespan*). In the context of advanced planning systems, those primary requirements arise from supply network planning (cf. Speranza and Stähly 2000, Chapter 2, for a survey of state of the art models and algorithms). The makespan objective is particularly important in the context of batch production, where typically a large number of different products are processed on multi–purpose equipment (cf. Pinto and Grossmann 1998) and where the production plant is configured according to the required final products. Before processing the next set of final products, the plant has to be reconfigured. This requires the termination of all operations.

A variety of technological constraints have to be taken into account. A task generally takes up two types of resources: *processing units* with sequence–dependent cleaning times (e.g. reactors or filters) and *storages* (e.g. tanks or silos). Some tasks may be performed on alternative non–identical processing units. Processing units and storages are available in limited capacity only. For all tasks, a lower and an upper bound on the respective batch sizes are given. The minimum batch size generally arises from a minimum filling level, whereas the maximum batch size coincides with the capacity of the corresponding processing unit. Moreover, certain intermediate products are perishable and thus cannot be stored.

There is an extensive literature dealing with short–term planning in process industries. Basic issues are discussed in Applequist et al. (1997), Blömer and Günther (1998), and Pinto and Grossmann (1998). Most of the solution approaches proposed in literature are based on MIP formulations, cf. e.g. Blömer (1999), Blömer and Günther (1998, 2000), Burkhard et al. (1998b), Kondili et al. (1993), or Pinto and Grossmann (1995). For a detailed literature review, we refer to Blömer (1999) and Schwindt and Trautmann (2000).

The specific feature of our solution method is the decomposition of the short–term planning problem into finding feasible batch sizes (*batching problem*) and scheduling the corresponding operations on the processing units subject to storage constraints (*batch scheduling problem*). A similar technique has been used by Brucker and Hurink (1999) for solving a special case of the short–term planning problem discussed in this paper. This heuristic approach offers the advantage of efficiently modelling and (approximately) solving even large–scale practical problems. In particular, the performance of our algorithm is independent of the time grid chosen. The heavy impact of this time grid on model size and computational effort seems to be the main drawback of time–indexed MIP formulations.

The remainder of this paper is organized as follows. In Section 2 we illustrate all constraints of our problem using a case study described in Westenberger and Kallrath (1995). Section 3 deals with the batching problem, which is modelled as a nonlinear mixed–integer program. In Section 4 we present a resource–constrained project scheduling model for batch scheduling. Section 5 sketches the solution procedure. We demonstrate the efficiency of our algorithm on the basis of a benchmark instance by Westenberger and Kallrath (1995), called *WK instance* for short. Section 6 is devoted to concluding remarks and directions for further research.

2 Example

Westenberger and Kallrath (1995) have presented a case study that covers most of the features occurring in short–term planning problems in process industries. The papers by Ahleff (1995), Blömer (1999), Blömer and Günther (1998, 2000), Burkhard et al. (1998a,b), and Rosenau (1996) have been inspired by this case study and show that it is extremely difficult to obtain feasible solutions within a reasonable amount of computing time. Figure 1 illustrates the production structure, which consists of 19 storages for products $P1$ to $P19$ and nine processing units (reactors) $R1$ to $R9$. The storages and processing units are linked by divergent, convergent, as well as cyclic material flows. The primary requirements for the final products $P15, \ldots, P19$ are given by demand vector $(30, 30, 40, 20, 40)$, cf. task 4 of the WK instance (Westenberger and Kallrath 1995).

The problem is to explode the primary requirements into batches and to schedule these batches on scarce resources. For each task, a lower and an upper bound on the corresponding batch sizes are prescribed (cf. Table 1). The resulting operations can be carried out on multi–purpose processing units (cf. Blömer and Günther 1998), i.e. facilities which can operate several kinds of tasks (but only one at a time). At some production levels, there are alternative processing units, e.g. $R6$ and $R7$. These alternative processing units are not identical, that is, the processing and cleaning times depend on the particular processing unit used (cf. Table 1). Recall that all processing times are independent of the respective batch size. Each operation uses one

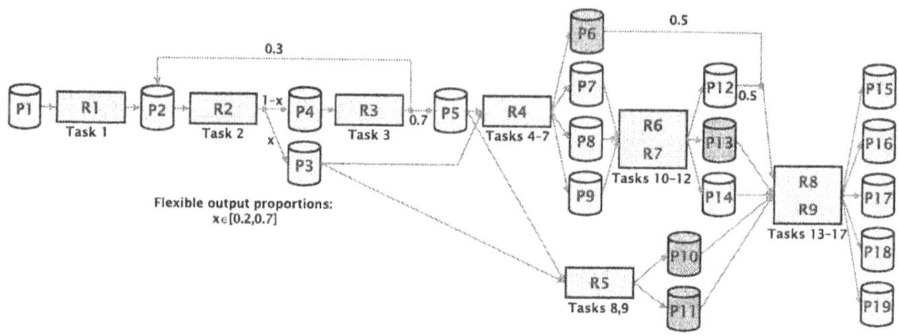

Figure 1: Example of a production structure

processing unit. In Figure 1, the processing units are labelled with the tasks executed on them.

Table 1: Task settings

Task	Batch size [min, max]	Alternative processing units	Alternative durations	Cleaning times	Materials consumed	Materials produced
1	[3,10]	*R*1	2	1	*P*1	*P*2
2	[5,20]	*R*2	4	2	*P*2	*P*3, *P*4
3	[4,10]	*R*3	2	1	*P*4	*P*2, *P*5
4	[4,10]	*R*4	4	2	*P*3	*P*6
5	[4,10]	*R*4	4	2	*P*3	*P*7
6	[4,10]	*R*4	4	2	*P*5	*P*8
7	[4,10]	*R*4	4	2	*P*5	*P*9
8	[4,10]	*R*5	6	3	*P*3	*P*10
9	[4,10]	*R*5	6	3	*P*5	*P*11
10	[3,7]	*R*6 / *R*7	4 / 5	2 / 2.5	*P*7	*P*12
11	[3,7]	*R*6 / *R*7	5 / 6	2.5 / 3	*P*8	*P*13
12	[3,7]	*R*6 / *R*7	6 / 6	3 / 3	*P*9	*P*14
13	[4,12]	*R*8 / *R*9	4 / 6	2 / 3	*P*10	*P*15
14	[4,12]	*R*8 / *R*9	4 / 6	2 / 3	*P*11	*P*16
15	[4,12]	*R*8	4	2	*P*6, *P*12	*P*17
16	[4,12]	*R*8 / *R*9	6 / 6	3 / 3	*P*13	*P*18
17	[4,12]	*R*8 / *R*9	6 / 6	3 / 3	*P*14	*P*19

In order to guarantee purity of products, cleaning of a processing unit after the completion of an operation becomes necessary if one passes to a task with higher number (the tasks are supposed to be numbered according to increasing quality of output products) or if there is no operation on the processing unit which is started immediately after the completion of the preceding one. Note that the cleanings between operations cannot be modelled by time lags

Table 2: Inventories

	$P1$	$P2$	$P3$	$P4$	$P5$	$P7$	$P8$	$P9$	$P12$	$P14$	$P15$	$P16$	$P17$	$P18$	$P19$
Initial stock	∞	20	20	0	20	0	0	0	0	0	0	0	0	0	0
Max. stock	∞	30	30	15	30	10	10	10	10	10	∞	∞	∞	∞	∞

because their durations depend on the product sequence.

Each task consumes and produces materials. Table 1 lists the corresponding input and output products. Tasks 2 and 3 produce two output products and task 15 consumes two input products. The respective proportions of the output products are shown in Figure 1. The output proportions of task 2 are flexible, that is, $100x\%$ of the total output is allotted to product $P3$ and the remaining part to product $P4$, where x can vary between 0.2 and 0.7.

Intermediate products $P6$, $P10$, $P11$, and $P13$ cannot be stored. For the storable materials, the inventory is bounded from above by some storage capacity (cf. Table 2). We assume that sufficient capacity is available to store the required raw material $P1$ and final products $P15$ to $P19$, that there is a sufficient initial stock of $P1$, and that there is no initial stock of $P15$ to $P19$. A task may deplete and/or replenish storages. Depletion occurs at the start and replenishment occurs at the completion of an operation. Backlogging of materials is not allowed, that is, the minimum inventories equal zero. Precedences between tasks resulting from the production structure are taken into account by the constraints on the minimum inventories of input products. This approach offers more flexibility compared to the linking of operations of consecutive production levels by precedence relationships (cf. e.g. Günther 1992 or Neumann and Schwindt 1997). Such a linking would require a fixed matching between producing and consuming operations.

3 Batching Model

Batching is concerned with the problem of translating the primary requirements for final products into sets of batches for each task such that the bounds on the batch sizes as well as the inventory constraints are observed and a given objective function is minimized. In what follows, we only consider solutions of the batching problem for which all batch sizes belonging to one and the same task are identical. Let $\mathcal{T}$ denote the set of all tasks. A solution is then given by a pair $(\beta_\tau, \varepsilon_\tau)$ of batch size β_τ and integral number ε_τ of executions for each task $\tau \in \mathcal{T}$ (e.g., $(\beta_1, \varepsilon_1) = (10, 14)$ means that there are 14 operations corresponding to the execution of task 1 with a batch size of 10 each). β_τ is bounded from below by some minimum batch size $\underline{\beta}_\tau$

and from above by some maximum batch size $\overline{\beta}_\tau$, i.e.

$$\underline{\beta}_\tau \le \beta_\tau \le \overline{\beta}_\tau \quad (\tau \in \mathcal{T}) \tag{1}$$

Now let $\mathcal{P}$ be the set of all products. By $\alpha_{\tau\pi}$ we denote the negative input proportion (if $\alpha_{\tau\pi} < 0$) or the output proportion (if $\alpha_{\tau\pi} > 0$) of product π for task τ. If π is neither input nor output of task τ, we put $\alpha_{\tau\pi} := 0$. The quantities $\alpha_{\tau\pi}$ are decision variables with

$$\underline{\alpha}_{\tau\pi} \le \alpha_{\tau\pi} \le \overline{\alpha}_{\tau\pi} \quad (\tau \in \mathcal{T}; \pi \in \mathcal{P}) \tag{2}$$

where $\underline{\alpha}_{\tau\pi}$ and $\overline{\alpha}_{\tau\pi} \ge \underline{\alpha}_{\tau\pi}$ designate the prescribed lower and upper bounds on $\alpha_{\tau\pi}$ (e.g. $\underline{\alpha}_{2,3} = 0.2$ and $\overline{\alpha}_{2,3} = 0.7$). If $\alpha_{\tau\pi}$ is fixed, we have $\underline{\alpha}_{\tau\pi} = \overline{\alpha}_{\tau\pi}$. Let $\mathcal{T}_\pi^-$ and $\mathcal{T}_\pi^+$ be the sets of tasks $\tau \in \mathcal{T}$ consuming and producing, respectively, product π. With γ_π denoting the primary requirement for product $\pi \in \mathcal{P}$, the inequalities

$$\sum_{\tau \in \mathcal{T}} \alpha_{\tau\pi}\beta_\tau\varepsilon_\tau - \gamma_\pi \ge 0 \quad (\pi \in \mathcal{P}) \tag{3}$$

ensure that the total quantity $\sum_{\tau \in \mathcal{T}_\pi^+} \alpha_{\tau\pi}\beta_\tau\varepsilon_\tau$ of product π produced is sufficient to match the respective total requirement $\sum_{\tau \in \mathcal{T}_\pi^-} \alpha_{\tau\pi}\beta_\tau\varepsilon_\tau + \gamma_\pi$. $\sum_{\tau \in \mathcal{T}} \alpha_{\tau\pi}\beta_\tau\varepsilon_\tau - \gamma_\pi$ equals the surplus of product π after the completion of all operations. Obviously, this final inventory must not exceed the capacity σ_π of the storage stocking product π, i.e.

$$\sum_{\tau \in \mathcal{T}} \alpha_{\tau\pi}\beta_\tau\varepsilon_\tau - \gamma_\pi \le \sigma_\pi \quad (\pi \in \mathcal{P}) \tag{4}$$

where $\sigma_\pi = 0$ if π cannot be stored.

We now turn to conditions on the inventory after the completion of individual operations. Let μ_τ be the number of alternative processing units task τ can be executed on. The maximum simultaneous depletion of the storage stocking π is given by $\sum_{\tau' \in \mathcal{T}_\pi^-} \alpha_{\tau'\pi}\beta_{\tau'}\mu_{\tau'}$. Hence, for all tasks τ producing π, $\alpha_{\tau\pi}\beta_\tau + \sum_{\tau' \in \mathcal{T}_\pi^-} \alpha_{\tau'\pi}\beta_{\tau'}\mu_{\tau'}$ is a lower bound on the inventory of π after the completion of (one execution of) task τ. This inventory must not exceed capacity σ_π, i.e.

$$\alpha_{\tau\pi}\beta_\tau + \sum_{\tau' \in \mathcal{T}_\pi^-} \alpha_{\tau'\pi}\beta_{\tau'}\mu_{\tau'} \le \sigma_\pi \quad (\tau \in \mathcal{T}; \pi \in \mathcal{P} \text{ where } \alpha_{\tau\pi} > 0) \tag{5}$$

The analogue to inequality (5) for the case of input products π says that the quantity $-\alpha_{\tau\pi}\beta_\tau$ consumed by task τ must not exceed the upper bound $\sigma_\pi + \sum_{\tau' \in \mathcal{T}_\pi^+} \alpha_{\tau'\pi}\beta_{\tau'}\mu_{\tau'}$ on the inventory of product π available when executing task τ, i.e.

$$-\alpha_{\tau\pi}\beta_\tau - \sum_{\tau' \in \mathcal{T}_\pi^+} \alpha_{\tau'\pi}\beta_{\tau'}\mu_{\tau'} \le \sigma_\pi \quad (\tau \in \mathcal{T}; \pi \in \mathcal{P} \text{ where } \alpha_{\tau\pi} < 0) \tag{6}$$

As our goal is to minimize the makespan and since the mean processing time ψ_τ of task τ on alternative processing units is independent of the respective batch size β_τ, the objective function to be minimized is chosen to be the total mean processing time $\sum_{\tau\in\mathcal{T}} \psi_\tau \varepsilon_\tau$. The batching problem can now be stated as follows:

$$\left.\begin{array}{ll} \text{Min.} & \sum_{\tau\in\mathcal{T}} \psi_\tau \varepsilon_\tau \\ \text{s.t.} & (1) \text{ to } (6) \\ & \varepsilon_\tau \in \mathbb{Z}_{\geq 0} \end{array}\right\} \qquad (7)$$

4 Batch Scheduling Model

After having determined appropriate batches, we proceed with scheduling the processing of those batches (i.e. the operations). Each operation is characterized by the underlying task and batch size. In this section, we will show how the execution of the operations on alternative processing units subject to inventory constraints can be modelled as a resource–constrained project (cf. e.g. Brucker et al. 1999, Neumann et al. 2000, or Schwindt and Trautmann 2000).

4.1 Basic concepts

Suppose that n operations numbered from 1 to n have to be scheduled. The project consists of a set $V = \{0, 1, \ldots, n, n+1\}$ of activities i with *duration* p_i and *cleaning time* c_i which require *resources* and which are connected by prescribed *minimum and maximum time lags*. Each operation is identified with exactly one real activity $i \in \{1, \ldots, n\}$ of the project. Dummy activity 0 represents the production start and dummy activity $n+1$ corresponds to the production end, where $p_0 = p_{n+1} = 0$ and $c_0 = c_{n+1} = 0$. Let S_i denote the start time of activity $i \in V$. We assume that the production starts at time zero, i.e. $S_0 := 0$. The makespan of the production then equals S_{n+1}. A vector $S = (S_i)_{i\in V}$ of start times is termed a *schedule*. Batch scheduling refers to the problem of determining a schedule S such that all time lags and all resource constraints are observed and the makespan S_{n+1} is minimized.

4.2 Time lags

In project scheduling, minimum and maximum time lags may be given between the execution of different activities $i, j \in V$. Without loss of generality we assume that all time lags refer to start times. We denote a minimum (or maximum) time lag between activities $i, j \in V$ by $d_{ij}^{min} \geq 0$ (or $d_{ij}^{max} \geq 0$, respectively).

It is customary to represent the project in question by a network $N = \langle V, E; \delta \rangle$ with node set V, arc set E, and arc weights δ. To this end we assign activity i to node i and identify node i with activity i ($i \in V$). Arc set E consists of arcs between activities $i, j \in V$ which are linked by time lags: If there is a prescribed minimum time lag d_{ij}^{min} between the start of activities i and j, we introduce an arc $\langle i, j \rangle$ with weight $\delta_{ij} := d_{ij}^{min}$. In case of a maximum time lag d_{ij}^{max} between the start of activities i and j, we have an arc $\langle j, i \rangle$ with weight $\delta_{ji} := -d_{ij}^{max}$.

Since no operation can be begun before the start of production, we have $S_i \geq 0$ for all $i \in V$. If there is no path in N from 0 to i ($i \in V$) of nonnegative length, we add an arc $\langle 0, i \rangle$ with weight $\delta_{0i} = 0$. Similarly, it has to be ensured that $S_i + p_i + c_i \leq S_{n+1}$ holds for all $i \in V$ because all operations and cleanings have to be completed by the termination of the production: If there is no path in N from i to $n+1$ ($i \in V$) with a length of at least $p_i + c_i$, we introduce an arc $\langle i, n+1 \rangle$ with weight $\delta_{i,n+1} = p_i + c_i$. A schedule S is called *time-feasible* if it satisfies

$$S_0 = 0 \text{ and } S_j \geq S_i + \delta_{ij} \quad (\langle i, j \rangle \in E). \tag{8}$$

It is well-known that a time-feasible schedule exists exactly if N does not contain any cycle of positive length (cf. Bartusch et al. 1988).

We now consider some particular time lags between operations i and j which will be used when dealing with resource constraints:

- j has to wait for the completion of i because both operations are executed on the same processing unit or because j requires (a part of) the output of i as input: $d_{ij}^{min} := p_i$
- j cannot be completed until the start of i frees storage capacity for the output product of j: $d_{ji}^{max} := p_j$
- Some perishable output product of i must be consumed by j immediately after the completion of i: $d_{ij}^{min} := d_{ij}^{max} := p_i$

Figure 2 shows a part of some project network N. Activities 57, 60, and 63 correspond to the processing of tasks 10, 11, and 12, respectively, on reactor $R7$ and activities 75, 79, and 82 correspond to the processing of tasks 15, 16, and 17, respectively, on reactor $R8$. We assume that the storage stocking product $P12$ is completely filled and that there is no inventory of product $P14$. Thus, the completion of activity 57 (producing $P12$) has to wait for the start of activity 75 (consuming $P12$) and the start of activity 82 (consuming $P14$) has to wait for the completion of activity 63 (producing $P14$). Activity 60 produces the perishable intermediate product $P13$. Thus, the corresponding consuming activity 79 has to start immediately after the completion of activity 60.

4.3 Resource constraints

We first deal with **processing units**. Processing units are modelled as specific *renewable resources* with capacity 1 (cf. Brucker et al. 1999) which have

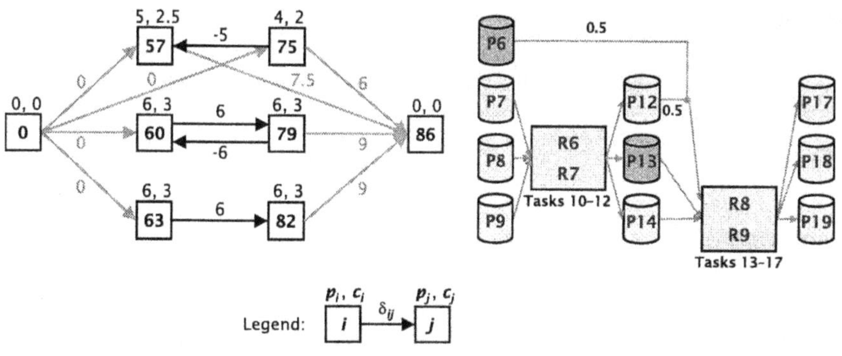

Figure 2: Part of project network and corresponding production structure

to be cleaned between subsequent operations. The need for cleanings depends on the sequence in which activities are processed on the processing unit. Each processing unit corresponds to one renewable resource.

The set of renewable resources is denoted by $\mathcal{R}^\rho$ and $\mathcal{R}_i^\rho \subseteq \mathcal{R}^\rho$ is the set of all (alternative) renewable resources on which activity i can be executed. Let x_{ik} be a binary decision variable which equals 1 exactly if activity i is carried out on resource k. Then equations

$$\sum_{k \in \mathcal{R}_i^\rho} x_{ik} = 1 \quad (i = 1, \ldots, n) \tag{9}$$

say that all real activities must be executed on exactly one of the alternative renewable resources.

Each processing unit $k \in \mathcal{R}^\rho$ can process at most one operation at a time. Moreover, between the completion of activity i and the start of that activity j which is processed immediately after i on the same processing unit $k \in \mathcal{R}_i^\rho \cap \mathcal{R}_j^\rho$, a cleaning time c_i may be necessary. Let $\tau(i)$ be the task belonging to operation i and let p_τ^k and c_τ^k denote the processing time and cleaning time, respectively, of task τ if executed on processing unit k. Then $p_i = \sum_{k \in \mathcal{R}_i^\rho} p_{\tau(i)}^k x_{ik}$ equals the processing time of activity i and $c_i = \sum_{k \in \mathcal{R}_i^\rho} c_{\tau(i)}^k x_{ik}$ is the cleaning time of activity i. For each renewable resource $k \in \mathcal{R}^\rho$, there must exist a permutation $(i_1, \ldots, i_\nu)$ of the $\nu = \sum_{i \in V} x_{ik}$ activities $i \in V$ being processed on k such that between two successive activities $i_\mu, i_{\mu+1}$ either a cleaning is performed or $\tau(i_{\mu+1}) \leq \tau(i_\mu)$ and $i_{\mu+1}$ starts immediately after the completion of i_μ. Accordingly, a schedule S is called *process–feasible* if it satisfies

$$\left.\begin{array}{l} S_{i_{\mu+1}} \geq S_{i_\mu} + p_{i_\mu} + c_{i_\mu}, \text{ if } \tau(i_{\mu+1}) > \tau(i_\mu) \text{ or } S_{i_{\mu+1}} > S_{i_\mu} + p_{i_\mu} \\ S_{i_{\mu+1}} = S_{i_\mu} + p_{i_\mu}, \text{ otherwise} \\ \hfill (k \in \mathcal{R}^\rho; \mu = 1, \ldots, \nu - 1) \end{array}\right\} \quad (10)$$

where $S_{i_1} \leq S_{i_2} \leq \cdots \leq S_{i_\nu}$.

Next, we turn to **inventories** that are modelled as so-called *cumulative resources* (cf. Neumann and Schwindt 1999). A cumulative resource k is bounded from below by a safety stock and from above by its capacity and is depleted and replenished by activities. For each product $\pi \in \mathcal{P}$, there is one cumulative resource k keeping its inventory. Let $\mathcal{R}^\gamma$ denote the set of cumulative resources. For each resource $k \in \mathcal{R}^\gamma$, there are a prescribed minimum inventory $\underline{R}_k$ (the safety stock) and a prescribed maximum inventory $\overline{R}_k \geq \underline{R}_k$ (the storage capacity). Each activity $i \in V$ has a *demand* r_{ik} for resource $k \in \mathcal{R}^\gamma$. If $r_{ik} > 0$, the demand is termed *replenishment* and occurs at time $S_i + p_i$; if $r_{ik} < 0$, the demand is termed *depletion* and occurs at time S_i. Since cumulative resource k corresponds to product π, we have $\underline{R}_k = 0$ and $\overline{R}_k = \sigma_\pi$ for all $k \in \mathcal{R}^\gamma$ and $r_{ik} = \alpha_{\tau(i)\pi}\beta_{\tau(i)}$ for all $i = 1, \ldots, n$ and all $k \in \mathcal{R}^\gamma$. r_{0k} corresponds to the initial stock of product π and $r_{n+1,k}$ equals zero for all $k \in \mathcal{R}^\gamma$.

Let $V_k^- := \{i \in V \mid r_{ik} < 0\}$ be the set of activities depleting resource $k \in \mathcal{R}^\gamma$ and $V_k^+ := \{i \in V \mid r_{ik} > 0\}$ be the set of activities replenishing resource $k \in \mathcal{R}^\gamma$. Then $\mathcal{A}_k(S,t) := \{i \in V_k^- \mid S_i \leq t\} \cup \{i \in V_k^+ \mid S_i + p_i \leq t\}$ is called the *active set* of activities which deplete or replenish resource $k \in \mathcal{R}^\gamma$ by time t for given schedule S. Schedule S is termed *storage-feasible* if it satisfies

$$\underline{R}_k \leq \sum_{i \in \mathcal{A}_k(S,t)} r_{ik} \leq \overline{R}_k \quad (k \in \mathcal{R}^\gamma; t \geq 0) \qquad (11)$$

Obviously, $\underline{R}_k \leq \sum_{i \in V} r_{ik} \leq \overline{R}_k$ for all $k \in \mathcal{R}^\gamma$ is a sufficient and necessary condition for the existence of a storage-feasible schedule (cf. Neumann and Schwindt 1999).

A schedule which is time–, process–, and storage–feasible is called *feasible.* The batch scheduling problem consists of finding a feasible schedule S with minimum makespan S_{n+1}. This problem can be stated as follows:

$$\left.\begin{array}{ll} \text{Min.} & S_{n+1} \\ \text{s.t.} & (8) \text{ to } (11) \end{array}\right\} \qquad (12)$$

5 Solution Method

We (approximately) solve the batching problem modelled in Section 3 using some standard software for nonlinear integer programming (branch-and-bound in combination with the generalized reduced gradient method of Frontline Systems Premium Solver Plus Version 3.5, cf. Lasdon et al. 1978). For the WK instance, we obtain the solution given in Table 3 within 10 seconds of computing time on a Pentium III–800 PC with 512 MB memory operating under MS Windows 2000. This solution corresponds to 85 operations, where for the output proportion of product $P3$ for task 2 we have $x = 0.3684$.

Table 3: Batching solution

Task τ	1	2	3	4	5	6	7	8	9	10	11	12	13	14	15	16	17
Batch size β_τ	10	19	10	5	10	7	9	10	10	7	7	7	10	10	10	7	10
No. of replications ρ_τ	14	10	11	4	3	3	5	3	3	3	3	6	3	3	4	3	4

Next, we briefly sketch the generation scheme of a branch–and–bound algorithm for solving the resource–constrained project scheduling problem (12) from Section 4. The constraints that make the problem intractable are the scarcity of resources: the limited availability of processing units, the minimum inventory of intermediate products, and the capacity of storages. By relaxing the corresponding constraints (9), (10), and (11), we obtain a *temporal scheduling* (TS) problem, where for each activity i which can be executed on more than one processing unit (i.e. $|\mathcal{R}_i^\rho| > 1$), we set $x_{ik} := 0$ for all $k \in \mathcal{R}_i^\rho$, $p_i := \min_{k\in\mathcal{R}_i^\rho} p_{\tau(i)}^k$ and $c_i := \min_{k\in\mathcal{R}_i^\rho} c_{\tau(i)}^k$. The TS problem represents a longest path problem and can be solved by a label correcting algorithm (cf. Lawler 1976). An optimal solution to this *relaxation* may correspond to an infeasible schedule due to two reasons: there may be activities with $|\mathcal{R}_i^\rho| > 1$ for which no processing unit $k \in \mathcal{R}_i^\rho$ has been selected so far (i.e. $\sum_{k\in\mathcal{R}_i^\rho} x_{ik} = 0$ and thus equation (9) is violated), or one of the resource constraints (10) and (11) may not be met. In the former case, we select some $k \in \mathcal{R}_i^\rho$ for processing i by putting $x_{ik} := 1$ and replace p_i by $p_{\tau(i)}^k$, c_i by $c_{\tau(i)}^k$, and $\mathcal{R}_i^\rho$ by $\{k\}$. Violations of the constraints (10) and (11) can be avoided by introducing appropriate time lags between activities and corresponding arcs in network N (*constraint generation*, cf. Figure 3). By selecting processing units and adding time lags we obtain a new batch scheduling problem with a tighter relaxation. The selection of processing units and the addition of time lags is repeated until the temporal scheduling yields a feasible schedule or the TS problem is unsolvable because N contains a cycle of positive length.

We now consider in more detail how to determine appropriate time lags during the constraint generation. Let us assume that schedule S under consider-

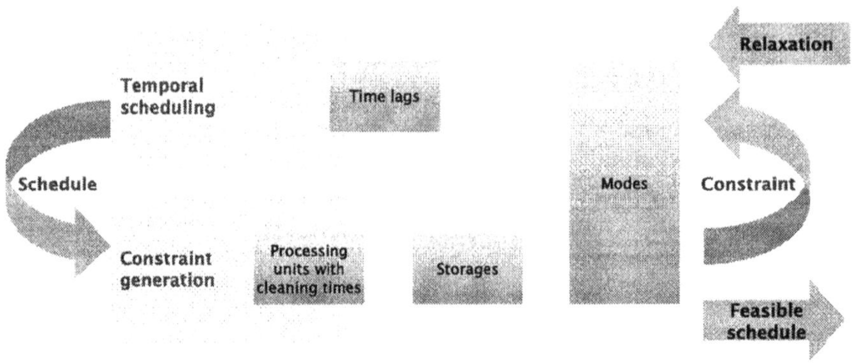

Figure 3: Temporal scheduling and constraint generation for components of the batch scheduling problem

ation is not process–feasible, where for the verification of (10), we only take into account activities whose execution mode has been selected, i.e. $|\mathcal{R}_i^\rho| = 1$. Then there exist activities i, j being executed on the same processing unit k (i.e. $\mathcal{R}_i^\rho = \mathcal{R}_j^\rho = \{k\}$) with $S_j > S_i$ such that

(*i*) $\tau(j) > \tau(i)$ and $S_j < S_i + p_i + c_i$, or

(*ii*) $\tau(j) \leq \tau(i)$ and $S_j < S_i + p_i$, or

(*iii*) $\tau(j) \leq \tau(i)$ and $S_i + p_i < S_j < S_i + p_i + c_i$.

Case (*i*) can be dealt with by considering two alternatives. First, we can introduce the minimum time lag $d_{ij}^{min} := p_i + c_i$ delaying activity j up to the point in time where the cleaning of processing unit k is terminated. Second, the infeasibility can be resolved by introducing the minimum time lag $d_{ji}^{min} := p_j$ saying that activity i cannot start before activity j has been completed (note that in this case, cleaning of k is not necessary). Case (*ii*) can be addressed similarly by interchanging the roles of activities i and j: The two alternatives consist of introducing minimum time lag $d_{ij}^{min} := p_i$ or minimum time lag $d_{ji}^{min} := p_j + c_j$.

The conditions of case (*iii*) say that there is a positive time lag between the completion of activity i and the start of activity j which is not sufficiently large for cleaning k. Then the first alternative is to delay j up to the end of the cleaning after the execution of i by introducing the time lag $d_{ij}^{min} := p_i + c_i$. Analogously, i can be delayed up to the end of the cleaning after the execution of j, i.e. $d_{ji}^{min} := p_j + c_j$. A third alternative arises from avoiding the cleaning of k before j starts. The latter can be ensured by introducing the maximum time lag $d_{ij}^{max} := p_i$.

The cumulative resource constraints are violated if some inventory falls below zero or exceeds the storage capacity. At first, we consider the case where at some time $t \geq 0$ the inventory of a storage k is negative. We chose an activity i with $S_i + p_i > t$ and $r_{ik} > 0$ and an activity j with $S_j \leq t$ and $r_{jk} < 0$. By introducing the minimum time lag $d_{ij}^{min} := p_i$ we then delay the start of activity i (i.e. the depletion of k) up to the completion of activity j (i.e. the replenishment of k). The case where at time $t \geq 0$ the inventory exceeds the capacity of storage k can be dealt with as follows. We select an activity i with $S_i > t$ and $r_{ik} < 0$ and an activity j with $S_j + p_j \leq t$ and $r_{jk} > 0$. The completion of activity j (i.e. the replenishment) is then delayed up to the start of activity i (i.e. the depletion) by introducing the maximum time lag $d_{ji}^{max} := p_j$.

A branch–and–bound algorithm based on the above generation scheme has been implemented in C under MS–Visual C++ 6.0. Batch sizes and numbers of execution for the WK instance have been determined by (approximately) solving the nonlinear mixed–integer batching program (cf. Table 3) within 10 seconds of computing time. The resulting batch scheduling problem has been (approximately) solved using a truncated beam search version of the branch–and–bound algorithm. On a Pentium III–800 personal computer with 512 MB memory operating under MS Windows 2000, we have obtained a feasible solution with a makespan of 101 units of time within 50 seconds. Figure 4 shows the corresponding Gantt chart. The white rectangles correspond to the execution of operations, which are numbered according to increasing task numbers. The shaded rectangles represent cleanings required when passing to higher quality output products, and the shaded triangles stand for cleanings which become necessary due to an idle time on the respective processing unit.

In sum, the short–term planning problem has been (approximately) solved within one minute of computing time. To the best of our knowledge, this is the first time that a feasible solution to the (genuine) WK instance has been found.

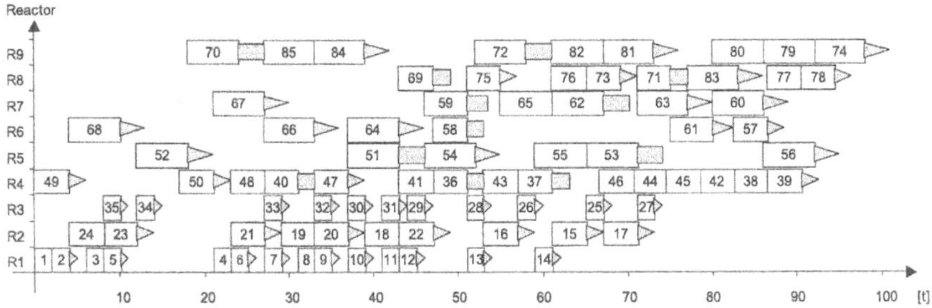

Figure 4: Gantt chart for solution of the batch scheduling problem

6 Conclusions and Further Research

We have dealt with the problem of short–term planning in process industries. A decomposition approach has been proposed consisting of the successive solution of a batching and a batch scheduling problem. The batching problem has been modelled as a mixed–integer nonlinear program that can be solved using standard software. The batch scheduling problem has been addressed within the framework of resource–constrained project scheduling. The corresponding scheduling procedure is based on the relaxation of the constraints limiting the availability of processing units, inventories, and storage capacities. In a branch–and–bound algorithm, those constraints are enforced by introducing minimum and maximum time lags between conflicting operations. For the first time, the benchmark instance by Westenberger and Kallrath (1995) has been solved to feasibility.

Some important aspects of practical short–term planning problems are subject to further research. Often manpower (possibly varying over time) is needed for executing tasks. Specific tasks cannot be processed during given production breaks. Tasks which can be interrupted (e.g. packaging) have to be resumed immediately after a production break. Other tasks (e.g. chemical reactions) must not be interrupted at all.

In practice, certain input data like processing times may often not be estimated with sufficient reliability (cf. Kanakamedala et al. 1994). Thus, in the course of the production process, the production schedule computed originally may become infeasible (e.g. due to breakdowns of processing units). Reactive planning aims at finding a feasible schedule while keeping the system nervousness as small as possible by computing a feasible schedule sharing a maximum number of properties (e.g. start times or operation sequences) with the original schedule. Using the relaxation–based approach presented, new constraints arising from modified input data can easily be integrated.

Another important area of future research is the generalization of the problem to continuous or semicontinuous material flows. In contrast to batch mode production, here the problem of finding appropriate time lags arises when resolving cumulative resource infeasibilities.

References

[1] Ahleff J (1995) Analyse von mathematischen Modellen zur Reihenfolgeplanung in der Prozeßindustrie. Master thesis, RWTH Aachen, Germany

[2] Applequist G, Samikoglu O, Pekny J, Reklaitis GV (1997) Issues in the use, design and evolution of process scheduling and planning systems. ISA Transactions 36: 81–121

[3] Bartusch M, Möhring R, Radermacher FJ (1988) Scheduling project networks with resource constraints and time windows. Annals of Operations Research 16: 201–240

[4] Blömer F (1999) Produktionsplanung und -steuerung in der chemischen Industrie — Ressourceneinsatzplanung von Batchprozessen auf Mehrzweckanlagen. Gabler, Wiesbaden.

[5] Blömer F, Günther HO (1998) Scheduling of a multi-product batch process in the chemical industry. Computers in Industry 36: 245–259

[6] Blömer F, Günther HO (2000) LP-based heuristics for scheduling chemical batch processes. International Journal of Production Research 35: 1029–1052

[7] Brucker B, Drexl A, Möhring R, Neumann K, Pesch E (1999) Resource-constrained project scheduling: notation, classification, models, and methods. European Journal of Operational Research 112: 3–41

[8] Brucker P, Hurink J (1999) Solving a chemical batch scheduling problem by local search. Osnabrücker Schriften zur Mathematik, Heft 215, University of Osnabrück

[9] Burkhard RE, Hujter M, Klinz B, Rudolf R, Wennink M (1998a) A process scheduling problem arising from chemical production planning. Optimization Methods & Software 10: 175–196

[10] Burkhard RE, Kocher M, Rudolf R (1998b) Rounding strategies for mixed integer programs arising from chemical production planning. Yugoslav Journal of Operations Research 8: 9–23

[11] Günther, HO (1992) Netzplanorientierte Auftragsterminierung bei offener Fertigung. OR Spektrum 14: 229–240

[12] Kanakamedala KB, Reklaitis G, Venkatasubramanian V (1994) Reactive schedule modification in multipurpose batch chemical plants. Industrial & Engineering Chemistry Research 33: 77–90

[13] Kondili E, Pantelides CC, Sargent RWH (1993) A general algorithm for short-term scheduling of batch operations — I. MILP formulation. Computers & Chemical Engineering 17: 211–227

[14] Lasdon LS, Waren AD, Jain A, Ratner M (1978) Design and testing of a generalized reduced gradient code for nonlinear programming. Transactions on Mathematical Software 4: 34–50

[15] Lawler EL (1976) Networks and Matroids. Rinehart and Winston, New York

[16] Neumann K, Schwindt C (1997) Activity–on–node networks with minimal and maximal time lags and their application to make–to–order production. OR Spektrum 19: 205–217

[17] Neumann K, Schwindt C (1999) Project scheduling with inventory constraints. Report WIOR–572, University of Karlsruhe

[18] Neumann K, Schwindt C, Zimmermann J (2000) Project scheduling with time windows and scarce resources I. Report WIOR–600, University of Karlsruhe

[19] Pinto M, Grossmann IE (1995) A continuous time mixed integer linear programming model for short term scheduling of multistage batch plants. Industrial & Engineering Chemistry Research 34: 3037–3051

[20] Pinto M, Grossmann IE (1998) Assignment and sequencing models for the scheduling of process systems. Annals of Operations Research 81: 443–466

[21] Rosenau B (1996) Bearbeitung eines Losgrößenproblems aus der chemischen Industrie mit Schnittebenenenverfahren. Diploma thesis, University of Marburg, Germany

[22] Schwindt C, Trautmann N (2000) Batch scheduling in process industries: an application of resource–constrained project scheduling. OR Spektrum 22, to appear

[23] Speranza MG, Stähly P (2000) New Trends in Distribution Logistics. Springer, Berlin

[24] Westenberger H, Kallrath J (1995) Formulation of a job shop problem in process industry. Unpublished working paper, Bayer AG, Leverkusen and BASF AG, Ludwigshafen

Local Search for a Travelling Salesman Problem in Production Control - A Case Study

Gerhard Wäscher, Jörg Heuer, Volker Reschke, Petra Schwerin

Wirtschaftswissenschaftliche Fakultät

Martin-Luther-Universität Halle-Wittenberg, Germany

Abstract

During the past two decades significant progress could be observed in the development of heuristic solution methods. In particular, Local Search Methods have attracted considerable interest, as they have been applied successfully to various difficult combinatorial problems in business management. However, only few articles exist in which these methods are compared to each other. The authors report some experience from a study in which classic (Descent Method) and modern (Simulated Annealing, Threshold Accepting, Great Deluge, Tabu Search) Local Search Methods have been implemented in order to solve a real-world Travelling Salesman Problem in production control. Simulated Annealing turned out to be superior to all other methods with respect to implementation requirements and solution quality. By replacing the previously implemented method the utilization of the respective production unit – which represented a bottleneck – could be increased significantly.

Introduction

The development of new heuristic solution methods has to be considered as one of the most fascinating areas in modern Operations Research/Management Science. During the last two decades, various meta-heuristics have been suggested in the literature (for an overview see Osman/Kelly 1996) that can be applied to a wide range of difficult combinatorial optimization problems in business management. From those methods based on analogies with biological systems and processes (*"Heuristics from Nature"*: Genetic Algorithms (Goldberg 1989, Michalewicz 1992, Mühlenbein 1997); Artificial Neural Networks (Peterson/Söderberg 1997); Ant Systems (Colorni/Dorigo/Maniezzo 1991); etc.), in particular *Local Search Methods* have attracted considerable attention. The latter include both traditional improvement methods (*classic* Local Search Methods) such as 2-OPT-, 3-OPT-, and Or-OPT-methods (Or 1976, Golden/Stewart 1985, p. 220), and more recent developments (*modern* Local Search Methods) like Simulated Annealing (Aarts/Korst/van Laarhoven 1997, Dowsland 1993, Eglese 1990), Threshold Accepting (Dueck/Scheuer 1990, Dueck/Scheuer/Wallmeier 1993), and Tabu Search (Glover/Laguna 1997).

From a given initial solution, classic Local Search Methods successively proceed to better solutions in the corresponding "neighbourhood". They terminate when no superior solution can be identified. The final solution represents a local, but usually not a global optimum. Traditional improvement methods are not able to leave such local optima. Modern Local Search Methods, on the other hand, incorporate special strategies which prohibit that they get stuck in a local optimum, e.g. by allowing them to proceed to inferior solutions, too.

Even though the body of literature on modern Local Search Methods has grown rapidly over the last twenty years (a good impression of the developments is given by Pesch/Voß 1995), only few articles actually compare them to each other and try to identify whether and under which conditions a particular method is to be favoured. The authors take the opportunity to contribute to narrowing this gap by reporting some experience from a study concerning a real-world production control problem. For this problem, which turned out to be equivalent to the Travelling Salesman Problem (TSP), several Local Search Methods have been implemented, the Descent Method as a classic, and special variants of Simulated Annealing, Great Deluge and Tabu Search as representatives of modern Local Search Methods. A series of numerical experiments with non-trivial problem instances from practice has been performed in order to gain some insight into the behaviour of these methods. A comparative analysis of the results, in particular with respect to solution quality and computing times, forms a central chapter of this paper.

In general, the material will be structured as follows: In section 1, the production control problem from practice, that will be considered in this paper, is introduced. Section 2 deals with Local Search Methods. Their common basic structure is presented and it is demonstrated how the implemented variants can be derived from it as special cases. Design of the numerical experiments, which have been performed in order to evaluate the different methods, the set of tests problems, and the test environment, are described in section 3. Test results are presented and discussed in section 4. Also the economic benefits from the methods under discussion are analysed. The paper finishes with some general conclusions in section 5.

1 A Travelling Salesman Problem from Industrial Practice

The study to be presented here has been carried out for a German manufacturer of trams and railway carriages. At an early production stage small parts belonging to a specific order have to be cut from a plate of steel. In the corresponding planning process, a cutting pattern is determined by means of a software package, which is being used for several years already. An example of such a cutting pattern is depicted in Fig. 1.

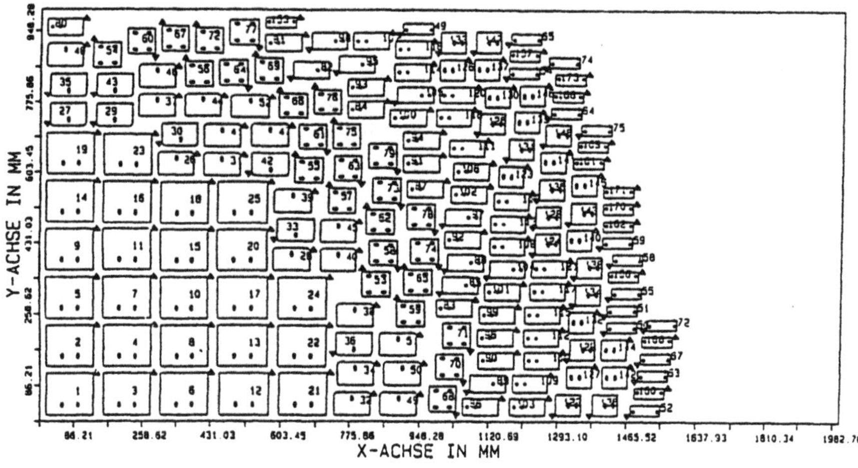

Fig. 1: Cutting pattern for the parts of an order

The cutting pattern is translated into an NC-program and transferred to a laser cutting system that carries out the actual cutting process automatically. The program contains a sequence according to which the small parts have to be cut (indicated by numbers in Fig. 1), and, for each small part, both the coordinates of a particular point (*stitch point*), where the corresponding cutting path starts and terminates (indicated by small triangles in Fig. 1), and a call of a subprogram, which basically controls the status (on/off) of the laser and the movements of the laser head. When the program has been started, the laser head moves from a resting position (in the bottom-left corner) to the stitch point of the first small part. There the laser head is positioned precisely, the laser is switched on and the laser head performs the necessary movements. The cutting process for the small part is completed and the laser is switched off again when the laser head has returned to the stitch point. From there the laser head proceeds to the second stitch point, where the cutting process continues, etc. When all small parts have been cut, the laser head returns to its original resting position.

The completion of a cutting pattern is a rather time-consuming task. It may take between one and three hours, depending on the type of material, the number of small parts, and the complexity of the contours to be cut. Even though the company was running ten laser-cutting systems of the described type, the cutting shop used to be a permanent bottleneck in production. In order to overcome this problem, the company considered to increase its capacity by introducing two additional cutting systems, which would have meant an investment of 1.5-5 million deutschmarks each. Alternatively, the company wanted to know whether it would be possible to reduce the capacity requirements by improving the processes in the cutting shop.

An initial problem analysis revealed that a considerable imbalance existed between the times the lasers were actually productive (i.e. the cutting times) and auxiliary times needed for positioning and moving the laser heads between stitch points (including the resting position). For example, the total processing time for the cutting pattern of Fig. 1 amounted to 120 minutes, of which more than 40 minutes (i.e. more than one third) had to be attributed to auxiliary times. The cutting times had to be looked upon as technically fixed, however, a considerable potential for reducing the auxiliary times could be identified. In particular is the time the laser head spends travelling between the stitch points immediately dependent on the total length of the corresponding distances. This length, again, is a function of the sequence according to which the stitch points are approached by the laser head (i.e. the sequence according to which the small parts are cut, respectively). Thus, in order to reduce the travel times between the stitch points to a minimum, one has to determine a sequence of the stitch points such that the total distance to be travelled by the laser head is minimized. This problem is identical with a Travelling Salesman Problem, in which a tour of all stitch points (including the resting position) has to be determined such that each point is visited exactly once and the total length of all distances to be travelled is minimized.

In the past, the software for the generation of cutting patterns had also provided the sequence of the stitch points. Unfortunately, which particular algorithm was actually used for this purpose, could not be identified from the sources available to the authors. Fig. 2 presents a typical solution of the sequencing problem. Depicted are the movements of the laser head between the stitch points and the resting position only, while the actual cutting paths are omitted from the picture. Obviously, the solution is far from an optimal one, as can be seen from the various intersections of the travel path. Because such intersections appeared in almost every solution checked during the problem analysis phase, the authors concluded that improving the sequence in which the stitch points are approached by the laser head would make a good point of departure for reducing the processing times. Consequently, it was decided to replace the present procedure of determining the stitch point sequence by a more appropriate one.

Fig. 2: Example for the solution of the sequencing problem

It was planned to implement the computer program on a personal computer that was available in the cutting shop. Furthermore, the program was required to provide a stitch point sequence even for the largest problem instance within at most one hour of computing time. (This time limit was basically set in order to avoid idle times of the cutting systems due to long computer running times.) As the TSP is NP-complete (Garey/Johnson 1979, p. 29), one can expect only small instances being solvable by *exact solution methods* in reasonable computing times.

In our case, in which the cutting patterns contained up to 800 or even 1000 stitch points (nodes in the terminology of the TSP), the choice of a *heuristic solution method* appeared to be more appropriate. Which particular method finally was to be implemented still had to be decided on. An analysis of the published literature turned out to be of limited help only. Initially, just methods of the "Heuristics-from-Nature"-type could be excluded from further considerations. Due to the experience published for the application of Genetic Algorithms (Chatterjee/Carrera/Lynch 1996, Dowsland 1996), Artificial Neural Networks (Potvin 1993), or for the Ant-System (Colorni/Dorigo/Maniezzo 1991) to the TSP, the authors did not expect that competitive results in terms of solution quality and computing times could be achieved with these methods. With respect to the application of Local Search Methods to the TSP there are some comprehensive publications (Golden/Stewart 1985, Reinelt 1994) available, however, for traditional methods only. Systematic comparisons of modern Local Search Methods applied to the TSP did not exist at the time when this study was carried out. Thus, in order to determine an appropriate method for implementation, the authors carried out their own numerical experiments with real-world data sets.

2 Local Search Methods

In this section the general principle and the basic modules of Local Search Methods are presented (also see Wäscher 1998). It is also demonstrated how the modules have to be specified in order to obtain the various methods described in the literature.

2.1 General Principle

In general, Local Search Methods for minimization problems proceed according to the principle depicted in Fig. 3. For a TSP each tour represents a solution of the problem, its length corresponds to the objective function value. Different ways of specifying the modules (in Fig. 3 highlighted in italics) give rise to different types of Local Search Methods.

The *initial solution* may be chosen randomly or generated by means of a constructive method. The *neighbourhood* of the current solution can be considered as the set of all solutions, which can be accessed from the current one by a specific "minor" operation. A 2-opt move, for example, is a typical operation of this kind (Fig. 4). When applied to a TSP, two non-adjacent edges of the current tour/solution are replaced by two new - uniquely determined - ones (pairwise exchange of edges) in such a way that a new tour is obtained. Thus, the neighbourhood of a tour/solution can be defined as the set of tours (then also called neighbour solutions) resulting from all the 2-opt moves feasible for this tour. Likewise, 3-opt moves, 4-opt moves, etc., can be defined.

begin
  choose an *initial solution* `initial_sol;`
  `current_sol := initial_sol;`
  repeat
    according to a *selection rule* choose a neighbour solution
      `neighb_sol` from the *neighbourhood* of `current_sol;`
    compute the corresponding change in the objective function value:
      `delta_z := z(neighb_sol) - z(current_sol);`
    determine the value `accept` of the *acceptance criterion* for
      `neighb_sol;`
    if `(accept =` true) **then**
      `current_sol := neighb_sol;`
      keep track of best solution so far;
    endif
  until (*stopping criterion* is fulfilled);
end

Fig. 3: General principle of Local Search Methods

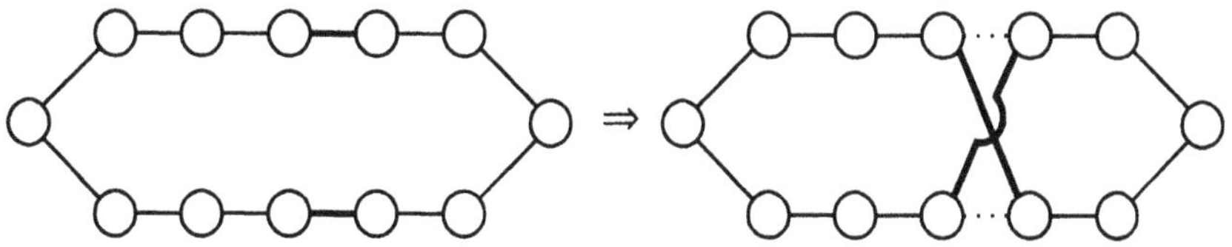

Fig. 4: 2-opt move

Various rules can be specified for the selection of a solution from the neighbourhood of the current solution. Among other options, the *selection rule* may determine to choose the first or the best solution from it or from a specific subset. Also, the rule may consist of a random choice.

Whether or not a neighbourhood solution is accepted as the new current solution is usually decided with respect to the corresponding change in the objective function value. Traditionally, a solution only gets accepted if it improves the objective function value. New Local Search Methods also allow the objective function value to deteriorate. The *acceptance criterion* can be a deterministic or a stochastic one. In the latter case, inferior solutions get accepted with a certain probability.

An (artificial) *stopping criterion* is necessary for methods, which allow an inferior solution to be chosen as a new current solution. Artificial stopping criteria are also used in order to restrict the computing times.

2.2 Classic and Modern Local Search Methods

In this section the authors show how specific Local Search Methods can be deduced from the general principal presented above (also see Aarts/Lenstra 1997 and Pirlot 1996).

- **(Classic) Descent Method (DM)**

  A solution from the neighbourhood of the current solution only gets accepted if it represents an improvement, i.e. its objective function value is smaller than that of the current one. The procedure terminates automatically when a neighbourhood has been searched completely without having identified a superior solution.

The disadvantage of the Descent Method lies in the fact that the current solution cannot be improved if the corresponding neighbourhood does not contain a better solution. The method gets stuck in a local minimum. Modern Local Search Methods try to avoid this trap by accepting inferior solutions as new current solutions, too.

- **Simulated Annealing (SA)**

  (Aarts/Korst/van Laarhoven 1997, Dowsland 1993, Eglese 1990) Simulated Annealing accepts solutions inferior to the current one with a certain probability. The value of the acceptance parameter `accept` is determined as depicted in Fig. 5. `random(0,1)` is a random variable uniformly distributed over the interval [0,1]. Thus, Simulated Annealing will accept an inferior solution with probability `exp(-delta_z/TEMP)` dependent on the size of the change in the objective function value `delta_z` and on a parameter `TEMP`, called *temperature*. Initially, a high temperature is chosen which means that almost every solution, including those causing a deterioration in the objective function value, will replace the current one. In the course of running the algorithm, the probability of accepting a solution inferior to the current one is slowly decreased by reducing the temperature (according to a certain "cooling" scheme). Finally, hardly any inferior solution will be accepted any more and the procedure becomes more or less identical with the Descent Method. Because the temperature usually does not assume the value zero, the method is aborted if no solution has been accepted "for a long time".

```
if (delta_z ≤ 0) then
      accept := true;
else
      if (random(0,1) < exp(-delta_z/TEMP)) then
         accept := true;
      endif
endif
```

Fig. 5: Acceptance of a neighbour solution in Simulated Annealing

A disadvantage of Simulated Annealing has to be seen in the fact that both a random number and the value of the exponential function for `-delta_z/TEMP` have to be determined for each solution which is inferior to the current one. This will make the algorithm time-consuming for problems in which a large number of neighbour solutions have to be evaluated. Consequently, in order to reduce the computing times, in Threshold Accepting and the Great Deluge-Method the decision on whether a neighbour solution should be accepted or not is made deterministically. From this point of view, they can be interpreted as deterministic variants of Simulated Annealing.

- **Threshold Accepting (TA)**

(Dueck/Scheuer 1990, Dueck/Scheuer/Wallmeier 1993) In Threshold Accepting a neighbour solution replaces the current one if the corresponding change in the objective function value `delta_z` is smaller then a threshold of acceptance `THRES` (`THRES` > 0). Thus, improvements get always accepted, deteriorations only as long as `delta_z` is smaller than the value of the threshold. Again, `THRES` is a parameter, which is slowly reduced in the course of running the algorithm, and for `THRES` = 0 Threshold Accepting is identical with the Descent Method. The method is terminated artificially if there has been no improvement "for a long time" for a given value of `THRES`.

- **Great Deluge-Method (GD)**

(Dueck 1993, Dueck/Scheuer/Wallmeier 1993) The Great Deluge-Method is very similar to Threshold Accepting, apart from the definition of the acceptance criterion. Here, the objective function value `z(neighb_sol)` of the neighbour solution is compared directly to the value of a parameter `WATER`, also called "water level". `WATER` serves the same purpose as `TEMP` in Simulated Annealing and `THRES` in Threshold Accepting, i.e. it controls whether an inferior solution should be accepted as a new current solution or not. Similarly, `WATER` is reduced over time as the algorithm proceeds.

- **(Short Term) Tabu Search (TS)**

(Glover 1989, p. 192; for a more general description see Glover/Laguna 1997) Starting from the current solution, Tabu Search always tries to proceed in the best possible way, i.e. to proceed to a neighbour solution which leads to the largest improvement, or, if no improvement can be achieved, to the least deterioration of the objective function value. Special features of the method prevent the algorithm from returning to solutions visited immediately before, in particular solutions, which represent local minima. In order to do so, certain solution properties are declared "tabu" for a pre-specified number of iterations. Generally, a solution which has (one of) these properties cannot be selected as a new current solution. However, the tabu status is suspended if this solution represents the best one found so far. Whether a neighbour solution is tabu or not, can be checked against a so-called "tabu list" which contains all properties (tabu criteria) currently active. The tabu list can be considered as a parameter of the method, which has to be administered in the course of application. The algorithm has to be terminated artificially, usually after a certain number of solutions have been generated.

3 Test Design

3.1 Implementations of Local Search Methods

An implementation of the described methods still requires their parameters to be specified. The tuning of the parameters is a critical procedure because solution quality and computational requirements are strongly dependent on the values chosen. Therefore, pre-tests have been carried out in order to determine the best possible parameter values. Special care has been taken of the fact that the final solutions have to be provided in a limited amount of time.

3.1.1 Problem-Specific Parameters

The first parameter all methods have in common is the determination of the initial solution. Several construction methods (Next Best, Nearest Insertion, Convex Hull & Nearest Insertion, CCA, Savings; cf. Golden/Stewart 1985, Reinelt 1994) were tested. In general, satisfactory results were achieved for the Next Best (Nearest Neighbour) Method, which was chosen for implementation. However, it was also found that in some cases better solutions could be generated by specific combinations of construction and improvement methods (see comments below).

The solution quality of Local Search Methods usually improves with the number of edges considered for an exchange. On the other hand, also the computing times increase dramatically when, instead of a pairwise exchange of edges, 3-opt or 4-opt moves are introduced. With respect to the fact that the production control problem under discussion requires to solve quite large problems, all our implementations of Local Search Methods carry out 2-opt moves only.

3.1.2 Generic Parameters

For the classic Descent Method, Simulated Annealing, Threshold Accepting and the Great Deluge-Method it has to be determined according to which sequence the solutions are to be selected from the current neighbourhood. Here, the 2-opt moves, which are feasible for the current tour, are checked in the natural order, i.e. exchanges of edges no. 1 and no. 3, no. 1 and no. 4, ..., are considered first, then those of edges no. 2 and no. 4, no. 2 and no. 5, etc. A solution gets immediately accepted as the new current solution if the acceptance criterion is satisfied. After the exchange has been carried out, the generation of new neighbour solutions proceed from the corresponding position.

The successive generation of neighbour solutions is quite common for the classic Descent Method, but not necessarily for Simulated Annealing. *Dowsland* (1993), for example, suggests to select the neighbour solutions randomly from the current neighbourhood, instead. However, our pre-tests indicated that a random selection does not necessarily improve the solution quality, neither for Simulated Annealing, Threshold Accepting, nor for the Great Deluge-Method.

A large number of variants have been described in the literature for the specification of the parameters (start temperature, cooling scheme, stopping criterion; see Connolly 1990, pp. 95ff. or Dowsland 1993, pp. 44ff.) of Simulated Annealing. The pre-tests showed that a start value TEMP(0) = 100 for the temperature and a reduction factor RF = 0.995 gained good results. The temperature is reduced to 0.995 times of its current value (i.e. TEMP(k+1) = TEMP(k)·0.995) after 100·n neighbour solutions have been checked (successfully or not) at the present temperature, or, otherwise, after 10·n neighbour solutions have been accepted as new current solutions (n: problem size; number of stitch points/nodes of the TSP). The procedure terminates if 100·n neighbour solutions have been checked for a given temperature without having accepted one of it.

In a similar way are the parameters THRES of Threshold Accepting and WATER of the Great Deluge-Method handled. The start value for THRES was found to work satisfactory if it was set to 0.15 times the length of the initial tour and combined with a reduction factor RF = 0.99. For the Great Deluge-Method the start value of the water level was set to 1.2 times the length of the initial tour. The reduction of the water level follows a scheme with a constant step size:

WATER(k+1) = WATER(k) − 25 (dimensions denoted in mm). Both methods terminate by application of the same artificial stopping criterion as in Simulated Annealing.

Tabu Search requires to specify the tabu criterion (tabu criteria), the (maximum) length of the tabu list, and the stopping criterion. For doing so, the authors have tried to follow the ideas which have been presented in the literature. *Knox* (1994) builds a tabu list from those edges which are eliminated when a new tour replaces the previous one. If such an edge is not on the list yet, it is appended to it. At the beginning the tabu list is empty. It is filled up successively until it has reached its maximum length. After that, for every new edge which has to be appended to the list, another one is removed from the top. A 2-opt move becomes tabu if it requires the introduction of two edges from the list. According to the results from numerical experiments with relatively small TSPs (the largest problem instance consisted of n = 105 nodes), *Knox* (1994, p. 872) suggests to limit the length of the tabu list to TLIST = 3·n and the number of exchanges to MOVES = $0.0003 \cdot n^4$. Furthermore, he recommends to start the procedure from several randomly generated initial solutions (diversification). These suggestions, however, proved completely inadequate for the TSPs to be solved here. For small instances the computing times turned out to be totally unacceptable, while the objective function values of the solutions were significantly worse than those provided by the other methods. Therefore, our implementation does not include a diversification phase. Instead, like in the other methods, it starts with a solution generated by the Next Best Method. Of several parameter combinations which have been tested only `TLIST` = n and `MOVES` = 2·n gained acceptable results.

3.1.3 Implementation Requirements

With respect to implementation requirements (determination of parameter values, in the first place) the methods under discussion could be divided into three classes. The Descent Method is the least demanding one and constitutes the first class. Simulated Annealing, Threshold Accepting and the Great Deluge-Method belong to the second class. They require to set three main parameters each (namely start temperature, initial threshold of acceptance, or water level; reduction scheme; stopping criterion). The insignificant sensitivity to variations of parameter values and initial solutions made it easy to identify suitable parameter combinations. This corresponds to the experience reported by the developers of Threshold Accepting and the Great Deluge-Method, *Dueck* and *Scheuer* (1990). They point out that usually relatively straightforward parameter combinations are sufficient in order to obtain good solutions. Their claim, however, that adjusting the parameters of Threshold Accepting and of the Great Deluge-Method is far less demanding than for Simulated Annealing could not be verified. Tabu Search, finally, represents the third class which is the most demanding one in terms of implementation requirements. The determination of suitable parameter values turned out to be rather difficult and time-consuming. Among other reasons this was due to the fact that the parameter values suggested in the literature did not turn out to be helpful at all.

3.2 Test Problems

In order to evaluate our implementations of the Local Search Methods, the 20 largest TSPs of a typical working day have been extracted from the NC-programs which the cutting software had provided for the laser cutting systems. This set of test problems covers a large variety of problem sizes and types. The number of nodes/stitch points varies between n = 58 and n = 461. For some problem instances the distribution of stitch points on the metal sheet looks rather unstructured while for other instances it appears to follow certain patterns. Furthermore, there are instances for which the points are distributed almost evenly over the cutting pattern, while they seem to concentrate in one or several spots for others. With respect to these properties we conclude that the problem instances chosen as test problems have to be looked upon as non trivial ones. (More information on the problem instances and some examples are available in Wäscher/Heuer/Reschke/Schwerin 1997.)

3.3 Determination of Solution Quality

The solution quality of an algorithm is usually expressed by the deviation of the objective function value from a reference point. *Stefan Thienel*, University of Cologne, was so kind to solve the test problem instances for us with codes developed by him (cf. Naddef/Thienel 1998a, 1998b). He managed to solve all test problems to an optimum, thus all errors claimed below represent deviations from the optimal objective function value.

3.4 Encoding and Hardware

Tabu Search has been implemented in C++ using the Watcom Compiler (version 10.0), the tests have been run under OS/2 Warp 3. All other methods have been programmed in Borland PASCAL 7.0. The experiments were executed under Windows 95 on a PC with an INTEL 90 processor and 16 MB RAM.

4 Test Results

The results from the numerical experiments are summarized in Table 1. The good solution quality of all methods catches instant attention. As expected, the Descent Method came out last. However, considering that implementation of this method was fast and did not bring about any difficulties, the average relative error of 4.93 percent appears to be acceptable.

Simulated Annealing provided the best results. The total relative error amounted to about one percent, and the largest deviation from the optimum was 2.90 percent, observed for instance no. 90. No other method came close to these results. In 18 out of 20 cases Simulated Annealing generated the best solution, of which five were optimal. Also worth noting is the extraordinary stability of the solution quality when solutions others than those from the Next Best-Method are taken as a basis. When Simulated Annealing was applied to solutions from Farthest Insertion, Convex Hull & Farthest Insertion, or CCA, almost the same results – in terms of the total relative error - were obtained (results not documented here). Starting from solutions provided by the Savings Method provided slightly better results (total relative error: 0.90 percent), and even for randomly generated initial solutions the error turned out to be only marginally larger than one percent. On the other hand, computing times were considerably larger than those of Threshold Accepting and the Great Deluge-Method, even though far from being critical with respect to the time which is available on the shop floor for solving such problems.

The solution quality of Threshold Accepting and the Great Deluge-Method has proven to be significantly worse than that of Simulated Annealing. The total relative error amounted to 2.17 (TA) and 2.57 (GD) percent, the maximal relative deviation 4.98 (TA) and 6.17 (GD) percent, respectively. Again, the results were found very stable for different initial solutions. Computing times were shorter for Threshold Accepting than for the Great Deluge-Method. This suggests that the gap between the solution quality of the two methods would diminish if the same computing times were adopted for the Great Deluge-Method (by a suitable selection of values for the parameters). Over all, the computing times of both Threshold Accepting and the Great Deluge-Method were significantly shorter than those of Simulated Annealing, however, they seem to grow faster with an increase in the size of the problems. For the largest problem instances, Threshold Accepting already required more computing time than Simulated Annealing but also provided an inferior solution.

Table 1: Results from numerical experiments

problem #	problem size n	optimal length [m]	Method														
			Descent Method			Simulated Annealing			Threshold Accepting			Great Deluge			Tabu Search		
			length [m]	error [%]	time [s]	length [m]	error [%]	time [s]	length [m]	error [%]	time [s]	length [m]	error [%]	time [s]	length [m]	error [%]	time [s]
20	461	43,34	45,25	4,41	5,76	44,58	2,86	633,51	45,49	4,98	721,06	46,01	6,17	518,61	44,13	1,84	8024,90
6	257	18,50	19,73	6,66	1,54	18,71	1,13	549,26	18,93	2,33	361,47	19,01	2,75	191,64	18,88	2,02	1395,00
90	176	12,51	13,03	4,22	0,77	12,87	2,90	473,13	13,08	4,56	250,57	13,13	5,00	62,67	12,65	1,19	443,94
62	151	18,92	19,45	2,80	0,60	19,15	1,21	276,77	19,51	3,11	171,32	19,25	1,75	86,34	19,25	1,74	282,13
98	137	19,21	20,83	8,41	0,77	19,25	0,22	296,76	19,82	3,16	145,61	19,97	3,93	87,93	19,37	0,81	209,94
87	133	15,34	15,75	2,68	0,60	15,46	0,79	188,01	15,65	2,02	137,48	15,59	1,67	44,43	15,67	2,16	191,25
35	127	13,93	14,89	6,89	0,77	13,95	0,15	209,59	14,06	0,92	124,18	14,18	1,83	46,58	14,55	4,44	165,66
50	110	8,68	9,29	7,02	0,27	8,68	0,03	206,47	8,69	0,07	92,27	8,73	0,52	40,59	8,77	1,06	107,62
72	108	11,96	12,72	6,36	0,22	12,10	1,12	245,85	12,33	3,11	118,69	12,15	1,60	49,05	12,17	1,72	101,56
40	97	10,46	10,89	4,14	0,17	10,46	0,00	138,91	10,46	0,00	102,22	10,52	0,54	20,77	10,53	0,69	73,75
13	93	14,84	15,57	4,94	0,22	15,01	1,16	137,97	15,04	1,34	87,88	15,34	3,38	48,83	15,13	1,96	64,69
83	93	10,65	11,42	7,24	0,16	10,72	0,64	168,84	10,83	1,68	93,87	10,95	2,85	25,16	11,34	6,52	64,72
45	86	11,32	11,56	2,09	0,22	11,49	1,47	209,48	11,49	1,49	104,86	11,45	1,14	31,53	11,36	0,32	51,28
53	81	3,75	3,82	1,78	0,17	3,75	0,00	143,79	3,77	0,37	68,27	3,82	1,71	4,95	3,81	1,50	42,81
39	76	13,97	14,32	2,49	0,05	14,00	0,17	166,48	14,16	1,29	82,01	14,16	1,36	22,96	14,29	2,29	35,57
18	72	12,17	13,56	11,49	0,10	12,17	0,00	128,36	12,17	0,00	80,25	12,18	0,10	29,83	13,02	7,01	29,97
68	66	12,89	13,29	3,07	0,11	12,92	0,21	149,35	13,03	1,07	75,41	13,20	2,35	19,45	13,02	0,97	22,94
37	58	13,43	13,85	3,12	0,06	13,49	0,46	126,55	13,51	0,64	54,65	13,52	0,66	15,38	13,67	1,76	15,50
48	58	10,17	10,83	6,48	0,06	10,17	0,00	62,45	10,21	0,41	41,08	10,22	0,47	20,22	10,31	1,33	15,56
91	58	9,25	9,29	0,48	0,06	9,25	0,00	63,93	9,25	0,00	42,02	9,25	0,00	12,36	9,26	0,14	15,50
total		285,28	299,35		12,68	288,17		4575,46	291,46		2955,17	292,62		1379,28	291,17		11354,29
total error [%]				4,93			1,01			2,17			2,57			2,06	
minimal error [%]				0,48			0,00			0,00			0,00			0,14	
maximal error [%]				11,49			2,90			4,98			6,17			7,01	

The average solution quality of Tabu Search is similar to that of Threshold Accepting (total relative error: 2.06 percent), even though the largest error was observed at 7.01 percent for instance no. 18. In contrast to the methods discussed so far, Tabu Search reacted rather sensitive to parameter variations and to different initial solutions. Problematic are the long computing times. They are acceptable for instances with less than 200 nodes/stitch points (for which they are even shorter than the times of Simulated Annealing), but they become prohibitive for large ones (particularly for the two largest problem instances no. 6 and no. 20, respectively). The strong increase in the computing times can be attributed to the fact that Tabu Search always tries to carry out the best possible move (which is not tabu). This means that the set of possible 2-opt moves has to be searched completely at each iteration, which requires $O(n^2)$ steps.

5 Conclusions

According to the results discussed above, Simulated Annealing had to be considered as the best of the methods under discussion. It could be implemented relatively easily, in particular because the determination of suitable parameter values was rather straightforward. The question which then did arise was what economic benefits could be achieved if it was used in the cutting shop. In Table 2 the objective function values of the solutions provided by the software package for the determination of cutting patterns and by Simulated Annealing are compared to each other. It can be seen that the application of Simulated Annealing brings about significant improvements (between 19.24 and 78.00 percent; 30.35 percent on the average). More important, however, is the question how the reduction of the distances to be travelled by the laser translates into savings of production times. It could be demonstrated that the average proportion of the auxiliary times could be reduced from almost 34 percent to approximately 25 percent. The corresponding capacity effect was large enough to reduce the proposed investment by one laser system.

Table 2: Improvements brought about by Simulated Annealing

problem #	problem size n	solution provided by cutting software		solution provided by Simulated Annealing		improvement	
		length [m]	error [%]	length [m]	error [%]	absolut [m]	relative [%]
20	461	53,15	22,65	44,58	2,86	8,58	19,24
6	257	26,90	45,38	18,71	1,13	8,19	43,75
90	176	15,70	25,54	12,87	2,90	2,83	22,01
62	151	26,11	38,03	19,15	1,21	6,96	36,37
98	137	27,24	41,82	19,25	0,22	7,99	41,51
87	133	23,50	53,21	15,46	0,79	8,04	52,01
35	127	20,53	47,39	13,95	0,15	6,58	47,17
50	110	13,04	50,25	8,68	0,03	4,36	50,21
72	108	20,47	71,11	12,10	1,12	8,37	69,22
40	97	14,95	42,90	10,46	0,00	4,49	42,90
13	93	19,39	30,67	15,01	1,16	4,38	29,17
83	93	15,14	42,21	10,72	0,64	4,43	41,31
45	86	15,99	41,24	11,49	1,47	4,50	39,19
53	81	5,39	43,56	3,75	0,00	1,64	43,56
39	76	24,88	78,04	14,00	0,17	10,88	77,74
18	72	21,66	78,00	12,17	0,00	9,49	78,00
68	66	19,89	54,25	12,92	0,21	6,97	53,93
37	58	20,84	55,18	13,49	0,46	7,35	54,46
48	58	16,79	65,07	10,17	0,00	6,62	65,07
91	58	12,18	31,78	9,25	0,00	2,94	31,78
total		413,74		288,17		125,57	30,35
total error [%]			45,03		1,01		
minimal error [%]			22,65		0,00		
maximal error [%]			78,04		2,90		
minimal improvement [%]							19,24
maximal improvement [%]							78,00

Acknowledgements

The authors would like to thank *Alexander Dahlke* for extracting the problem data from the NC programs. Special thanks goes to *Stefan Thienel* who provided the optimal solutions for the test problems.

References

Aarts, E.H.L.; Korst, J.; van Laarhoven, P.J.M. (1997): Simulated Annealing. *Local Search in Combinatorial Optimization* (Aarts, E.H.L.; Lenstra, J.K.; eds.). Chichester et al., 91-120

Aarts, E.H.L.; Lenstra, J.K. (eds.) (1997): Local Search in Combinatorial Optimization. Chichester et al.

Chatterjee, S.; Carrera, C.; Lynch, L.A. (1996): Genetic Algorithms and Traveling Salesman Problems. *European Journal of Operational Research* 93, 490-510

Colorni, A.; Dorigo, M.; Maniezzo, V. (1991): Distributed Optimization by Ant Colonies. *Proceedings of ECAL'91 - European Conference on Artificial Life* (Varela, F.J.; Bourgnine, P.; eds.). Paris, 134-142

Connolly, D.T. (1990): An Improved Annealing Scheme for the QAP. *European Journal of Operational Research* 46, 93-100

Dowsland, K.A. (1993): Simulated Annealing. *Modern Heuristic Techniques for Combinatorial Problems* (Reeves, C.R.; ed.). Oxford, 20-69

Dowsland, K.A. (1996): Genetic Algorithms - A Tool for OR? *Journal of the Operational Research Society* 47, 550-561

Dueck, G. (1993): New Optimization Heuristics - The Great Deluge Algorithm and the Record-to-Record Travel. *Journal of Computational Physics* 104, 86-92

Dueck, G.; Scheuer, T. (1990): Threshold Accepting: A General Purpose Optimization Algorithm Appearing Superior to Simulated Annealing. *Journal of Computational Physics* 90, 161-175

Dueck, G.; Scheuer, T.; Wallmeier, H.-M. (1993): Toleranzschwelle und Sintflut: Neue Ideen zur Optimierung. *Spektrum der Wissenschaft*, No. 3 (March), 42-51

Eglese, R.W. (1990): Simulated Annealing: A Tool for Operational Research. *European Journal of Operational Research* 46, 271-281

Garey, M.R.; Johnson, D.S. (1979): Computers and Intractability: A Guide to the Theory of NP-completeness. San Francisco

Glover, F. (1989): Tabu Search - Part I. *ORSA Journal on Computing* 1, 190-206

Glover, F.; Laguna, M. (1997): Tabu Search. Boston, Dordrecht, London

Goldberg, D.E. (1989): Genetic Algorithms in Search, Optimization and Machine Learning. Reading

Golden, B.L.; Stewart, W.R. (1985): Empirical Analysis of Heuristics. *The Traveling Salesman Problem - A Guided Tour Through Combinatorial Optimization* (Lawler, E.L. et al.; eds.). Chichester et al., 207-249

Knox, J. (1994): Tabu Search Performance on the Symmetric Traveling Salesman Problem. *Computers and Operations Research* 21, 867-876

Michalewicz, Z. (1992): Genetic Algorithms + Data Structures = Evolution Programs. 2nd ed., Berlin et al.

Mühlenbein, H. (1997): Genetic Algorithms. *Local Search in Combinatorial Optimization* (Aarts, E.H.L.; Lenstra, J.K.; eds.). Chichester et al., 137-171

Naddef, D.; Thienel, S. (1998a): Efficient separation routines for the symmetric travelling salesman problem I: general tools and comb separation. Technical Report, Universität zu Köln

Naddef, D.; Thienel, S. (1998a): Efficient separation routines for the symmetric travelling salesman problem II: separating multi-handle inequalities. Technical Report, Universität zu Köln

Or, I. (1976): Traveling Salesman-Type Combinatorial Problems and their Relation to the Logistics of Regional Blood Baking. Ph.D. Thesis, Northwestern University, Evanston, IL

Osman, I.H.; Kelly, J.P. (1996): Meta Heuristics - An Overview. *Meta Heuristics - Theory and Applications* (Osman, I.H.; Kelly, J.P.; eds.). Boston, London, Dordrecht, 1-21

Pesch, E.; Voß, S. (eds.) (1995): Special Issue: Applied Local Search. *Operations Research-Spektrum* 17, No. 3/4

Peterson, C.; Söderberg, B. (1997): Artifical Neural Networks. *Local Search in Combinatorial Optimization* (Aarts, E.H.L.; Lenstra, J.K.; eds.). Chichester et al., 173-213

Pirlot, M. (1996): General local search methods. *European Journal of Operational Research* 92, 493-511

Potvin, J.-Y. (1993): The Traveling Salesman Problem: A Neural Network Perspective. *ORSA Journal on Computing* 5, 328-348

Reinelt, G. (1994): The Traveling Salesman - Computational Solutions for TSP Applications. Berlin et al.

Wäscher, G. (1998): Local Search. *Das Wirtschaftsstudium* 27, 1299-1307

Wäscher, G.; Heuer, J.; Reschke, V.; Schwerin, P. (1997): Local Search-Verfahren für ein Traveling Salesman-Problem in der Produktionssteuerung. *Betriebswirtschaftliche Diskussionsbeiträge Nr. 97/14,* Martin-Luther-Universität Halle-Wittenberg, Wirtschaftswissenschaftliche Fakultät, Halle (Saale)

Transportation Problems *

Rainer E. Burkard
Department of Mathematics
University of Technology, Graz, Austria.

Abstract

Starting from historical remarks on transportation problems and early applications we discuss the various connections between Monge matrices and transportation problems. In particular, we survey time transportation problems, algebraic transportation problems with applications in scheduling theory and minimax flow transportation problems. Finally we report on a recent case study for a large capacitated facility location model.

Keywords:
Transportation problem, Monge matrix, facility location

1 Historic remarks on the classical transportation problem

The classical transportation problem is attributed to Hitchcock [16] who published the article *The distribution of a product from several sources to numerous localities* in the Journal of Mathematics and Physics in 1941. Around the same time Kantorovich [19] published his seminal study on mathematical methods in the organization and planning of production where he also addressed transportation problems. Today we describe the classical transportation model in the following way: Let m production centers be given which produce a_i, $i = 1, 2, ..., m$, units of a good. Further let n consumers be given which need a supply of b_j, $j = 1, 2, ..., n$, units of the good. For sake of simplicity we assume that

$$\sum_{i=1}^{m} a_i = \sum_{j=1}^{n} b_j.$$

The good has to be transported from the factories to the consumers. The

*This research has been supported by the Spezialforschungsbereich F 003 "Optimierung und Kontrolle", Projektbereich Diskrete Optimierung.

cost to transport one unit from factory i to customer j is given by c_{ij}. We ask now in which way the good is to be distributed such that the total transportation costs are minimum?

One of the first practical applications of this model is reported by Knödel [21]. In the fifties the author undertook a case study which concerned the distribution of sugar from seven sugar plants to 300 warehouses in Austria and which achieved a reduction of 10% compared with the transportation plan in use. Thus the original annual transportation costs of 22,000.000 Austrian Schilling were cut and the costs for modelling and computation were amortized within ten days. A similar study was performed for the Austrian salt industry. There the gain was not so high, since due to the simpler structure of the model the transportation plan in use was already closer to optimality. Again, the modelling and computation costs were only a small fraction of the yearly achievable gain.

Hitchcock and Kantorovich, however, were not the first who realized the importance of transportation problems. As Schrijver [22] found out recently, A. Tolstoĭ [24] published a study on methods for finding the minimum total kilometrage for cargo transportation planning already in 1930. Tolstoĭ considers among others the transportation problem for the case of only two production sites. He observes that in this case one can order the customers with respect to the difference between the distances to the two production sites. The first site supplies the nearer customers until its supply is used up. The other site supplies the remaining customers. Here two remarks are in order: first, this rule is independent of the supplies and demands and secondly, it resembles very much an observation made by the French geometer and engineer Monge in 1781: If unit quantities have to be transported from locations P_1 and Q_1 to locations P_2 and Q_2 in such a way as to minimize the total distance traveled, then the route from P_1 and the route from Q_1 must not intersect. This follows from the quadrangle inequality for convex quadrangles.

In 1961 Alan J. Hoffman [18] used this observation of Monge to introduce so-called *Monge properties for matrices*. Hoffman showed that the Hitchcock transportation problem can be solved by a very simple greedy approach if its underlying cost matrix satisfies the so-called *Monge property*:

$$c_{ij} + c_{rs} \leq c_{is} + c_{rj} \qquad \text{for all } 1 \leq i < r \leq m, \ 1 \leq j < s \leq n. \qquad (1)$$

A matrix fulfilling (1) is called a *Monge matrix*. In the next section we discuss transportation problems whose cost matrix fulfills the Monge property.

2 Transportation problems and the Monge property

Let the classical *Hitchcock transportation problem* (TP) be given:

$$\min \quad \sum_{i=1}^{m}\sum_{j=1}^{n} c_{ij}x_{ij} \tag{2}$$

$$\text{s.t.} \quad \sum_{j=1}^{n} x_{ij} = a_i \qquad \text{for all } i = 1,\dots,m, \tag{3}$$

$$\sum_{i=1}^{m} x_{ij} = b_j \qquad \text{for all } j = 1,\dots,n, \tag{4}$$

$$x_{ij} \geq 0 \qquad \text{for all } i,j. \tag{5}$$

A method for finding a feasible solution of the TP is the *north-west corner rule:* Start with the first factory and try to fulfill the demands of customers $1, 2, \ldots$ until the supply of this factory is used up. Then proceed with the second factory and so on.

It follows from a more general result of Hoffman [18] that this rule generates an optimal solution of TP, if the cost matrix C is a Monge matrix. Thus the transportation problem can be solved in $O(m+n)$ time when we know that matrix C has the Monge property. Indeed, the following theorem holds.

Theorem 2.1 The north-west corner rule produces an optimal solution of (TP) for all supply and demand vectors a and b with $\sum_{i=1}^{m} a_i = \sum_{j=1}^{n} b_j$ if and only if the cost matrix C is a Monge matrix.
Let us illustrate this approach by the following example.

Example. We consider 3 facilities (sources) which produce

$$a_1 = 10, \quad a_2 = 20, \quad a_3 = 20$$

units of a good. Further we have 5 customers (destinations) which need

$$b_1 = 7, \;\; b_2 = 8, \;\; b_3 = 12, \;\; b_4 = 10, \;\; b_5 = 13$$

units. The transportation costs are given by the following matrix C:

$$C = \begin{pmatrix} 8 & 7 & 11 & 15 & 10 \\ 9 & 7 & 10 & 13 & 8 \\ 8 & 1 & 4 & 6 & 1 \end{pmatrix}.$$

It can easily be checked that this matrix fulfills the Monge property (1). Using the north-west corner rule we get the following optimal solution of TP

$$X^* = \begin{pmatrix} 7 & 3 & - & - & - \\ - & 5 & 12 & 3 & - \\ - & - & - & 7 & 13 \end{pmatrix}.$$

Thus, facility 1 will supply 7 units to customer 1, and 3 units to customer 2, facility 2 supplies customers 2, 3 and 4 and facility 3 supplies customers 4 and 5. ∎

If we number the facilities (and customers) in the above example differently from 1, 2, 3, e.g. as 2, 1, 3, then the corresponding matrix would not fulfill the Monge property. Thus the matrix C being Monge depends on a suitable numbering of the rows and columns of matrix C. This leads to the following definition. We say matrix $C = (c_{ij})$ is a *permuted Monge matrix* if there exists a permutation φ of the rows of C and a permutation ψ of the columns of C such that $C_{\varphi,\psi} = (c_{\varphi(i),\psi(j)})$ is a Monge matrix. This definition immediately leads to the question whether or not we can efficiently recognize that a matrix C is a permuted Monge matrix. This question has been answered by Deĭneko and Filonenko [10] who present an $O(mn + m \log m + n \log n)$ time algorithm which, given an $m \times n$ matrix C, either finds a pair of permutations (φ, ψ) such that $C_{\varphi,\psi}$ becomes a Monge matrix or proves that no such permutations exist. This algorithm together with many further results on Monge properties can be found in Burkard, Klinz and Rudolf [6].

Note that any $(2 \times n)$-matrix $C = (c_{ij})$ is a permuted Monge matrix: just order the columns j according to increasing values of $c_{1j} - c_{2j}$. This is exactly the way how Tolstoĭ [24] solved transportation problems with 2 sources. Adolphson and Thomas [1] showed that $2 \times n$ transportation problems can even be solved in linear time.

3 Time transportation problems

When we replace the sum objective function in the classical transportation problem

$$\sum_{i=1}^{m} \sum_{j=1}^{n} c_{ij} x_{ij}$$

by the objective function

$$\max_{x_{ij} > 0} c_{ij},$$

we get the so-called *time transportation problem.* The time transportation problem asks for a transportation plan which minimizes the time needed to ship all goods. Formally this problem can be stated as

$$\begin{array}{lll} \min & \max_{x_{ij}>0} c_{ij} & \\ \text{s.t.} & \sum_{j=1}^{n} x_{ij} = a_i & \text{for all } i = 1, \ldots, m, \end{array}$$

$$\sum_{i=1}^{m} x_{ij} = b_j \qquad \text{for all } \; j = 1, \dots, n,$$

$$x_{ij} \geq 0 \qquad \text{for all } \; i, j.$$

The time transportation problem was first studied by Hammer [15] and can be solved in various ways, in particular by a threshold method. A fast solution routine for time transportation problems has been published by Derigs and Zimmermann [9]. As in the case of the classical transportation problem one can ask if there exist specially structured matrices for which this problem can be solved faster than in the general case. And, indeed, if the matrix $C = (c_{ij})$ fulfills the so-called *bottleneck Monge* property

$$\max\{c_{ij}, c_{rs}\} \leq \max\{c_{is}, c_{rj}\} \qquad \text{for all } \; 1 \leq i < r \leq m, 1 \leq j < s \leq n,$$

then the time transportation problem can again be solved directly by the north-west corner rule. As in the case of the classical Monge property (1) one can ask whether there exists a permutation φ of the rows of C and a permutation ψ of the columns of C such that $C_{\varphi,\psi} = (c_{\varphi(i),\psi(j)})$ is a bottleneck Monge matrix. The recognition of permuted bottleneck Monge matrices is more difficult than in the sum case. Whereas permuted bottleneck Monge matrices with 0 and 1 entries can be recognized in linear time due to their staircase structure, general permuted bottleneck Monge matrices can be recognized in $O((n+m)nm)$ time, see Klinz, Rudolf and Woeginger [20].

Again it is easy to show that $(2 \times n)$-matrices are always permuted bottleneck Monge matrices, see Burkard [4]. In this case the permutations φ and *psi* can very easily be found. Hochbaum and Woeginger [17] showed that any time transportation problem with a fixed number of sources can be solved in linear time. Whether, however, their algorithm is practicable, may be questionable, since this algorithm considers all (exponentially many) subsets of sources explicitly.

4 Algebraic transportation problems

The classical transportation problem and the time transportation problem differ only in the form of their objective functions. Moreover, the solution routines for these problems show an amazing similarity. Thus the question arises: what is the mathematical structure behind these problems and their solution routines? An answer to this question has been given by the introduction of so-called *algebraic transportation problems*, see Burkard [2]. There an algebraic model is derived which comprises both, the classical transportation problem and the time transportation problem as well as several other types of transportation problems. The underlying algebraic structure is a totally ordered, commutative semigroup $(S, *, \preceq)$ with neutral element e. This means that the composition of two elements a and b of S is always defined and $a \preceq b$ implies $a * c \preceq b * c$ for all $c \in S$. Moreover, we require a reducibility axiom of the form

$$\text{If } a \preceq b, \text{ there exists an element } c \in S \text{ with } a * c = b.$$

The elements of the set S describe the transportation costs per unit. These unit costs have to be multiplied with the amount of the good shipped. Thus we define an outer composition $\Box : \mathbb{R} \times S \to S$ which is distributive and obeys $n \Box a = a^n = a * a * \ldots * a$ (n times) as well as

$$n \leq \alpha < n+1 \text{ implies } a^n \preceq \alpha \Box a \preceq a^n + 1 \text{ for } \alpha \in \mathbb{R},\ a \in S,\ n \in \mathbb{N}.$$

For the sake of simplicity we introduce the notation

$$[x \Box c] := (x_{11} \Box c_{11}) * (x_{12} \Box c_{12}) * \cdots * (x_{mn} \Box c_{mn}).$$

With this notation we can write the algebraic transportation problem as follows

$$\begin{array}{lll} \min & [x \Box c] & \\ \text{s.t.} & \sum_{j=1}^{n} x_{ij} = a_i & \text{for all } i = 1, \ldots, m, \\ & \sum_{i=1}^{m} x_{ij} = b_j & \text{for all } j = 1, \ldots, n, \\ & x_{ij} \geq 0 & \text{for all } i, j. \end{array}$$

In [2] a solution routine for algebraic transportation problems has been described. Burkard and Zimmermann [7] developped an improved method under slightly more special assumptions on the algebraic system $(S, *, \preceq)$.
By specifying the algebraic structure one obtains from this general model specific models, for example:

1. If $S = \mathbb{R}$, $*$ is the addition and $\Box$ is the multiplication of real numbers and if $\preceq$ is the usual order $\leq$ in the reals, then we get the classical transportation problem.

2. If $S = \mathbb{R}$, $\preceq$ is again the usual order $\leq$ in the reals, $a * b$ is $\max(a, b)$ and $\Box$ is defined by $x \Box a = a$ for $x > 0$ and $x \Box a = -\infty$ for $x = 0$, then we get the time transportation problem.

3. A lexicographical transportation problem is obtained by: $S = \mathbb{R}^n$, $*$ is the addition of vectors and $\Box$ is the multiplication of a vector with a scalar x. In this case $\preceq$ is the lexicographic order of vectors.

4. An interesting model is the so-called time-cost transportation problem which minimizes first the time needed to ship all goods and minimizes secondly under all time-minimal solutions the costs. This time-cost transportation problem can also be modeled within the framework of algebraic transportation problems, see e.g. [2].

We can also consider Monge properties within this algebraic framework. An $(m \times n)$ matrix $C = (c_{ij})$ with $c_{ij} \in S$ is called an *algebraic Monge matrix* if

$$c_{ij} * c_{rs} \leq c_{is} * c_{rj} \qquad \text{for all } 1 \leq i < r \leq m, \ 1 \leq j < s \leq n.$$

We get:

Theorem 4.1 ([6]) The north-west corner rule produces an optimal solution of the algebraic transportation problem for all supply and demand vectors a and b with $\sum_{i=1}^{m} a_i = \sum_{j=1}^{n} b_j$ if and only if the cost matrix C is an algebraic Monge matrix.

The problem of recognizing permuted algebraic Monge matrices is $\mathcal{NP}-$ hard in general, but simple in the case of matrices with only two rows.

Algebraic transportation problems can be used to bound the objective function value in certain machine scheduling problems see [3]. Let n jobs be given which are to be processed on m identical machines subject to precedence constraints in a non-preemptive way. Several different objective functions are considered in scheduling theory like the makespan (maximum completion time), the weighted sum of completion times of the jobs (which comprises the average completion time), the maximum lateness, the sum of total latenesses, the maximum tardiness and the average tardiness. All these objective functions can be modelled by means of the ordered semigroup introduced above: For every job i let $k_i(c_i)$ be a monotone cost function where c_i denotes the completion time of job i. We assume that $k_i(c_i)$takes values in S. The objective function of the scheduling problem can be written in the form

$$z(c_1, c_2, \ldots, c_n) := k_1(c_1) * k_2(c_2) * \cdots * k_n(c_n).$$

For example, set $S = (\mathbb{R}, +, \leq)$ and $k_i(c_i) := \alpha_i \cdot \max(0, c_i - d_i)$, where d_i is the due date of job i. This leads to the objective function which describes the weighted sum of tardinesses. If we consider the same functions $k_i(c_i)$ with respect to the system $S = (\mathbb{R}, \max, \leq)$ we model the maximum tardiness. In Burkard [3] it has been shown that by solving an algebraic transportation problem lower bounds on the objective function for the scheduling problem under consideration can be computed. These bounds are exact (i.e., equal to the optimal solution value of the scheduling problem) if there are no precedence constraints. In the important special case where the cost functions k_i

are monotone increasing, concave or convex and differ only by an additive constant in their argument, i.e., if

$$k_i(t) = k(t + p_i) \quad \text{for all jobs} \quad i,$$

then the cost matrix of the algebraic transportation problem fulfills the algebraic Monge property. In these cases the optimal solution of the algebraic transportation problem can easily be found by the north-west corner rule.

5 The transportation paradoxon

Let us now modify the classical transportation problem by requiring that the sources supply *at least* a_i units of the good and the customers need *at least* b_j units:

$$\begin{aligned}
\min \quad & \sum_{i=1}^{m}\sum_{j=1}^{n} c_{ij}x_{ij} & \\
\text{s.t.} \quad & \sum_{j=1}^{n} x_{ij} \geq a_i & \text{for all } i = 1, \ldots, m, \\
& \sum_{i=1}^{m} x_{ij} \geq b_j & \text{for all } j = 1, \ldots, n, \\
& x_{ij} \geq 0 & \text{for all } i, j.
\end{aligned}$$

This version of the classical transportation problem shows sometimes a strange behaviour, known as ***transportation paradox:*** The optimal solution can be improved by shipping more units than required ***(overshipments).*** This transportation paradox seems to have first been observed by Charnes and Klingman [8] and independently by Szwarc [23].

Another way to improve the optimal solution are so-called *reshipments* from the customers to the suppliers. The reshipment version of the transportation problem can be modelled in the following form:

$$\begin{aligned}
\min \quad & \sum_{i=1}^{m}\sum_{j=1}^{n} c_{ij}x_{ij} & \\
\text{s.t.} \quad & \sum_{j=1}^{n} x_{ij} = a_i & \text{for all } i = 1, \ldots, m, \\
& \sum_{i=1}^{m} x_{ij} = b_j & \text{for all } j = 1, \ldots, n, \\
& x_{ij} \in \mathbb{R} & \text{for all } i, j.
\end{aligned}$$

In a series of papers Finke [12, 13, 14] derived conditions for both the classical and for the time transportation problem which can be used to decide whether a given optimal solution can be improved by overshipments or reshipments.

In the following we briefly discuss the analoguous question for so-called minimax flow transportation problems. The exposition here follows the paper of Eiselt and Burkard [11]. The aim of minimax flow transportation problems is to minimize the maximum flow from a source to a sink, i.e.

$$\begin{aligned} \min \quad & \max x_{ij} \\ \text{s.t.} \quad & \sum_{j=1}^{n} x_{ij} = a_i \qquad \text{for all } i = 1, \ldots, m, \\ & \sum_{i=1}^{m} x_{ij} = b_j \qquad \text{for all } j = 1, \ldots, n, \\ & x_{ij} \geq 0 \qquad \text{for all } i, j. \end{aligned}$$

If we allow reshipments, i.e., if the flows are no longer restricted to source - destination pairs, but destinations can reroute goods, then we obtain the problem

$$\begin{aligned} \min \quad & \max |x_{ij}| \\ \text{s.t.} \quad & \sum_{j=1}^{n} x_{ij} = a_i \qquad \text{for all } i = 1, \ldots, m, \\ & \sum_{i=1}^{m} x_{ij} = b_j \qquad \text{for all } j = 1, \ldots, n, \\ & x_{ij} \in \mathbb{R} \qquad \text{for all } i, j. \end{aligned}$$

The overshipment version of the minimax transportation problem can be formulated as

$$\begin{aligned} \min \quad & \max x_{ij} \\ \text{s.t.} \quad & \sum_{j=1}^{n} x_{ij} \geq a_i \qquad \text{for all } i = 1, \ldots, m, \\ & \sum_{i=1}^{m} x_{ij} \geq b_j \qquad \text{for all } j = 1, \ldots, n, \\ & x_{ij} \geq 0 \qquad \text{for all } i, j. \end{aligned}$$

Let z_S, z_R, z_O denote the optimal objective function values of the standard minimax flow transportation problem, the reshipment version thereof and the overshipment version of this problem, respectively. The following small example shows the improvements which may be obtained by reshipments and overshipments:

Example. Consider three sources with supplies $a_1 = 33$, $a_2 = 33$ and $a_3 = 6$. Moreover we have three destinations with demands $b_1 = 33$, $b_2 = 33$ and $b_3 = 6$. The optimal solution of the standard minimax flow transportation problem has the form

	33	33	6
33	15	15	3
33	15	15	3
6	3	3	0

with $z_S = 15$. The optimal solution of the reshipment problem has the form

	33	33	6
33	12	12	9
33	12	12	9
6	9	9	−12

with $z_R = 12$. Finally, the optimal solution of the overshipment problem is

	33	33	6
33	11	11	11
33	11	11	11
22	11	11	0

with $z_O = 11$.

Since reshipment and overshipment problems cannot have worse solution values than the standard problem because they are relaxations of it, we have $z_S \geq \max\{z_R, z_O\}$. Secondly, the overshipment solution value cannot be worse than the value of the reshipment problem, since setting negative values in the reshipment solution to zero will yield a feasible solution of the overshipment problem. Thus we get

$$z_S \geq z_R \geq z_O.$$

In [11] is shown that the values z_S and z_R can be obtained from an explicit formula of the form

$$z = \max_{i,j} h_{ij},$$

where the values h_{ij} can be evaluated in constant time for any fixed i and j, provided some preprocessing is done which takes $O(m+n)$ time. Moreover, the matrix $H = (h_{ij})$ fulfills a Monge property of the form

$$h_{ij} + h_{rs} \geq h_{is} + h_{rj} \qquad \text{for all } 1 \leq i < r \leq m,\ 1 \leq j < s \leq n.$$

This fact can be exploited to obtain an $O(m+n)$ time algorithm for computing the optimal values z_S and z_R and an $O((m+n)^2)$ time algorithm for computing corresponding optimal transportation plans.

6 Location and transportation problems

An important model in the OR practice is the so-called *capacitated facility location model* which combines facility location with transportation. Let $\{1, 2, \ldots, m\}$ be a set of m possible sites for establishing new facilities or redimensioning already existing facilities. The facilities should serve n customers which need b_j, $j = 1, 2, \ldots, n$, units of a good. Opening a new facility or redimensioning an existing facility incurs costs d_i, $i = 1, 2, \ldots, m$. The facility at location i can supply at most a_i units of the good. Customer j needs b_j units. Finally, the unit transportation costs from location i to customer j are c_{ij}. The question underlying the capacitated facility location problem is then: If we want to open or redimension at most p facilities, where should they be located such that the installing and transportation costs become minimum?

This problem can be modeled as a (mixed-)integer linear program. Recently we performed a case study, see [5], for a large European group with around 10 production sites all over Europe and around 20 costumers (warehouses). The company produces around 1500 different products which were grouped into 300 product classes. The transportation costs involved the pure transportation costs per truck, customs clearance costs per shipment for every origin-destination pair (i, j), and different custom tariffs depending on the product k and the pait (i, j). These custom tariffs applied only for certain origin-destination pairs, and did not arise for shipments within the EU. Finally, transportation limitations occured concerning the maximum allowed weight of a truckload from i to j and concerning the maximum number of pallets allowed for a truck moving from i to j.

The basic model turned out to be a mixed-integer program with about 190000 variables among which there were around 2500 binary or integer variables. There were around 135000 constraints and 960000 nonzero entries in the coefficient matrix of the system. Since the current MIP-sovers cannot handle systems of this size, we solved the underlying linear program and used various rounding strategies to find feasible solutions. Within 48 hours of CPU time on a HP RISC7200 workstation with 1.5GB RAM the gap between the linear programming relaxation and the best feasible solution could be closed up to 5%. The overall costs of the obtained solution result in a saving of about 6-7% compared to the present solution implemented by the company.

References

[1] D.L. Adolphson and G.N. Thomas, A linear-time algorithm for a $2 \times n$ transportation problem. *SIAM J. Comput.* **6** 1977, 481–486.

[2] R.E. Burkard, A general Hungarian method for the algebraic transportation problem. *Discrete Math.* **22**, 1978, 219–232.

[3] R.E. Burkard, Über eine Anwendung algebraischer Transportprobleme bei Reihenfolgeproblemen. In *Numerische Methoden bei graphentheoretischen und kombinatorischen Problemen Vol.2* , (L. Collatz, G. Meinardus and W. Wetterling, eds.), Basel: Birkhäuser Verlag, 1979, pp. 22–36.

[4] R.E. Burkard, On the role of bottleneck Monge matrices in combinatorial optimization. *Operations Res. Letters* **17**, 1995, 53–56.

[5] R.E.Burkard and E. Çela, Optimal location of facilities involving a two stage production process. In preparation.

[6] R.E. Burkard, B. Klinz and R. Rudolf, Perspectives of Monge properties in optimization. *Discrete Applied Mathematics* **70**, 95–161, 1996.

[7] R.E. Burkard and U. Zimmermann, Weakly admissible transformations for solving algebraic assignment and transportation problems. *Math. Programming Study* **12**, 1980, 1–18.

[8] A. Charnes and D. Klingman, The more-for-less paradox in the distribution model. *Cah. Centre Etud. Rech. Oper.* **13**, 1971, 11–22.

[9] U. Derigs and U. Zimmermann, An augmenting path method for solving linear bottleneck transportation problems. *Computing* **22**, 1979, 1–15.

[10] V.G. Deĭneko and V.L. Filonenko, On the reconstruction of specially structured matrices. *Aktualnyje Problemy EVM i programmirovanije*, Dnepropetrovsk, DGU, 1979, (in Russian).

[11] H.A. Eiselt and R.E. Burkard, Reshipments and overshipments in transportation problems with minimax objective. *OR Spektrum* **13**, 1991, 133–140.

[12] G. Finke, A unified approach to reshipment, overshipment and postoptimization problems. In *Optimization Techniques, Lect. Notes in Control, Inform. Sci.* **7**, Berlin: Springer, 1978, pp. 201–208.

[13] G. Finke, Bottleneck problems with overshipments. In: *Methods of Operations Research*, (R.E. Burkard and Th. Ellinger, eds.) **40**, 1981, Königstein/Ts.: Athenäum, pp. 307–310.

[14] G. Finke, Minimizing overshipments in bottleneck transportation problems. *INFOR* **21**, 121–135.

[15] P.L. Hammer, Time minimizing transportation problems. *Naval Res. Log. Quart.* **16**, 1969, 345–357.

[16] F.L. Hitchcock, The distribution of a product from several sources to numerous localities. *Journal of Mathematics and Physics* **20**, 224–230, 1941.

[17] D. Hochbaum and G. Woeginger, A linear-time algorithm for the bottleneck transportation problem with a fixed number of sources. *Operations Research Letters* **24**, 1999, 25–28.

[18] A.J. Hoffman, On simple linear programming problems, in: *Proceedings of Symposia in Pure Mathematics*, Convexity, Vol. VII, V. Klee (ed.), AMS, Providence, RI, 1963, pp. 317–327.

[19] L.V. Kantorovich, Mathematical methods in the organization and planning of production [Russian, 1939]. English translation in *Man. Sci.* **6**, 1960, 366–422.

[20] B. Klinz, R. Rudolf and G. Woeginger, On the recognition of permuted bottleneck Monge matrices. *Discrete Appl. Maths.* **63**, 1995, 43–74.

[21] W. Knödel, Lineare Programme und Transportaufgaben. *MTW, Z. modern. Rechentechn. Automat.* **7**, 63–68, 1960.

[22] A. Schrijver, On the history of the transportation and maximum flow problems. Presented at the Math. Programming Symposium, Atlanta, August 2000.

[23] W. Szwarc, The transportation paradox. *Naval Res. Log. Quarterly* **18**, 1971, 185–202.

[24] A.N. Tolstoĭ, Metody nakhozhdenyianaimenshego summovogo kilometrazha pri planirovanii perevosok b prostranstve [Methods of finding the minimum total kilometrage in cargo transportation planning in space], in: *Planirovanie Perevozok* [Transportation Planning, Vol. 1], NKPS [Trans Press of the National Commissariat of Transportation], Moscow, 1930, pp. 23–55.

Operational Planning and Optimization of Hub-and-Spoke Transportation Networks for Area Wide Groupage Services

Günther Zäpfel, Michael Wasner

University of Linz, Austria

Abstract

Increased competition in the transport market has led to new cooperative arrangements between third-party logistics providers in the form of hub-and-spoke systems. In addition to the design problem, the operative planning task of a hub-and-spoke network is a challenging task for the management of such transportation networks. In particular, the transport management has to decide whether a pure hub-and spoke system should be realized, where all quantities within the transportation network flow over the hub from or to the depots, or whether a hybrid hub-and-spoke network is preferred in which direct transports also take place. Mathematical models for these operative planning tasks are developed and applied to a real case of an Austrian parcel service provider. Cost savings of the hybrid hub-and-spoke system are described.

1 Introduction: Transportation problems of a parcel service provider

One typical example of an area wide groupage service can be seen in the parcel industry. Parcels of a region respectively a depot are transferred to another region respectively depot of this area. Transportation in the parcel industry can take place in the following manner (Figure 1):

- Pure direct transport system
- Pure hub-and-spoke transport system
- Mixed transport system

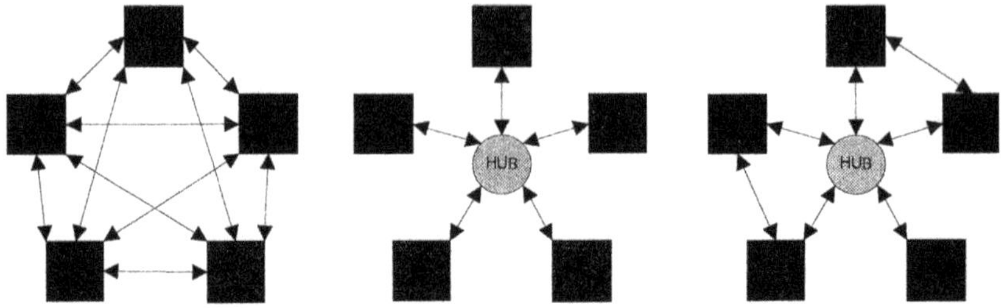

pure direct transport system | pure hub-and-spoke transport system | mixed transport system

Figure 1: Three alternative transport systems

Pure direct transport is characterised by sending the goods directly to the receiving depots. Today, new innovative transportation networks have been formed as *pure hub-and-spoke systems*. This transportation system has the form of a organizational structure in which the single depots (terminals, spokes) cover an area with specific collection and delivery points for every terminal. The depots are connected by at least one transshipment center, or hub. Coordination of the logistic flows is achieved by bunching all shipments from one depot to another using the transshipment center. Mixed systems contain both alternatives: direct and hub-and-spoke transports.

In the following we describe a real parcel service provider covering the area of Austria. The parcel service provider maintain 10 depots (terminals) and one hub (Figure 2). The ten terminals handle about ten million parcels per year. As the service provider guarantees delivery within 24 hours, material flow is organized by tightly coupled processes. During the day the parcels are picked up at the customer points and must arrive at the regional depot not later than 7 p.m. Next, the line haul must be executed from every depot to the hub. That is, the parcels are transferred from the sending depots to the transshipment center (hub), where the parcels are sorted according to their target area and redirected to their respective destinations (receiving depots). This we call *hub transports*.

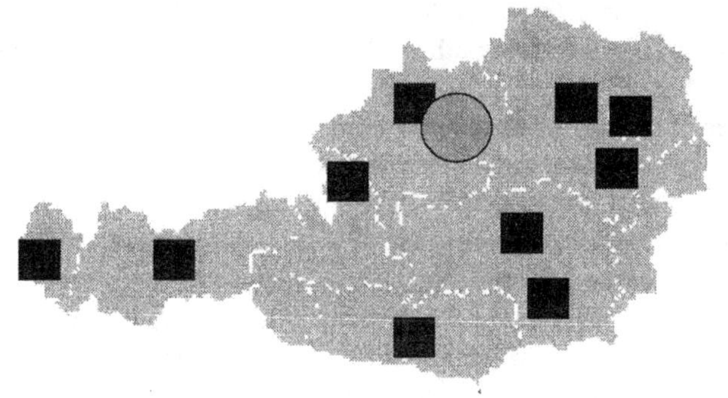

Figure 2: Location of the terminals and the hub of the analysed service provider

In this case transportation takes place on trucks loaded with one or two containers, depending on the current quantity. At 2 a.m. the last truck leaves the hub and arrives at the receiving depot early in the morning. The parcels are delivered by 12 noon via delivery tours.

The quantity of a typical day is shown in Table 1 for the transportation network.

from \ to depot	1	2	3	4	5	6	7	8	9	10	Sum
1	38	137	143	191	47	125	224	70	41	48	1.064
2	108	164	83	324	196	156	98	222	113	129	1.593
3	114	90	145	435	401	154	350	127	460	279	2.555
4	57	143	242	627	386	441	154	217	386	443	3.096
5	68	134	133	329	268	183	473	481	450	299	2.818
6	62	182	189	430	175	263	421	114	192	200	2.228
7	99	189	147	158	417	332	70	389	188	448	2.437
8	47	101	208	425	163	89	270	277	165	324	2.069
9	69	376	87	399	493	134	456	123	109	236	2.482
10	162	296	397	540	376	278	171	368	124	38	2.750
Sum	824	1.812	1.774	3.858	2.922	2.155	2.687	2.388	2.228	2.444	23.092

Table 1: Number of parcels from one depot to another depot on a typical day

The described pure hub-and-spoke system has the advantage that the logistic flows are bunched for shipment from one terminal to another. Nevertheless the system has two disadvantages: The first is that all parcels run over the hub, even parcels with sending and receiving terminals situated quite close together. The second is that the number of parcels from and to the hub can differ significantly; this means that containers that are fully loaded in one direction are underutilized in the other direction, or even that an unequal number of trucks are necessary in the two directions. Therefore, the (additional) use of direct transports can reduce costs and decrease mean distances between depots (especially relatively close ones). The study set out to determine whether the introduction of direct transport pattern in a network of a pure hub-and-spoke structure (Figures 1 and 2) can increase the efficiency of the transportation system. In this sense the connections between the depots can consist of pure hub transports, pure direct transports or any combination of hub and direct transport patterns. This article demonstrates what cost reductions are possible by additionally introducing direct transports between depots into the hub-and-spoke structure.

Because the amount of parcels changes from day to day, the decision has to be reached every day anew. This requires high flexibility in the disposition on the number and destination of the trucks and necessitates a well-developed connected information and communication system between the partners in the transportation network.

2 General problem description

Similar problems as in the parcel industry (goods up to 31.5 kg) arise in other freight service markets for example in the groupage services which are specialized in transports of piece goods (weight above 31.5 kg). For these services, deregulation under European Union law has led to increasing competition in freight service markets within the EU, especially due to the release of transport tariffs in recent years. Aggressive competition on the carrier sector for market shares has been the consequence. In order to compete against big carrier companies and foreign competitors, small- and medium-sized carriers are also offering more and more complete logistics services and have changed to third-party logistics service providers. Furthermore, they are starting to form cooperations or strategic alliances with other third-party logistics region providers to offer transport logistics services over a (nation-wide, EU-wide or even world-wide), e.g., for parcel distribution. Therefore, many cooperative arrangements have been created in the general freight service industry whereby several third-party logistics providers located in different geographical positions build a common transportation network acting under a single name as a joint venture.

The movement of goods in hub-and-spoke-transportation networks can be divided into two parts (Figure 3):

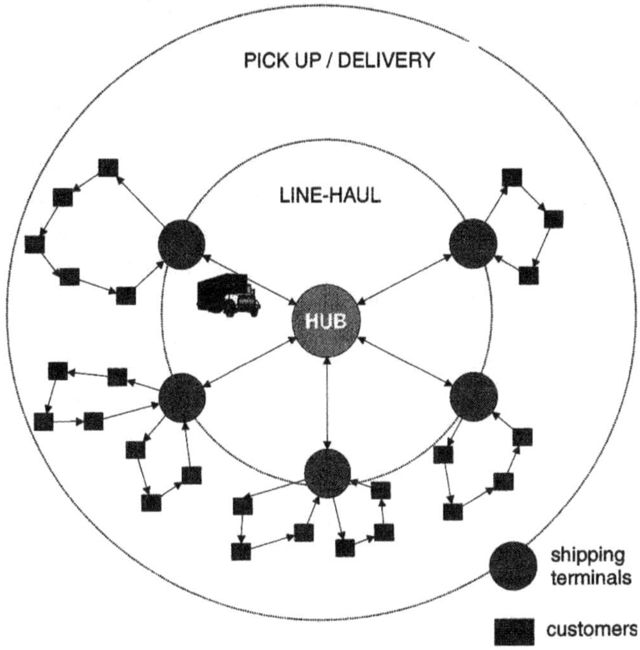

Figure 3: Organisation can be divided into the pick up/delivery and the line haul

- Line-haul (trunk haulage) is usually long-distance transportation between the sending depots and the hub(s) and between the hub(s) and the receiving depots.

- Local pickup/delivery tours involve transportation over short distances with smaller trucks and are carried out by the receiving depots in their regions.

For hub-and-spoke transportation systems the following strategic and operational decisions can be identified:

- Strategic decisions for a hub-and-spoke transportation system include: selection of suitable locations for consolidation (number and location of depots and hubs), assignments of customers to sending and receiving depots, determination of the routing of the line haul and the kind of transportation facilities (e.g., trucks).

- Operational decisions, which are based on results of the strategic decisions, include: (daily) disposition of the number of trucks (or other transportation facilities) for line haul, planning of pick-up/delivery tours for parcels or piece goods to the customers by every depot. In the context of the operational decisions, *pure hub transports*, where the quantities within a transportation network run over the hub from and to a depot, are not the only alternative. It is also possible to execute *pure direct transports*, sending depot delivers directly to the receiving depot without using the hub. In this paper we analyze and develop decision models for these alternatives. In this case the pure hub-and-spoke structure is transformed into an *extended hub-and-spoke or mixed transport system* (compare Figure 1). In a hybrid hub-and-spoke system further alternatives to pure hub and direct transport can exist: triangular and groupage transports. In Section 6 we briefly discuss these transport alternatives.

For the strategic decision problems of hub-and-spoke systems, a lot of literature is available. O'Kelly (1986, 1987) was the first to examine the problem of designing hub-and-spoke systems through their formulation as a quadratic programming problem. Since the number of possible sets of hub locations increases exponentially with the size of the problem, the proposed solution method is limited to very small-scale transportation networks. Some researchers have decomposed the hub location problem into two sub-problems (hub location and routing) and applied different solution methods. For example, Skorin-Kapov (1994) used tabu search to find good solutions to each subproblem. Aykin (1995) investigates two different variants of the hub design problem. In the first variant, all traffic from a given point must flow through a specific hub before proceeding to its destination. The second variant permits trips from a given origin to different hubs depending on the destination (single versus multiple hub design problem). Aykin develops an enumeration method for the multiple allocation and a branch-and-bound method for the single allocation case. Campell (1996) proposes heuristics which rely on first solving the multiple assignment problem via a greedy exchange method and then using this solution to develop a network of hubs and allocations for the single assignment problem. A more comprehensive review of mathematical modeling for hub design can be found in Campell (1994), O'Kelly/Miller (1994) and O'Kelly et al. (1997). A related problem is discussed by the paper of Bruns/Klose/Stähly (2000). The authors discuss the location problem (number, locations, sizes, and service areas of transshipments points) for a new logistics system of the Swiss postal services and develop a discrete facility location model.

The general operational decisions of hub-and-spoke systems have found little attention in the literature, although a lot of publications exist to a related problem: the vehicle routing problem (see Golden/Assad (1988)). The incorporation of direct transports in pure hub-and-spoke systems is discussed in Lumsden/Dalleri/Ruggeri (1999). These authors provide an overview of hub-and-spoke systems and propose some possible improvements to this practice for freight transportation (trucking industry); In particular, in a case study involving the SKE European distribution network, they have applied reallocation of transport resources and direct connection between pairs of nodes on the distribution networks. Stumpf (1998) deals with the daily control of the vehicles in a network of less-than-truckload carriers and analyzes the trunk haulage problem by developing a new heuristic; he also provides reports on computational tests with real data. Donaldson et. al. (1998) also discuss the daily control of hub-and-spoke networks. They develop methods for solving a real case study and refer the results to self created lower bounds. Some further aspects of operational decisions (without focusing on hub-and-spoke systems) can be found in Fleischmann et al. (1998).

We particularly lack research results concerning the connection of the line haul and the pickup/delivery tours. This paper begins to bridge this gap by investigating the *operational decisions* for the mixed hub-and-spoke transportation systems and proposing new mathematical models. The results are based on a case study of a medium-sized Austrian parcel service provider that has built up a hub-and-spoke transportation system.

The paper is structured as follows: In Section 3 we provide a precise mathematical model of the line haul problem of a mixed hub-and-spoke system. Section 4 describes a method for solving the problem. In Section 5 we present the results for the real case of the Austrian parcel service provider. Finally we make some concluding remarks regarding triangular and groupage transport patterns into the line haul problem.

3 Mathematical formulation of the line haul problem

Mathematically, the problem can be formulated as follows:

(P) Minimize:

$$\sum_{\substack{d,d' \in D \\ d \neq d'}} (C^2_{dd'} * x^2_{dd'} + C^1_{dd'} * x^1_{dd'}) \rightarrow \min! \qquad (1)$$

subject to

$$m_{dh} + \sum_{d' \in D-\{h,d\}} m_{dd'} = \sum_{d' \in D-\{d\}} M_{dd'}, \forall d \in D \setminus \{h\} \qquad (2)$$

$$m_{hd} + \sum_{d' \in D-\{h,d\}} m_{d'd} = \sum_{d' \in D-\{d\}} M_{d'd}, \forall d \in D \backslash \{\mathrm{h}\} \tag{3}$$

$$m_{dd'} \leq M_{dd'}, \qquad \forall (d, d' \in D \backslash \{\mathrm{h}\}; d \neq d') \tag{4}$$

$$m_{dd'} \leq x^2_{dd'} * K^2 + x^1_{dd'} * K^1, \qquad \forall (d, d' \in D; d \neq d') \tag{5}$$

$$x^2_{d'd} = x^2_{dd'}, x^1_{d'd} = x^1_{dd'}, \qquad \forall (d, d' \in D; d \neq d') \tag{6}$$

$$m_{dd'} \geq 0, \qquad \forall (d, d' \in D; d \neq d') \tag{7}$$

$$x^2_{dd'}, x^1_{dd'} \in N_0, \qquad \forall (d, d' \in D; d \neq d') \tag{8}$$

whereby the symbols are:

Indices:

D... set of all depots, inclusive the hub h

Decision variables:

$m_{dd'}$... quantity that will be redirected from depot d to depot d' (d, d'$\in$D; d$\neq$d').

Thereby $m_{dd'}$ (d, d'$\in$D\{h}; d$\neq$d') defines the quantity that will be redirected from depot d to depot d' by direct transport and $m_{dd'}$ (d$\in$D\{h}; d'=h) defines the quantity which will be redirected from depot d to depot d' by hub transport.

$x^2_{d,d'}$.. number of trucks with two containers from depot d to depot d'

$x^1_{d,d'}$... number of trucks with one container from depot d to d'

Constants:

$M_{dd'}$... total quantity from depot d to depot d' by customer orders (M_{dh}:=0; M_{hd}:=0)

K^2... capacity of one truck with two containers (measured in parcels)

K^1... capacity of one truck with one container (measured in parcels)

$C^2_{dd'}$ ... cost for one truck with two containers from depot d to depot d'

$C^1_{dd'}$ ... cost for one truck with one container from depot d to d',

The objective function (1) states that the sum of transport costs depends on the number and type of the means of transport (truck with one or two containers, van, etc.) and the cost of each type from a depot d to a depot d'. In the objective function only transport costs are considered. Sorting costs can be included as well. But in our case of operative planning, these costs can be assumed to be fixed due to the already existing automatic sorting capacity in the hub. The costs for personal processing in the depots and the hubs are approximately equal and depend on the total sorting quantity, which is given by the total customer orders in the planning period. Thus these costs are also not variable with respect to the variables of the decision model.

A more generalized objective function can be defined if we permit any alternative means of transports A (vans, trucks, ships, trains with different capacities, e.g., containers, wagons, load areas, etc.). These different transport alternatives $a \in A$ can be modeled by the more general objective function:

$$\sum_{\substack{d,d \in D \\ d \neq d'}} \sum_{a \in A} C^a_{dd'} \cdot x^a_{dd'} \rightarrow \min!$$

Restriction 2 defines for every depot d that the sum of the outgoing quantities to the hub (hub transports) and direct transports to every other depot d' must be equal to the total quantity that must be redirected from depot d to each other depot d' due to the customer orders (expressed in parcels). Analogously, restriction 3 ensures that the sum of all quantities from hub h to depot d (hub transports) or from direct transports coming in from all other depots d' are equal the customer orders that must be delivered by depot d.

Restriction 4 defines that the chosen quantity for a transport alternative (hub or direct transport) cannot exceed the total quantity that the customers want to ship and deliver from every depot d to d'.

The number and the types of the means of transports are determined by restriction 5. The chosen capacities of all types of means of transports, e.g., expressed in number of parcels, must be at least adequate to fulfill the capacity requirements resulting from all chosen $m_{dd'}$. If between two depots the capacities of the means of transports differ in the two directions (for example two trucks each with two containers in one direction and one truck with two containers in the other direction), the larger capacity has to be used in both direction. This is ensured by equation 6.

Restriction 7 presents the non-negativity conditions, and integrality condition 8 concerns the number of transports.

4 A solution method for the line haul problem

As described above, the underlying mathematical formulation leads to a mixed-integer problem. Such problems are NP-hard and can no longer be solved exactly for medium and large dimensions. The reason is integrality condition 8.

If n describes the number of terminals, the mathematical optimization model (1)-(8) consists of O(n) integer variables resulting from the hub transfers and O(n*(n-1)) integer variables resulting from the direct transports. The dominating term is thereby $O(n^2)$ due to direct transport.

To develop an efficient solution algorithm the statements of the following theorem 1 are quite helpful.

Theorem 1: Let d,d'∈D\{h}, d≠d'.

If $\frac{C^2_{d,d'}}{K^2} < \frac{C^1_{d,d'}}{K^1}$, whereby $K^2=2\,K^1$, than in the optimum solution of (P) the number of transports $x^a_{d,d'}$, fulfill the following conditions (a=2 with two swaps, a=1 with one swap):

1. $$\left\lceil \frac{\min\{M_{d,d'}, M_{d',d}\}}{K^2} \right\rceil - 1 \le x^2_{d,d'} \le \left\lceil \frac{\max\{M_{d,d'}, M_{d',d}\}}{K^2} \right\rceil$$

2. $$\max\{M_{d,d'}, M_{d,d'}\} \le K^1 \quad \Rightarrow \quad x^2_{d,d'} = 0$$

3. $x^{1}_{d,d'} \in \{0,1\}$

Sketch of Proof:

1. a) We first show that $x^{2}_{d,d'} \le \left\lceil \frac{\max\{M_{d,d'}, M_{d',d}\}}{K^2} \right\rceil$.

Assume that $x^{2}_{d,d'} > \left\lceil \frac{\max\{M_{d,d'}, M_{d',d}\}}{K^2} \right\rceil$

(1.1)

Then $x^{2}_{d,d'} - 1 \ge \left\lceil \frac{\max\{M_{d,d'}, M_{d',d}\}}{K^2} \right\rceil \ge \frac{\max\{M_{d,d'}, M_{d',d}\}}{K^2}$ (1.2)

• Let x represent the optimal solution and lets select a solution $\overline{x}$

(that is $\overline{x}^{1}_{i,j} = \overline{x}^{1}_{j,i} := x^{1}_{i,j}$, $\overline{x}^{2}_{i,j} = \overline{x}^{2}_{j,i} := x^{2}_{i,j}$, $(\forall i,j \in D;\quad \{i,j\} \neq \{d,d'\})$ and $\overline{x}^{1}_{d,d'} = \overline{x}^{1}_{d',d} := x^{1}_{d,d'}$, $\overline{x}^{2}_{d,d'} = \overline{x}^{2}_{d',d} := x^{2}_{d,d'} - 1$).

• We show that the solution $\overline{x}$ is feasible for (P):

The restrictions (2), (3), (4), (6), (7) are fulfilled, as the $m_{dd'}$ did not change. (8) is fulfilled according to (1.1). With (1.2) $\overline{x}^{2}_{d,d'} := x^{2}_{d,d'} - 1 \ge \frac{\max\{M_{d,d'}, M_{d',d}\}}{K^2}$ and restriction (4) $m_{dd'} \le M_{dd'}$ it follows, that restriction (5) is also fulfilled and the solution $\overline{x}$ is feasible.

• Now we show that the solution x is not optimal for (P):

$$C(x) - C(\overline{x}) = C^{2}_{d,d'} \cdot x^{2}_{d,d'} + C^{2}_{d',d} \cdot x^{2}_{d',d} - C^{2}_{d,d'} \cdot \overline{x}^{2}_{d,d'} - C^{2}_{d',d} \cdot \overline{x}^{2}_{d',d} =$$

$$= x^{2}_{d,d'} \cdot (C^{2}_{d,d'} + C^{2}_{d',d}) - (C^{2}_{d,d'} + C^{2}_{d',d}) \cdot (x^{2}_{d,d'} - 1) = C^{2}_{d,d'} + C^{2}_{d',d} > 0.$$

This is a contradiction to the assumption that x is optimal.

b) The proof to show that $\left\lceil \frac{\min\{M_{d,d'}, M_{d',d}\}}{K^2} \right\rceil - 1 \le x^{2}_{d,d'}$ is similar to a).

2., 3.: Can be proved in an analog manner. ♦

These statements influence the mathematical model (P) of chapter 2.2 as follows: The theorem first shows, that the integer variables $x^2_{d,d'}$, describing the direct transfers, can be restricted to a certain interval (1.) . Furthermore these variables can be uniquely determined with zero, if the quantities in both directions are very low ($\max\{M^2_{d,d'}, M^2_{d',d}\} \leq M^1$). Also the number of means of transport, loaded with only one swap, can be restricted. The variables $x^1_{d,d'}$ reduce to binary variables (3.) and are no longer general integers.

If we consider the problem specific data of table 1, we see that the condition $\max\{M^2_{d,d'}, M^2_{d',d}\} \leq M^1$ is fulfilled for nearly all direct transfers. According to theorem 1 all variables $x^2_{d,d'}$ in the mathematical model (P) can be fixed with zero for the direct transfers. The theorem further states, that in the optimum solution the variables for the direct transfers are binary ($\in \{0,1\}$).

With these results the mathematical model (P) is much simplified and it results the following solution method: a complete enumeration of the direct transfers (of the binary variables) and for every combination then determining the hub transports.

Lets give an example for n=3 depots: For the binary variables x^1_{12}, x^1_{13}, x^1_{23} (which correspond to the variables $x^1_{dd'}$ for the direct transfers in the upper mathematical model) define whether the parcels are transferred directly ($x^1_{dd'}=1$) or over the hub ($x^1_{dd'}=0$), the following 8 combinational possibilities have to be tested: $(x^1_{12}, x^1_{13}, x^1_{23})$ = (0,0,0); (0,0,1); (0,1,0); (0,1,1); (1,0,0); (1,0,1); (1,1,0); (1,1,1). Alternative (0,0,0) describes a pure hub-and-spoke structure, whereby alternative (1,1,1) uses only direct transfers.

If the direct transfers are fixed, the solution (which is equal to a determination) of the resulting mathematical model is easy. As all direct transfer variables are fixed, only the hub variables have to be determined. Therefore we can apply theorem 2:

Theorem 2: Let $d \in D\backslash\{h\}$.

If $\frac{C^2_{d,h}}{K^2} < \frac{C^1_{d,h}}{K^1}$, whereby $K^2=2\ K^1$, then for a pure hub-and-spoke-system the number of hub transports is given by:

1. $x_{h,d}^2 = x_{d,h}^2 = \max\{0, \left\lceil \frac{\max\{M_{d,h}, M_{h,d}\} - K^1}{K^2} \right\rceil\}$

2. $x_{h,d}^1 = x_{d,h}^1 = \max\{0, \left\lceil \frac{\max\{M_{d,h}, M_{h,d}\} - K^2 \cdot x_{h,d}^2}{K^1} \right\rceil\}$

Sketch of Proof:

1. a) Assume that $x_{h,d}^2 > \max\{0, \left\lceil \frac{\max\{M_{d,h}, M_{h,d}\} - K^1}{K^2} \right\rceil\}$

$$\Rightarrow x_{h,d}^2 - 1 > \max\{0, \left\lceil \frac{\max\{M_{d,h}, M_{h,d}\} - K^1}{K^2} \right\rceil\} \geq \left\lceil \frac{\max\{M_{d,h}, M_{h,d}\} - K^1}{K^2} \right\rceil \geq \frac{\max\{M_{d,h}, M_{h,d}\} - K^1}{K^2}$$

$$\Rightarrow \max\{M_{h,d}, M_{d,h}\} \leq K^2 \cdot x_{d,h}^2 - K^2 + K^1 = K^2 \cdot (x_{d,h}^2 - 1) + K^1$$

$\Rightarrow$ A truck capacity of ($x_{d,h}^2 - 1$) with two swaps and 1 with one swap is sufficient and therefore feasible.

As $C_{d,h}^2 \cdot x_{d,h}^2 - [C_{d,h}^2 \cdot (x_{d,h}^2 - 1) + C_{d,h}^1 \cdot 1] = C_{d,h}^2 - C_{d,h}^1 > 0$ the assumed solution is not cost optimal.

b) is similar to a).

2. Can be proved in an analog manner. ♦

Thus the number of $x^1_{h,d}$ and $x^2_{h,d}$ is determined unique and the remaining MIP-problem reduces to the two equations of theorem 2. The running time for one combination is O(1) and moreover the complete enumeration leads to the optimum solution of (P).

Nevertheless running time grows very fast: The number of possibilities grows exponentially with the number of terminals (compare Table 2) and is determined by $2^{(n \cdot (n-1)/2)}$. The table shows that for n=7 more than 2 million possibilities have to be tested in order to guarantee the optimal solution. A pentium II, 400 MHz computer like the one used in our simulation calculates about 30 minutes for one million possibilities. If the optimization algorithm is to be utilized daily, the computing time of an acceptable solution must not exceed 30 minutes. If n is larger than seven (see Table 2) such times are impossible; thus other algorithms, especially approximation methods, have to be developed.

n = number of terminals	possibilities
2	2
3	8
4	64
5	1.024
6	32.768
7	2.097.152
10	35.184.372.088.832
15	4,1 * 10^31

Table 2: Number of possibilities of alternative direct transfers for different values of n

As the number of terminals in the case study is ten, a complete enumeration leads to computing times of some thousand years and is thus impossible. Therefore other methods have to be used – for example, an partial enumeration, as done here. The idea is to restrict the search space so much, that the number of possibilities (35.184.372.088.832 for the case study, where n=10; compare Table 2) are reduced to about one million, which means a reduction by a factor 10^7.

The number of alternative direct transports can be determined by the formula n*(n-1)/2. As shown above for n=3, three direct transports result. In the case study, where n=10, there are 45 possibilities. These direct transfers can be represented by the 45-tupel

$(y_1, y_2, y_3, y_4, y_5, y_6,..., y_{45}) := (x^1_{1,2}, x^1_{1,3}, x^1_{1,4}, x^1_{1,5}, x^1_{1,6}, x^1_{1,7}, x^1_{1,8}, x^1_{1,9}, x^1_{1,10}, x^1_{2,3}, x^1_{2,4}, x^1_{2,5},.., x^1_{2,10}, x^1_{3,1},... x^1_{9,10})$. As every variable can be 0 or 1, this leads to the 2^{45} = 35.184.372.088.832 combinations.

The following idea is to reduce the number of 2^{45} possibilities by using problem-specific knowledge. Despite this reduction to about 1 million possibilities (because of computing time), the quality of the solution should not decline much. In other words, the idea is to construct an expert system: If-then-inquiries shall test, whether a combination of direct transports is allowed. Important criteria for the reduction of the search space were the following:

(1) If the hub is located between two terminals, then a direct connection will not lead to high cost reductions and can be eliminated. This rule is especially valid when a direct transfer does not reduce the empty miles.

This rule means for the 45-tupel $(y_1, y_2, y_3, y_4, y_5, y_6,..., y_{45})$ that some y_i can be fixed, i.e., set to zero. For example, if the hub is located between terminal 9 and 10, the variable $y_{45} := x^1_{9,10}$ can be set to zero and the resulting 45-tupel is $(y_1, y_2,$

y_3, y_4, y_5,..., y_{44}, 0). Thus the number of possibilities can be reduced from 2^{45} to 2^{44}.

(2) If the quantities, that is, the number of parcels between two terminals, is quite small in relation to the truck capacity and they are not directly connected, then a direct transport will lead to no or only small savings.

The effect for the 45-tupel is analogous to rule 1. Some direct transfers can be eliminated, i.e., set to zero. For the underlying case study it is possible to fix 13 direct transfers with the rules 1 and 2 (without loss of generality the last ten y_i), which leaves the 45-tupel (y_1, y_2, y_3,..., y_{34}, y_{32}, 0, 0, ..., 0). Thus the number of possibilities can be reduced from 2^{45} to 2^{32} = 4.294.967.296.

(3) A further reduction of the search space can be achieved by concentrating some direct transfers to a group that has to fulfill some conditions. For example, consider the parcel flow of depot 1 in Table 1. It is (1064-38) and (824-38) parcels, whereby the smallest truck capacity is 1000 parcels. A pure hub-and-spoke transfer requires at least two trucks (number of parcels ≥ 1000). If exactly one direct transfer is used (no matter which one), the remaining parcel flow reduces to less than 1000 – less than the minimum truck capacity. Thus it can be easily proved that for depot 1 it is only useful to allow no, exactly one or exclusively direct transfers.

For the 45-tupel (y_1, y_2, y_3,..., y_{34}, y_{32}, 0, 0,..., 0) this means the following: The direct transfers of depot 1 are represented by the first nine y_i of the 45-tupel. As only one, no or exclusively direct transfers are allowed, the variables (y_1, y_2, y_3,..., y_9) can only take on eleven different combinations: (0,0,0,0,0,0,0,0,0), (1,0,0,0,0,0,0,0,0), (0,1,0,0,0,0,0,0,0), (0,0,1,0,0,0,0,0,0), (0,0,0,1,0,0,0,0,0), (0,0,0,0,1,0,0,0,0), (0,0,0,0,0,1,0,0,0), (0,0,0,0,0,0,1,0,0), (0,0,0,0,0,0,0,1,0), (0,0,0,0,0,0,0,0,1), (1,1,1,1,1,1,1,1,1). The other 23 variables (y_{10}, y_{11}, y_{12},..., y_{32}) are not fixed. The number of remaining possibilities can easily be computed by 92.274.688 (=11*2^{23}). It can be seen that rule (3) reduces the number of possibilities to about 92 million. Furthermore, similar rules can reduce the search space additionally to a number of not more than 1 million.

The remaining one million possibilities are all tested; i.e., the costs are calculated for all possibilities and the best is defined as the solution of the incomplete enumeration algorithm.

Therefore the algorithm developed for the case study can be represented by the following flow chart:

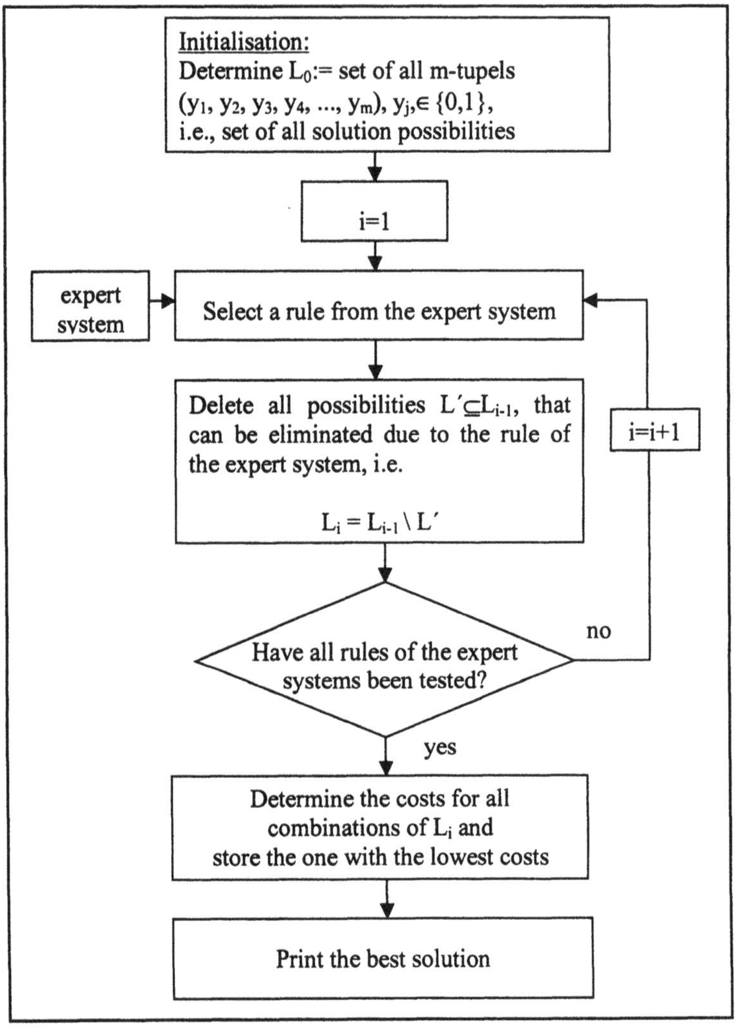

The developed algorithm was especially designed for the underlying case study. For large n it is no longer directly transferable because the search space cannot be reduced sufficiently. In that case other algorithms have to be used, e.g., local search algorithms.

The application of such methods are the subject of present research. Especially approaches that are based on genetic algorithms are being examined. A promising attempt is to combine these with an expert system, i.e., a rule-based approach.

5 Solution of the case study of section 1

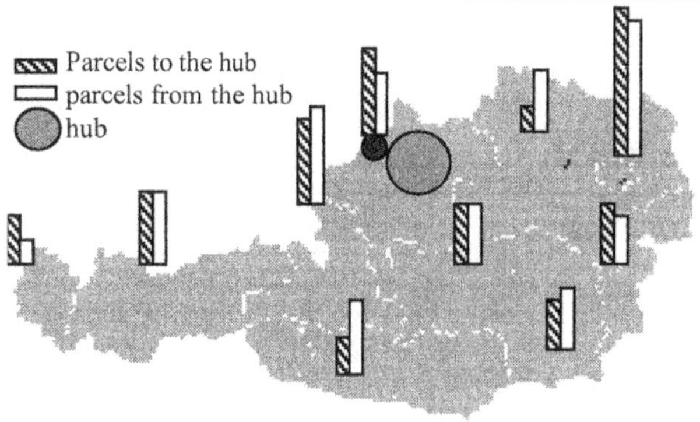

Figure 4: Number of parcels to be transferred from the alternative depots. Costs in a pure hub-and-spoke structure: 100,000 money units

Using the data from Section 1 and applying the mathematical model of Section 3 yields the following result (Figure 4): Without permitting direct transports, which is the practice of the third-party logistics provider, the quantities to and from the hub differ considerably (disequilibrium of quantities). The costs total 100,000 money units and are standardized to protect secrecy. Permitting direct transports produces costs of 89,840 money units, a reduction of 10.16%. As a rule, the differences in quantities from and to the hub for the depots have been reduced by direct transports (Figure 5). A simulation study of the line haul problem of the logistics service provider for 50 days showed that the average cost reductions are about 10% by additionally permitting direct transports, whereby the interval varies between 6% and 15%. Introducing direct transports counteracts the disadvantages of the hub-and-spoke system. Transport kilometers decline. Direct transport occurs mostly between nearby depots, while on the whole the number of truck transports stays almost the same.

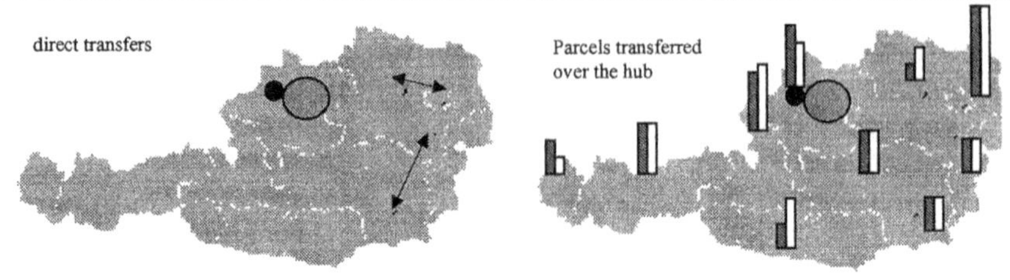

Figure 5: Permitting direct transports reduces the differences between quantities from and to the hub for the depots (in comparison to Figure 4)

The resulting question concerns the quality of the developed solution method. Is it possible to improve the potential of 10.16% by applying better algorithms? To give an answer the optimum solution has to be known. As the problem is NP-complete, we will only be able to find upper and lower bounds. To represent the quality of the solution method, good lower bounds are of special interest. Three lower bounds have been developed and tested:

The first one is quite simple: Solve the optimization problem (P) and neglect the integer conditions (8). Then a LP-problem has to be solved. For the underlying input data (compare table 1), where in den LP-solution nearly all $x^2_{d,d'}$ vary between 0 and 1, the bound is about 50% below the simulation results and thus (hopefully) useless.

The second approach for a lower bound tries to apply theorem 1 of chapter 4. With theorem 1.1. the optimum number of direct transports can be limited:

$$x^{2L}_{d,d'} := \left\lceil \frac{\min\{M_{d,d'}, M_{d',d}\}}{K^2} \right\rceil - 1 \leq x^2_{d,d'} \leq \left\lceil \frac{\max\{M_{d,d'}, M_{d',d}\}}{K^2} \right\rceil =: x^{2H}_{d,d'} \qquad (1)$$

A solution with $x^2_{d,d'} := x^{2L}_{d,d'}$ for all direct transfers can be used as the second lower bound. The only problem is, that the input data of table 1 are so specific, that nearly all $x^{2L}_{d,d'}$ are 0. Thus the bound is even worse than the upper LP-bound.

Nevertheless, for higher quantities of parcels the theorem yields an interesting result. If the high quantities are beyond well-balanced (equilibrium of quantities), it follows from (1) that $x^{2L}_{d,d'} = x^{2H}_{d,d'} - 1$. As the solution (S1):= $x^2_{d,d'} := x^{2L}_{d,d'}$

$(x^1_{d,d'} = x^2_{d,h} = x^1_{d,h} = 0)$ is a lower bound for the optimum solution and the solution (S2):= $x^2_{d,d'} := x^{2H}_{d,d'}$ ($x^1_{d,d'} = x^2_{d,h} = x^1_{d,h} = 0$, i.e. no hub traffic) is feasible, the variation between (S2) and the optimum solution is less than $1 / x^{2L}_{d,d'}$.[1] I.e. If the quantities delivered to all destinations are e.g. greater than 20 trucks (with two swaps), a use of pure direct transfers leads to a solution that is closer than 5% to the optimum.

This is one reason, why large logistics service providers (e.g. train and postage services) use direct transport systems and no hub systems. Hub systems are mostly the union of small and medium enterprises who build a strategic alliance to use synergies.

As discussed above, the underlying problem is NP-complete and thus not solvable for big dimensions. For a network with (only) 10 terminals good algorithms can generate the optimum solution and thus the exact lower bound. Using the commercial software CPLEX the optimum solution can be found for our case study. In figure 6 the deviation between the heuristic of chapter 4 and the optimum solution is represented.

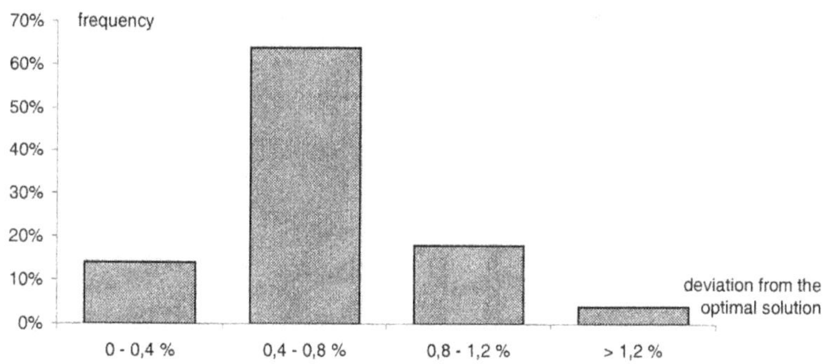

Figure 6: Bar chart of the deviation of the solution method presented in chapter 4.

It can be seen that the developed solution method generates quite good results and the simulated cost savings of 10,16 % exhaust nearly the whole potential.

[1] exactly: $1/\min\{ x^{2L}_{d,d'}: d, d' \in D\backslash\{h\}, d \neq d' \}$

6 Summary and further extension

The results of the paper can be summarized as follows:

- The operational decisions of hub-and-spoke transportation systems have received relatively little attention in the literature. This paper investigates these decisions for hub-and-spoke systems and develops a new mathematical model.

- For a real case study of a mid-sized Austrian parcel service provider, we showed that on average 10% of the total transport costs for the line haul can be reduced by applying the model of Section 4 and solving it with a heuristic combining expert rules with an enumeration scheme.

The proposed model was not only applied to a parcel service provider, but also to a hub-and spoke-system in Germany which executed less than truckload transportation. Therefore the new mathematical models are applicable in the general cargo industry, too.

Future directions of our research not only take into consideration the development of efficient solution methods, especially combining expert rules with local search methods, but moreover analyze further alternatives to the direct and hub transports: triangular and groupage transport services. Because different pickup and delivery tours can influence the line haul and vice versa a simultaneous solution of the two interrelated problems is the next step of a more sophisticated planning concept. First results can be found in Zäpfel/Wasner (2000b).

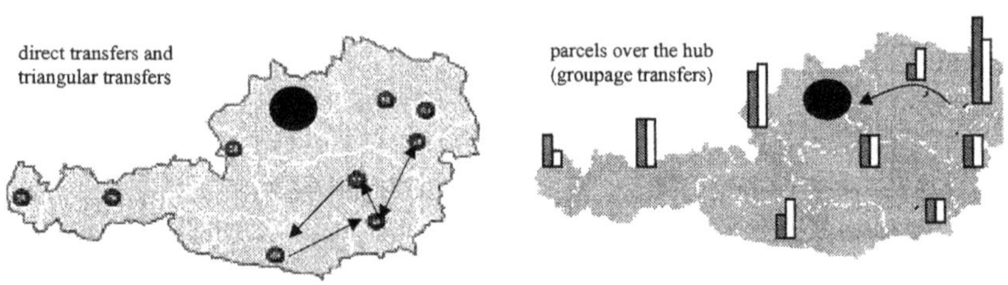

Figure 7: The system costs can be reduced by 16.64 % to 83,360 by using direct and hub as well as triangular and groupages transport services (for the case study of Section 5)

Similar to direct transport, triangular transports can be characterized in a way that three (nearby) depots directly change their incoming and outgoing quantities by a connected tour (see Figure 7, left). Groupage transport services redirecting the quantities to and from the hub, but on the way unloading and loading, can take place at several depots. For our case study in Section 1, we could show in Zäpfel/Wasner (2000a) that about 16,5% of the total costs can be reduced by simultaneously using direct and hub as well as triangular and groupages services to prevent empty miles. The resulting saving potential justifies the development of such sophisticated planning tools.

References

Aykin, T.(1995): Networking policies for hub-and-spoke systems with applications to the air transportation system, in: Transportation Science, vol. 26, 201-221

Bruns, A.; Klose, A.; Staehly, P. (2000): Restructuring of Swiss parcel delivery services, in: OR Spectrum, vol 22(2), 285-302

Campbell, J.F. (1996): Hub location and the p-hub median problem, in: Operations Research, vol. 44, 387-405

Donaldson, H. et al (1998): Schedule-Driven Cross-Docking Networks, in: conference proceedings of "Tristan III – Triannual Symposium on Transportation Analysis", held in Puerto Rico, June 17-23, 1998, 1-13

Fleischmann, van Nunen, J.A., Speranza,M.G., Stähly, P. (1998): Advances in Distribution Logistics, Berlin-Heidelberg-New York

Golden, B.L., Assad, A.A. (Eds.) (1988): Vehicle Routing: Methods and Studies, Amsterdam et. al.

Lumsden, K., Dalleri, F., Ruggeri, R. (1999): Improving the efficiency of the hub and spoke system for the SKF European distribution network, in: International Journal of Physical Distribution & Logistics Management, vol. 29, 50-64

O'Kelly, M.E. (1986): The location of interacting hub facilities, in: Transportation Science, vol. 29, 92-106

O'Kelly, M.E., Miller, H.J: (1994): The hub network design problem: A review and sythesis, in: Journal of Transport Geography, vol. 2, 31-40

O'Kelly; M.E. (1987): A quadratic integer program for location of interacting hub facilities, in: European Journal of Operational Research, vol.32, 393-404

O'Kelly, M.E. , Bryan, D. Skorin-Kapov, D, Skorin-Kapov, J. (1997): Hub network design with single and multiple allocation: a computational study, In : Location Science, vol. 4, 125-138

Savelsberg, M.W.P., Sol, M. (1995): The general pickup and delivery problem, in: Transportation Science, vol 29, 17-29.

Skorin-Kapov, D., Skorin-Kapov, J. (1994): On tabu search for the location of interacting hub facilities, in: European Journal of Operational Research, vol. 73, 501-508

Stumpf, P. (1998): Vehicle Routing and Scheduling for Trunk Haulage, in: Fleischmann. B. van Nunen, J.A. et al. (editors): Advances in Distribution Logistics, Berlin-Heidelberg-New York, 341-371

Zäpfel, G., Wasner, M. (2000a): Planung und Optimierung von virtuellen Hub-and-Spoke-Transportnetzwerken kooperativer Logistikdienstleister im Sammelgutverkehr, in: Zeitschrift für Betriebswirtschaft (ZfB), Ergänzungsheft 2, 243-260

Zäpfel, G., Wasner, M. (2000b): Planning and Optimization of hub-and-spoke transportation networks of cooperative third-party logistics provider, accepted for: European Journal of Production Economics

Stochastic Programming: Achievements and Open Problems

Peter Kall

University of Zurich, Switzerland

1 Introduction

As is well known, many applied problems may be modelled as linear programs of the standard type

$$\left.\begin{array}{rrl} & \min c^{\mathrm{T}}x & \\ \text{subject to} & Ax = & b \\ & x \geq & 0, \end{array}\right\} \tag{1.1}$$

where $A \in \mathbb{R}^{m\times n}$, $b \in \mathbb{R}^m$, $c \in \mathbb{R}^n$ are fixed data and $x \in \mathbb{R}^n$ is to be determined as a vector of optimal decisions satisfying the given constraints. However, as was observed already more than 40 years ago, it may also happen in applications, that modelling the linear structures as in (1.1) is justified, but not all of the data in A, b, c are fixed (and known) before the decision on x has to be taken. If those data happen to be random variables with known distributions, we face a problem of *stochastic linear programming* (SLP). Among the first papers discussing those problems are Beale [2], Charnes–Cooper [7], Dantzig [8], Dantzig–Madansky [9] and Tintner [33].

Hence, denoting random data by $\tilde{A}$, $\tilde{b}$ and $\tilde{c}$, respectively, instead of (1.1) we have in general a basic problem structure like

$$\left.\begin{array}{rrl} & \text{"min" } \tilde{c}^{\mathrm{T}}x & \\ \text{subject to} & \tilde{A}x \propto & \tilde{b} \\ & x \geq & 0, \end{array}\right\} \tag{1.2}$$

where "$\propto$" may stand for "=" and/or "$\geq$". The first difficulty, if we have to decide on x before knowing the realization of $\tilde{A}$, $\tilde{b}$, $\tilde{c}$, is that (1.2) is not a well defined problem. That is why we have written "min" in quotes, since it is not at all clear what had to be understood by minimization in this situation. Therefore, we need to restate the model such that it implies a meaningful task. There are different possibilities for reformulations, but before discussing the most relevant ones we shall make once and for all the following

Assumption **A1**: The probability distribution $\mathcal{P}_{(\tilde{A},\, \tilde{b},\, \tilde{c})}$ does not depend on the choice of the decision x.

Basically, two different types of models have been discussed with respect to their theoretical properties as well as in applications, *stochastic programs with chance (or probabilistic) constraints* and *stochastic programs with recourse.* To simplify the following presentation, with respect to the structure of random elements in the various models we shall make the

Assumption **A2**: Given the probability space $(\Xi, \mathcal{F}, P)$ defined by $\Xi \subset \mathbb{R}^k$, $\mathcal{F} \subset \{\Xi \cap Z \mid Z \in \mathcal{B}_k\}$ ($\mathcal{B}_k$ the Borel σ-algebra in $\mathbb{R}^k$), and a probability measure P on $\mathcal{F}$, the random elements in our SLP-models, i.e. the matrices and vectors—given that they are random—are linear affine transforms on Ξ; hence, with $\xi \in \Xi$,

$$\tilde{A} := A^0 + \sum_{j=1}^{k} \xi_j A^j \ , \quad \tilde{b} := b^0 + \sum_{j=1}^{k} \xi_j b^j \ , \quad \tilde{c} := c^0 + \sum_{j=1}^{k} \xi_j c^j \ , \tag{1.3}$$

where $A^j \in \mathbb{R}^{m \times n}$, $b^j \in \mathbb{R}^m$, $c^j \in \mathbb{R}^n$ for $j = 0, 1, \cdots, k$ are fixed matrices and vectors, respectively.

2 SLP with chance constraints

First instances of this model type have been discussed long time ago, e.g. in Charnes–Cooper [7]. Essentially, SLP with chance constraints come in two different variants: Either they have to satisfy (among others) *joint chance constraints* yielding—with X being some fixed convex polyhedral set, e.g. like $X = \{x \in \mathbb{R}^n \mid Dx \propto d,\ x \in [l, u]\}$, and $\alpha \in [0, 1]$—model types as

$$\min_{x \in X} \{c^{\mathrm{T}} x \mid P(\{\xi \mid \tilde{A}x \geq \tilde{b}\}) \geq \alpha\} \ , \tag{2.1}$$

or they are required to satisfy *separate chance constraints* with $\alpha_i \in [0, 1]$ resulting in model types as

$$\min_{x \in X} \{c^{\mathrm{T}} x \mid P(\{\xi \mid \tilde{a}_i^{\mathrm{T}} x \geq \tilde{b}_i\}) \geq \alpha_i \ , \ i = 1, \cdots, m\} \ , \tag{2.2}$$

where the vector $\tilde{a}_i$ conicides with the i-th row of the random matrix $\tilde{A}$.

2.1 Convexity

Unfortunately, in this general setting problems of type (2.1) turn out very likely to be nonconvex optimization problems as long as the matrix $\tilde{A}$ contains stochastic elements—even if the underlying probability distributions are "nice" like e.g. the uniform or the multinormal distribution. On the other hand, if in (2.1) only $\tilde{b}$ is random (but all elements of $\tilde{A}$ are deterministic), i.e. if we deal with the problem

$$\min_{x \in X}\{c^{\mathrm{T}}x \mid P(\{\xi \mid Ax \geq \tilde{b}\}) \geq \alpha\}, \tag{2.3}$$

we know for rather wide classes of probability distributions (of $\tilde{b}$) that we have a convex optimization problem. This was first shown by Prékopa [23, 24] for logarithmic concave distributions which may be defined as follows:

Definition 2.1 *The probability measure P on $\mathcal{F}$ is log-concave if for any two convex events M, $N \in \mathcal{F}$ and arbitrary $\lambda \in (0,1)$ holds*

$$P(\lambda M + (1-\lambda)N) \geq P^{\lambda}(M)P^{1-\lambda}(N),$$

where $\lambda M + (1-\lambda)N := \{z \mid z = \lambda x + (1-\lambda)y,\ x \in M,\ y \in N\}$.

For our purposes, the central result of Prékopa is stated as

Theorem 2.1 *The probability measure $P_{\tilde{b}}$, given on $\mathbb{R}^m$ (the support of $\tilde{b}$) by a density function $f_{\tilde{b}}$, is log-concave if and only if $f_{\tilde{b}}$ is log-concave, i.e. $\log(f_{\tilde{b}})$ is a concave function.*

This way he characterized a relatively broad class of distributions being log-concave, containing e.g. the multinormal, the uniform, the Wishart, and further distributions.

More generally, if the probability distribution is quasi-concave, i.e. if for any two convex events M, N and arbitrary $\lambda \in (0,1)$ holds

$$P_{\tilde{b}}(\lambda M + (1-\lambda)N) \geq \min[P_{\tilde{b}}(M), P_{\tilde{b}}(N)],$$

implying immediately the quasi-concavity of the distribution function $F_{\tilde{b}}$, the feasible set of our problem

$$\{x \in X \mid F_{\tilde{b}}(Ax) \geq \alpha\}$$

is obviously convex. Observe that any log-concave distribution is trivially also quasi-concave, saying that Prékopa had dealt with a—rather broad—subclass of quasi-concave distributions.
For any m-dimensional probability distribution P with density f, lateron Borell [3] and Rinott [29] proved the following

Theorem 2.2 *The probability measure $P_{\tilde{b}}$, given on $\mathbb{R}^m$ (the support of $\tilde{b}$) by a density function $f_{\tilde{b}}$, is quasi-concave if and only if $f_{\tilde{b}}^{-1/m}$ is convex.*

We thus have a fairly broad class of *continuous type* probability distributions for which the convexity of problems of type (2.3) can be asserted.

Whereas for continuous type distributions we get convexity under certain assumptions, this may not be expected for discrete distributions as is easily demonstrated by simple examples, or else may be seen from the validity of the following reformulations of (2.1) and (2.3), respectively. Assume that we have the finite discrete distribution

$$\{(\xi^{(i)}, p_i),\ i = 1, \cdots, K\} \text{ with } p_i > 0\ \forall i \text{ and } \sum_{i=1}^{K} p_i = 1 \tag{2.4}$$

and let $A^{(i)} := \tilde{A}(\xi^{(i)})$, $b^{(i)} := \tilde{b}(\xi^{(i)})$, $i = 1, \cdots, K$.
Under these assumptions Raike [28] was the first to state the relation of problem type (2.1) to mixed integer programming:

Theorem 2.3 *Given the discrete distribution (2.4), solving problem (2.1) is equivalent to solving the mixed integer program*

$$\left.\begin{array}{llcll} \min c^{\mathrm{T}} x & & & & \\ A^{(i)} x & + M \cdot (1 - z_i) e & \geq & b^{(i)} & i = 1, \cdots, K\,, \\ & \sum_{i=1}^{K} p_i z_i & \geq & \alpha & \\ x & & \in & X & \\ & z_i & \in & \{0,1\} & i = 1, \cdots, K\,, \end{array}\right\} \tag{2.5}$$

where $e = (1, 1, \cdots, 1)^{\mathrm{T}} \in \mathbb{R}^m$ *and* M *is to be chosen "big enough".*

Lateron, Prékopa [25] succeeded in proving an equivalent reformulation of (2.3) which in turn does not require the "big enough" M:

Theorem 2.4 *Solving problem (2.3) is equivalent to solving the mixed integer program*

$$\left.\begin{array}{llcll} \min c^{\mathrm{T}} x & & & & \\ A x & - \sum_{i=1}^{K} b^{(i)} z_k & \geq & 0 & \\ & \sum_{i=1}^{K} F_{\tilde{b}}(b^{(i)}) z_i & \geq & \alpha & \\ & \sum_{i=1}^{K} z_i & = & 1 & \\ x & & \in & X & \\ & z_i & \in & \{0,1\} & i = 1, \cdots, K\,, \end{array}\right\} \tag{2.6}$$

where $F_{\tilde{b}}$ *is the multivariate distribution function of* $\tilde{b}$.

Further equivalent reformulations of the discrete distribution case may be found in the monograph of Prékopa [26].

Finally, for the case of separate chance constraints (2.2) for various classes of distributions statements of the type hold:

For a specific bound $\overline{\alpha}_i$ *the set* $\{x \mid P(\{\xi \mid \tilde{a}_i^{\mathrm{T}} x \geq \tilde{b}_i\}) \geq \alpha_i\}$ *is convex for* $\alpha_i \geq \overline{\alpha}_i$.

In particular we have

Theorem 2.5 *If the random vector* $(\tilde{a}_i^{\mathrm{T}}, \tilde{b}_i)^{\mathrm{T}}$ *has a joint (nondegenerate) normal distribution, then*

$$\{x \mid P(\{\xi \mid \tilde{a}_i^{\mathrm{T}} x \geq \tilde{b}_i\}) \geq \alpha_i\}$$

is convex for all $\alpha_i \geq \frac{1}{2}$.

This and similar convexity statements for other distribution types were found by Marti [16].

Particularly simple becomes the situation if only the right hand side is random, i.e. if we deal with the the constraint

$$P(\{\xi \mid a_i^{\mathrm{T}} x \geq \tilde{b}_i\}) \geq \alpha_i \ .$$

With the distribution function $F_{\tilde{b}_i}$ of $\tilde{b}_i$ this is equivalent with

$$F_{\tilde{b}_i}(a_i^{\mathrm{T}} x) \geq \alpha_i$$

and hence with

$$a_i^{\mathrm{T}} x \geq F_{\tilde{b}_i}^{-1}(\alpha_i) \ ,$$

where $F_{\tilde{b}_i}^{-1}(\alpha_i) := \min\{\xi \mid F_{\tilde{b}_i}(\xi) \geq \alpha_i\}$. Therefore, in this case the chance constraints reduce to linear constraints.

2.2 Algorithmic approaches

For discrete distributions (2.4) the problems (2.1) and (2.3)—according to Theorems 2.3 and 2.4—may be solved with methods of the ordinary mixed integer programming toolkit.

For separate chance constraints, under the assumptions of Theorem 2.5 for $(\tilde{a}_i^{\mathrm{T}}, \tilde{b}_i)^{\mathrm{T}}$ having a joint multivariate normal distribution with expectation $\mu \in \mathbb{R}^{n+1}$ and positive definite (i.e. nondegenerate) $(n+1)\times(n+1)$-covariance matrix S it can be shown (see e.g. Kall-Wallace [14]) that the feasible set can be rewritten as

$$\begin{aligned}\mathcal{B}_i(\alpha_i) &:= \{x \mid P(\{\xi \mid a_i^{\mathrm{T}} x \geq \tilde{b}_i\}) \geq \alpha_i\} \\ &= \{x \mid -\Phi^{-1}(1-\alpha_i)\,\sigma_{\tilde{\zeta}}(x) - m_{\tilde{\zeta}}(x) \leq 0\}\end{aligned}$$

with Φ the standard normal distribution function, and

$$m_{\tilde{\zeta}}(x) := \mu^{\mathrm{T}} z(x) \quad \text{and} \quad \sigma_{\tilde{\zeta}}^2(x) := z^{\mathrm{T}}(x) S z(x)$$

with $z(x) := (x_1, \cdots, x_n, -1)^{\mathrm{T}}$. Since $\sigma_{\tilde{\zeta}}(x)$ is a convex function, this proves the convexity of $\mathcal{B}_i(\alpha_i)$ for $\alpha_i \geq 0.5$, again, and the probabilistic constraint may be handled as deterministic convex constraint due to this reformulation. Considering now (2.3) under the assumptions of Theorems 2.1 or 2.2, the solution methods discussed so far are adaptations of convex optimization methods with some specializations to deal with the distribution function included in the constraints. For one of these approaches, based on the reduced gradient algorithm of Abadie-Carpentier [1], we may rewrite the problem as

$$\left.\begin{array}{rcl} \multicolumn{3}{l}{\min c^{\mathrm{T}} x} \\ F(x) & \geq & \alpha \\ Dx & = & d \\ x & \geq & 0, \end{array}\right\} \tag{2.7}$$

with $F(x) := F_{\tilde{b}}(Ax) = P(\{\xi \mid Ax \geq \tilde{b}\})$ and $\mathcal{B}(\alpha) := \{x \mid F(x) \geq \alpha\}$. Assuming that rank$(D) = m$, that we have a feasible solution x of (2.7), and that we can partition D (if necessary after rearranging its columns) into $D = (B, N)$, B nonsingular, and correspondingly then also partition the vectors $x^{\mathrm{T}} = (y^{\mathrm{T}}, z^{\mathrm{T}})$, $c^{\mathrm{T}} = (f^{\mathrm{T}}, g^{\mathrm{T}})$ as well as a descent direction $w^{\mathrm{T}} = (u^{\mathrm{T}}, v^{\mathrm{T}})$, and finally that x is strictly nondegenerate with respect to B, i.e.

$$y_j > \varepsilon\,(> 0)\ \forall j\,, \tag{2.8}$$

the descent direction is determined by solving

$$\left.\begin{array}{rcrcll} \multicolumn{6}{l}{\max \tau} \\ f^{\mathrm{T}} u & + & g^{\mathrm{T}} v & \leq & -\tau & \\ \nabla_y^{\mathrm{T}} F(x) u & + & \nabla_z^{\mathrm{T}} F(x) v & \geq & \theta \cdot \tau & \text{if } F(x) \leq \alpha + \varepsilon \\ Bu & + & Nv & = & 0 & \\ & & v_j & \geq & 0 & \text{if } z_j \leq \varepsilon \\ & & \|v\|_\infty & \leq & 1\,, & \end{array}\right\} \tag{2.9}$$

where $\theta > 0$. Inserting $u = -B^{-1} N v$ we get the equivalent problem

$$\left.\begin{array}{rcll} \multicolumn{4}{l}{\max \tau} \\ r^{\mathrm{T}} v & \leq & -\tau & \\ s^{\mathrm{T}} v & \geq & \theta \cdot \tau & \text{if } F(x) \leq \alpha + \varepsilon \\ v_j & \geq & 0 & \text{if } z_j \leq \varepsilon \\ \|v\|_\infty & \leq & 1 & \end{array}\right\} \tag{2.10}$$

with

$$\begin{aligned} r^{\mathrm{T}} &= g^{\mathrm{T}} - f^{\mathrm{T}} B^{-1} N \\ s^{\mathrm{T}} &= \nabla_z^{\mathrm{T}} F(x) - \nabla_y^{\mathrm{T}} F(x) B^{-1} N \,. \end{aligned}$$

Now the procedure, proposed by Mayer [17], may be described as follows:

S1 Solve (2.10) yielding a solution $(\tau^\star, u^{\star\mathrm{T}}, v^{\star\mathrm{T}})$.

S2 Continue according to one of the following cases:

C1 If $\tau^\star = 0$, then let $\varepsilon = 0$ and solve (2.10) again. If you get still $\tau^\star = 0$, then the feasible solution $x^{\mathrm{T}} = (y^{\mathrm{T}}, z^{\mathrm{T}})$ is optimal.

Otherwise, reset ε to its original (positive) value; go to case *C2*.

C2 If $0 < \tau^\star \leq \varepsilon$, begin the following cycle:

i): Let $\varepsilon := 0.5\varepsilon$.

ii): Solve (2.10). If afterwards still $\tau^\star \leq \varepsilon$, go to *i)*; otherwise go on to *C3*.

C3 If $\tau^\star > \varepsilon$, then $w^{\star\mathrm{T}} = (u^{\star\mathrm{T}}, v^{\star\mathrm{T}})$ is accepted as search direction, and we continue with step **S3**.

S3 Determine by line search $\tilde{x} \approx \{\eta \mid \eta \geq 0;\ \eta = x + \mu w^\star,\ \mu \geq 0\} \cap \operatorname{bd} \mathcal{B}(\alpha)$ with a tolerance of ε.

S4 If $\tilde{x}$ still satisfies the strict nondegeneracy condition (2.8), repeat from **S1** with $x := \tilde{x}$ and the same partition of D;
otherwise exchange the basis in D such that with the new basis and $x := \tilde{x}$ (2.8) is satisfied, and return to **S1**.

The particular difficulty in this algorithm is the evaluation of $F(x)$ and $\nabla F(x)$, which are represented by multivariate integrals and hence cannot be computed in closed form. Hence, for $\tilde{b}$ having a multivariate normal distribution, Mayer proposed to use a fast simulation method developped by Szántai [31] and yielding simultaneously the function values of $F(x)$ and its gradient. In this version the method denoted as PROCON was implemented by Mayer [18].

Replacing in (2.7) the equalities $Dx = d$ by inequalities $Dx \geq d$ and imposing the following assumptions

- $\tilde{b}$ has a nondegenerate multinormal distribution;
- $M := \{x \mid Dx \geq d,\ x \geq 0\}$ is a bounded set;
- M contains a Slater point for the chance constraint, i.e. $\exists x^S \in M : F(x^S) > \alpha$;

Szántai [32] proposed for this problem an algorithm based on the supporting hyperplane method of Veinott [35] as follows:

S1 Choose $z^1 := x^S$, $k := 1$, $\mathcal{M}^1 := M$.

S2 Solve the linear programm $\min\{c^{\mathrm{T}}x \mid x \in \mathcal{M}^k\}$ yielding a solution x^k.

S3 If $F(x^k) \geq \alpha - \varepsilon$, stop;
else add a *feasibility cut* (see Figure 2.1) and go on to **S4**.

S4 Determine

$$\begin{aligned}
&y^k \in \overline{[z^k, x^k]} \cap \{x \mid F(x) = \alpha\};\\
&\mathcal{M}^{k+1} := \mathcal{M}^k \cap \{x \mid \nabla^{\mathrm{T}} F(y^k)(x - y^k) \geq 0\};\\
&z^{k+1} := z^k + \frac{1}{k+1}(y^k - z^k);\\
&k := k + 1 \text{ and go to step } \mathbf{S2}.
\end{aligned}$$

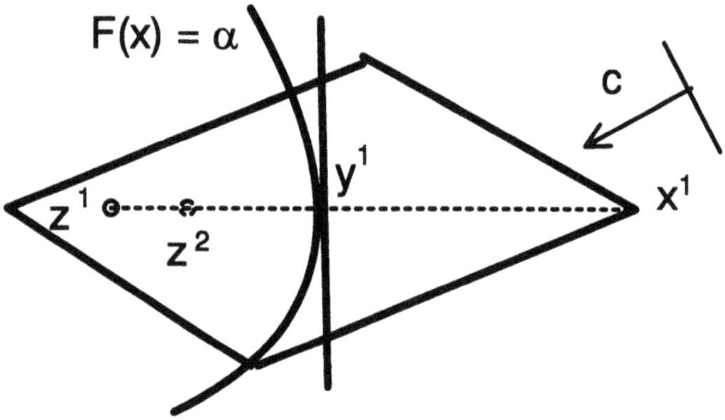

Figure 2.1: One iteration in PCSPIOR

This method was denoted as PCSPIOR and implemented by Mayer [18] as well.

Finally, under the additional assumption that the objective is bounded above on the feasible set by some U, Mayer [18] proposed and implemented a cutting plane method called PROBALL based on the central cutting plane method by Elzinga–Moore [11], which briefly may be described as follows:

S1 Let $z^1 := x^S$, $k := 1$ and
$\mathcal{P}^1 := \{(x^{\mathrm{T}}, \eta)^{\mathrm{T}} \mid D_i^T x - \|D_i\|\eta \geq d_i \; \forall i, \; c^{\mathrm{T}}x + \eta \leq U\}$ (with D_i the i-th row vector of D).

S2 Solve the linear program $\max\{\eta \mid (x^{\mathrm{T}}, \eta)^{\mathrm{T}} \in \mathcal{P}^k\}$, yielding a solution $({x^k}^{\mathrm{T}}, \eta^k)^{\mathrm{T}}$.

S3 If $\eta^k \leq \varepsilon$, then stop; else

- if $F(x^k) < \alpha$, then add a *feasibility cut*, go on to step **S4**;
- else add an *objective (central) cut* (see Figure 2.2), go on to step **S5**.

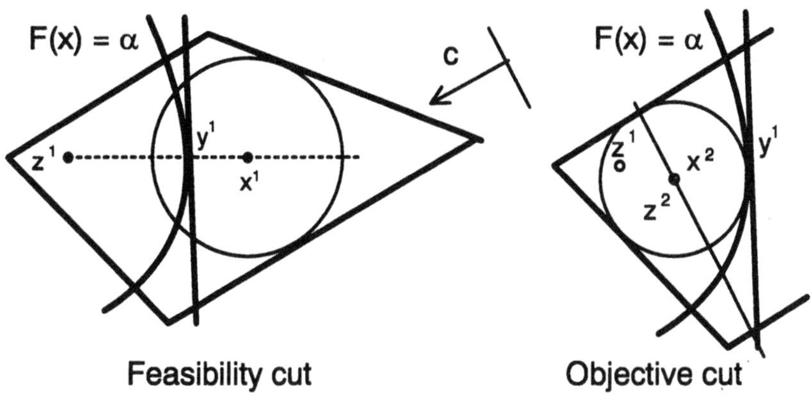

Figure 2.2: PROBALL: Feasibility cut and objective cut

S4 Determine

$y^k \in \overline{[z^k, x^k]} \cap \{x \mid F(x) = \alpha\}$;
$\mathcal{P}^{k+1} := \mathcal{P}^k \cap \{(x^{\mathrm{T}}, \eta)^{\mathrm{T}} \mid \nabla^{\mathrm{T}} F(y^k)(x - y^k) - \|\nabla F(y^k)\|\eta \geq 0\}$;
$z^{k+1} := z^k$, $k := k + 1$; go to step **S2**.

S5 Replace the objective cut by $c^{\mathrm{T}}x + \eta \leq c^{\mathrm{T}}x^k$;
if $F(x^k) > \alpha$, then let $z^{k+1} := x^k$,
else $z^{k+1} := z^k$, $k := k + 1$, and go to step **S2**.

The iterates generated in this method, due to Nemhauser–Widhelm [22], allow for an intuitive interpretation:

With

- $J^k := \{j \mid 1 \leq j \leq k$, feasibility cut in iteration $j\}$,
- $I^k := \{1, \cdots, k\} \setminus J^k$, i.e. iterations with objective cuts in the first k cycles,
- $U^k := \min[U, \min_{i \in I^k} c^{\mathrm{T}} x^i]$

we have:

x^k is the center and η^k the radius of the largest sphere inscribed to the convex polyhedron given by

$$\left.\begin{array}{rcll} D_i^{\mathrm{T}} x & \geq & d_i & \forall i \\ c^{\mathrm{T}} x & \leq & U^k & \\ \nabla^{\mathrm{T}} F(y^j)(x - y^j) & \geq & 0 & \forall j \in J^k. \end{array}\right\} \tag{2.11}$$

To implement any one of these three methods for any other quasi-concave distribution $F_{\tilde{b}}$ requires the availability of a fast Monte Carlo method to compute F and its gradient.

3 SLP with recourse

In general, multistage SLP's with recourse may be stated as follows:
Given

- a probability space $(\Omega, \mathcal{G}, P)$;
- random vectors $\xi_t : \Omega \longrightarrow \mathbb{R}^{r_t}$ (with $\xi_1 \equiv 0$) such that $\xi_t \in L^2(\Omega, \mathbb{R}^{r_t})$ (with respect to $(\Omega, \mathcal{G}, P)$);
- the joint distributions of $\vec{\xi}_t := (\xi_1^{\mathrm{T}}, \cdots, \xi_t^{\mathrm{T}})^{\mathrm{T}}$, $t = 1, \cdots, T$;
- the σ-algebras $\mathcal{F}_t := \sigma(\vec{\xi}_t)$, $t = 1, \cdots, T$, (with $\mathcal{F}_1 := \{\Omega, \emptyset\}$) such that $\mathcal{F}_t \subset \mathcal{G}$, $\mathcal{F}_t \subset \mathcal{F}_{t+1}$ $\forall t$ (i.e. $\{\mathcal{F}_t,\ t = 1, \cdots, T\}$ being a *filtration*);
- $\mathcal{F} := \{\mathcal{F}_1, \cdots, \mathcal{F}_T\}$, where possibly $\mathcal{F}_T = \mathcal{G}$;
- the $m_t \times n_\tau$- matrices $\tilde{A}_{t\tau} := A_{t\tau}(\cdot)$, m_t-vectors $\tilde{b}_t := b_t(\cdot)$ and n_t-vectors $\tilde{c}_t := c_t(\cdot)$ being linear affine in $\vec{\xi}_t$ (and hence being $\mathcal{F}_t$-measurable and having finite second moments);
- X_t a linear subspace of $L^2(\Omega, \mathbb{R}^{n_t})$ (with respect to $(\Omega, \mathcal{G}, P)$), including the set of $\mathcal{F}_t$-simple functions;
- M_t the set of $\mathcal{F}_t$-measurable functions $\Omega \longrightarrow \mathbb{R}^{n_t}$, and hence $X_t \cap M_t$ being a closed linear subspace of X_t;

the T-stage stochastic linear program with recourse is formulated as

$$\left.\begin{array}{rcll} \min E\left\{\sum_{t=1}^{T} \tilde{c}_t^{\mathrm{T}} x_t\right\} & & & \\ \sum_{\tau=1}^{t} \tilde{A}_{t\tau} x_\tau & = & \tilde{b}_t & \text{a.s., } t = 1, \cdots, T, \\ x_t & \geq & 0 & \text{a.s., } t = 1, \cdots, T, \\ x_t & \in & X_t \cap M_t, & t = 1, \cdots, T. \end{array}\right\} \tag{3.1}$$

The interpretation of this model is the following: We decide first—i.e. in the first stage—on x_1, feasible for the first block of constraints $A_{11}x_1 = b_1$, $x_1 \geq 0$, (deterministic due to the above assumptions). Having observed the realization $\hat{\xi}_2$ of ξ_2, and thus a realization of $\vec{\xi}_2$, we decide on $x_2 \in X_2$ such that the constraints $A_{21}(\vec{\xi}_2)x_1 + A_{22}(\vec{\xi}_2)x_2 = b_2(\vec{\xi}_2)$, $x_2 \geq 0$, and $x_2(\omega) = \text{const}$ on $\vec{\xi}_2^{\,-1}[(\xi_1^{\mathrm{T}}, \hat{\xi}_2^{\mathrm{T}})^{\mathrm{T}}] \in \mathcal{F}_2$ according to $x_2 \in X_t \cap M_t$ are satisfied, the latter condition saying that x_2 may not depend on those events $D_t = \overrightarrow{\xi}_t^{-1}[B] \in \mathcal{F}_t,\ t > 2$, (with B a Borel set in $\mathbb{R}^{(r_1+\cdots+r_t)}$), not being events in $\mathcal{F}_2$, i.e. the decision on x_2 is to be *nonanticipative*. Analogously, we continue to decide on x_3, x_4, etc., for any t having a realization $\hat{\xi}_t$ of ξ_t, and thus of $\overrightarrow{\xi}_t$, for the corresponding data $A_{t\tau}, \tau = 1, \cdots, t;\ b_t$, observing the constraints $\sum_{\tau=1}^{t} A_{t\tau} x_\tau = b_t, x_t \geq 0$, and the nonanticipativity constraint $x_t \in X_t \cap M_t$ such that the *policy* $\{x_t(\overrightarrow{\xi}_t), t = 1, \cdots, T\}$ is $\mathcal{F}$*-adapted.*

3.1 Discrete distributions

Consider the case of $\overrightarrow{\xi}_t, t = 1, \cdots, T$, having finite discrete distributions. Then the filtration $\mathcal{F} = \{\mathcal{F}_1, \cdots, \mathcal{F}_T\}$ is finite, and the corresponding data $\{[A_{t\tau}(\overrightarrow{\xi}_t), \tau = 1, \cdots, t], b_t(\overrightarrow{\xi}_t), c_t(\overrightarrow{\xi}_t); t = 1, \cdots, T\}$ have finite discrete distributions as well.

The finite σ-algebras $\mathcal{F}_t = \sigma(\overrightarrow{\xi}_t)$ are generated by finite partitions of Ω given as

$$\Omega = \bigcup_{i=1}^{k_t} B_i^t \text{ with } B_j^t \cap B_\ell^t = \emptyset \text{ for } j \neq \ell. \tag{3.2}$$

If we have, analogously,

$$\Omega = \bigcup_{i=1}^{k_{t+1}} C_i^{t+1} \text{ with } C_j^{t+1} \cap C_\ell^{t+1} = \emptyset \text{ for } j \neq \ell, \tag{3.3}$$

then the filtration property $\mathcal{F}_t \subseteq \mathcal{F}_{t+1}$ implies:

$$\forall i : 1 \leq i \leq k_t\ \exists J_i^{t+1} \subset \{1, \cdots, k_{t+1}\} : \quad B_i^t = \bigcup_{k \in J_i^{t+1}} C_k^{t+1}. \tag{3.4}$$

Obviously (since $\mathcal{F}_t = \sigma(\overrightarrow{\xi}_t)$) we have

$$\overrightarrow{\xi}_t(\omega) \equiv \text{const} \text{ for } \omega \in B_i^t,\ i = 1, \cdots, k_t;\ t = 1 \cdots, T,$$

and for a policy $x = \{x_t(\overrightarrow{\xi}_t), t = 1, \cdots, T\} = \{x_1(\omega), \cdots, x_T(\omega)\}$ holds:

$$x \text{ is } \mathcal{F}\text{-adapted} \iff x_t(\omega) = \text{const}\ \forall \omega \in B_i^t, \forall i, t. \tag{3.5}$$

The filtration $\mathcal{F}$ may now be represented by a *scenario tree*, i.e. a rooted tree with nodes associated to the components B_i^t of partitions (3.2), for $i = 1, \cdots, k_t,\ t = 1, \cdots, T$. The construction of a scenario tree is indicated in Fig. 3.1, where e.g. node i in stage t corresponds to B_i^t in the partition (3.2) and the nodes $J_i^{t+1} = \{k1, \cdots, k4\}$ in stage t+1 correspond to $C_k^{t+1}, k \in J_i^{t+1}$, according to (3.4). Hence, the arcs of the tree reflect exactly the successive

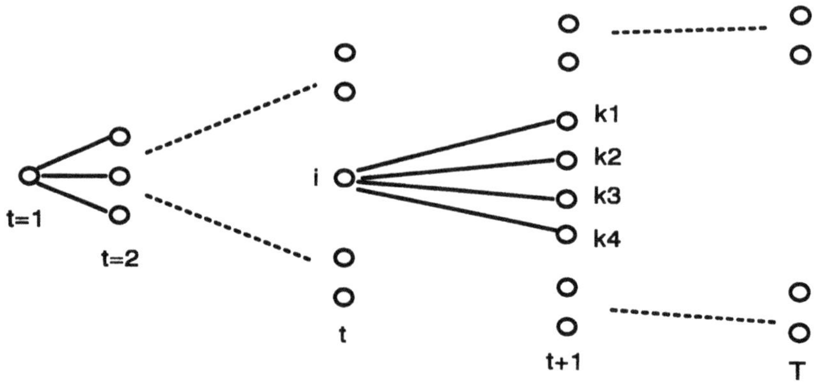

Figure 3.1: Scenario tree

subpartitions described in (3.4), i.e. node $i \sim B_i^t$ is connected to $k \sim C_k^{t+1}$ if and only if $k \in J_i^{t+1}$.

For the scenario tree we have the following notations:

- $\mathcal{T} = (\mathcal{N}, \mathcal{A})$, the scenario tree, is a rooted tree, the nodes $n \in \mathcal{N}$ in hierarchical levels t_n corresponding to stages, where
  - $n = 1$ with $t_1 = 1$ is the (only) root,
  - the nodes $\{n \mid t_n = T\}$ are the leaves, and
  - the unique path from the root $n = 1$ to any leaf n with $t_n = T$ is a *scenario*;
- S is the set of scenarios (*root-to-leaf paths*);
- p_s is the probability of scenario $s \in S$;
- S_n is the set of scenarios passing through node $n \in \mathcal{N}$;
- $\overline{p}_n = \sum_{s \in S_n} p_s$ is the probability to reach node n at all;
- $H_n \subseteq \mathcal{N}$ are the predecessor nodes of node n (*history*);
- $\overline{H}_n = H_n \cup \{n\}$;
- $C_n \subset \mathcal{N}$ are the immediate successor nodes of node n (*children of* n or *immediate future of* n);
- $\overline{B}_n \subseteq \Omega$ is the event in $\mathcal{F}_{t_n}$ belonging to node n.

Obviously, for any $n \in \mathcal{N}$ the random vector $\vec{\xi}_{t_n}(\omega)$ has a constant realization $\overline{\xi}_n$ on $\overline{B}_n$, with probability $\overline{p}_n = P(\overline{B}_n)\ \forall n \in \mathcal{N}$. Observing that the constraints are required a.s., and $\overline{p}_m = 0$ for some $m \in H_n$ implies $\overline{p}_n = 0$, it follows that the MSLP (3.1) may be written as

$$\left.\begin{array}{rrcll} \min & \displaystyle\sum_{n\in\mathcal{N}:\ \overline{p}_n>0} \overline{p}_n c_{t_n}^{\mathrm{T}}(\overline{\xi}_n)x_n & & & \\ & \displaystyle\sum_{\substack{m\,\in\,\overline{H}_n:\\ \overline{p}_m>0}} A_{t_n t_m}(\overline{\xi}_n)x_m & = & b_{t_n}(\overline{\xi}_n) & \forall n:\overline{p}_n>0 \\ & x_n & \geq & 0 & \forall n:\overline{p}_n>0. \end{array}\right\} \qquad (3.6)$$

x_m being associated to node m, i.e. to $\overline{B}_m$, and due to the measurability w.r.t. $\mathcal{F}_{t_m}$ being constant on $\overline{B}_m$.

Further, from (3.4) and (3.2) follows immediately

$$\overline{p}_n = \sum_{k\in C_n} \overline{p}_k\ \forall n: t_n < T \ \text{ and } \sum_{n\in\mathcal{N},\ t_n=t} \overline{p}_n = 1\ \forall t \in \{1,\cdots,T\},$$

such that the $\overline{p}_n$ yield in any particular stage a probability distribution on the nodes of this stage.

In particular, the $\overline{p}_n$ yield a probability distribution on the set of leaves $\{n \mid t_n = T\}$, which, in turn, are in a one-to-one relation with the root-to-leaf paths, i.e. with the scenarios; hence we also have the probability distribution $\{p_s\}$ on the set of scenarios, which may be understood as sample paths of a stochastic process on a finite state space in discrete time.

Models of this type, under further special assumptions like

- $c_{t_n}(\vec{\xi}_{t_n}) \equiv c_{t_n}$ and $A_{t_n t_n}(\vec{\xi}_{t_n}) \equiv A_{t_n t_n}\ \forall n$,
- a complete recourse assumption for $A_{t_n t_n}$, i.e. a condition usually stated as $\{y \mid A_{t_n t_n} y = z,\ y \geq 0\} \neq \emptyset\ \forall z$,

have been used in various applications, for instance in water storage problems as in Prékopa–Szántai [27], and in particular in finance, e.g. Cariño et al. [4, 5, 6] and Mulvey [19]; and solution methods were proposed adapted to special data structures arising in these applications, as e.g. by Mulvey–Ruszczyński [20, 21].

For the two stage case our problem (3.6) is reduced to

$$\left.\begin{array}{rrcll} \min c_1^{\mathrm{T}} x_1 + \displaystyle\sum_{n=2}^{K} p_n c_2^{\mathrm{T}} x_n & & & & \\ A_{11} x_1 & & = & b_1 & \\ A_{21}(\bar{\xi}_n) x_1 & + A_{22} x_n & = & b_2(\bar{\xi}_n)\,, & n = 2, \cdots, K\,, \\ & x_n & \geq & 0 & n = 1, \cdots, K\,, \end{array}\right\} \quad (3.7)$$

having a dual decomposition structure and therefore being efficiently solvable by especially designed methods, for instance the L-shaped decomposition of Van Slyke–Wets [34] or the regularized decomposition of Ruszczyński [30].

3.2 Continuous distributions

Coming back to our general problem (3.1) with arbitrary (continuous) distributions, we consider first the two stage case (with $A_{22}(\cdot)$ and $c_2(\cdot)$ constant) which obviously may be reformulated as

$$\left.\begin{array}{rcl} \min c_1^{\mathrm{T}} x_1 + E\{Q(x_1, \xi_2)\} & & \\ A_{11} x_1 & = & b_1 \\ x_1 & \geq & 0 \end{array}\right\} \quad (3.8)$$

with

$$\left.\begin{array}{rcl} Q(x_1, \xi_2) := \min c_2^{\mathrm{T}} x_2 & & \\ A_{22} x_2 & = & b_2(\xi_2) - A_{21}(\xi_2) x_1 \\ x_2 & \geq & 0. \end{array}\right\} \quad (3.9)$$

Assuming that $\Xi := \operatorname{supp} P$ is an interval in $\mathbb{R}^{r_2}$ such that $\bar{\xi}_2 := E\xi_2 \in \Xi$, and observing that—under the complete recourse assumption—$Q(x_1, \cdot) : \Xi \longrightarrow \mathbb{R}$ is convex, from Jensen's inequality [13] and the Edmundson–Madansky inequality [10, 15] (defining a particular discrete distribution $\tilde{P}$ on $\operatorname{extr} \Xi$, the vertices of Ξ) we get, for all feasible x_1, the bounds

$$Q(x_1, \bar{\xi}_2) \leq E\{Q(x_1, \xi_2)\} \leq \int_{\operatorname{extr} \Xi} Q(x_1, \xi_2) \tilde{P}(d\xi_2), \quad (3.10)$$

yielding in turn an error bound for approximating $E\{Q(x_1, \xi_2)\}$ by $Q(x_1, \bar{\xi}_2)$. If this bound is too large, we may partition Ξ into two subintervals Ξ_1, Ξ_2 and apply bounds analogous to (3.10), using the conditional distributions of ξ_2 with respect to the subintervals. If we continue to partition the subintervals in an appropriate way, it can be shown, that this leads to increasing the successive lower and decreasing the successive upper bounds such that we get convergence to $E\{Q(x_1, \xi_2)\}$ from both sides as well as convergence of the corresponding approximating solutions to the solution of (3.8). This approach is implemented and works as long as the dimension of the random vector ξ_2 is not too high ($\dim \xi_2 \leq 10$, say), since beyond that the size of the approximating problems exceeds our computational possibilities, in general. One exception from this fact is the special case of *simple recourse*, where $A_{21}(\cdot) \equiv A_{21}$ and $A_{22} = (I, -I)$. As was pointed out by Wets [36], then the objective of (3.8) is a separable function, the components depending on the components of $b_2(\cdot)$. Hence, in the above procedure instead of partitioning r_2-dimensional intervals we have to deal only with partitioning one-dimensional intervals corresponding to the components of $b_2(\cdot)$, and the number of these components is by far not as prohibitive for this algorithm as the dimension of ξ_2 for the general case. Nevertheless, also for the latter case methods have been developped which could be shown to succeed, e.g. the stochastic decomposition of Higle–Sen [12]. More details on these and other algorithmic approaches for problem (3.8) may be found in Kall–Wallace [14].

Unfortunately, for the general problem (3.1)—with continuous distributions and more than two stages—appropriate and computationally manageable approximation schemes, similar to those mentioned above for the two stage case, are not known up to now. One problem is that we do not know much about bounds derived from discretizations of the original distributions. To give an example: Under the assumptions that

- only the $\tilde{b}_t$ are random;
- the random vectors $\xi_2, \cdots, \xi_T$ are stochastically independent;
- there exist intervals $\Xi^t \subset \mathbb{R}^{r_t}$ such that range $\xi_t \subseteq \Xi^t$;
- A_{tt} are complete fixed recourse matrices $\forall t \geq 2$;

and further, that by successively partitioning the intervals Ξ^t and constructing accordingly scenario trees, it can be shown that these discretized problems yield lower bounds for the optimal value of the original problem. However, if only one of the above assumptions, the mutual independence of the random vectors ξ_t, does not hold, we find immediately counterexamples to the conjecture that the discretization yields a lower bound. And about upper bounds we know practically nothing for the general multistage case.

It seems that there is still a long way to go until we have operational approximation schemes for multistage problems with arbitrary distributions at our disposal. Nevertheless, there is a broad activity on the discrete case, considering practically relevant issues like scenario generation, scenario reduction, appropriate (and efficient) solution methods applicable to scenario trees, and—last but not least—modelling practical problems as multistage stochastic programs.

References

[1] J. Abadie and J. Carpentier. Generalization of the Wolfe reduced gradient method to the case of nonlinear constraints. In R. Fletcher, editor, *Optimization*, pages 37–47. Academic Press, London, 1969.

[2] E.M.L. Beale. The use of quadratic programming in stochastic linear programming. Rand Report P-2404, The RAND Corporation, 1961.

[3] C. Borell. Convex set functions in *d*-space. *Period. Math. Hungar.*, 6:111–136, 1975.

[4] D.R. Cariño et al. The Russell-Yasuda Kasai Model: An asset/liability model for the Japanese Insurance Company using multistage stochastic programming. *Interfaces*, 24:29–49, 1994.

[5] D.R. Cariño and W.T. Ziemba. Formulation of the Russell-Yasuda Kasai financial planning model. *Oper. Res.*, 46:433–449, 1998.

[6] D.R. Cariño, D.H. Myers, and W.T. Ziemba. Concepts, technical issues and uses of the Russell-Yasuda Kasai financial planning model. *Oper. Res.*, 48:450–462, 1998.

[7] A. Charnes and W.W. Cooper. Chance-constrained programming. *Management Sci.*, 5:73–79, 1959.

[8] G.B. Dantzig. Linear programming under uncertainty. *Management Sci.*, 1:197–206, 1955.

[9] G.B. Dantzig and A. Madansky. On the solution of two-stage linear programs under uncertainty. In I.J. Neyman, editor, *Proc. 4th Berkeley Symp. Math. Stat. Prob.*, pages 165–176, Berkeley, 1961.

[10] H.P. Edmundson. Bounds on the expectation of a convex function of a random variable. Technical Report Paper 982, The RAND Corporation, 1956.

[11] J. Elzinga and T.G. Moore. A central cutting plane method for the convex programming problem. *Math. Prog.*, 8:134–145, 1975.

[12] J.L. Higle and S. Sen. *Stochastic Decomposition. A Statistical Method for Large Scale Stochastic Linear Programming.* Kluwer Academic Publ., 1996.

[13] J.L. Jensen. Sur les fonctions convexes et les inégalités entre les valeurs moyennes. *Acta Math.*, 30:173–177, 1906.

[14] P. Kall and S.W. Wallace. *Stochastic Programming.* John Wiley & Sons, Chichester, 1994.

[15] A. Madansky. Bounds on the expectation of a convex function of a multivariate random variable. *Ann. Math. Statist.*, 30:743–746, 1959.

[16] K. Marti. Konvexitätsaussagen zum linearen stochastischen Optimierungsproblem. *Z. Wahrsch. theorie u. verw. Geb.*, 18:159–166, 1971.

[17] J. Mayer. Probabilistic constrained programming: A reduced gradient algorithm implemented on PC. Working Paper WP-88-39, IIASA, Laxenburg, 1988.

[18] J. Mayer. *Stochastic Linear Programming Algorithms: A Comparison Based on a Model Management System.* Gordon and Breach Science Publishers, 1998.
(Habilitationsschrift, Wirtschaftswiss. Fakultät, Universität Zürich, 1996).

[19] J.M. Mulvey. Financial planning via multi-stage stochastic programs. In J.R. Birge and K.G. Murty, editors, *Mathematical Programming – State of the Art 1994*, pages 151–171. University of Michigan, 1994.

[20] J.M. Mulvey and A. Ruszczyński. Diagonal quadratic approximation method for linear multistage stochastic programming problems. In P. Kall, editor, *System Modelling and Optimization*, pages 588–597, Berlin, 1992. Springer-Verlag. Lecture Notes in Contr. Inf. Sci. 180.

[21] J.M. Mulvey and A. Ruszczyński. A new scenario decomposition method for large-scale stochastic optimization. *Oper. Res.*, 43:477–490, 1995.

[22] G.L. Nemhauser and W.B. Widhelm. A modified linear program for columnar methods in mathematical programming. *Oper. Res.*, 19:1051–1060, 1971.

[23] A. Prékopa. On probabilistic constrained programming. In H.W. Kuhn, editor, *Proc. of the Princeton Symposioum on Math. Programming*, pages 113–138. Princeton University Press, Princeton, New Jersey, 1970.

[24] A. Prékopa. Logarithmic concave measures with applications to stochastic programming. *Acta Sci. Math. (Szeged)*, 32:301–316, 1971.

[25] A. Prékopa. Numerical solution of probabilistic constrained programming problems. In Y. Ermoliev and R.J-B. Wets, editors, *Numerical Techniques for Stochastic Optimization*, pages 123–139. Springer-Verlag, Berlin, 1988.

[26] A. Prékopa. *Stochastic Programming.* Kluwer Academic Publ., 1995.

[27] A. Prékopa and T. Szántai. On multistage stochastic programming (with application to optimal control of water supply). In *Progress in Operations Research*, pages 733–755. North-Holland Publ. Co., 1976. Proceedings Eger Hungary 1974, Coll. Math. Soc. J. Bolyai 12.

[28] W. M. Raike. Dissection methods for solution in chance constrained programming problems under discrete distributions. *Management Sci.*, 16:708–715, 1970.

[29] Y. Rinott. On convexity of measures. *Ann. Prob.*, 4:1020–1026, 1976.

[30] A. Ruszczyński. A regularized decomposition method for minimizing a sum of polyhedral functions. *Math. Prog.*, 35:309–333, 1986.

[31] T. Szántai. Calculation of the multivariate probability distribution function values and their gradient vectors. Working Paper WP-87-82, IIASA, Laxenburg, 1987.

[32] T. Szántai. A computer code for solution of probabilistic-constrained stochastic programming problems. In Y. M. Ermoliev and R. J.-B. Wets, editors, *Numerical Techniques for Stochastic Optimization*, pages 229–235. Springer-Verlag, Berlin, 1988.

[33] G. Tintner. Stochastic linear programming with applications to agricultural economics. In H.A. Antosiewicz, editor, *Proc. 2nd Symp. Linear Programming*, volume 2, pages 197–228, Washington D.C., 1955. National Bureau of Standards.

[34] R. Van Slyke and R. J-B. Wets. *L*-shaped linear programs with applications to optimal control and stochastic linear programs. *SIAM J. Appl. Math.*, 17:638–663, 1969.

[35] A.F. Veinott. The supporting hyperplane method for unimodal programming. *Oper. Res.*, 15:147–152, 1967.

[36] R. Wets. Programming under uncertainty: The complete problem. *Z. Wahrsch. theorie u. verw. Geb.*, 4:316–339, 1966.

Part 3:

Decision Support and Management Systems

Infrastructure for CRISIS-2000

A Distributed Disaster Management System

Nenad Marovac

Department of Mathematical and Computer Sciences

San Diego State University, USA

Abstract

Either nature-caused and man-made disasters seem to be occurring more frequently and are more severe, or our communication technology has advanced considerably and we are made aware more quickly and completely of disasters happening everywhere in the world. Such disasters can cause a large number of injured, dead and homeless. Some disasters are small and can be handled by the local authorities. On the other hand, some of them may be large in magnitude and spread over large geographical areas and therefore require coordination by authorities in many localities, as well as authorities of county, region, state and country levels - as in the case of very large earthquakes, coordinated worldwide distributed terrorist activities, etc.

This paper[1] presents the infrastructure for CRISIS-2000 system, a worldwide distributed system for crisis management. The purpose of the system is to enable optimal management of activities and resources in handling disasters in an arbitrary large geographical area, i.e. it allocates the resources in a manner so that effects of the crises, e.g. number of fatalities and human suffering, are minimized. The system applies the most recent advances in methodologies of Operations Research, Artificial Intelligence, Information Management and Web Technology.

---

[1] Parts of this paper are based on the paper „Marovac, N. and Staehly, P. :CRISIS-2000: A Decision Support System for Major Disasters, presented at the conference OR-2000, October 2000, Dresden, Germany".

1 Introduction

Disasters caused by nature and man, e.g. earthquakes, airplane crashes, terrorist attacks, etc., can result in a large number of deaths, injured, and homeless. When a crisis occurs in an area, authorities responsible for that area respond quickly but efficiently to minimize the number of casualties, suffering, and economic effects. If the response is fast but not optimal, due to lack of sufficient and correct information, it may result in unnecessary additional loss of life and property. The responses include:

- ❖ allocating resources to handle the effects of disasters, e.g. distributing the injured with certain type of injuries to the nearest and most adequate emergency stations and hospitals

- ❖ dispatching transportation resources that are most suitable and that would require the least time to get to the crisis location and from the disaster area to designated treatment facilities, and

- ❖ placing homeless people into existing shelters and to set up new shelters and kitchens if needed.

Complete, precise, and immediately available information regarding crisis type, location and severity, as well as resource availability, types and locations are imperative to make fast and optimal decisions. Once the optimal decisions are made, it is important to issue associated commands to resources using most efficient means. Furthermore, it is imperative to process progress reports from the resources and to fine-tune the decision as the situation unfolds.

In dealing with crisis we address three possible **crisis situations**:

1. The local authorities have adequate resources at their disposal and can effectively manage the crisis.

2. The crisis is large and the local authorities do not have enough resources to handle all wounded and homeless persons involved in the crisis. In this case, the local authorities need to approach neighboring localities to obtain additional resources.

3. A disaster may be too large to be handled by the local authorities alone. They, i.e. the local authorities, either do not have enough resources, or they may lack special resources required for proper handling of the disaster (e.g. large military transport planes), or they may lack authority to contain and respond

to a crisis of a certain type, e.g. terrorist attack. In this case, the local authorities contact the next higher level of authority and request that the management decisions and resource coordination be done by authorities on that level. In most cases the authorities on this higher level may be able to coordinate and allocate the resources and delegate the implementation to the lower, i.e. local authorities. In other cases, the authorities on the next level may decide that the crisis must be handled by the authorities on a higher level of authority, (maybe state or province or even on the federal level), and they pass the information about the crisis to the next level. This may continue until the proper level of authority is reached.

A similar, but somewhat more complex situation occurs when a disaster is very large and spans a number of localities and may be distributed over a number of cities, counties and maybe states. In this case, all decisions should defer to a higher authority; a single locality should not make any decisions about handling of the crisis even in its own area. The effort in handling the crisis should typically be coordinated by the authority on the lowest level that has responsibility over all affected areas.

The aim of a project initiated jointly between research teams at the San Diego State University and the University of St. Gallen, is to develop a web based computer-aided information and decision support system, which assists the crisis specialist staff in optimally handling major disasters. The system integrates Web Technology, Information Management, Operations Research and Artificial Intelligence methodologies and techniques.

At the onset of the research the following goals were clear and specified:

- The system should be distributed and based on the Internet. It should cover an arbitrary large geographical area. This is a very important aspect. The system should be usable to manage disasters over areas of any size and should be able to utilize or suggest resources both within these and outside these areas.

- It would be useful and desirable to utilize the system to coordinate activities when managing multiple crises in a very large area, e.g. multiple terrorist attacks simultaneously happening in a number of areas that could be in different cities or countries.

- The system should be as automatic as possible. When making management decisions it is common today to use computer based optimizing systems that use complex algorithms and methods. However, in most cases the data gathering and input is manual causing unacceptable time delays.

- It should support all three crisis situations identified above.

- It should be platform independent

For our system to be successful it must emphasize three features:

- ❖ Very efficient infrastructure that would provide for:
  - ➢ Prompt and precise reporting of disasters, and
  - ➢ Fast communication between all concerned parties, i.e. crisis management centers, hospitals, shelters, fire brigades, police and transportation units.
- ❖ Enable decision-making and management centers to automatically make optimal decisions to minimize the number of deaths due to injuries and to help the maximum number of people in the shortest time, and to keep the suffering of injured and homeless to a minimum. The crisis management specialist staff reviews the decisions and accepts them as such or modifies them as needed.
- ❖ Monitor the progress of handling the resolution of the crisis.

This paper presents the infrastructure for the CRISIS-2000 Disaster Management System. It describes the overall organization of the system and the information flow in gathering of information, decision making, issuing of commands to resources, processing progress reports and tuning the decisions as the progress of handling the crisis evolves.

All models included in the paper are presented in the Unified Modeling Language (UML). The models are generated using The Rational Corporation Suite Enterprise 1.5.

2 The Model of the Problem

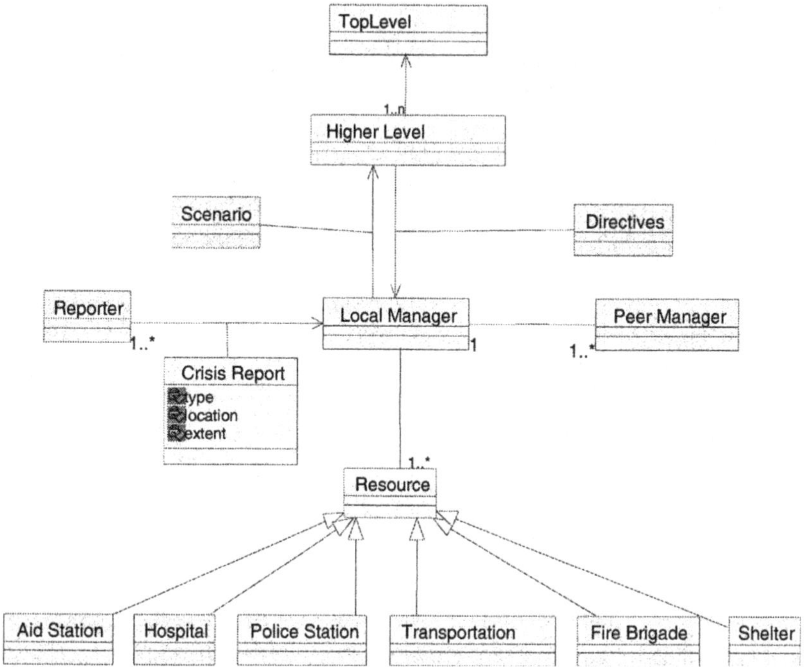

Figure 1: Model for crisis

The conceptual model for the problem is shown in Figure 1. It depicts all entities involved in the crisis reporting and management. In the figure we identify:

1. **Reporter** is a person reporting crises. The crisis report contains information about the type, location and the extent of the crisis.

2. **Local Manager** is the entity responsible for managing the crisis in the vicinity in which the crisis occurred. The **vicinity** term as used here is a very flexible one: it may mean the a village, a section of a city, an entire city, a county, a state or a country depending on the type, size and number of disasters.

3. **Resource** (s) includes all resources that are used in handling the crisis. These resources include those under direct jurisdiction of the local manager. The resources are:

    - ❖ First-Aid Stations, i.e. emergency receiving stations erected at critical points in the crisis locality;
    - ❖ Hospitals;
    - ❖ Police Stations and other entities responsible for maintaining the order in handling the disaster;
    - ❖ Shelters;
    - ❖ Fire Brigades; and
    - ❖ Transportation Units, i.e. ambulances, trucks and other vehicles used in transportation of injured and homeless.

4. **Peer Managers** are entities responsible for managing crises in neighboring vicinities. They might be contacted to provide some resources under their jurisdiction if there are not sufficient resources available to the local manager for optimal crisis management.

5. **Higher Level Manager** represents the manager responsible for handling crises in the territory that encompasses the vicinity of the current crisis.

6. **Scenario,** or **crisis scenario,** is an information entity completely describing the crises-related situation in the vicinity. In normal circumstances the scenario only contains information about the available resources at the vicinity. This information is obtained from the periodic reporting by all the resources in the vicinity (see the next section). As the first report about a crisis is received the information about the crisis is added into the scenario. It is constantly updated as more information about that crisis is obtained. If any additional crisis at that vicinity occurs that may or may not be related to the original crisis the information about the new crisis is used to update the scenario. This is very important because crises should not be handled in isolation; the optimal decision must be made on handling all simultaneous crises in the area. Additional information about available resources, issued commands and progress in handling the crisis or multiple crises are added to the scenario as described below.

7. **Directives** are addressed below.

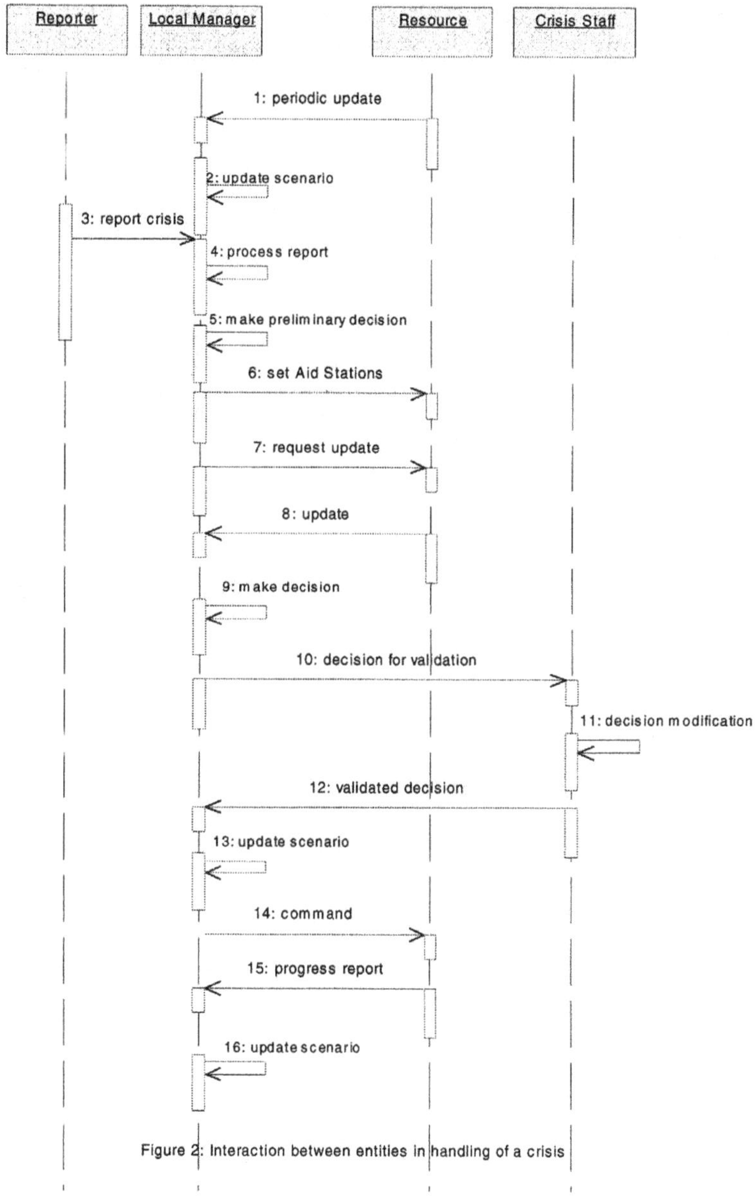

Figure 2: Interaction between entities in handling of a crisis

Figure 2 presents the interaction between the entities introduced in the Figure 1 in managing a crisis. These interactions are described below:

1. Periodic update – All resources in the vicinity send information about their available capacity to the local manager. These periodic updates are done once a day, e.g. in the morning. A resource may send additional periodic updates if its situation changes considerably during the day.

2. The local manager uses the information in these periodic updates to bring up to date the resource portion of the scenario.

3. A reporter sends a crisis report to the local manager. This report contains information about the type, location and extent of the crisis.

4. Process report. If this is the first report about a crisis it is processed and the crisis section of the scenario is updated and the information about the crisis is stored in the database. On the other hand if reports about crises have been received previously and there are situations that have not been closed yet, then the information in this current report must be consolidated with the information in the other previously received reports. Careful analysis has to be made to determine whether the information just received duplicates the information in previous reports, i.e. to determine whether the current crisis has already been reported. When the processing of this current report has been completed and the information consolidated, the scenario is updated. The appropriate information is stored in the database.

5. Make preliminary decision. If the local manager has determined that the crisis report just received indeed deals with a new crisis or at least a new section (location) of an already known crisis, it can make a preliminary decision about setting up First-Aid receiving stations. It does that on the basis of the information about resources as contained in the scenario, i.e. the information obtained through the periodic updates is precise enough for that decision.

6. Set First-Aid stations. The local manager issue commands to appropriate resources to establish First-Aid and receiving stations.

7. Request update. At this point the local manager issues requests to all local resources for updates about available capacities and whether any additional capacities can be made available, e.g. police stations can summon registered volunteers, or non-urgent operations can be rescheduled, non-critical patients may be converted to outpatients, etc.

8. Updates from local resources are being received and the scenario is updated.

9. The local manager makes the decision regarding optimal allocation of resources

    - ❖ distribution of the injured with certain types of injuries to the nearest and most adequate emergency stations and hospitals

    - ❖ allocation of transportation resources that are most suitable and would require the least time to get to the crisis location and from the disaster area to designated treatment facilities, and

    - ❖ transportation and placement of people made homeless by the disaster into existing shelters and to set up new shelters and kitchens if needed.

10. Decision validation. Information gathering and decision making is automatic applying the latest Operations Research and Management methodologies and techniques. Once the local manager system makes the decision that decision is presented to crisis managing specialist staff.

11. Decision modification. The crisis management specialist staff may either accept the decision made by the local manager (the system) or perform what-if analyses and modify the decision if needed.

12. Once the management staff accepts the decision it is submitted to the system for execution.

13. The local manager updates the scenario by adding the decision information to it. Also, the decision is translated into commands to individual resources.

14. The local manager issues commands to resources.

15. Resources execute requested activities and send progress reports to inform the local manager of their success or any problems.

16. As the progress reports are received the local managers fine tune the decision and update the scenario. This continues until the crisis situation is closed, i.e. all wounded and homeless are placed in the appropriate places of care and the crisis location is declared safe.

At this point an observation can be made. Automatic information gathering and decision making has a distinct advantage. As the first crisis report is received the system has enough information both about the crisis and available resources to make a preliminary decision and direct both setting up of First-Aid and receiving stations at strategic places, and dispatching fire brigade units if needed. At the same time the local manager can dispatch observation resources, e.g. helicopters and police units to gather more precise reports about the crisis. As these units are dispatched the system can request more precise information about the existing and additional emergency resources that can be made available. At that point in time more precise reports about the crisis or crises may be received, the information consolidated and the optimal decision made in the quickest possible time. This means also that the consolidation of information from multiple reports present much less of a problem than it may seem.

The step 9: make decision, as presented above can only handle properly the first crisis situation as identified in the Section One. If the local manager, while making the decision, realizes that the nature of the crises falls into one of the other two crisis situations the step 9 is expanded with additional steps as shown in interaction activity sub-diagrams in Figures 3 and 4.

Figure 3 shows the interactions and activities that take place when the crisis situation falls under the crisis situation 2.

1. Make decision, is the same as under the step 9 in Figure 2. However, the local manager realizes that it does not have enough resources in general or resources of a certain type, e.g. clinics that can handle burns, to satisfactory manage the crisis.

2. Ask for additional resources. In this case the local manager contacts one or more peer managers. These are local managers of the neighboring vicinities. The local manager requests additional resources located in neighboring vicinities and under the jurisdiction of the peer managers.

3. If the peer managers can free requested resources they send instructions to these resources that they will be delegated to the neighboring local manager, i.e. they will be under temporary jurisdiction of that local manager.

4. A peer manager informs the local manager about temporary delegation of requested resources.

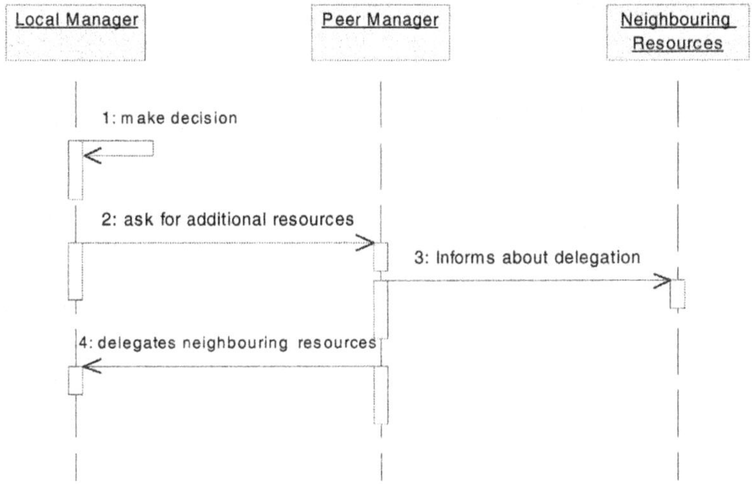

Figure 3: Interaction with Peer Managers

Figure 4 depicts the additional interactions and activities that take place when the crisis situation falls under the crisis situation 3:

1. Make decision, is the same as under the step 9 in Figure 2. However, the local managers realizes that the crisis is either too large or it is of a type it is not authorized to handle. Alternatively, another reason may be that the local manager cannot get enough additional resources from peer managers.

2. The local manager sends a complete scenario with the request for help to the higher level manager. Then the higher level manager makes the decision. It may also delegate some additional or special resources under its jurisdiction to the local manager. Alternatively, these special resources may stay under the control of the higher level manager but are sent to the vicinity of the local manager. In order for the higher level manager to make an optimal decision it is important to have complete information describing the crisis situation as well as all the available local resources. This is the reason that the local manager sends the complete crisis scenario. The decision the higher level manager makes is translated into a set of directives to the local manager.

3. The higher level manager informs the resources that they were delegated to the local level manager.

4. Directives are sent to the local manager. The local manager translates these directives into commands for individual resources.

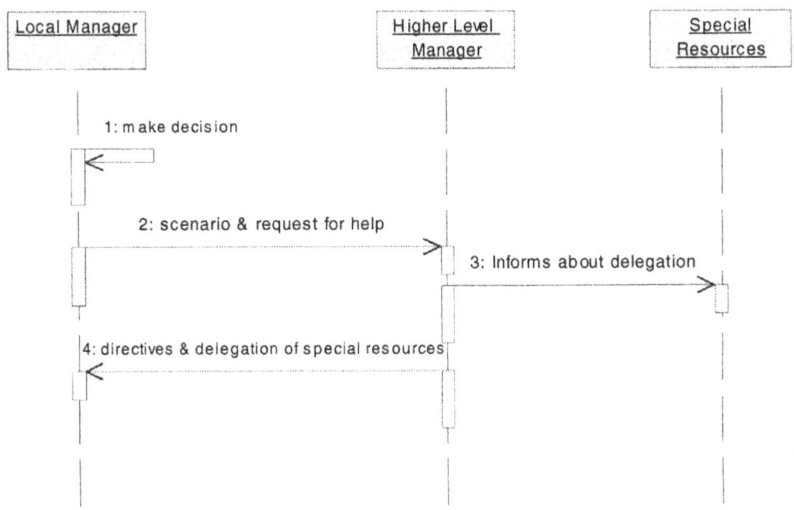

Figure 4: Interaction with Higher Level Manager

There are two observations that we should make at this point:

1. If a crisis is so large that a local manager is required to contact a higher level manager, it means most likely that one or more neighboring vicinities are also affected by the crisis, and that all local managers of the affected areas have also sent their crisis scenarios to the higher level manager. The higher level manager has the complete picture of the overall situation, and it is in the best position to make the optimal decision. It then translates the decision into responsibilities of the local managers for their vicinities and compiles these responsibilities into directives that are sent to respective local managers.

2. It may happen that the size or the nature of the crisis is such that this higher level manager can not nor is authorized to handle the crisis. In that case it forwards all scenarios it has received to the next level higher level manager, and this may be repeated until the appropriated level has been reached. Then the manager on that level makes the optimal decision and that decision in the form of a set of directives is passed "downstream" the chain of authority until the appropriate subset of directives reaches the local manager(s). It is important that the authority on the lowest level that has responsibility over all affected areas makes the decision and coordinates the management of the crisis.

3. Logical System Design

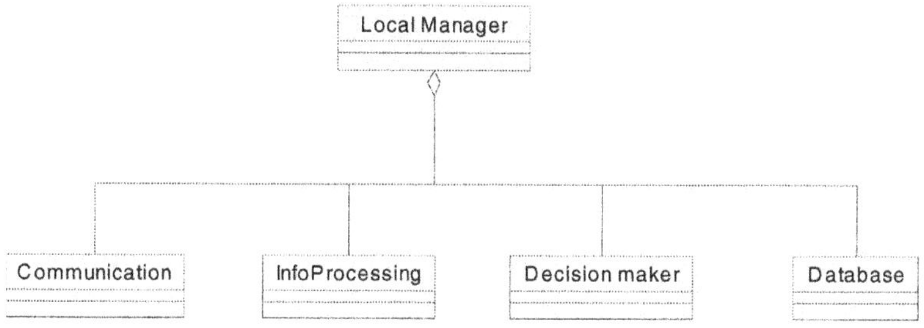

Figure 5: Local Manager components

The basic structure of the local manager entity is shown in Figure 5. We identify four components:

- **Communication** that handles all communication between reporters, resources, peer managers, and higher level managers.

- **InfoProcessing** contextually processes all information coming into the local manager system. It consolidates information contained in multiple crises reports. It also processes all available capacity and progress reports from resources. Furthermore, it maintains the crisis scenario.

- **Decision Maker** is the "brain" of the local manager. It initiates all requests for additional information and it makes all crisis management decisions concerning utilization of resources and required operations to handle the crisis. It also translates the decision or directives from higher level managers into commands to individual resources. Furthermore, it decides when to contact peer or higher level managers. Finally, it analyses the progress reports to fine tune the decision and to declare the crisis closed.

- **Database** is a persistent information storage device containing all operational data.

The basic structure of a resource entity is shown in Figure 6. We also identify four components:

- **Communication** that handles all communication with the local manager.

- **InfoProcessing** processes all requests coming from the local managers. It extracts from the associated database information about the available capacity. It cooperates with the Operations component to identify "current" capacity and the additional emergency capacity. This information is then sent to the local manager as the response for the update request.

- **Operations** is the software system used by the resource personnel for normal every day operations of the resource

- **Database** is a persistent information storage component containing all operational data.

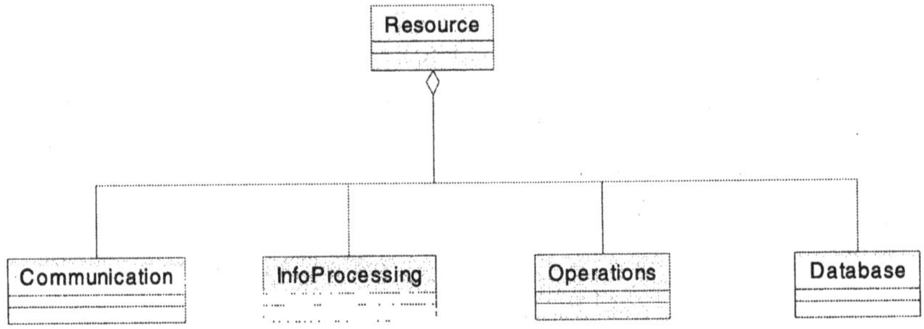

Figure 6: Resource components

4 Optimization Environment

Discussion of the optimization algorithms used in the decision making is not in the scope of this paper. They are discussed elsewhere [15].

Here we are only briefly addressing the methods used to model a crisis environment with regard to the geographical, topological and traffic loads issues. Currently, we use the map information (of cities, counties, and any larger units, e.g. countries, etc.) about the distances and main street routes between crises locations to required resources. Obviously one should also consider available air transport in inaccessible areas and for covering larger distances.

We are researching a model that continuously maintains traffic delay information on main streets. The method under consideration is similar to the traffic delay tables mechanism used in the original Arpanet routing mechanism. In this model emergency transport units continuously transmit travel time they spent between key points. A component in the local manager is responsible to maintain routing delay tables. The local manager in allocating resources and routing transportation units uses these tables. Such mechanism does add considerable overhead and increases communication load on the infrastructure. However, it promises to add another dimension in the optimization of transportation of wounded to required places of care. This is particularly important when the main routes are congested due to the effects of crises on traffic.

Conclusion

This paper presents the model and the infrastructure for a world wide distributed disaster management system. A number of prototypes have been successfully implemented. The system is build over the Internet using Web technology and Internet protocols. The entire infrastructure has been implemented using Perl.

A new system is currently being developed. We are considering the idea of developing the system to be location independent. The system will be based on a number of replicated servers. The servers will house all the optimization components, i.e. the InfoProcessing and DecisionMaking components. A local manager will maintain the crisis scenario and its database and the mechanism to communicate with peer managers, higher level managers, local resources and the well known decision making servers. This configuration will enable sharing of optimization components through a very large community. We successfully used such idea on another project [16]. The new version of the system will be implemented using Java and Java Servlets.

References

[1] Bhargava, H. K. und Krishnan, R.(1998): The World Wide Web: Opportunities for Operations Research and Management Science, in: INFORMS Journal on Computing, Vol. 10, Nr. 4, S. 359-383, 1998.

[2] Comfort, L., Metzler, D., Sungu, Y., Dunn, M., Selavo, L., Brown, K., Myung, J.(1998): An Interactive Intelligent Spatial Information System (IISUS) for Disaster Management: A Community Model for Hazardous Material Management, Proceedings of the Environmental Systems Research Institute's User Conference, Palm Springs, CA, July 27- 31, 1998.

[3] Cosgrave, J.(1996): Decision Making in Emergencies, in: Disaster Prevention and Management, Vol. 5, Nr. 4, S. 28-35, 1996.

[4] Czyzyk, J., Owen, J. H., Wright, S. J.(1997): Optimization on the Internet, in: OR/MS Today, Vol. 24, Nr. 5, S. 48-51, 1997.

[5] Dhar, V. und Stein, R.(1997): Intelligent Decision Support Methods: The Science of Knowledge work, Upper Saddle River, NJ Prentice-Hall, 1997.

[6] Fischer, H.W.(1998): The Role of the New Information Technologies in Emergency Mitigation, Planning, Response and Recovery, in: Disaster Prevention and Management, Vol. 7, Nr. 1, S. 28-37, 1998.

[7] Gruntfest, E. und Weber, M.(1998): Internet and Emergency Management: Prospects for the Future, in: International Journal of Mass Emergencies and Disaster, Vol. 16, Nr. 1, S. 55-72, 1998.

[8] Guarniéri, F. und Wybo, J.L.(1995): Spatial Decision Support and Information Management Applications to Wildland Fire Prevention: The WILFRIED System, in: Safety Science, Vol. 20, Nr. 1, S. 3-12, 1995.

[9] Heath, R.(1995): The Kobe Earthquake: Some Realities of Strategic Management of Crises and Disasters, in: Disaster Prevention and Management, Vol. 4, Nr. 5, S. 11-24, 1995.

[10] Herrmann, P.(1997): Hightech im Notfall: Internationales Fachsymposium für Kommunikation und elektronische Innovation in der Notfallmedizin,

Regensburg, 7. März, in: Notfall und Rettungsmedizin, Vol. 0, Nr. 0, S. 55-59, 1997.

[11] IDNDR(1999): Final Report of the Scientific and Technical Committee of the International Decade for Natural Disaster Reduction (IDNDR), Vereinte Nationen, 1999.

[12] Kleiboer, M.(1997): Simulation Methodology for Crisis Management Support, in: Journal of Contingencies and Crisis Management, Vol.5, Nr.4, S. 198-206, 1997.

[13] La Porte, T.M.(1999): Contingencies and Communications in Cyberspace: The World Wide Web and Non-Hierarchical Co-Ordination, in: Journal of Contingencies and Crisis Management, Vol.7, Nr.4, S. 215-224, 1999.

[14] Marovac, N. (1999): Design and Implementation of the Infrastructure for Crisis Management System, Technical Report of The Multimedia and Software Engineering Laboratory, Department of Mathematical and Computer Sciences, San Diego State University, MSEL-1-99.

[15] Marovac, N. and Stähly, P. Crisis–2000: A Distributed Crisis Management System, *To be submited.*

[16] Nenad Marovac, N. and Harrer,N. (1999): Virtual Laboratory for Image Processing,

WebNet 99--World Conference on the WWW, Honolulu, Hawaii,1999.

[17] McEntire, D.A.(1999): Issues in Disaster Relief: Progress, Perpetual Problems und Prospective Solutions, in: Disaster Prevention and Management, Vol. 8, Nr. 5, S. 351-361, 1999.

[18] Mor, B.D.(1993): Decision and Interaction in Crisis: A Model of International Crisis Behavior, Praeger, Westport, Connecticut, 1993.

[19] Riley , J. und Meadows, J.(1997): The Role of Information in Disaster Planning: A Case Study Approach, in: Disaster Prevention and Management, Vol. 6, Nr. 5, S. 349-355, 1997.

[20] Schenker-Wicky, A.G.M.(1990): The Conceptual Definition of a Crisis Management Decision Support System CMDSS, Universitätsverlag Freiburg Schweiz, Freiburg, 1990.

[21] Stähly, P. (1994): Erste Erfahrungen beim Einsatz des rechnergestützten St. Galler Modellsystems zur Analyse der Notfallversorgung bei Grossschadensereignissen, in: Biethahn, J., Hummeltenberg, W. und Schmid, B. (Hrsg.). Simulation als betriebliche Entscheidungshilfe (Band 4). Fachberichte Simulation. Springer Verlag, Berlin et al., 1994.

[22] Stähly, P. (1989): Simulationsmodelle zur Bewältigung medizinischer Notfallsituationen, in: Output, Vol. 18. Nr. 12, 1989.

[23] Swiss Re(1999): Natural Catastrophes and Man-Made Disasters 1998: Storms, Hails and Ice Cause Billion-Dollar Losses, Sigma, Nr. 1, 1999.

[23] Weber, P.(1992): Krisenmanagement, Organisation, Ablauf und Hilfsmittel der Führung in Krisenlagen, Peter Lang, Bern, 1992.

Decision Making Based on Causal Graphs

Dietrich Eherler, Peter Kischka

Lehrstuhl für Wirtschafts- und Sozialstatistik,
Wirtschaftswissenschaftliche Fakultät,

Friedrich-Schiller-Universität Jena, Germany

Abstract

Graphs have been used since quite long in statistics as tools to represent probabilistic dependencies. The origins can be traced back to first applications in path analysis (Wright 1921). During the last decade developments took place that involved an improved understanding of the relationships between graphs and probabilities, on the one hand, and graphs and causal inference on the other (e. g. Pearl 1988, Spirtes et al. 1993). Graphical modeling has emerged as a key component of the KDD (knowledge discovery in databases) process in the way of extraction and depiction of dependencies from data. Further, graphical modelling provides a powerful symbolic machinery for causal analysis e. g. the problem of covariate selection and the assessment of causal effects in the sense of the potential response framework. If a decision maker fixes the value of a treatment variable the effects of this decision can easily be computed using the causal graph associated with this model.

1 Introduction

The following quotes capture some of the major ideas of graphical modeling 'Graphical Models, a marriage between probability theory and graph theory, provide a natural tool for dealing with two problems that occur through applied mathematics and engineering - uncertainty and complexity. Fundamental to the idea of graphical models is the notion of modularity: a complex systems is built by combining simpler parts' (Jordan 1998, p. 1).

Another issue that attracted a lot of attention with the emergence of graphical models is causality, 'owing partly to advancements in graphical models, causality has undergone a major transformation from a concept shrouded in mystery into a mathematical object with well-defined semantics and well-founded logic' (Pearl 2000, p. xiii).

In this report we aim to introduce these core ideas as well as some new results. Some issues can at most only be mentioned. Nevertheless we hope to raise attention onto this subject. Introductory texts to causal graphs are Pearl (1993, 1995) and Kischka (2000). During the text remarks indicate further readings on the specific topics.

2 Basics

2.1 Probability Theory

We want to start with some simple concepts of probability theory. Given is a set of random variables $\{X_1,\ldots,X_n\}$. For notational reasons we consider only discrete variables with a finite range of instantiations. Let these variables have a joint distribution $P(X_1=x_1,\ldots,X_n=x_n)$ abbreviated as $P(x_1,\ldots,x_n)$. From this distribution marginals of subsets of $\{X_1,\ldots,X_n\}$ can be derived, as well as (conditional) independence properties of subsets can be verified. The approach to model uncertainty in a domain with a joint probability distribution leads even in small problems to an enormous number of elementary probabilities that have to be handled. Therefore it is important to find a representation of this probability distribution that leads to more economical and algorithmically tractable solutions. The key to this challenge is a simple result of probability theory - the factorization chain rule. If all conditional probabilities are well-defined, a joint probability distribution can be factorized

$$P(x_1,\ldots,x_n)=P(x_1)P(x_2\mid x_1)\cdot\ldots\cdot P(x_n\mid x_1,\ldots,x_{n-1}) \qquad [1]$$

for any permutation of the variables $X_1,\ldots,X_n$. Above was already mentioned the notion of marginal and conditional independence. A characterization of conditional independence is, that if $\boldsymbol{X}$, $\boldsymbol{Y}$ and $\boldsymbol{Z}$ are disjoint subsets the conditional probability $P(\boldsymbol{x}|\boldsymbol{z},\boldsymbol{y})$ reduces to $P(\boldsymbol{x}|\boldsymbol{z})$ if $\boldsymbol{X}$ is conditionally independent of $\boldsymbol{Y}$ given $\boldsymbol{Z}$, denoted as $I(\boldsymbol{X},\boldsymbol{Z},\boldsymbol{Y})$. The task is to make use of as many as possible of such independence relations to reduce the number of parameters required for modeling the joint distribution on the left hand side of equation [1]. A generalization of [1] can be stated. If $\boldsymbol{S}_1,\ldots,\boldsymbol{S}_m$ are a disjoint decomposition of the set $\{X_1,\ldots,X_n\}$ then the joint distribution can be factorized to

$$P(x_1,\ldots,x_n)=P(\boldsymbol{s}_1)P(\boldsymbol{s}_2\mid \boldsymbol{s}_1)\cdot\ldots\cdot P(\boldsymbol{s}_m\mid \boldsymbol{s}_1,\ldots,\boldsymbol{s}_{m-1}) \qquad [2]$$

This factorization is useful, when the consideration of singleton variables is not sensible for a given problem.

In order to simplify and decompose a given joint probability distribution thorough studies on conditional independence have been undertaken (e. g. Dawid 1979, Spohn 1980). Further investigation in connection to graphical graphical models are due to Pearl (1988).

Let $\boldsymbol{X}$, $\boldsymbol{Y}$, $\boldsymbol{Z}$, $\boldsymbol{W}$ be disjoint subsets of $X_1,\ldots,X_n$ with a joint distribution P. Then conditional independence fulfils

1) Symmetry

$$I(\boldsymbol{X}, \boldsymbol{Z}, \boldsymbol{Y}) \Leftrightarrow I(\boldsymbol{Y}, \boldsymbol{Z}, \boldsymbol{X})$$

2) Decomposition

$$I(\boldsymbol{X}, \boldsymbol{Z}, \boldsymbol{Y} \cup \boldsymbol{W}) \Rightarrow I(\boldsymbol{X}, \boldsymbol{Z}, \boldsymbol{Y}) \,\&\, I(\boldsymbol{X}, \boldsymbol{Z}, \boldsymbol{W})$$

3) Weak Union

$$I(\boldsymbol{X}, \boldsymbol{Z}, \boldsymbol{Y} \cup \boldsymbol{W}) \Rightarrow I(\boldsymbol{X}, \boldsymbol{Z} \cup \boldsymbol{Z}, \boldsymbol{W}) \,\&\, I(\boldsymbol{X}, \boldsymbol{Z} \cup \boldsymbol{W}, \boldsymbol{Y})$$

4) Contraction

$$I(\boldsymbol{X}, \boldsymbol{Z} \cup \boldsymbol{Y}, \boldsymbol{W}) \,\&\, I(\boldsymbol{X}, \boldsymbol{Z}, \boldsymbol{Y}) \Rightarrow I(\boldsymbol{X}, \boldsymbol{Z}, \boldsymbol{W} \cup \boldsymbol{X})$$

If P is strictly positive there is another property

5) Intersection

$$I(\boldsymbol{X}, \boldsymbol{Z} \cup \boldsymbol{Y}, \boldsymbol{W}) \,\&\, I(\boldsymbol{X}, \boldsymbol{Z} \cup \boldsymbol{W}, \boldsymbol{Y}) \Rightarrow I(\boldsymbol{X}, \boldsymbol{Z}, \boldsymbol{Y} \cup \boldsymbol{W}).$$

Whereas the joint probability function itself hardly reveals anything about the structure of the considered variables, the independence properties give some insight about the interaction of the domain.

2.2 Graph Theory

'The power and appeal of probabilistic networks stems from the pictorial representation they provide of the structural inter-relationships and dependencies between the variables of a problem, and the fact that these pictures have a formal definition as graphs' (Cowell et al. 1999, S. 43). The type of graphs used in graphical modeling are *undirected graphs*, *directed acyclic graphs* (henceforth DAGs) and a kind of mixture of these two types called *chain graphs*. Figure 2.1 shows examples of the three kind of graphs. Formal definition of undirected and directed acyclic graphs can be found in any book on graph theory. Chain graphs were introduced in Lauritzen and Wermuth (1984). One approach to chain graphs is the following. The vertex set V is partitioned into disjoint blocks $V = V(1) \cup \ldots \cup V(T)$ such that each of the blocks $V(t)$ has only undirected between its vertices, and any directed edges point from vertices in blocks with lower number to those with higher number.

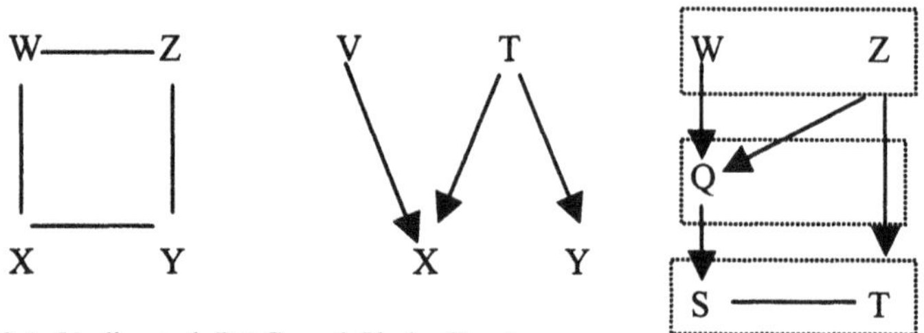

Figure 2.1: Undirected, DAG, and Chain Graph

When a graph is used each node in the graph represents a random variable and the edges different kind of dependencies or respectively missing edges independencies with respect to the kind of graph. These interpretations vary with the kind of graph considered. In the following we concentrate on DAGs.

3 Dependency Models and Their Representation as Graphs

3.1 Dependency Model

The approach to graphical modeling rests on so called *dependency models*. A dependency model consists of a finite set of random variables $X_1, \ldots, X_n$, and a list of independence statements of the form *I*(***X***,***Z***,***Y***) where ***X***, ***Z***, ***Y*** are disjoint subsets of $X_1, \ldots, X_n$. These independence statements can be given explicitly (3.1.2) or implicitly (3.1.1, 3.1.3). This is a quite general concept of mere qualitative statements (see 3.1.2, 3.1.3). The aim is now to find a graph for a given dependency model that separation properties in the graph imply the corresponding independence statement in the dependency model. In the next three subsection we consider special kinds of dependency models and describe how to obtain a DAG for that model.

3.1.1 Joint Distributions as Dependency Models

Given a joint probability distribution P for a set of variables $\{X_1,\ldots,X_n\}$ we can always decide for any subsets of variables whether a particular independence statement is true. Thus, joint probability distributions are special kind of dependency models. Let a set of variables $\{X_1,\ldots,X_n\}$ be given and a fixed order of that variables (without loss of generality by the numbering of the variables). In applications this order is often derived from subject matters e.g. a chronological order. A procedure to construct a directed acyclic graph for a given distribution is as follows (Pearl 1988, p. 119).

1) Fix an order of the variables $X_1,\ldots,X_n$

2) Find minimal boundary sets $\mathbf{PA}_i \quad (2 \le i \le n), \quad \mathbf{PA}_1 = \varnothing$

   i $\mathbf{PA}_i \subset \{X_1,\ldots,X_{i-1}\}$

   ii $P(x_i \mid x_1,\ldots,x_{i-1}) = P(x_i \mid \mathbf{pa}_i)$

3) Draw from every variable $X_j \in \mathbf{PA}_i$ a directed edge to X_i.

Note, that for the same distribution P the resulting graph strongly depends on the order fixed in advance. It is clear from property (2ii) that the joint probability factorizes to

$$P(x_1,\ldots,x_n) = \prod_{i=1}^{n} P(x_i \mid \mathbf{pa}_i)\,. \qquad [3]$$

If P is strictly positive, then the sets $\mathbf{PA}_i$ are unique and so is the resulting graph for the specified order (Pearl and Paz 1985). Other properties of the graph constructed by the procedure above will be discussed in Section 3.3.

3.1.2 Input Lists as Dependency Models

An *input list* is defined as a finite set of independence statements $I(\boldsymbol{X}, \boldsymbol{Z}, \boldsymbol{Y})$ where $\boldsymbol{X}$, $\boldsymbol{Y}$, and $\boldsymbol{Z}$ are disjoint subsets of the considered variables $\{X_1,\ldots,X_n\}$ (Castillo et al. 1997, p. 185). These statements may be derived from a joint probability distribution or may be given as an assessment of an expert about the considered domain. Thus, this approach is feasible in cases, when the joint probability is not known a priori. Given an initial set of triples the list can be logically expanded by the properties of conditional independence. For instance, if the two statements $I(\boldsymbol{X}, \boldsymbol{Z} \cup \boldsymbol{Y}, \boldsymbol{W})$ and $I(\boldsymbol{X}, \boldsymbol{Z}, \boldsymbol{Y})$ are given it is deducible that $I(\boldsymbol{X}, \boldsymbol{Z}, \boldsymbol{W})$ is valid, too.

Particular attention received so called *causal input lists* (Castillo et al. 1997, p. 245) also named as recursive basis (Geiger et al. 1990). Given the variables $X_1,\ldots,X_n$ in this order, a causal input list consists of one independence statement for each variable, i. e. $I(X_i,\mathbf{\Pi}_i,\{X_1,\ldots,X_{i-1}\}\setminus\mathbf{\Pi}_i)$ where $\mathbf{\Pi}_i$ is a minimal subset of the predecessors $\{X_1,\ldots,X_{i-1}\}$ of X_i that renders X_i conditionally independent of all its other predecessors $\{X_1,\ldots,X_{i-1}\}\setminus\mathbf{\Pi}_i$.

Given a causal input list a DAG can be constructed by the following procedure.

1) Fix an order of the variables $X_1,\ldots,X_n$

2) Confirm the validity of $I(X_i,\Pi_i,\{X_1,\ldots,X_{i-1}\}\setminus\Pi_i)$

3) Draw from every variable $X_j \in \mathbf{\Pi}_i$ a directed edge to X_i.

With $\mathbf{PA}_i = \Pi_i$ and because of (2) the joint distribution adheres to the factorization [3]. Properties of input lists are discussed in Geiger et al. (1990). Some major results follow in Section 3.3.

3.1.3 Equation Systems as Dependency Models

Let $\{U_1,\ldots,U_n\}$ be a set of mutually independent random variables and f_i measurable but elsewise unspecified functions. An equation system $X_i = f_i(\mathbf{PA}_i,U_i)$ with $1 \le i \le n$ where $\mathbf{PA}_i$ is a subset of $\{X_1,\ldots,X_n\}\setminus\{X_i\}$ defines a structural equation model M for the variables $\{X_1,\ldots,X_n\}$. The corresponding graph is given by drawing from every variable $X_j \in \mathbf{PA}_i$ a directed edge to X_i. Procedural we can summarise

1) Let $\{X_1,\ldots,X_n\}$ be the relevant variables

2) Assign to each variable X_i its direct influences $\mathbf{PA}_i$

3) Link every variable $X_j \in \mathbf{PA}_i$ with a directed edge into X_i.

If the resulting graph is acyclic we call it a *causal graph* of the structural equation model M. The assumptions of independence of the U_i and of an acyclic resulting graph is called Markov assumption (Pearl 2000, p. 30) and the model is called *Markovian.* If a model is Markovian the joint distribution factorizes according to [3] (Pearl 1996). In the following we always assume that a structural model is Markovian.

Structural models and their graphical representation, which are also known as path diagrams, have a long history (Wright 1921) as well as a wide scope of applications in social sciences and economies. The work of Pearl (2000) has put new focus on them with respect to causality. This and other aspects as well as properties will be given in the section 3.3 and 4.2.

3.2 Separation in Graphs

Before we will see some of the major merits of graphical models, we need additional tools that enable us to perform graphical examinations of the specified graphs. These tools are the following separation notions. In an undirected graph two set of vertices $\boldsymbol{X}$ and $\boldsymbol{Y}$ are *u-separated* by a set of vertices $\boldsymbol{Z}$ ($\boldsymbol{X}$, $\boldsymbol{Y}$ and $\boldsymbol{Z}$ are assumed to be disjoint), denoted as $\langle \boldsymbol{X}, \boldsymbol{Z}, \boldsymbol{Y} \rangle$, if all paths from nodes in $\boldsymbol{X}$ to nodes in $\boldsymbol{Y}$ are intercepted by a node in $\boldsymbol{Z}$.

In DAGs a more complex separability criterion is used. This criterion is due to Pearl (1988, p. 93) and it takes the directionality of edges into account.

Definition 3.1. If X, Y, and $\mathbf{Z}$ are three disjoint subsets of nodes in a DAG then $\mathbf{Z}$ is said to *d-separate* $\boldsymbol{X}$ from $\boldsymbol{Y}$ denoted as $\langle \boldsymbol{X}, \boldsymbol{Z}, \boldsymbol{Y} \rangle$, if along every connection between a node in $\boldsymbol{X}$ and a node in $\boldsymbol{Y}$ there is a node W satisfying one of the following conditions. (1) W has converging arrows and none of W or its descendants are in $\boldsymbol{Z}$ or (2) W does not have converging arrows and W is in $\boldsymbol{Z}$.

Another separation criterion which is equivalent to d-separation in DAGs was introduced by Lauritzen et al. (1990). It is based on the moral graph. For DAGs moralization correspondents to connecting all nodes that have a child in common and stripping of all arrowheads.

D-separation can be verified by a procedure consisting of three steps (Castillo et al. 1997, S. 183).

1) Identify the smallest subgraph containing $\boldsymbol{X}$, $\boldsymbol{Y}$, $\boldsymbol{Z}$ and their ancestral sets

2) Moralize the obtained subgraph

3) Use the separation criterion for undirected graphs to verify $\langle \boldsymbol{X}, \boldsymbol{Z}, \boldsymbol{Y} \rangle$.

Example:

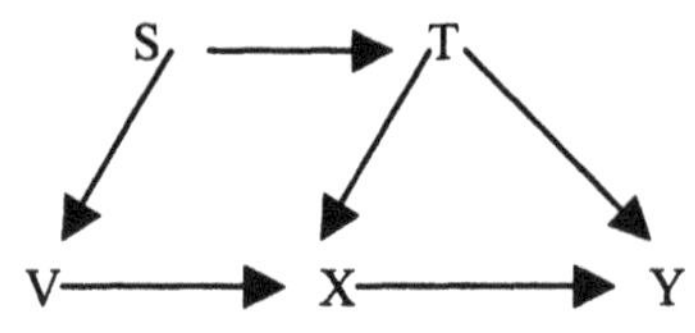

Graph 3.1

In Graph 3.1 V is d-separated from Y by for instance, $\mathbf{Z} = \{X, T\}$. The nodes are not d-separated by $\{S, X\}$ because on the path $V \to X \leftarrow T \to Y$, X has converging arrows and no other node except X belongs to the separation set on this path. The moral graph to this task contains the path V — T— Y that is not intercepted by $\{S, X\}$.

3.3 Graphical Representations

A graphical representation of a dependency model intends to capture as many properties of this model as possible. With a one to one correspondence between the variables in a dependency model and the set of vertices the topology of the graph is supposed to reflect the structure of the domain under investigation.

3.3.1 Perfect Maps

Definition 3.2. A graph is said to be a *perfect map* of a dependency model, if independence relations and separation properties coincide, i. e. $I(\mathbf{X}, \mathbf{Y}, \mathbf{Z}) \Leftrightarrow \langle \mathbf{Y}, \mathbf{Z}, \mathbf{X} \rangle$ for all disjoint subsets of the considered variables (Pearl 1988).

Depending on the type of graph either u- or d-separation is applied. Many problems do have perfect maps. In particular, if a dependency model is derived from a Markovian structural model M where the parameters can vary freely, the corresponding causal graph is almost surely a perfect map (Meek 1995b). Necessary conditions for the existence of a perfect map can be found in Pearl (1988, p. 128). A weaker condition, introduced in Section 3.3.2 that still renders graphs a very powerful inference instruments, can always be met.

3.3.2 Independency Maps

Instead of requiring perfect coincidence of independence and separation, the definition of an independency map (I-map) (Pearl 1988, p. 92, 119) demands that separation in the graph implies independence in the dependency model.

Definition 3.3. A graph is said to be an *independency map* (I-map) of a dependency model (I-map) if separation properties entail the corresponding independence relations, i. e. $\langle \boldsymbol{X}, \boldsymbol{Z}, \boldsymbol{Y} \rangle \Rightarrow I(\boldsymbol{X}, \boldsymbol{Z}, \boldsymbol{Y})$ for all disjoint subsets of the considered variables. A minimal I-map is an I-map where none of its edges can be deleted without destroying its I-mapness.

In addition, if the graph is a DAG, the minimal I-map is also called *Bayesian network.*

Most attention in recent research activities has received the approach with DAGs as maps of dependency models. Proposition 1 (Pearl 1988, Castillo et al., 1997) states a central result.

Proposition 1. Let G be a DAG. Then the following statements are equivalent

1) The joint distribution factorizes to

$$P(x_1,\ldots,x_n)=\prod_{i=1}^{n}P(x_i\,|\,\mathbf{pa}_i)$$

where $\mathbf{PA}_i$ are the parent nodes in G.

2) G is an I-map of the considered dependency model.

3) X_i is independent of its nondescendants given its parents $\mathbf{PA}_i$ $(1 \le i \le n)$.

Note that for the construction procedures in 3.1.1, 3.1.2, and 3.1.3 statement (1) is always fulfilled given the respective assumptions.

The first item allows to decompose the joint distribution into conditional subdistributions. This is particularity helpful if the task is to specify the joint distribution. Instead of dealing with the complete set of parameters one can specify the different components. The reduction of complexity can be enormous.

Secondly, the I-map property allows to infer valid characteristics about the underlying distribution by only graphical analysis. Without knowing the specifications of the probability the graph informs us which variables are independent.

The third item in Proposition 1 is also known as the Markov Condition for graphs (Spirtes et al., 1993). If the graph simplifies to a chain, this condition coincides with the Markov property of Markov chains. Thus graphs allow us to model more complex problems. Additionally, the Markov property has also an intuitive causal interpretation, i. e., once the direct causes are known there is no other systematic influence on a variable.

In the next section the usefulness and power of DAGs will be portrayed and exposed. Nevertheless, there are limitations, too. Sometimes these limitations can be overcome by choosing another graphical representation (see 3.4).

3.4 Extensions

Consider the dependency model with only two valid independence statement $I(X, \{Y, W\}, Z)$, $I(Y, \{X, Z\}, W)$ and symmetric images. For any order of the variables, a DAG will portray at most one of the independence relations, where as an undirected graph with edges $Y — X$, $X — W$, $W — Z$, $Z — Y$ would be a perfect map (see Figure 2.1).

An extension to DAGs are chain graphs. Key to their interpretation is a more general Markov condition, the so called *block-recursive Markov property* (Cowell et al. 1999, p. 76). A missing edge between a pair of variables means that the two variables are conditionally independent given all its remaining concurrent variables. A set of concurrent variables is the union of a chain element with chain elements from which directed edges could be pointing to it (Wermuth and Lauritzen, 1990). A chain graph that would perfectly display the dependency model is depicted in Graph 3.2.

Graph 3.2

4 Predictions with Graphs

A decision A is preferred to a decision B if the effects of A are preferred to the effects of B. Of course the computation of effects always depends strongly on the correctness of the framework the computations are made. In this subsection we introduce the notion of a causal effect of a treatment variable on a response variable, i. e., we consider the effects of different values of treatments (decisions) on some response variable. The framework is given by a structural model as introduced in 3.1.3. In the second part of this section we give some results concerning the correctness of the framework. Decision making based on causal graphs is a method which seems to be more reliable for decision making than e. g. decisions based on regression (see Spirtes et al. 1993, Chapter 8).

Another application of DAGs are to compute diagnostic predictions. Although graphical models have been used for quite a while their gain in importance and attention is due to the desire to model uncertainty in expert systems. A Bayesian network can not only be viewed as a 'passive code for storing knowledge but also as a computational architecture for reasoning about that knowledge' (Pearl 1988, p. 145). It became clear that in high dimensional problems 'brute force' probabilistic propagation is not feasible. Graphical models offer an approach to split up complex and large problems into small manageable pieces. Within this framework techniques have been developed that are able to perform the required tasks of reasoned guidance on the considered problem. More details are given in Pearl (1988), Jensen (1996), Jordan (1998) and Cowell et al. (1999). Due to the limited space and yet committed to decision making it can here only be mentioned that Bayessian networks can be extended to influence diagrams. An influence diagram is a DAG with three kind of nodes, that are, decision nodes, chance nodes, and a value node. Suggested literature to this topic is, for instance, Pearl (1988), Shachter (1986), Cowell et al. (1999). For propagation in Bayesian networks several software packages are available (see Murphy 2000).

4.1 Prediction of Effects

The fundamental aim of any empirical studies is to predict the effect of changes that are imposed by deliberate decisions. How will be the effect petrol consumption if an additional tax is imposed on the price per litre? To what extent does a marketing compaign (hopefully) increase a firm's profit? What will be the effect of an social welfare program a government is planing to implement? If this kind of predictions are to be made with statistical methods, a sample is required from the very distributions that would result if the corresponding treatments were actually applied everywhere. This situation can be created with randomized trials, in fact, this is the essence of randomization. However, the real world is seldom a laboratory where this technique can be applied. In the following we will show how advancements in graphical modeling have opened avenues to this kind of predictions of effects solely based on observational data. Of course some, further assumptions will be needed. Nevertheless it is astonishing how weak the additional requirements are to come to these kind of treatment-effect conclusions. These achievements are mainly due to research from groups at Carnegie Mellon University (Spirtes et al. 1993) and around Pearl (2000). Some further contributions to this endeavour are presented in section 4.2.

4.1.1 Manipulation

To predict the effect of a treatment with statistical tools one needs, as already mentioned above, the distribution or respectively a sample of this distribution, as if the treatments were imposed. Observational data alone is not sufficient to mount this task, however, data plus a directed acyclic graph representing the causal structure will do. Here we will present the structural modeling approach (see 3.1.3).

Definition 4.1. Given is Markovian a structural model M with the equation $X_i = f_i(\mathbf{PA}_i, U_i)$ for $1 \le i \le n$. Let x_k be a fixed realization of X_k. A manipulation is the replacement of the k-th equation by $X_k = x_k$. The resulting equation system $X_i' = f_i(\mathbf{PA}_i', U_i)$ where $\mathbf{PA}_i' = \mathbf{PA}_i$ if $X_k \notin \mathbf{PA}_i$ and $\mathbf{PA}_i' = (\mathbf{PA}_i \setminus \{X_k\}) \cup \{x_k\}$ if $X_k \in \mathbf{PA}_i$ for $1 \le i \le n$, $i \ne k$ is called manipulated system.

$$\widetilde{P}_{x_k}(x_1, \ldots, x_{k-1}, x_{k+1}, \ldots, x_n) := P(X_1' = x_1, \ldots X_{k-1}' = x_{k-1}, X_{k+1}' = x_{k+1,\ldots}, X_n' = x_n)$$

symbolises its distribution.

Graphically, a manipulation can be presented by the removal of all arcs that enter the manipulated variable X_k while leaving the rest of the graph intact. The impact on the distribution is content of the next proposition (Pearl 1993).

Proposition 2. The distribution $\widetilde{P}_{x_k}(x_1, \ldots, x_{k-1}, x_{k+1}, \ldots, x_n)$ of a manipulated systems given the manipulation $X_k = x_k$ is given by

$$\widetilde{P}_{x_k}(x_1, \ldots, x_{k-1}, x_{k+1}, \ldots, x_n) = \prod_{i \ne k} P(x_i \mid \mathbf{pa}_i').$$

Note, that on the distributional level a manipulations corresponds to the removal of the k-th term in the factorization of the joint probability. Alternatively it can be seen as a generalized form of conditioning. Instead of dividing the joint distribution by $P(x_k)$ the division is made by $P(x_k \mid pa_k)$.

Definition 4.2. Let X_k be a treatment variable and $Y \in \{X_1,\ldots,X_{k-1},X_{k+1},\ldots,X_n\}$ a response variable. The marginal of $\widetilde{P}_{x_k}$ with respect to Y is called *causal effect* of the manipulation $X_k = x_k$ on Y.

Note, that a causal effect is defined starting from a Markovian structural model M by a manipulation of the treatment variable. Therefore, the interpretability of the obtained causal effects with those a randomized experiment would give rests on the appropriateness of the model, i. e., whether all relevant variables and equations are included (Common Cause Principle, Reichenbach 1956), and whether the actual performance of the manipulation would not change the causal structure elsewise. The latter is given if the equations can be regarded as autonomous mechanisms (Pearl 2000, p. 22).

4.1.2 The Backdoor Criterion

To compute the causal effects of a treatment variable X on a response variable Y one does not have to refer to the manipulated distribution as a whole. The graphical structure can be exploited to ease the effort for calculations. The simple graphical backdoor criterion can be applied (Pearl 1993).

Proposition 3. Let M be a Markovian structural model and G be the corresponding causal graph. Further let $\mathbf{T} \subset \{X_1,\ldots,X_n\}$ and $X, Y \notin \mathbf{T}$. If

1) For all $X_j \in \mathbf{T}: X_j$ is not a descendant of X

2) $\mathbf{T}$ d-separates X from Y on every path (so called backdoor path) between X and Y, that has an arrow into X,

then

$$\widetilde{P}_x(y) = \sum_{\mathbf{t}} P(\mathbf{T} = \mathbf{t}) P(Y = y \mid \mathbf{T} = \mathbf{t}, X = x).$$

If a model M is completely specified any effect of a treatment variable on a response variable can be ascertained by this formula. In particular the parents of X

do satisfy the above criterion. Note, that all terms on the right hand side can be estimated from data. The name of the criterion echoes the second condition because paths are considered that enter X. The formula correspondences to the adjustment formula suggested by Rosenbaum and Rubin (1983).

A complete characterization when effects of singleton variables can be computed as well as an algorithm how to perform this calculations is given in Pearl (2000, pp. 114-8).

4.2 Confounding

Until now we have always assumed that we know the complete structural model M. This is a rather strong requirement because in general we will not be sure whether we have indeed included all relevant variables into the model. The other way round, it may happen that we have included wrong variables in our computation and therefore get false results. For decision making purposes this situation is not desirable. In both described situations, omitting variables or including wrong variables, we have to deal with confounding.

4.2.1 Definition and Characterization

Pearl (1998) suggested a definition of stable unconfoundedness that is based on structural models and can be characterised in graphical terms. Moreover he stated an operational criterion that yields a necessary statistical test for stable no-confounding. We generalize this definition with respect to known confounders that can be adjusted for. Nevertheless the question prevails, whether other not yet considered confounders still bias the effect of a treatment on a response variable. Partial answers to this problem follow. We start with the definition of stable unconfoundedness.

Definition 4.3. Given is a Markovian structural model M. X and Y are *stably unconfounded* with respect to a set of variables **T**, if $T_i \in \mathbf{T}$ is observable and the following equality holds

$$\widetilde{P}_x(y) = \sum_{\mathbf{t}} P(y \mid \mathbf{t}, x) P(\mathbf{t})$$

regardless of the distribution of the U_i and of the special form of the functions f_i ($1 \leq i \leq n$).

If X and Y are stably unconfounded with respect to **T**, then the variables in **T** suffice for an adjustment in the computation of causal effects on the response variable Y. The variables in **T** can be seen as potential confounders. A graphical characterization of stable unconfoundedness states the following proposition (Kischka and Eherler 1999).

Proposition 5. Let M be a Markovian structural model X and Y variables, and let **T** be observable subset of other variables. X and Y are stably unconfounded with respect to **T**, if and only if X and Y are d-separated on every backdoor path by **T** in the corresponding causal graph.

Where this proposition is applicable, it provides a simple graphical test to verify whether two variables are stably unconfounded. It also suggests how to compute the desired effect, namely by an application of the backdoor formula.

4.2.2 Operational Criteria with Nondescendants

In a decision making process one might seldom expect to have a completely specified model in order to predict unconfounded effects nor one can be safe to assume that all relevant variables are included. This is in particular true when we suppose to deal with latent common causes. In this situation it would be desirable if we could judge whether a pair of treatment response variables is unconfounded or not on using available information. As the following propositions 6-9 will show we can derive statistical tests about unconfoundedness only based on rather weak structural knowledge. Technically we assume a model M to compute the causal effect of X on Y, which induces by Proposition 1 theoretical independence relations. On the other hand there is a (i.g. unknown) structural model M' which generated the data. The true causal effect of X on Y is given within the model M'. The theoretical independence relations induced by the assumed model M are compared to independence statements derived from data generated by M'.

The following propositions give necessary and sufficient conditions for computing this true effect within the model M. The first proposition rules out stable unconfoundedness (Kischka and Eherler 2000). Hence it bears a necessary test for stable unconfoundedness.

Proposition 6. Assume X and Y are stably unconfounded in M with respect to **T**. Let V be an additional variable with

1) V is a nondescendant of X

2) Y is a descendant of V

3) a) X is not independent of V given **T**

b) Y is not independent of V given $\mathbf{T} \cup \{X\}$.

Then X and Y are not stably unconfounded in M'.

A special case with $\mathbf{T} = \varnothing$ of this proposition is due to Pearl (1998). The ratio of Proposition 6 is based on an assumed structural model where X and Y appear to be unconfounded with respect to **T** and on the additional, rather modest, structural knowledge that 1) X is not affected by V and 2) V possibly affects Y. Given these, we can perform the two independence tests. If both hypothesis of independence are rejected, X and Y are not stably unconfounded with respect to **T** in the unknown data generating model M'.

A necessary test for stable unconfoundedness of X and Y with respect to **T** in an assumed model M with an additional variable V is that given the conditions 1) and 2) of Proposition 6 at least one of the independence hypothesis of condition 3) is rejected. A sufficient criterion states the following proposition (Kischka and Eherler 2000).

Proposition 7. Assume X and Y are stably unconfounded in M with respect to **T**. Let V be an additional variable with

1) V is an ancestor of X

2) V is not independent of X given **T**

3) V is independent of Y given $\mathbf{T} \cup \{X\}$

Then X and Y are stably unconfounded with respect to **T** in M', if the corresponding graph to M' is a perfect map.

Again, if we think of X and Y being unconfounded in a supposed model M and we possess an additional variable V that has influence on X we can perform the two independence tests to decide whether X and Y are stably unconfounded. As stated, we need the additional assumption that G' is a perfect map of M'. In almost every situation this assumption is valid (Meek 1995b).

4.3.4 Operational Criteria with Descendants

For an application of the proposition above one requirement is that we need to find variables that are nondescendants of the treatment or respectively ancestors of the treatment. When no such variables can be found, we still have the possibility to apply one of the following propositions to yield similar conclusions. As assumption of these propositions it is explicitly required that we find additional variables that are also affected by the treatment variable.

Proposition 8. Assume X and Y are stably unconfounded with respect to **T**. Let **Q** be a set of variables satisfying

1) **Q** intercepts every directed path from X to Y

2) X and Y are not independent given $\mathbf{Q} \cup \mathbf{T}$.

Then, X and Y are not stably unconfounded with respect to **T** in M'.

Proof.: **Q** intercepts every directed path from X to Y. Assuming that X and Y are stably unconfounded with respect to **T** implies that there are no further backdoor paths between X and Y that are not already d-separated by **T**. Hence any connection between X and Y is d-separated by $\mathbf{T} \cup \mathbf{Q}$. By Proposition 1 X and Y are then independent given $\mathbf{T} \cup \mathbf{Q}$ in contradiction to 2).

A sufficient criterion states the next proposition.

Proposition 9. Assume X and Y are stably unconfounded with respect to **T**. Let **Q** be a set of other variables with

1) Every $Q \in \mathbf{Q}$ is a descendant of X

2) X and Y are independent given $\mathbf{Q} \cup \mathbf{T}$.

Then, X and Y are stably unconfounded with respect to **T** in M', if the corresponding graph G to M' is a perfect map.

Proof.: Let **Q** be a set satisfying 1.) and let X and Y be d-separated by $\mathbf{Q} \cup \mathbf{T}$. Consequently, all paths between X and Y with non-converging arrows are via nodes of $\mathbf{Q} \cup \mathbf{T}$. In particular there are no further backdoor paths between X and Y that are not yet d-separated by **T**.

Note, that condition 1) in Proposition 8 is stronger than condition 2) in Proposition 9 in the sense the first implies the latter. Therefore, if a set **Q** meets condition 1) of Proposition 8) and the hypothesis of independence 2) can not be rejected, the effect of X on Y is unconfounded with respect to **T** in M'.

An interesting area of application of the last proposition is in the long lasting 'smoking X – lung cancer Y' debate. Most controversially discussed is the question, whether there is a latent variable 'genotype' causing both, smoking and lung cancer.

$X \longrightarrow Y$ $\qquad\qquad$ $X \longrightarrow Q \longrightarrow Y$

Graph 4.2a $\qquad\qquad$ Graph 4.2b

The simple model with Graph 4.2a is appropriate to compute the causal effect if, e.g. for the variable tar deposits Q we can ascertain that X is independent of Y given Q (see Graph 4.2b). Consequently as a result of Proposition 9, the genotype theory that assumes a common ancestor of X and Y, could be rejected.

5 Learning Graphical Models

Up to now we have assumed that a graph for a considered problem is given by an expert whose expertise about the subject matter guided the model specification. Depending on the nature of the problem this approach is not everywhere applicable. Recently methods have been developed how graphs can be learned from data. There are two aspects of learning with respect to graphical models. Given the graph, the first target is to fit parameters and therefore this aspect is refereed to parametric learning. This problem belongs to the classical statistical field of parameter estimation. We will not focus on it here. The new methods to extract the structure from data are refereed as structural learning. Some aspects of this challenge will be dealt in the remaining part of this contribution. The focus will be on directed acyclic graphs. Methods for learning undirected graphs can be found in Meek (1995a), Edwards (1995), Whittaker (1990). Aspects of learning chain graphs are considered in Meek (1995a), Wermuth and Lauritzen (1990), and Lauritzen (1996).

5.1 The Search Space

Learning DAGs requires to search a vast space of possible structures. There are $2^{n(n-2)/2}$ undirected graphs with n vertices, the number of directed graphs is $3^{n(n-1)/2}$. Cooper (1999, p. 43) gives exact numbers for DAGs up to six vertices which is 3.781.053, an enormous number of possible structures. Learning DAGs by any means is NP-hard (Burckhard 1995, Chickering 1996). Yet, from a statistical point of view the search space can be reduced by dividing it into equivalence classes. Formally two DAGs are said to be Markov equivalent, if the graphs entail the same set of independence constraints. For a graphical characterization of this definition we need the notion of an unshielded collider. A node Y in a DAG a substructure of 3 nodes of called unshielded collider, if X and Y, and Z and Y are adjacent, Z and X are not adjacent and if the edges between X and Y, and Z and Y collide in Y, i. e. $X \rightarrow Y \leftarrow Z$. With this definition it is graphically a simple task to see whether two graphs are Markov equivalent (Spirtes et al., 1994, p. 34).

Proposition 10. Two directed acyclic graphs are Markov equivalent if and only if they have the same adjacencies and the same unshielded colliders.

The property of Markov equivalence has several impacts when we want to learn structure from data. If, for instance, we observe an independence $I(X, Z, Y)$ there are three possible DAGs that display this independence relation, i. e. they belong to the same equivalence class.

$X \rightarrow Z \rightarrow Y$	$X \leftarrow Z \rightarrow Y$	$X \leftarrow Z \leftarrow Y$
A	B	C

Causally interpreted with respect to X and Y, graph A asserts that X affects Y, and the effect is given by $P(y|x)$. In graph C and B the effect of X on Y is the marginal $P(y)$, that is, X has no effect on Y. Note, that additional variables may help to distinguish this structures while keeping the observed independence intact.

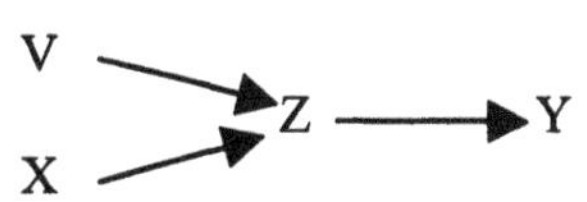

D

For example, if V is a variable marginally independent of X, and Y is conditionally independent of V given Z, figure D would be the only graph consistent with the observational evidence.

The implied factorization of the joint distribution can be used for diagnostic predictions. If we want to use the elicited structure for a causal analysis, additional assumptions are required. We will discuss them below.

5.2 Learning Approaches

A coarse taxonomy an learning approaches can be done by the method the structure is derived. One class of methods are constraint – based methods. These methods exploit the independence constraints that a graphical structure imposes on a distribution. A represent of these methods is the later explained PC-algorithm. A second class of procedures is score-driven. Different structures are evaluated by a score how well the data fit. The structure with the highest score is chosen. This approach is exemplified by the K2-Algorithm. We can further distinguish learning approaches whether prior knowledge can or must be incorporated. Some methods require a complete ordering of the variables, e. g. the Wermuth-Lauritzen Algorithm (cited in Spirtes et al. 1993, p. 111) or the K2-Algorithm (Cooper and Herskovitz 1991). Other methods allow the inclusion of uncertain expert knowledge into a learning process (Heckerman et al. 1994, Hunscher 1998). Also some hybrid forms of construction algorithms have been suggested where the constraint based search procedures are supported by a score, i. e. the independence test are replaced by other decision, mechanisms, e. g. the Bayes information criterion (Steck and Tresp 1999) or a Bayesian score.

5.2.1 Constraint Based Methods

As one representant of these methods we want to give an outline of the PC-Algorithm (Spirtes and Glymour 1991). This algorithm is implemented in the Tetrad software (Scheines et al. 1994). Given data and assuming that this data is sampled from a distribution that has a perfect map, the PC-algorithm constructs a pattern which represents the equivalence class of the DAGs that are perfect maps of the distribution. A pattern Π is a mixed graph with directed and undirected edges. A DAG G is in the Markow equivalence class represented by Π if and only if

1) G has the same adjacencies as Π,

2) if the edge between two nodes X and Y is oriented $X \rightarrow Y$ in Π it is oriented $X \rightarrow Y$ in G,

3) if X, Y and Z form an unshielded collider in G, then X, Y and Z form an unshielded collider in Π (Spirtes et al. 1993, p. 90).

The PC-Algorithm is described in detail in Scheines et al. (1994, p. 236-243). It is remarkable that without any prior knowledge this algorithm can elicit useful structural substance from data alone. It is not surprising that there is still a controversial debate going on, whether and how to use this methods. The authors of the PC-algorithm have also developed other techniques to discover structural knowledge which can be found in Spirtes et al. (1993, 1999) and Scheines et al. (1998).

5.2.2 Score Based Methods

The first score based method to learn a graph was introduced by Cooper and Herkovitz (1991). The basic idea of these methods is that a score is calculated for each considered structure and finally, the structure with the highest score is chosen as output candidate. Several scores or quality measures have been proposed that can be categorized into (1) Bayesian quality measures, (2) minimum description length measures and (3) information measures. Bayesian quality measures have the merit that uncertain expert knowledge about the structure can be incorporated. Heckerman et al. (1994) use a global approach to find an appropriate prior on the structure. They propose priors for Gaussian as well as for multinomial networks (Heckerman, et al. 1994). Another local approach where to each single edge a priori probability is assigned, has been suggested by Hunscher (1998). The score introduced there is, however, only applicable for multivariate normal domains. An overview of different scoring functions can be found in Castillo et al. (1997, p. 484 – 510) and Sangüsa and Cortés (1997). As search strategies, there have been suggested among others the later described K2-algorithm (Cooper and Herkovitz 1992), local search (Heckerman 1995), Occams Window (Madigan and Ratery 1994) and Simulated Annealing (Metropolis et al. 1953).

5.2.3 Hybrids

Several hybrid forms of the two essential approaches to learn graphical model have been proposed. The combination is made in two stages. The task being solved on the first stage is to select a graph using a constraint based search method. The second stage starts with that structure and applies a Bayesian method to refine the structure. Algorithms of this form have been developed by Singh and Valtorta (1993) and by Spirtes and Meek (1995). Another kind of hybrid form is to use the search procedure of the PC-algorithm but to apply instead of the independence tests some other quality measure to find valid d-separation relations in the graph. Steck and Tresp (1999) achieved promising results by the application of the Bayesian information criterion as d-separation oracle. Another possibility that allows smoothly the incorporation of uncertain expert knowledge is the utilisation of the score proposed by Hunscher (1998) as a decision tool for d-separation. There are also attempts to include other methods from the field of artificial intelligence to support the learning process (de Campos and Huete 2000) like genetic algorithms.

5.3 Final Remarks

Learning graphs from data or from a mixture of expert knowledge and data is a challenging task for the research community. Despite the advancements that have already been achieved there are many problems left. Most methods require a complete set of data. In practical applications, however, missing data is the reality. Score based methods tend to get stuck at a local maximum white constraint based approaches show an undesirably huge sensitivity on the choose of the significance level used in independence test. Nevertheless, any efforts are with taken because graphical models have enormous potentials for explanation and description of phenomena, for diagnostics and reasoning, and for predictions about interventions. All these are essentials for well founded decision making.

References

Bishop, Y., Fienberg, S. Holland, P. (1975): Discrete Multivariate Analysis, MIT Press, Cambridge.

Bouckaert, R. (1995): Bayesian Belief Networks, From Construction to Inference, Ph.D. Dissertation, Computer Science Department, University of Utrecht.

Castillo, E., Gutiérrez, J. M., Hadi, A. S. (1997): Expert Systems and Probabilistic Networks Models, Springer-Verlag, New York.

Chickering, M. (1996): Learning Bayesian Networks is NP-Complete, in: Fisher, D., Lenz, H. (eds.) Learning from Data, Lecture Notes in Statistics, Springer-Verlag, New York, 121 – 30.

Cooper, G. F. (1999): An Overview of the Representation and Discovery of Causal Relationships Using Bayesian Networks, in: Glymour, C., Cooper, G. F. (eds.), Computation, Causation, and Discovery, MIT Press, Menlo Park, 3 – 62.

Cooper, G. F., Herskovitz, E. (1991): A Bayesian Method for constructing Bayesian Belief Networks from Databases, in: Proceedings of the 7th Conference on Uncertainty in Artificial Intelligence, LA, 86 – 94.

Cowell, R. (1998): Introduction to Inference for Bayesian Networks, in: Jordan, M. I., Learning in Graphical Models, MIT Press, Cambridge.

Cowell, R. G., Dawid, A. P., Lauritzen, S. L., Spiegelhalter, D. J. (1999): Probabilistic Networks and Expert Systems, Springer-Verlag, New York.

Cox, D. R., Wermuth, N. (1993): Linear Dependencies Represented in Chain Graphs, Statistical Science, Vol 8, No. 3, 204 – 18.

Dawid, A. P. (1979): Conditional Independence in Statistical Theory, Journal of the Royal Statistical Society, Ser. B. 41, 1 – 31.

De Campos, L. M., Huete, J. F. (2000): Approximating Causal Orderings for Bayesian Networks using Genetic Algorithms and Simulated Annealing, in: Proceedings 8th International Conference on Information Processing and Management of Uncertainty in Knowledge Based Systems Universidad Politécnica de Madrid, Madrid, Vol. I, 333 – 40.

Edwards, D. (1995): Introduction to Graphical Modelling, New York.

Geiger, D., Verma, T. S., Pearl, J. (1990): Identifying Independence in Bayesian Networks, Networks 20, 507-34.

Heckerman, D. (1995): A Tutorial on Learning with Bayesian Networks, Technical Report MSR-TR-95-06, Microsoft Research, Redmond.

Heckerman, D., Geiger, D. Chickering, D. M. (1994): Learning Bayesian networks: The Combination of Knowledge and Statistical Data. Microsoft Research, Technical Report MSR-TR-94-09, Redmond.

Heckerman, D., Meek, C., Cooper, G. F. (1999): A Bayesian Approach to Causal Discovery, in: Glymour, C., Cooper, G. F. (eds.), Computation, Causation, and Discovery, MIT Press, Menlo Park, 141 – 65.

Hunscher, M. (1998): Abhängigkeitsanalyse unter Einbeziehung exogener Informationen als Data-Mining Instrument, Dissertation, Friedrich-Schiller-Universität Jena, Jena.

Jordan, M. I. (1998): Learning in Graphical Models, (Editor), Kluwer Academic Publishers, Dordrecht.

Kischka, P. (2000): Graphentheoretische Modelle in der Statistik, in: Voss, H. (ed.), Taschenbuch der Statistik, Leipzig.

Kischka, P., Eherler, D. (1999): Causal Graphs and Unconfoundedness, Diskussionspapier, Reihe B, Nr. 99/5, Friedrich-Schiller-Universität Jena, Jena.

Kischka, P., Eherler, D. (1999): Causal Graphs and Unconfoundedness, Diskussionspapier, Reihe B, Nr. 99/5, Friedrich-Schiller-Universität Jena, Jena.

Kischka, P., Eherler, D. (2000): Uncounfounded Effects Derived from Graphical Structures, in Proceedings 8th International Conference on Information Processing and Management of Uncertainty in Knowledge Based Systems Universidad Politécnica de Madrid, Madrid, Vol. III, 1278-84.

Lauritzen, S. L. (1996): Graphical Models, Clarendon Press, Oxford.

Lauritzen, S. L., Dawid, A. P., Larsen, B. N., Leimer, H. G. (1990): Independence Properties of Directed Markov Fields, Networks 20, 491 – 505.

Lauritzen, S. L., Wermuth, N. (1984): Mixed Interaction Models, Technical Report R-84-8, Institute of Electronic Systems, Aalborg University.

Madigan, D., Rafberg, A. (1994): Model Selection and Accounting for Model Uncertainty in Graphical Models Using Occam's Window. Journal of the Amer. Stat. Ass., 89 (428), 1535 – 46.

Meek, C. (1995a): Relating Graphical Framework; Undirected, Directed Acyclic, and Chain Graph Models, Carnegie Mellon University, Technical Report CMU-Phil-64, Pittsburgh.

Meek, C. (1995b): Strong Completeness and Faithfulness in Bayesian Networks. In Besnard, P., Hanks, S. (eds.), Uncertainty in Artificial Intelligence: Proceedings of the 11th Conference, Morgan Kaufmann, San Francisco, 403 – 410.

Metropolis, N., Rosenbluth, A. W., Rosenbluth, M., Teller, A. U., Teller, E. (1953): Equation of State Calculations by Fast Computing Machines, The Journal of Chemical Physics, 21, 1087 – 92.

Murphy, K. P. (2000): Bayesian Network Software Packages, URL:http://HTTP.CS.Berkeley.EDU/~murphyk/Bayes/bnsoft.html.

Pearl, J. (1988): Probabilistic Inference in Intelligent Systems, Morgan Kaufmann, San Mateo.

Pearl, J. (1993): Comment: Graphical Models, Causality, and Intervention, Statistical Science, Vol. 8, 266 – 9.

Pearl, J. (1995): Causal Diagrams for Empirical Research, Biometrica 82, 669 – 710.

Pearl, J. (1996): A Causal Calculus for Statistical Research, in: Fisher, D., Lenz, H. J. (eds.), Learning from Data, Springer-Verlag, New York, 23 – 33.

Pearl, J. (1998): Why there is no Statistical Test of Confounding, Why many think is, and why the are almost right, Technical Report R – 256, Cognitive Systems Laboratory, UCLA, Los Angeles.

Pearl, J. (2000): Causality, Models, Reasoning, and Inference, Cambridge University Press, Cambridge.

Pearl, J., Paz, A. (1985): Graphoids: A Graph Based Logic for Reasoning About Relevance Relations, Technical Report R – 93 – III, Cognitive Systems Laboratory, UCLA, Los Angeles.

Reichenbach, H. (1956): The Direction of Time, University of California Press, Berkeley.

Rosenbaum, P, Rubin, D. (1983): The Central Role of Propensity Score in Observational Studies for Causal Effects, Biometrics 70, 41 – 55.

Sangüsa, R., Cortés, U (1997): Learning Causal Networks from Data: A Survey and a New Algorithm for Reasoning Possibilistic Causal Networks, AI Communications, Vol. 10, No. 1, 31 – 61.

Scheines, R., Spirtes, P., Glymour C., Meek, C. (1994): Tetrad II – Tools for Causal Modeling, Lawrence Erlbaum Ass., New York.

Scheines, R., Spirtes, P., Glymour, C., Meek, C., Richardson, T. (1998): The Tetrad Project: Constraint Based Aids to Causal Models Specification, Multivariate, Behavioural Research, 33, 65 – 117.

Shachter, R. D. (1986): Evaluating Influence Diagrams, Operations Research 34, 6, 871-82.

Singh, M., Valtorta, M. (1993): An Algorithm for the Construction of Bayesian Network Structure from Data, in: Proceedings of the Conference on Uncertainty in Artificial Intelligence, Morgan Kaufmann Publishers, San Francisco, 259 – 65.

Spirtes, P., Glymour, C. (1991): An Algorithm for Fast Recovery of Sparse Causal Graphs. Social Science Computer Review, 9, 62-72.

Spirtes, P., Glymour, C., Scheines, R. (1993): Causation, Prediction, and Search, Springer-Verlag, New York.

Spirtes, P., Meek, C. (1995): Learning Bayesian Networks with Discrete Variables form Data. In: Proceedings of the 1st International Conference on Knowledge Discovery and Data Mining, AAAI Press., Menlo Park, 294 – 9.

Spirtes, P., Meek, C., Richardson, T. (1999): An Algorithm for Causal Inference in the Presence of Latent Variables and Selection Bias, in: Glymour, C., Cooper, G. F. (eds.), Computation, Causation, and Discovery, MIT Press, Menlo Park, 211 – 52.

Spohn, W. (1980): Stochastic Independence, Causal Independence, and Shieldability, Journal of Philosophical Logic, 9, 73 – 99.

Steck, H., Tresp, V. (1999): Bayesian Belief Networks for Data Mining, Proceedings, 2nd Workshop, DMDW99, University of Magdeburg, Germany, 145-54.

Wermuth, N., Lauritzen, S. L. (1990): On Substantive Research Hypothesis, Conditional Independence Graphs and Graphical Chain Models, Journal of the Royal Statistical Society, Ser. B. 52, No. 1, 21 – 50.

Whittacker, J. (1990): Graphical Models in Applied Multivariate Statistics, Wiley, Chichester.

Wright, S. (1921): Correlation and Causation, Journal of Agricultural Research, 20, 557 – 85.

On the Effect of the Bargaining Context on Bargaining Behaviour

Maximilian K. P. Jung[1] and Ulrike Leopold-Wildburger[2]

[1] Department of Accounting and Auditing

[2] Department of Statistics and Operations Research

University of Graz, Austria

Abstract

This paper analyses three and two person bargaining experiments with respect to the question of the ability of players to push through their own interests. It is shown that the success of the players strongly depends on the circumstances under which bargaining takes place.

Acknowledgements. Financial support of the Austrian Science Fund (FWF P 13919-OEK) is gratefully acknowledged.

1 Introduction

The bargaining context is often thought to essentially influence bargaining behaviour and results. Selten/Schuster 1970 recommend to enhance the influence of bargaining theories which consider forces emerging from the social field that "is automatically set up (...) if you bring together several people in one room" (p. 100). Roth 1995 (p.254) argues that in experimental bargaining theory it can be observed that the extreme positions of the game theory purists and the social norm purists move towards each other. This also supports the view that the social field represented by social norms is now widely accepted to influence bargaining behaviour and results.

The effect of individual factors of the social field on bargaining is analysed in Hoffmann/Spitzer 1985, Ostmann 1992a, 1992b, Leopold-Wildburger 1992b, Ostmann/Leopold-Wildburger 1995 and Solnick/Schweitzer 1999 for example.

In Hofmann/Spitzer 1985 it is shown that the way in which roles are assigned to players will make a difference. Subjects regard differences in roles which are assigned randomly as unfair and tend to compensate for these inequalities in the bargaining process.

Ostmann 1992a, 1992b and Ostmann/Leopold-Wildburger 1995 analyse the effect of different bargaining styles on bargaining results. In Ostmann/Leopold-Wildburger 1995 it is found that the style of the friendly collaborator is favourable to the degree of success.

Leopold-Wildburger 1992b demonstrates that the success of players in three person bargaining games depends on the value of the grand coalition and the aspiration levels.

In Solnick/Schweitzer 1999 the effect of the physical attractiveness and the gender of the bargaining partners on bargaining outcome is analysed. It is asserted that attractive people tend to receive better results.

In this paper three person face to face and anonymous two person bargaining experiments are analysed. The three person bargaining experiments take place in a neutral labor environment. The two person experiments are conducted under two circumstances: First, in the neutral frame bargaining takes place without any cover story. Second, in the collusive frame one bargaining partner is labelled as a defrauder before bargaining starts. The main question of research is whether players are able to realise their own interests. We suppose that players who are in a weak position will not succeed. However, the weakness or strength of ones position in a bargaining game does not only depend on the economic factors characterising it. It is but also influenced by the social interpretation of the role.

Section 2 presents the experiments. The results are summarised in section 3 and interpreted in section 4.

2 The Experiments

This section briefly describes the two experiments analysed. The first experiment implements three person face-to-face bargaining, the second experiment consists of anonymous two person bargaining situations.

Three Person Bargaining

Briefly described, a 3-person game in characteristic function form is defined by a pair (N, v), where $N = \{1,2,3\}$ is the set of the players and v is a real valued function on the set of coalitions $P(N) = \{S: S \subset N\}$. The possible subsets of players are called coalitions. The value of a coalition can be interpreted as a measure of the utility controlled by the corresponding subset of players in a coalition against all the other players in the game. The payoff amount which is assigned to a coalition can be distributed among its members in various ways. It is a matter of bargaining, which distribution actually prevails. In the games played in the experiment we always have:

$$v(\{1\}) = v(\{2\}) = v(\{3\}) = 0 \tag{2.1}$$

$$v(\{1,2\}) = a = 80 \tag{2.2}$$

$$v(\{1,3\}) = b = 60 \tag{2.3}$$

$$\mathrm{v}(\{2,3\}) = \mathrm{c} = 40 \tag{2.4}$$

$$v(\{1,2,3\}) = g = 80, 85, ..., 120 \tag{2.5}$$

Thus, due to (2.1) all games considered in the experiment are so-called zero-normalised games, implying that the players will receive nothing, if they are unable to form coalitions. Following (2.2), (2.3) and (2.4) player 1 contributes most to any two-person coalition, whereas player 3 contributes least. The contribution of player 2 to any two-person coalition lies between player 1 and player 3. Due to (2.5) the value of the grand coalition consisting of all three players is varied systematically. All games are superadditive games, which means that $g \geq a$ is satisfied.

The subjects were male and female undergraduate students of economics and/or business administration at the Universities of Graz and Klagenfurt in Austria.

The experiment had been carried out with 12 independent subject groups. There were nine subjects in each group. So the total number of participants was 108. Each subject participated in three different games, which means that each individual played all player roles in the game exactly once, however two subjects never met twice.

The first six groups with 54 subjects received monetary rewards and are denoted by subset I, the second six groups with 54 subjects, denoted as subset II, didn't receive any rewards. If one considers typical income of Austrian students and the time spend in the experiment, one can speak about substantial monetary incentives in the case of subset I.

The procedure permitted free and unrestricted face-to-face communication between the players. However, only payoff divisions with integer payoffs for each player were permitted. When a group of players had formed a coalition and when they had agreed upon a the payoff distribution they could announce this to their referee. If a two-person coalition was formed, the referee would then inform the outside player about the agreed upon payoff division. Agreements were taken as final if they had been stable for ten minutes. Within this time an agreement could be nullified by an unilateral decision of one of the members of the coalition. During the final waiting time of ten minutes the individuals usually discussed their bargaining behaviour. Bargaining time was unrestricted.

Before the beginning of the bargaining, during the so called offer stage, each player had the possibility to ask questions referring to the understanding of the procedure. Each player was asked to write down two things: First, a proposal for an intended coalition together with a payoff division. Second, the value of the first definite offers. These initial proposals had to be made independently and separately by the tree players. Before bargaining was permitted to start, the three proposals were announced publicly. The first definite offers are in nearly all cases the same as the proposals for the first payoff division.

On the average one game of subset I lasted for approximately 45 minutes. The average game of subset II took about 23 minutes.

Two Person Bargaining

Figure 1 illustrates the sequential structure of bargaining process implemented in the two person bargaining games.

The two players $N = \{1,2\}$ have to bargain about the division of a given sum of money, the initial value of which is denoted by B. The bargaining process can last for several rounds $t = 0, 1, ..., n$. Due to bargaining costs the pie is reduced by a constant discount factor $\rho \leq 1$ each time the bargaining process is extended by one further round. The value of the pie at the beginning of each round is therefore given by $B_t = \rho^t \cdot B$.

Each round consists of one player making an offer about the division of the remaining amount of money and the other player deciding whether to accept the offer or to reject it or to continue the bargaining process by submitting a counteroffer. In even rounds offers are submitted by player 1 in odd rounds by player 2.

The division of the remaining amount of money proposed in round t is denoted by $(x_t, \rho^t \cdot B - x_t)$ with x_t being the intended share of player 1. If a proposal is accepted bargaining ends and the players will receive their respective shares. If one player rejects an offer the bargaining process is also terminated and the players get their outside opportunities denoted by δ_1 and δ_2, respectively. We have set $\delta_1 < 0$, $\delta_2 > 0$. The parameter δ_1 can be interpreted as the outside opportunity or fine player 1 has to pay if bargaining does not end in agreement, the parameter δ_2 is the outside opportunity or premium player 2 gets paid if bargaining is unsuccessful. In order to get non trivial bargaining situations $\delta_1 + \delta_2 < B$ is assumed. Let x denote the final bargaining outcome of player 1. The final outcome is either $x = x_t$ if an agreement is reached in round t or $x = \delta_1$ if bargaining does not succeed. The final outcome of player 2 is denoted by y and it is either $y = B_t - x_t$ if bargaining succeeds or $y = \delta_1$ if bargaining ends in disagreement.

If the players are not able to reach an agreement within 20 rounds the bargaining process is terminated automatically leaving the players with their outside opportunities δ_1 and δ_2.

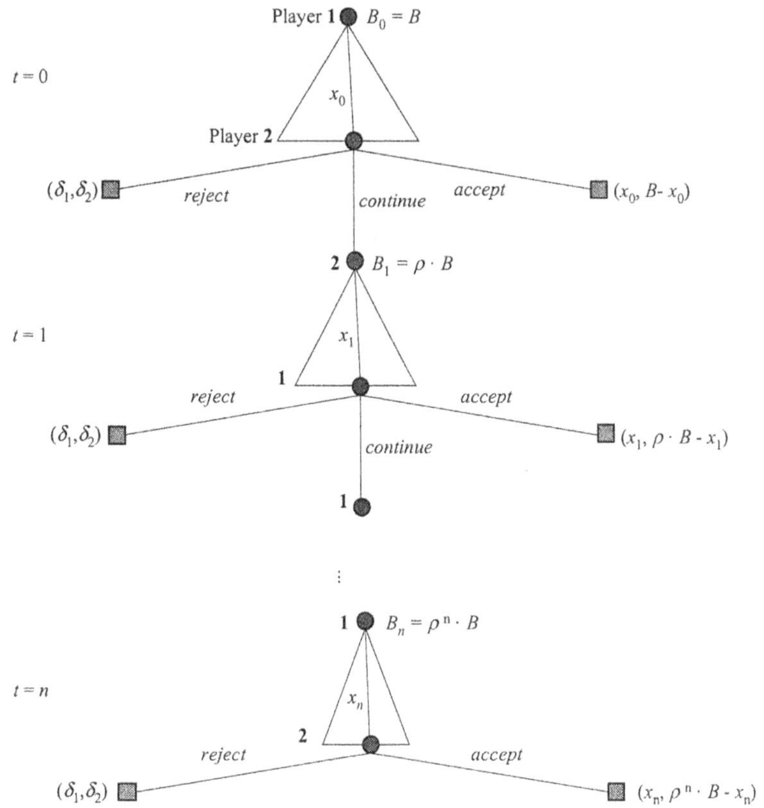

Figure 1: The implemented sequential bargaining process

The subjects were male and female undergraduate students of business administration at the University of Graz.

The experiment was carried out in eight sessions. There were 16 subjects in each session, eight in the role of player 1 and eight in the role of player 2. The total number of participants was 128. Each player had to participate in eight bargaining encounters which were different with respect to the values of the parameters B, δ_1 and δ_2 as well as with respect to the bargaining partner. Two subjects never met twice. Table 1 summarises the eight different treatments which each subject was confronted with. In order to avoid position effects the order of treatments was balanced.

	TR 1	TR 2	TR 3	TR 4	TR 5	TR 6	TR 7	TR 8
B	10.000	10.000	10.000	10.000	40.000	40.000	40.000	40.000
δ_1	-2.000	-6.000	-2.000	-6.000	-8.000	-24.000	-8.000	-24.000
δ_2	4.000	4.000	8.000	8.000	16.000	16.000	32.000	32.000

Table 1: Treatments TR 1 –TR 8

In the experiment a currency called Monetary Unit was used to denote amounts of money. Participants received their payments in Austrian Schillings at the end of each session. The exchange rate was set to 1 Austrian Schilling for 1.000 Monetary Units. Note that 13,7603 Austrian Schillings are equal to 1 Euro.

The first four sessions with 64 subjects were part of the so called neutral frame. In the neutral frame negotiations took place in an usual labor environment. No special cover story was presented to the subjects. They were told that they would receive the amount B provided that they could agree about its division. If they failed to reach any agreement they would have to pay δ_1 or would receive δ_2, respectively. To avoid that players 1 lost real money if all of their eight bargaining encounters ended in disagreement they were granted ex-ante payments of 80.000 Monetary Units.

Bargaining took place anonymously by using a computer network. The workstations of players 1 and players 2 were located in two different rooms of the computer laboratory. Within one room there was enough space between the computer terminals to avoid mutual disturbances. Furthermore, verbal communication was prohibited. Each subject had to log in the computer network by using a code-number which he was assigned randomly at the beginning of the session.

The collusive frame consisted of the second four session with 64 subjects. In the collusive frame the 32 subjects in the role of player 1 were told that they should act as managers being in charge of a small firm. The other 32 subjects in the role of player 2 were requested to behave as auditors. Each session had two stages:

At stage one each manager had to play a small computerised business simulation game for several time periods. In each time period decisions concerning the price of the product of the firm, about marketing expenditures, about the acquisition of further information and about the amount of profit reported to the owner of the firm had to be made. The manager had the opportunity to increase his own compensation by illegally underreporting the profits of the firm. However, in doing so he ran the risk of being detected by the auditors of the firm, being delivered to the court and being punished. The business simulation was terminated either if the accumulated underreporting of the manager exceeded 280.000 Monetary Units or if more than 60 time periods have been played. In the first case the manager was notified that the eight auditors of the firm had been able to detect frauds of 200.000 Monetary Units in total. The manager was also informed of the possibility to persuade each of the auditors to conceal his findings by offering him an adequate bribe. In the second case the manager was just notified of the end of the game. Actually, 31 of the 32 managers decided to underreport profits in a way that triggered termination before 60 time periods were played. Termination due to exceeding the time limit occurred only once. Since the one subject concerned had committed minor frauds he/she was asked to continue at stage two. During the play of the business simulation game the auditors were taught their professional responsibilities.

At the second stage the manager could negotiate with the eight auditors of the firm. The circumstances of each bargaining encounter are defined in Table 1. The parameter B is interpreted as the fraction of the total amount illegally acquired by the manager which a particular auditor had been able to discover. If the bargaining partners were not able to reach an agreement the manager had to pay the fine δ_1, whereas the auditor received the premium δ_2.

Bargaining took place anonymously by using the computer network. Unlike in the neutral frame the software used a value laden terminology in order to remind the subjects of the collusive bargaining environment.

On average one session in the neural frame lasted for about 110 minutes. The average session in the collusive frame took about 130 minutes. Players 1 could expect to earn about 90 Austrian Schillings. Players 2 could receive about 150 Austrian Schillings.

3 Results

The main question of research is whether the players are able to succeed in pushing through their own interests.

Three Person Bargaining

In the three person bargaining experiment the outcome target of each player is measured by his essential first offer made during the offer stage. In order to analyse the influence of outcome targets on realised outcome the following linear regression model is specified:

$$OR_i = \alpha_i + \beta_{1i} \cdot g + \beta_{2i} \cdot OT_{Ai} + \beta_{3i} \cdot OT_{Bi} + \beta_{4i} \cdot OT_{Ci} + u \tag{2.6}$$

Therein, OR_i denotes the final payoff of player i, with $i = A, B, C$. The parameters OT_{Ai}, OT_{Bi} and OT_{Ci} represent the initial offers of players in role A, B and C during the offer stage. The parameter u denotes the residuum with $\mathbf{E}(u) = 0$.

The coefficients as well as R^2 are listed in Table 2:

	α_i	β_{1i}	β_{2i}	β_{3i}	β_{4i}	R^2
$i = A$	-10,8588	<u>0,37301</u>	<u>0,45938</u>	0,06919	-0,09591	0,717643
$i = B$	18,5558	<u>0,29619</u>	<u>-0,30513</u>	0,02341	0,01766	0,650964
$i = C$	-5,2145	<u>0,32937</u>	<u>-0,16377</u>	-0,12367	0,04562	0,536473

Table 2: Regression coefficients

All coefficients which are statistically significant on a 95% level are underlined. Due to Table 2 the final outcomes are influenced by the value of the grand coalition and further by the aspiration level of each player. The final results of players A who actually are in the strongest position from the economic point of view strongly depend on their initial intentions. The results of players B and C are still positively influenced by their initial offers. However, the regressions are low and insignificant. Note that the frame of the three person games was a neutral one.

Two Person Bargaining

In order to measure the outcome target of player 1 we use the following proxy:

$$OT_{1j} = \frac{1}{8} \cdot \sum_{i=1}^{8} \frac{x_{0ij} - \delta_{1i}}{B_i - \delta_{1i} - \delta_{2i}} \tag{2.7}$$

The index j denotes the number of the subject in the role of player 1. Let $j = 1, 2, \ldots, 32$ and $j = 33, 34, \ldots, 64$ be the subjects of the neutral and collusive frame, respectively. The index i denotes the treatment number. Due to (2.7) the outcome target is defined as the average fraction of the total gain from bargaining which subject j in the role of player 1 demands for himself in round $t = 0$ in all of his eight treatments. Equivalently, we use the following proxy to measure the level of generosity of the bargaining partners of player 1:

$$LG_{1j} = \frac{1}{8} \cdot \sum_{i=1}^{8} \frac{\tilde{x}_{1ij} - \delta_{1i}}{B_i - \delta_{1i} - \delta_{2i}} \tag{2.8}$$

The level of generosity is defined as the average fraction of the total gain from bargaining which subject j in the role of player 1 is offered by his bargaining partners in round $t = 1$ of all eight treatments. For bargaining encounters ending in $t = 0$, realised payoffs are used instead of proposals. The realised outcome of subject j in the role of player 1 is defined as:

$$OR_{1j} = \frac{1}{8} \cdot \sum_{i=1}^{8} \frac{x_{ij} - \delta_{1i}}{B_i - \delta_{1i} - \delta_{2i}} \qquad (2.9)$$

In the collusive frame players 1 are labelled as defrauders. We, therefore, conjecture that they will demand less, will be treated less friendly by players 2 and will end up with a smaller share of the total gain of bargaining than in the neutral frame. Formally, we test the following hypotheses:

H_{01}: $F_N(OT_1) \leq F_C(OT_1)$ H_{A1}: $F_N(OT_1) > F_C(OT_1)$

H_{02}: $F_N(LG_1) \leq F_C(LG_1)$ H_{A2}: $F_N(LG_1) > F_C(LG_1)$

H_{03} $F_N(OR_1) \leq F_C(OR_1)$ H_{A3}: $F_N(OR_1) > F_C(OR_1)$

Using the Mann-Whitney-U-Test all three hypotheses are rejected with $p \leq 0{,}01$. This supports our conjectures.

In order to get further insight into the forces that drive the results within each frame the dependencies between these parameters have to be identified. Table 3 summarises the results of an analysis of correlation between OT_1, LG_1 and OR_1 for both frames:

		OT_1	LG_1
OR_1	Neutral Frame	$\rho = -0{,}70$ $p \leq 0{,}01$	$\rho = 0{,}46$ $p \leq 0{,}01$
	Collusive Frame	$\rho < 0$ $p > 0{,}05$ (n.s.)	$\rho = 0{,}75$ $p \leq 0{,}01$

Table 3: Correlation Coefficients for the Outcome Received of Players 1

Table 3 shows a strong and highly significant negative correlation between the outcome targets of players 1 and the final results they receive in the neutral frame. In other words, in the neutral frame players 1 will get less if they demand more. In the collusive frame the same correlation is also negative but weak and insignificant, leading us to the conclusion that initial offers are almost without any effect on final outcomes in the collusive frame.

Table 3 also shows strong and highly significant positive correlations between the level of generosity of the bargaining partners of players 1 and the outcome players

1 finally receive. This correlation turns out to be stronger in the collusive frame than in the neutral one.

If players 1 insist on getting a large fraction of the total gain from bargaining in the neutral frame they will be punished by players 2. Table 4 shows that punishment actually takes place in two ways: First, there is a strong and highly significant correlation between the outcome targets of players 1 and the average length of their eight bargaining encounters denoted as *LENGTH*. This means that on average players 1 tend to bargain longer and therefore incur higher bargaining costs if their outcome targets are higher. Second, there also exists a strong and highly significant correlation between the outcome targets of players 1 and the number of their eight bargaining encounters ending in disagreement denoted as *REJECTION*. This implies that on average players 1 will be left with their negative outside opportunities more frequently the higher their outcome targets are.

	OT_1	LG_1
LENGTH	$\rho = 0{,}643$ $p \leq 0{,}01$	$\rho = -0{,}348$ $p > 0{,}05$ (n.s.)
REJECTION	$\rho = 0{,}682$ $p \leq 0{,}01$	$\rho = -0{,}224$ $p > 0{,}05$ (n.s.)
LG_1	$\rho = -0{,}258$ $p > 0{,}05$ (n.s.)	/

Table 4: Selected Correlation Coefficients for the Neutral Frame

Table 4 shows that there is no significant correlation between the level of generosity of the bargaining partners of players 1 and the average length of the bargaining encounters and the number of encounters not ending in agreement. Furthermore, the outcome target of players 1 do not seem to influence the level of generosity of players 2 significantly.

High outcome goals of players 1 seem to have different consequences in the collusive frame. As is shown in Table 5 there is a positive and highly significant correlation between the outcome targets of players 1 and the number of their eight bargaining encounters ending in disagreement. Therefore, players 1 who require a higher fraction of the total gain from bargaining at the beginning will end up with their negative outside opportunities more frequently. However, in contrast to the neutral frame there is no significant correlation between the average length of the eight bargaining encounters and the average outcome targets of players 1. Due to Table 5 the average length of the eight bargaining encounters of players 1 is influenced by the average level of generosity of their eight bargaining partners in a negative and highly significant way. This means that the bargaining encounters last for a smaller number of rounds if the bargaining partners turn out to be friendly.

	OT_1	LG_1
LENGTH	$\rho = 0{,}123$ $p > 0{,}05$ (n.s.)	$\rho = -0{,}571$ $p \leq 0{,}01$
REJECTION	$\rho = 0{,}436$ $p \leq 0{,}05$	$\rho = -0{,}308$ $p > 0{,}05$ (n.s.)
LG_1	$\rho = -0{,}113$ $p > 0{,}05$ (n.s.)	/

Table 5: Selected Correlation Coefficients for the Collusive Frame

Table 5 shows that there is no significant correlation between the outcome targets of players 1 and the average level of generosity of their bargaining partners. The number of bargaining encounters ending in disagreement is not significantly influenced by the average level of generosity of the bargaining partners.

In the two person experiments a questionnaire was used to ask subjects about their personal perceptions of the bargaining experiment. Table 6 shows three questions and the parameters used to denote them:

	Question	**Parameter**
1	In the experiment I made the same considerations as in real life (I completely agree I completely disagree)	*REAL*
2	In the experiment my main goal was to achieve a fair split of the given amount. (I completely agree I completely disagree)	$FAIR_1$
3	An equal split is always fair. (I completely agree I completely disagree)	$FAIR_2$

Table 6: Questionnaire

Subjects had to mark the degree of their agreement by drawing a vertical line in a given rectangle. The answers were evaluated by using a scale of ten intervals and a low value indicating high agreement. The parameters *REAL*, $FAIR_1$ and $FAIR_2$ do not depend significantly on the outcome targets of players 1. However, Table 7 shows that these parameters correlate with the level of generosity of the bargaining partners of players 1.

	LG_1	
	neutral frame	collusive frame
REAL	$\rho = -0,380$ $p \leq 0,05$	$\rho = 0,490$ $p \leq 0,01$
FAIR $_1$	$\rho = 0,377$ $p \leq 0,05$	$\rho = 0,285$ $p > 0,05$ (n.s.)
FAIR $_2$	$\rho = 0,397$ $p \leq 0,05$	$\rho = -0,012$ $p > 0,05$ (n.s.)

Table 7: Selected Correlation Coefficients for the Questionnaire

Due to Table 7 we observe a significant negative correlation between *REAL* and LG_1 in the neutral frame, whereas these parameters are correlate in a highly significant and positive way in the collusive frame. Players 1 interpret the experimental situation the more realistic the more friendly they are treated by their bargaining partners in the neutral frame, whereas a more friendly behaviour of their bargaining partners leads them to interpret the experimental situation as more unrealistic in the collusive frame. Table 7 also shows positive and significant correlations between $FAIR_1$ as well as $FAIR_2$ and LG_1 in the neutral frame. This means that players 1 find themselves less inclined to pursue fair splits of the given amounts if they are treated more friendly by their bargaining partners. In the collusive frame these correlations are insignificant.

4 Interpretations

The results show that the answer to the question if the players are able to push through their own intentions depends very much on the circumstances under which the bargaining takes place.

In the three person bargaining experiment all players will end up getting more if they demand more in the beginning. Their final payoffs are positively influenced by their aspiration levels.

If the two person bargaining experiment takes place in a neutral frame players 1 who require much at the beginning tend to insist on those high demands and will be punished by players 2 in the end. Punishment takes place either directly by ending the encounters in disagreement or indirectly by not accepting offers and thus increasing the length of the bargaining processes. The insistence on high demands may be explained by the fact that in the neutral frame players 1 interpret it as realistic to be treated friendly by their bargaining partners. It is shown that the more friendly players 1 are treated the more they try to pursue their own interests. Therefore, players 1 having high initial outcome targets will not be inclined to lower their demands sufficiently. In short, players 1 will be punished for their inflexibility not to adapt aspiration levels in an adequate way during the bargaining process.

In the collusive frame players 1 do not insist on their initial aspiration levels. They being labelled as defrauders perceive it as unrealistic to be treated in a friendly way by their bargaining partners. Therefore, players 1 tend to accept benevolent counteroffers of their bargaining partners early. However, if players 1 are treated unfriendly by their partners they continue bargaining in order to try to improve their position and end up getting less due the bargaining costs. In short, players 1 will be punished due to the fact that they are labelled as defrauders and not because of their inflexible bargaining behaviour.

It is concluded that the willingness to reduce aspiration levels is strongly influenced by factors of the frame in which bargaining takes place. This means that changing the moral position of bargaining partners actually affects their behaviour and as a consequence the results of bargaining encounters. Therefore, the recommendation to enhance bargaining theories which consider forces emerging from the social field is supported.

References

Corfman, K. & Lehmann, D. (1993). The importance of others' welfare in evaluating bargaining outcomes. Journal of Consumer Research 20, 124-37

Hoffman, E. & Spitzer, M. (1985) Entitlements, rights, and fairness: An experimental examination of subjects' concepts of distributive justice. Journal of Legal Studies 14, 259-97

Jung, M. (2000). Bargaining in criminal environments. Discussion Paper 3/2000. Department of Business. University of Graz

Leopold-Wildburger, U. (1992a). Payoff divisions on coalition formation in a three-person characteristic function experiment. Journal of Economic Behaviour and Organisation 17, 183-93

Leopold-Wildburger, U. (1992b). Regression analysis of co-operative payoff divisions. A contribution to experimental economics. Operations Research 91, 417-22

Ostmann, A. (1992a). On the relation between formal conflict structure and the social field. Small Group Research 23, 26-48

Ostmann, A. (1992b). The interaction of aspiration levels and the social field in experimental bargaining. Journal of Economic Psychology 13, 233-61

Ostmann, A. (1994). Anpassung und Einflußnahme im Verhandlungskontext. Gruppendynamik 25. 133-47

Ostmann, A. & Leopold-Wildburger, U. (1995). On Styles of Relating to Bargaining Partners. In Albers W., Güth, W., et al. (eds.): Understanding Strategic Interaction - Essays in Honour of Reinhard Selten, 430-43. Berlin: Springer

Roth, A. (1995). Bargaining experiments. In: Kagel, J. & Roth, A. (eds.): The handbook of experimental economics. 253-348. Princeton: Princeton University Press

Selten, R. & Schuster, K. (1970). Psychologische Faktoren bei Koalitionsverhandlungen. In Sauermann H. (ed.): Beiträge zur experimentellen Wirtschaftsforschung. Vol. II. 99-135. Tübingen: Mohr

Solnick, S. & Schweitzer, M. (1999). The influence of physical attractiveness and gender on ultimatum game decisions. Organizational Behaviour and Human Decision Processes 79, 199-215

Income Tax Rate: Properties and Implications

Wolfgang Eichhorn, Helmut Funke and Winfried Gleissner

Department of Economic Theory and Operations Research,
University Karlsruhe, Germany

Abstract

An income tax which is progressive and motivation preserving in the sense that income after tax increases with income before tax, satisfies interesting additional conditions that are somewhat surprising. This is shown without any differentiability assumptions

1. Introduction

If an income tax satisfies the conditions that

(i) the average tax rate is progressive, i.e., (weakly) increasing with income before tax, and

(iv) income after tax is weakly increasing with income before tax,

many interesting and several somewhat surprising phenomena are implied. For instance, condition (i) does *not* yield that

(ii) the marginal tax rate is progressive,

whereas (ii) yields (i), and conditions (i) and (iv) are, if conceived in a strict sense, *not* equivalent to a (strict) decrease of inequality in incomes after tax as compared with the inequality in incomes before tax; see Eichhorn/Funke/Richter [1982].

Without any differentiability assumptions it will be shown, among other things, that properties (i) and (iv) are compatible with the condition that

(v) the tax elasticity ("liability progression") is weakly increasing

if and *only if the income tax is proportional*, i.e., if conditions (i), (iv) and (v) are satisfied only in an extremely weak sense.

In this connection it should be noted that the tax elasticity plays an important role in many papers on income tax functions; see, for instance, Musgrave and Tun Thin [1948], Jakobsson [1976], Genser [1980].

2. Notation and Definitions

Let $\mathbb{R}_+$ be the nonnegative reals and $\mathbb{R}_{++}$ the positive reals. Any $x \in \mathbb{R}_+$ may be considered an *income before tax*. An *income tax rate* or *average tax rate* is a function $\mathrm{p}: \mathbb{R}_+ \to \mathbb{R}_+$ that assigns to each x a real number $\mathrm{p}(x)$ such that $x\,\mathrm{p}(x)$ is the *value of the income tax (income tax liability)*. Then $(1-\mathrm{p}(x))x$ is the *income after tax* or *net income* and, if p is differentiable, $d(x\,\mathrm{p}(x))/dx$ is the *marginal tax rate*. If we write $\mathrm{T}(x)$ for the (income) tax (amount) and $\mathrm{N}(x)$ for the net income, we have

$$\begin{aligned} \mathrm{T}(x) &= x\,\mathrm{p}(x), \\ \mathrm{p}(x) &= \mathrm{T}(x)/x \qquad \text{for } x \in \mathbb{R}_{++}, \end{aligned}$$

and

$$\mathrm{N}(x) = x - \mathrm{T}(x).$$

3. Properties

(i) **Progression of the Average Tax Rate**: The average tax rate p is weakly increasing, i.e., nondecreasing on $\mathbb{R}_+$: For any two incomes x_1, x_2 satisfying $x_1 < x_2$ we have $\mathrm{p}(x_1) \leqq \mathrm{p}(x_2)$.

(ii) **Progression of the Marginal Tax Rate**: The tax T is a convex function of x.

Note that T is not assumed to be differentiable. If so, Property (ii) can be formulated as follows: The marginal tax rate T' is nondecreasing.

(iii) **Bounded Burden**: There exists $r \in [0,1]$ such that $\mathrm{p}(x) \leqq 1-r$ for all $x \in \mathbb{R}_+$.

(iv) **Preservation of the Taxpayer's Motivation**: There exists $s \in [0,1]$ such that $\mathrm{N}(x)-\mathrm{N}(y) \geqq s\cdot(x-y)$ for all $x \in \mathbb{R}_+$, $y \in \mathbb{R}_+$ satisfying $x \geqq y$. In other words: Net income is a nondecreasing function of income before tax.

Note that $\mathrm{T}(0)=0$ and (ii) implies (i), but not conversely, and (iv) implies (iii) with $s=r$, but not conversely. Hence, conditions (i) and (iii) are weaker than conditions (ii) and (iv), respectively.

Examples of tax rates p that fulfil Properties (i) – (iv) are

$$(1)\quad \mathrm{p}(x)=\frac{1}{2},\ \mathrm{p}(x)=\frac{x}{2x+2},\ \text{and}\ \mathrm{p}(x)=\begin{cases}1/2 & \text{for } x\leqq 1\\ 1-1/\left(2x^{1/2}\right) & \text{for } x>1.\end{cases}$$

Hence, Properties (i) – (iv) are consistent.

4. Implications

Proposition 1. *Properties (i) (or (ii)) and (iv) imply continuity, but not differentiability, of the tax rate* p *on* $\mathbb{R}_{++}$.

Proof. From Properties (i) and (iv) we obtain, for every $\delta \in \mathbb{R}_{++}$,

$$0 \leqq \mathrm{p}(x+\delta)-\mathrm{p}(x) \leqq (1-\mathrm{p}(x))\delta/(x+\delta)\ ,$$

i.e., continuity of p for all $x \in \mathbb{R}_{++}$. Note that $\mathrm{p}(x) \leqq 1$ by (iv). The third example in (1) satisfies (i) and (iv), but is not differentiable at $x=1$.

Proposition 2. *Every tax rate* p *that satisfies Properties (ii) and (iv) on* $\mathbb{R}_{++}$ *can be written in the form*

$$(2)\qquad \mathrm{p}(x)=\frac{1}{x}\int_0^x \mathrm{t}(\xi)d\xi\ ,$$

where $\mathrm{t}: \mathbb{R}_{+} \rightarrow [0,1]$ *is a nondecreasing function. Conversely, every function* p *representable by (2) satisfies Properties (ii) and (iv).*

Proof. According to (ii), the income tax amount $x\,\mathrm{p}(x)$ is a convex function of the income x, hence differentiable with respect to x almost everywhere. Setting

$$\mathrm{t}(x)=d(x\,\mathrm{p}(x))/dx \quad \text{(for all } x \text{ at which the derivate exists)}$$

we obtain from (iv) (almost everywhere)

$$\mathrm{t}(x)=d(x\,\mathrm{p}(x))/dx+\mathrm{p}(x)\leqq 1\ ,$$

and from (ii) it follows that t is nondecreasing. Hence, the tax rate p can be written in the form (2). The second assertion of Proposition 2 can be shown by inserting (2) into the expressions occuring in (ii) and (iv).

In many papers on income tax functions both the tax elasticity ("liability progression") and the elasticity of income after tax (elasticity of net income, "residual progression") play an important role; see, for instance, Musgrave and Tun Thin [1948], Jakobsson [1976], Genser [1980].

Without any differentiability assumption we define the *tax elasticity* as

$$\eta(x,\delta)=\frac{T(x+\delta)-T(x)}{T(x)}:\frac{\delta}{x} \qquad (\delta \in \mathbb{R}_{++})$$

and the *elasticity of net income* as

$$\theta(x,\delta)=\frac{N(x+\delta)-N(x)}{N(x)}:\frac{\delta}{x} \qquad (\delta \in \mathbb{R}_{++}).$$

Are Properties (i) – (iv) compatible with the following two properties which have been required for several reasons, e.g., for decreasing income inequality?

(v) **Nondecreasing Tax Elasticity**: There exist $\delta \in \mathbb{R}_{++}$ and $x_1 \in \mathbb{R}_{+}$ such that $\eta(x,\delta)$ is, as a function of x, nondecreasing for all $x \geqq x_1$.

(vi) **Nonincreasing Elasticity of Net Income**: There exist $\delta \in \mathbb{R}_{++}$ and $x_1 \in \mathbb{R}_{+}$ such that $\theta(x,\delta)$ is, as a function of x, nonincreasing for all $x \geqq x_1$.

The answer is yes, but only in a very particular case. We will show this by Theorem 2 and its Corollary 2 which present characterizations of the proportional income tax. Before we show:

Theorem 1. a) *Properties (i) – (vi) are consistent.* b) *Properties (i) or (ii), (iii) or (iv), and (v) are logically independent.* c) *Properties (i) or (ii), (iii) or (iv), and (vi) are logically independent.*

Proof. a) The proportional tax, namely

$$p(x)=c\text{, that is, } T(x)=cx \quad (c \in (0,1))$$

satisfies Properties (i) – (vi) (if they are considered in their weakest possible sense).

b) We have to show that for any two of the three properties there exists a function that satisfies both of them but does not satisfy the remaining property. Obviously such a function is not necessarily an average tax rate. The function p given by

$$p(x)=\frac{1}{4}+\frac{1}{4}e^{-x}$$

satisfies (iii) and (iv) with $r = s = 1/2$, (v) with $x_1 = 2$, but neither (ii) nor (i).

$$p(x) = e^x$$

satisfies (i) and (ii), (v) with $x_1 = 1$, but neither (iv) nor (iii).

$$p(x) = \frac{1}{2}\frac{x}{x+1}$$

satisfies (i) and (ii), (iii) and (iv) with $r = s = 1/2$, but does not fulfil (v) for any x_1.

c) The function p given by

$$p(x) = \frac{1}{4} + \frac{1}{4}e^{-x}$$

satisfies (iii) and (iv) with $r = s = 1/2$, (vi) with $x_1 = 1$, but neither (ii) nor (i).

$$p(x) = 1 + \ln(1 + x)$$

satisfies (i) and (ii), (vi) with $x_1 = 1$, but neither (iv) nor (iii).

$$p(x) = \frac{1}{2}\frac{x}{x+1}$$

satisfies (i) and (ii), (iii) and (iv) with $r = s = 1/2$, but does not fulfil (vi) for any x_1.

In what follows we exclude the trivial tax rates $p(x) \equiv 0$ and $p(x) \equiv 1$. Hence, by Properties (i) and (iv), there exists x^* such that $0 < p(x^*) < 1$. The following lemma is essential for Theorem 2.

Lemma. *Properties (iii) (Bounded Burden) and*

(3) $\qquad \eta(x,\delta) \geqq \alpha > 1$ for all $x \geqq x_1$ ($x_1 \in \mathbb{R}_+$ *arbitrarily chosen*)

are incompatible.

Proof. The definition of η and (3) imply

$$p(x+\delta) = \frac{x + \delta\eta(x,\delta)}{x+\delta} p(x) \geqq \frac{x+\delta\alpha}{x+\delta} p(x) \text{ for all } x \geqq x_1 .$$

This yields

$$p(x+k\delta)=p(x)\prod_{j=1}^{k}\frac{x+j\delta \qquad +(\alpha-1)\delta}{x+j\delta}(x\geq x_1;k=1,2,\ldots)$$

The product on the right-hand side satisfies

$$\prod_{j=1}^{k}\frac{x+j\delta+(\alpha-1)\delta}{x+j\delta}=\prod_{j=1}^{k}\left(1+\frac{\alpha-1}{x/\delta+j}\right)>$$

$$1+(\alpha-1)\sum_{j=1}^{k}\frac{1}{x/\delta+j}>(\alpha-1)\sum_{i=[x/\delta+2]}^{[x/\delta+k+1]}\frac{1}{i}$$

Here, $[y]$ means the next integer number that is not greater than y. Since

$$\sum_{i=1}^{\infty}\frac{1}{i} \quad \text{(i.e., the harmonic series)}$$

is not bounded, we have

$p(x+k\delta)>1$ for sufficiently large k which contradicts (iii).

Theorem 2. *(A characterization of the proportional income tax).* a) *A tax rate* p *satisfying* $p(x)\not\equiv 0$ *and* $p(x)\not\equiv 1$ *fulfills conditions (i) (Progression of the Average Tax Rate), (iii) (Bounded Burden)*[1] *and (v) (Nondecreasing Tax Elasticity) if and only if*

$p(x)\equiv c \in (0,1)$ *for all* $x \geqq x_1$,

that is, if and only if the tax elasticity is equal to 1 *for all* $x \geqq x_1$.

b) *A tax rate* p *satisfying* $p(x)\not\equiv 0$ *fulfills conditions (i), (iii) with* $r>0$, *and (vi) (Nonincreasing Elasticity of Net income) if and only if*

$p(x)\equiv c \in (0,1)$ *for all* $x \geqq x_1$,

that is, if and only if the elasticity of net income is equal to 1 *for all* $x \geqq x_1$.

---

[1] Note that condition (i) is weaker than condition (ii) and that condition (iii) is weaker than condition (iv).

Proof. a) There does not exist any $x \geqq x_1$ satisfying $\eta(x,\delta) > 1$. Otherwise we would have had, by (v), for a suitably chosen $x_2 \geqq x_1$

$$\eta(x,\delta) \geqq \eta(x_2,\delta) =: \alpha > 1 \quad \text{for all} \quad x \geqq x_2 ;$$

that is, condition (3) would be fulfilled which is excluded by the Lemma. Since by condition (i) and the definition of η we have

$$\eta(x,\delta) \geqq \frac{p(x+\delta)}{p(x)} \geqq 1 ,$$

all that remains is $\eta(x,\delta) \equiv 1$ for all $x \geqq x_1$. Hence,

$$p(x+\delta) = p(x) \quad \text{for all} \quad x \geqq x_1 .$$

The monotonicity (i) of p yields the constancy of p, i.e.,

$$p(x) = c \in (0,1) \quad \text{for all} \quad x \geqq x_1 .$$

b) We use the identity

$$\text{(4)} \qquad p(x)\eta(x,\delta) + (1-p(x))\theta(x,\delta) = 1 \quad \text{for all } x, \delta,$$

rewritten as

$$\eta(x,\delta) = 1 + \frac{1-p(x)}{p(x)}(1-\theta(x,\delta))$$

in order to prove part b of Theorem 2 by analogous arguments as in the proof of part a.

Corollary 1 *(An impossibility assertion). There does not exist any income tax system which satisfies conditions (i), (iii) and (v) or (vi), assuming that the elasticities in (v) or (vi) are strictly monotonic in an arbitrarily small interval after* x_1.

We thank Johann Hermann v. Oehsen for suggesting the following remark.

Corollary 2 *(A Characterization of the proportional income tax). If we require, in addition to Properties (i), (iii) and (v) or (vi), Property (ii), that is the convexity of the tax* $T(x) = x\,p(x)$, *then we obtain proportionality of the tax for all* $x \in \mathbb{R}_+$.

Proof. We have to show proportionality for $x \in [0, x_1)$. By (i) we have

$$0 \leqq \mathrm{p}(x) \leqq \mathrm{c} = \mathrm{p}(x_1).$$

The case

$$\mathrm{p}(x_0) < \mathrm{c} \quad \text{for some} \quad x_0 < x_1$$

leads to a contradiction: Let $x_2 := 2x_1 - x_0$, whence $x_2 > x_1$, that is, $\mathrm{p}(x_2) = \mathrm{p}(x_1) = \mathrm{c}$ and $x_1 = x_0/2 + x_2/2$. Because $\mathrm{p}(x_0) < \mathrm{p}(x_1)$ we have

$$x_1\,\mathrm{p}(x_1) = \frac{1}{2}x_0\,\mathrm{p}(x_1) + \frac{1}{2}x_2\,\mathrm{p}(x_1) > \frac{1}{2}x_0\,\mathrm{p}(x_0) + \frac{1}{2}x_2\,\mathrm{p}(x_2)$$

which contradicts (ii).

The second and the third example in (1) show that conditions (i) – (iv) do *not* yield the proportionality of the income tax for incomes above a certain level. So it is not surprising that in most of the present income tax systems there does *not* exist any income x_1 such that the elasticities $\eta(x,\delta)$ and $\theta(x,\delta)$ are exactly equal to 1 for all $x \geqq x_1$. In this connection it is interesting to know whether conditions (i) – (iv) imply $\lim_{x\to\infty} \eta(x,\delta) = 1$ or $\lim_{x\to\infty} \theta(x,\delta) = 1$.

Theorem 3. a) *Properties (ii) (Progression of the Marginal Tax Rate), (iii) (Bounded Burden), and* $\mathrm{p}(x) \not\equiv 0$ *imply*

$$\lim_{x\to\infty} \eta(x,\delta) = 1.$$

b) *Properties (ii), (iii) with* $r > 0$, *and* $\mathrm{p}(x) \not\equiv 0$ *imply*

$$\lim_{x\to\infty} \theta(x,\delta) = 1.$$

Proof. a) We examine the convergence of the two factors of

$$\eta(x,\delta) = \frac{1}{\mathrm{p}(x)} \frac{(x+\delta)\mathrm{p}(x+\delta) - x\,\mathrm{p}(x)}{\delta}.$$

Since p is nondecreasing (by (ii) which implies (i)) and bounded from above (by (iii)), it converges,

$$\lim_{x\to\infty} \mathrm{p}(x) \in (0,1],$$

i.e., $1/\mathrm{p}(x)$ converges to a positive value. The second factor is also nonincreasing (by (ii)) and bounded from above (by (iii); see the Lemma), and hence converging. Hence, η converges. By the Lemma,

$$\lim_{x\to\infty}\eta(x,\delta)>1$$

is excluded. Since we have seen that (i), which is implied by (ii), yields $\eta(x,\delta)\geqq 1$, all what remains is

$$\lim_{x\to\infty}\eta(x,\delta)=1. \tag{5}$$

b) From the identity (4) we obtain

$$\theta(x,\delta)=1+\frac{\mathrm{p}(x)}{1-\mathrm{p}(x)}(1-\eta(x,\delta)).$$

Since $\lim_{x\to\infty}\mathrm{p}(x)\geqq 1$ is excluded by condition (iii) with $r>0$, $\mathrm{p}(x)/(1-\mathrm{p}(x))$ converges to a positive value. Hence, by (5),

$$\lim_{x\to\infty}\theta(x,\delta)=1.$$

Corollary. *An income tax that satisfies the conditions formulated in Theorem 3 behaves more and more like a proportional tax when income before tax grows more and more: For any* $\varepsilon\in(0,1)$ *there exists an income* x^* *such that for all incomes* $x>x^*$ *an increase of* 1% *in x yields an increase in the net income that lies between* $(1-\varepsilon)\%$ *and* 1%.

Remark 1. The following example shows that Properties (i) and (iii) or Properties (i) and (iv) do not necessarily imply the convergence of η or θ.

$$\mathrm{p}(x)=\frac{1}{4}\exp\left(\int_0^x\frac{\mathrm{f}(t)-1}{t}dt\right),$$

where

$$\mathrm{f}(t)=\begin{cases}\ln 2\left(t-2^n+1\right)2^{-n}t+1 & \text{for } t\in\left[2^n-1,2^n\right]\\ \ln 2\left(2^n+1-t\right)2^{-n}t+1 & \text{for } t\in\left(2^n-1,2^n\right]\\ 1 \text{ for all other } t\in\mathrm{I\!R}_+\end{cases}$$

(n an arbitrary natural number).

Remark 2. Part b of Theorem 3 would be wrong if $r > 0$ were not required. For instance, $p(x) = 1 - \ln(x+1)/x$ yields $\lim_{x\to\infty} \theta(x,\delta) = 0$, $p(x) = 1 - (x+1)^a/x + 1/x$ yields $\lim_{x\to\infty} \theta(x,\delta) = a$ ($a \in (0,1)$). For

$$p(x) = 1 - \frac{1}{x}\left(\sum_{i=1}^{j} a_i(x_i - x_{i-1}) + a_j(x - x_j)\right) \quad \left(x \in [x_j, x_{j+1}]\right),$$

where

$$\begin{aligned} a_i &= (i!)^{-1} \qquad i \in \mathbb{N} \\ x_i &= ((i+1)!)^2 \\ x_0 &= 0, \end{aligned}$$

every point of $[0,1]$ is limit point of $\theta(x,\delta)$.

References

Eichhorn, W., Funke, H., and Richter,W. F., 1984, Tax Progression and Inequality of Income Distribution, Journal of Mathematical Economics 13, 127 – 131.

Genser, B., 1980, Lorenzgerechte Besteuerung, Verlag der österreichischen Akademie der Wissenschaften, Wien.

Jakobsson, U., 1976, On the Measurement of Degree of Progression, Journal of Public Economics 5, 161 – 168.

Musgrave, R.A., and Tun Thin, 1948, Income Tax Progression 1929 – 48, The Journal of Political Economy **56**, 498 – 514.

Knowledge Management - Challenges and the "KNOWING"-Implementation Strategy

Dirk Solte

Forschungsinstitut für anwendungsorientierte Wissensverarbeitung

Helmholtzstr. 16, 89081 Ulm, Germany

Abstract

The fast globalization process of today has a strong impact on enterprises. They are confronted with the need to manage permanent change. Especially they have to build up more partnerships on a world-wide scale forming virtual enterprises. This is one reason to invest in internet-, intranet- and extranet-technology. From an organizational view point this needed change process from old economy to new economy has to consider on the one hand side an increasing explicitness. This means the organization of an enterprise is becoming more transparent because of the use of standard processes, standard software etc. On the other hand also non-explicit mechanisms of increased self organization have to be used and thus included into the organization harmonically. Examples are business units, self responsible teams and other fractal structuring forms.

Globalization leads to a dramatic increase in innovation speed. This is a big challenge for enterprises because faster innovation also requires a faster change process. Employees have to be supported always by the most modern information- and communication technology. This requires permanent investment, organizational change and employees that are willing and able for live-long learning.

Knowledge management is seen as a strategic methodology to define and set up the needed change process. To describe the knowledge management strategy, that has been developed in close partnership of FAW and its spin off company KNOWING GmbH with Prof. Dr. Paul Stähly at IfU-HSG we first explain a relatively general view onto enterprises as complex organisms. This view identifies the different aspects of knowledge management by exploiting an analogy to the functions of biological organisms. An enterprise is seen as a "body" that has to act in a permanent process of change. The enterprise can act "intelligent" because of the knowledge, embodied into it. Such a "surviving body" is orientated towards adaption to the future and knowledge management. The organizational structure supports and motivates live-long learning in a network of human resources (communities of practice) and technological components. The information networks become the enterprise's "nervous systems" and are extremely powerful because they build upon information- and communication technology with its high transmission speed.

Besides strategy aspects of knowledge management a supporting information- and communication-technology architecture are discussed as well. In addition concrete activities for a stepwise implementation of a technological support for knowledge management in enterprises are explained.

1 The new challenge

Enterprises, public authorities but also regions do have to accept that they currently are acting in an extremely fast process of globalization [6, 11, 15,] One of the reasons for globalization is the availability and use of modern information- and communication-technologies (ICT). In this process enterprises and regions are competing now on a world-wide scale, for markets and resources and they do this under the free-order regime of WTO, which is not concerned too much with social, cultural and environmental issues [8]. Capital and education, which are important enablers, can be made available everywhere in the world with the speed of light by the use of telecommunication networks. The result is, that now the importance of product quality is increasing because a permanent reduction of costs has to be reached in all value chains of an enterprise and there is no space anywhere for correcting mistakes later. Product live cycles are shorter. More and more "classical" product technologies are substituted by information- and communication-based technology. The organization has to be adapted always to the newest technologies and market needs. This describes roughly the framework for enterprises in the so called "new economy".

To survive in this framework, an enterprise has to be strictly customer focussed. It is more and more important to streamline the product and service portfolio to the customer value. Because of the increasing amount of competitors the enterprise's processes have to be optimized all the time. The product development cycle has to be shortened (time to customer). Products have to be available on the market fast (time to market). Not only local or regional markets have to be addressed, instead sales have to be organized on a world-wide basis. But not only sales have to be globalized. An enterprise has to access the best resources world-wide in networked processes. That means an enterprise is urged to network different locations and involve various resources temporarily, thus becoming a virtual enterprise [2, 6]. This effects all parts of an enterprise, research, development, production, administration etc. This virtualization also allows new forms for the design of the own legal positioning due to the regional differences (associated employer outlay, taxes etc.). By optimizing the placement of enterprise locations and optimizing the financial flew between the locations, tax, associated employer outlay etc. can be reduced significantly.

To make this potential available to an enterprise, it is a must to master modern information and communication technology as a core competency [10, 13]. Information and communication technology have to be optimally integrated and continuously made better use of.. This empowers human capital as the most important resource of an enterprise. People, departments and institutions have to be networked with knowledge, information and methods via processes.

Knowledge management is seen in this context as the organizational and technical strategy to build up the needed permanent process of change, and to manage this process successfully. As part of it an enterprise has to introduce an intranet for employee support and extranet/internet use to optimize its interaction with different partners, locations and customers.

2 Enterprises as complex organisms

As a basis for the developed knowledge management strategy an enterprise is seen as a complex organisms in analogy to biological organisms [9]. An enterprise is a "body" which has to adapt itself to a permanent process of change. This organism is acting in an environment that is defined by a society (e.g. population structure, mentality, preferences etc.), markets (the requirements of customers and partners), competition and a permanently increasing innovation speed. An enterprise thus is seen as an organism that is positioned in such an environment and acting in it. Its "live-objective" should be a long-term survival on a "high quality level". The experience of the last years have shown that the metric for this "quality of living" should not be restricted to measure shareholder values alone. It is more and more important to consider stakeholder values as the enterprise's objectives as well, if long term survival and profitability is the issue.

Knowledge (our understanding and structuring is explained in the next chapter) is seen as the potential, experience and intelligence of the enterprise. The "consciousness" of an enterprise is defined by its management. In this view of an enterprise as a complex organism, management is especially responsible for managing scarce resources and their controlled use. Management is also mainly responsible for the definition of the enterprise's identity (self-conception of the enterprise) and the outside appearance of the enterprise (corporate identity). The "body" of an enterprise comprises its employees, the technological components and the networks (biological networks as well as telecommunication networks). These components have to be integrated, via modern information- and communication technology, as an extremely powerful "nervous system". The enterprise's "mentality", its organization and behavior should be orientated towards innovation adaption, knowledge management and live-long learning.

3 Knowledge and knowledge management

To access the problem-complexity of knowledge management, we first describe an approach to structure knowledge (c. f. fig. 1, fig. 2). In our view to enterprises as complex organisms we structure knowledge in a four level architecture with respect to knowledge representation and processing [9]. This architecture can also be applied to biological organisms [5, 7].

Layer	Knowledge	Processing
Theory layer	Insight e. g. bar statics	Calculation and proof systems
Symbol layer	Experiences e. g. how to react to a bear in a forest or zoo	Rule processing
Neuronal layer	Recognizing e. g. moved object	Artificial neuronal networks
Signal layer	Feeling e. g. irritation of retina	Measuring, controlling, adjusting

Fig. 1: Knowledge and knowledge processing

The lowest layer – the layer of signals - we understand as direct interactions of an organism with its environment. E. g. the retina of a biological organism could be irritated by an electromagnetic wave. The result of the irritation of the retina is the "feeling" of a colored point. On the 2nd, so-called "neural layer", biological organisms are able to aggregate these elementary signals and reactions to patterns, and this is done via the neural network mechanism of the brain. This allows the cognition or re-cognition of patterns as objects and "intuitive" reactions on it. As an example, a moving bear is recognized via patterns like brown dots, a circle of black dots etc. Surviving people are those who intuitively run away (fear as a form of knowledge) when they see a bear approaching. As a next layer of knowledge representation higher mammals, especially human beings, have developed an explicit form of knowledge processing. This is the symbol layer in which the above described patterns and behavior are represented by symbols. This layer allows to make experiences explicit as rules in order to communicate them. We use e. g. a language to formulate knowledge on the symbol layer and make it explicit outside our biological organism. At the symbol layer e. g. an experience like "if a bear is coming close to you in a zoo enjoy it because bars are between you", can be formulated and can be learned by others. The highest quality of explicit knowledge is positioned in the theory layer. In the theory layer formal languages, i. e. modeling languages or theories are used to specify deterministic knowledge like mathematical theories, calculuses etc. E. g. a calculus like the method of finite elements allows to determine the needed static of a bar exactly, to protect us from a bear.

One has to consider, that for all these different knowledge representation layers, processing technologies are available now in ICT (Information and Communication Technology). The basis for this is a homogenous digital representation of knowledge of all this layers in ICT-components. Measuring / controlling / adjusting are the processing elements for the signal layer. Artificial neural networks are the processing mechanisms for the neural layer. For the symbol layer we do have rule processing engines, programming languages etc. Proof systems and dedicated calculation or solver programs process knowledge on the theory layer.

Layer	Knowledge
Theory Layer	Calculation methods e. g. FEM, bookkeeping
Symbol Layer	Rules and regulations e. g. design rules 4-eyes-principle
Layer of self-organization	Relations network e. g. brainstorming, teams
Signal layer (biological and technical infrastructure)	Individual abilities and sensibility e. g. employee-reaction to a design

Fig. 2: Enterprise knowledge

When we apply the four layer knowledge architecture to enterprises as complex organisms we identify e. g. individual abilities and emotions of employees as knowledge elements on the signal layer. The signal layer could thus be seen as the collection of the biological and technical infrastructure of an enterprise, including buildings, hardware etc. As an example the reaction of an employee on a specific design solution is part of the "emotional" knowledge of an enterprise. Relation-networks, e. g. a group of people with good harmony which is able to solve a heavy problem in a defined period of time is a knowledge element in the layer of self-organization. This layer is the neuronal layer of the enterprise. As a complex organism the experiences of the employees, the efficiency of teams etc. as elements of this layer should be considered in modern management strategies. The next higher and first explicit form of knowledge in an enterprise – the symbol layer – contains e. g. rules, constraints and regulations. These could be for example design instructions, organizational models, four-eyes-principle or others. One has to mention, that e. g. changes to regulations have to be learned by employees to be applied correctly. This makes it obvious that high regulated institutions loose flexibility. On the theory layer the used methodologies and evaluation schemas like e. g. tax-calculation, bookkeeping and others can be seen.

As an important prerequisite for its successful implementation a really powerful knowledge management strategy has to consider all layers of the above described architecture. The strategy should be orientated to the objective to optimally use and continuously enhance the knowledge on each layer by motivating a reasonable knowledge mentality. It should find and implement the best fitting enterprise organization and its supporting technical infrastructure (ICT).

3.1 The organizational dimension

When defining the most reasonable strategy to manage knowledge of an enterprise it is important to mention that this does not mean to try to have available all needed knowledge explicitly. Instead one has to find the right balance between implicit and explicit knowledge and support the problem-oriented access to it. A strategy that tries to make any kind of knowledge explicit would lead to motivation problems of the enterprise's employees due to the fear they have, that they are not needed any more if their knowledge is commonly available. Another aspect is that if knowledge is explicit, also competitors could have access to that knowledge and can make it available for their own use. Also, for principle reasons, it seems impossible to make all implicit knowledge explicit – not to talk about costs. Under this perspective an important management task is to find the right balance between explicit and implicit / fractal knowledge; one could also say that the task is to find the right balance between constraints and freedom, acting consciously or intuitively. Figuratively speaking, the question is, where decisions are made, in the head or in the stomach. Another important task is to set the most important constraints under which the employees can act self-organizing with freedom. Especially one has to give a clear orientation about the most important processes of the enterprise. These are how priorities are set, how resources are distributed and how decisions are made. It is also important to define and communicate the processes to come to products and services.

With respect to the enterprise's "live-metric" it is important to define all the criteria under which management is measuring the value of the enterprise, its "enterprise's fitness".

As mentioned earlier beside shareholder values like profits, efficiency and innovation potential also more stakeholder-like values such as responsibility, environmental awareness, caring for stuff and the local community, caring for life-long learning, protection of important information etc. should be considered.

3.2 The technical dimension

Knowledge Management has also to deal with the optimal technical support of the enterprise organization. The human capital has to be networked with knowledge and methodologies within workflows. The broad spectrum of modern information and communication technologies has to be managed as a complex network system inside the enterprise (intranet) and beyond (extranet/internet). The first attempts have been made for engineering/manufacturing with the CIM approach (computer integrated manufacturing) [1, 3]. Today this discipline is named "Enterprise Engineering and Enterprise Integration" which means that it is not only restricted to engineering/manufacturing but is now dealing with all parts of an enterprise [4, 16]. Besides the intranet it covers the supply chain and also the interaction with the enterprise's customers and other partners as well.

It is important to recognize from passed experience in thousands of companies that "integration" of ICT components can not be bought simply on the market [13]. Only with inside know how of the enterprise, integration can eventually be reached. Not only explicit knowledge, but also how people work together etc., has to be considered for an optimal ICT-support. This leads to the realization that the know how to adopt ICT-technologies and tools to the enterprise's "core-business" and its organization and processes has to be a core competency of (large) enterprises and will be a core competency for all companies in future as well.

The strategy for enterprise engineering and enterprise integration as described next thus only is meant as a guideline or strategic framework that should help to identify the best suited solution on an individual basis.

A central aspect of enterprise engineering is to build up a "development plan for the enterprise's application model". The application model consists of an information model and a process model. The information model could be seen as a framework for the documentation of products, services, resources, experiences etc. A process model uses the information model and defines the organization and methodologies to come to products and services. Information and process model have to be supported by information and communication technologies. This support is defined by the tools model. It is very important to understand that the application model and the tools model have to be defined in a co-design process. Co-design means that both definitions have to be done in parallel and in permanent reconciliation. This is because both models have impacts on each other; e. g. it is not optimal to buy desktop-computers if the organizational strategy motivates mobile work. A special aspect for the tools model is that one needs an architecture and (migration) strategy that allows to integrate (or federate) legacy systems, on the shelf products and own developments. As part of the knowledge management strategy we defined a concept of enterprise integration that structures the tools model architecture in three different layers (c. f. fig 3)

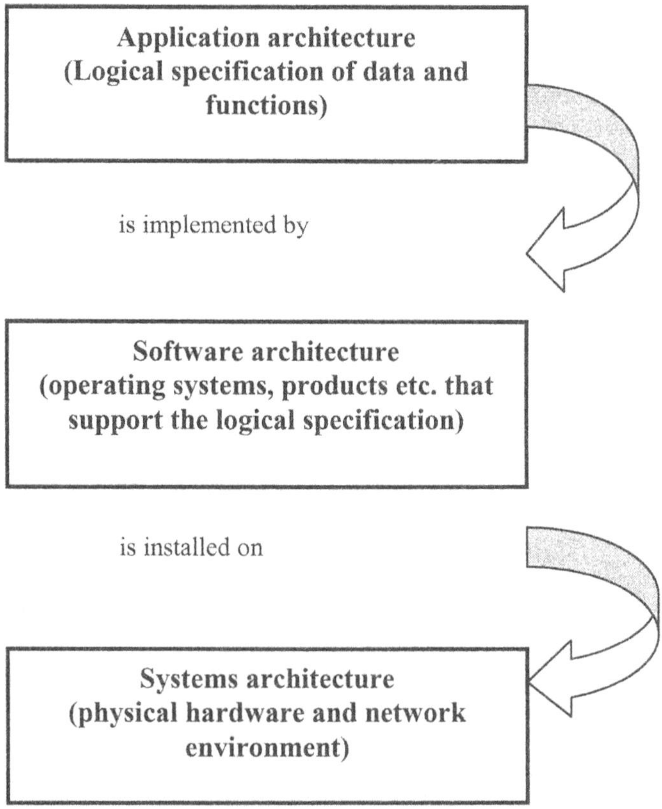

Fig. 3: The tools model architecture

The first layer is the application architecture. The application architecture defines all the functionalities and data-elements of the technical systems. We name the reasonable collection of function and data "logical roles". In the application architecture we strictly define the logical functions and the needed data but no software components and products. So the application architecture could be seen as a kind of principal view to which kind of support one would like to have available for the employees in a networked systems environment. The mapping of these logical roles onto products is done in the second layer which is the software architecture. In principle the software architecture could be seen as the definition of the technical components that fulfill the logically defined roles. These technical components are for example applications, operating-systems, web-server etc. The third layer is the systems architecture. The systems architecture is the definition of the network, the server-systems, firewall-systems and so on. The technical components, defined by the software-architecture, are installed on the systems architecture. So the systems-architecture defines the overall hardware and network environment, whereas the software-architecture defines the overall software-solution. Both architectures are implementing the application architecture.

4 Implementation strategy

Knowledge management has to cover a lot of aspects. So knowledge management is the sum of several tasks. These are firstly all the activities to strengthen the enterprise's fitness. An important task here is to set up an effective and permanent change process and to manage it. In this change process all the employees should be actively involved. As part of the change process the organization and the management tasks should be permanently adapted to the market needs. As another part the technological support of the enterprise's organization has to be adapted to changes and innovations. Enterprise engineering and enterprise integration – its content and the technology – are the topics of the change process. As one important aspect of it the "corporate memory" should be defined and further developed. That means the access to knowledge, the important capital of an enterprise, should be organizational and technically supported. In the technical dimension e. g. one defines and builds up knowledge repositories or market places for knowledge. In the organizational dimension one should support the distribution of knowledge between employees, departments etc. Implicit knowledge has to be considered as well e. g. the interaction of employees or departments. Communication platforms like cafeterias or social events are supporting these "biological" networking. As an important organizational concept, a system of incentives could be part of a framework that motivates a deliberate knowledge mentality.

As a second task to implement knowledge management a controlling system for the enterprise's fitness could be build up. This could consist e. g. of activities or methodologies for knowledge evaluation and balancing. One approach could be to view the quality and the status of the implementation of enterprise engineering and enterprise integration. Adapted to the enterprise's values and the enterprise's "self-conception" an evaluation scheme for the information model, the process model and the tools model could be defined. Another possibility is to set up activities that evaluate the enterprise's ability for innovation and migration. This could be done for example by defining a kind of "trial order" or to define a contest for the adoption of a new technology.

As an important prerequisite for a successful knowledge management, this kind of management has to be identified as an important issue and thus responsibility for knowledge management has to be clearly defined. Knowledge management is an important strategic element of an enterprise and should not been seen – as ICT has been looked to often in the past – only as a tool or a supporting technology. The responsibility for knowledge management, the management of change process and the co-design of organization and ICT, should be in the top-management. Knowledge management needs adequate resources and competence.

As mentioned earlier, a central question of knowledge management is to find a way of how a permanent change process could be implemented successfully in an enterprise. One could also say the question is how the speed of migration and change can be adapted to the permanently increasing speed of innovation. In a couple of consulting projects we identified that the implementation of knowledge management and of a change process could strongly be supported by setting up a so-called "vision team". The vision team should be empowered by the top-management and should work outside any operational responsibility. Its objective should be the definition respective further development of the enterprise's vision for five or ten years. This vision should define roughly a co-designed solution for human-resources development, organization and optimal ICT-support. It is important that this vision should mainly be basis for the decision of top management, to minimize the irritations, conflicts and the opposition of the employees. As part of the five/ten years perspective a rough migration time-schedule should be defined, that could also consider that old and new have to be managed in parallel for a longer period of time. This is due to the fact that not all employees are able or willing to change themselves with the same speed. As a next step after having made a decision about a long term strategy, the first milestone of the migration time schedule should be made public as the official enterprise's change aim with the definition of a change project. This project and the change aim should be discussed in a open process with all employees. This is important to motivate people and allow for compromises as long as the long term change aim could be reached.

Some hints about aspects of the vision plan should be made: In general it is reasonable to increase the migration and change potential by allowing more interaction and self-organization and to accept ownership of knowledge. From a technical view point one can support the change process by implementing a knowledge repository as a corporate memory. As mentioned, the focus of the managed information, respectively knowledge, should be the "know what, who and where" instead of the "know how". The structure of the corporate memory should consider this. So besides the explicit knowledge also organizational knowledge, resource knowledge (we call that communications infrastructure knowledge), process models, experiences (especially also why something was rejected) should be considered. Other knowledge is meta information such as key-words and synonyms for a document etc. The knowledge could be organized and made accessible via hypermedia technology. On the desktops a uniform access and uniform navigation to distributed locations should be installed. In addition also the implementation of electronic business process support could be done.

Over the past ten years, a complete software solution, to support knowledge management, has been developed [14]. It is available as products from the FAW spin off company Knowing GmbH. The software consists of a neutralizing integration platform for heterogeneous distributed environments [14] following an open reliability architecture (c. f. fig. 4). It supports an intranet view (for employee support) as well as an internet or an extranet view (for customer and supplier support). The software can be, stepwise, adapted to the enterprise's needs.

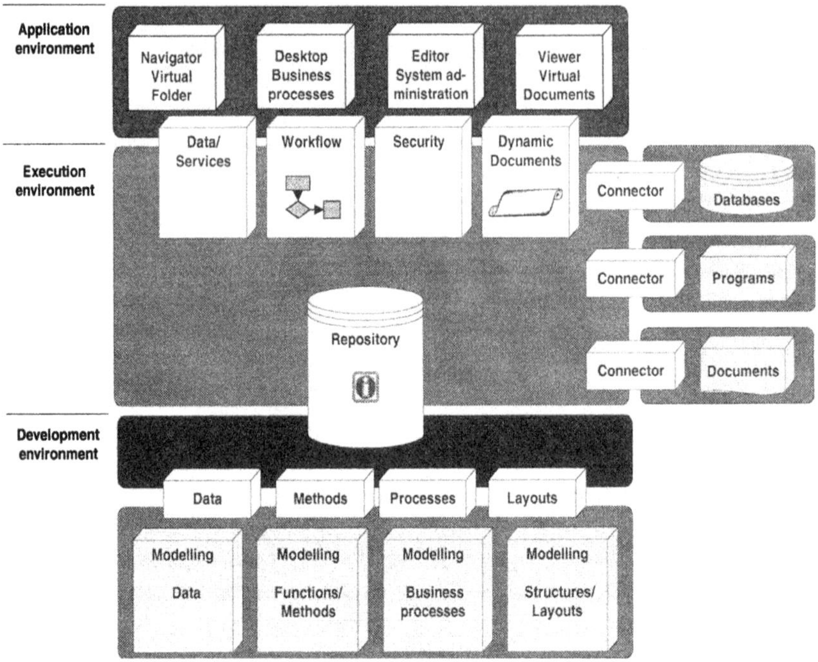

Fig. 4: KNOWING application architecture

As a first step it is reasonable to start with the tool for knowledge organization and navigation. The second step allows to define contexts, thus allowing to define views to the managed knowledge. As part of this context definition a tool to structure discussions, in a kind of structured chat forum, is available. This enhances the knowledge repository with the ability to manage also the "know why – know why not?" The integration platform as the fourth step for the implementation, supports the integration and federation of legacy systems and available data management systems. At the fifth step, a work-flow engine together with a desktop-client is available.

The knowledge repository is the central component, first at all, as an intranet application for employee support. Since it is possible to restrict the access (read, modification etc.) to the knowledge repository by the definition of access roles, a support system for customers as well as for suppliers could automatically be derived from the intranet knowledge repository. This could provide for example an electronic customer care and help system. In modern technology trends one would name this kind of systems enterprise portal or internet portal. The portal can be made more attractive – as a second step – by also making available the system for structured chats e. g. for frequently asked questions. After the installation of security technology (firewalls, digital signature, trust-center etc.)

this builds a basis for electronic business support. In a last step this could be enhanced to a supply chain support by also allowing electronic processes to be handled between the enterprise and its partners and customers.

5 Summary

In this paper we gave an overview about an approach for knowledge management, which is seen as an organizational and technological strategy. This approach has been developed in a close partnership between FAW / KNOWING and Prof. Dr. Paul Stähly at the IfU-HSG. Based on the experience of a couple of consultations and development projects the resulting implementation strategy has been described. This includes an architectural framework for information and communication technology. Beside that an integration platform and engineering environment to build up a supporting software solution has been developed that is available as product via the spin off company KNOWING GmbH.

References

(1) AMICE, CIMOSA (1992) Open System Architecture for CIM; 2nd extended and revised version Research Reports ESPRIT; Springer

(2) Gerybadze, A., F. Meyer-Krahmer und Guido Reger (1997) Globales Management von Forschung und Entwicklung; Schäffer Poeschel Verlag, Stuttgart

(3) Ladet, P., Vernadat, F. B. (eds.) (1995) Integrated Manufacturing Systems Engineering; Chapman & Hall, London

(4) Petrie, Cj J. (ed.) (1992) Enterprise Integration Modeling; MIT Press

(5) Radermacher, F. J., (1996) Cognition in Systems; Cybernetics and Systems: An International Journal, 27pp. 1-41; Taylor & Francis

(6) Radermacher, F. J., (Hrsg.), (1997) Globalisierung – Herausforderung für den Mittelstand. Ergebnisband Ulmer Forum 1997, Universitätsverlag Ulm, ISBN 3-89559-028-2

(7) Radermacher, F.J. (1998) Intelligenz - Kognition – Bewußtsein, Systemtheoretische Überlegungen, technische Möglichkeiten, philosophische Fragen; In: Interdisziplinäre Beiträge zur Kommunikation und zum Mensch-Technik-Verhältnis (C. Stadelhofer, ed.), Band 6, S. 146-193, Kleine Verlag GmbH, Bielefeld,

(8) Radermacher, F. J.,(1998) Globalisierung und Informationstechnologie; In: Internationale Tagung anläßlich des 85. Geburtstages von Carl-Friedrich von Weizsäcker (U. Bartosch und J. Wagner, eds.), S.105-117; LIT Verlag Münster

(9) Radermacher, F. J., (1999) Komplexe Systeme und lernende Unternehmen; In: Komplexe System und Nichtlineare Dynymik in Natur und Gesellschaft (K. Mainzer, ed.); S. 423-445; Springer-Verlag, Berlin, Heidelberg, New York

(10) Radermacher, F.J., (1999) Wissensmanagement: Herausforderung für Unternehmen. Beitrag für die Jubliäumsbroschüre zu den 20. Salemer Gesprächen

(11) Radermacher, F.J., (2000) New Economy – Börsenrausch und Greencard: Spielt die Welt verrückt oder hat alles seine Logik?; Beitrag für die Herbstakademie 2000, Veranstaltungsreihe des Zentrums für Allgemeine Wissenschaftliche Weiterbildung (ZaWiW), Universität Ulm

(12) Solte, D. (1999) The OPAL Platform – A CIMOSA Compliant Execution Environment. In: Kosanke, K.; Vernadat, F.; Zelm, M. (eds.): CIMOSA: CIM Open Systems Architecture, Evolution and Applications in Enterprise Engineering and Integration; Computers in Industry Vol. 40, pp. 293-303.

(13) Solte, D. (1997) ICT-Support for Enterprise Integration – Where are we?; in: Kosanke, K.; Nell, J. G.(eds.): Enterprise Engineering and Integration: Building International Consensus, Proceedings of the ICEIMT '97, Research Reports ESPRIT, Springer, ISBN 3-540-63402-9.

(14) Solte, D. (1999) Modellorientierte Entscheidungsunterstützung, Habilitationsschrift, Universität St. Gallen.

(15) Solte, D. (2000) Telemetropolis – Making the Potential of Telematics accessible in Rural Areas; in: Sturm, R.; Weinmann, G.; Will, O. (eds.): Information Society and the Regions in Europe; Nomos, Baden-Baden.

(16) Vernadat, F. B. (1996) Enterprise Modeling and Integration: principles and applications; Chapman & Hall, London

Perturbation Heuristics for Unconstrained Quadratic 0 -1 Programming and an Alternate Stopping and Comparison Criterium

Kim Allemand and Thomas Liebling

ROSO, Mathematics Dept., EPFL, Lausanne Switzerland

Abstract

Given quadratic function f, the unconstrained quadratic zero-one programming problem consists in minimizing $f(\boldsymbol{x})$ where $\boldsymbol{x}$ is a zero-one vector of dimension n. This problem is $\mathcal{NP}$-hard and therefore the most efficient results have been obtained by heuristics. As optimal solutions are in most cases unkown, comparisons between heuristics are usually based on the shortest time to reach the best known solution. This approach is arbitrary and depends on both problem size and computer speed. We present an alternate comparison and stopping criterium based on an approximate count evaluations of the objective function. This comparison technique will be applied on descent algorithms embedded in a multi-start heuristic scheme. Finally, some results for public instances of various sizes will be reported.

Keywords : Quadratic 0-1 Optimization, Heuristic, Criterium

1 Introduction

A *quadratic pseudo-boolean function* is a function

$$f(\boldsymbol{x}) = \boldsymbol{x}^T Q \boldsymbol{x} + \boldsymbol{c}^T \boldsymbol{x} + \text{cst} \quad \text{with} \quad \boldsymbol{x} \in \mathbb{B}^n \tag{1}$$

where Q is a $n \times n$ matrix, $\boldsymbol{c}$ a n-vector, $\mathbb{B} = \{0, 1\}$, and we note $\mathbb{F}^n$ the set of quadratic pseudo-boolean functions. For computational reasons, we assume that coefficients of f are rational numbers. Under this assumption and without loss of generality, we can assume that coefficients are integers.

The *quadratic 0-1 optimization problem* (Q01P) consists in minimizing a quadratic pseudo-boolean function $f \in \mathbb{F}^n$ in n variables :

$$\min\{\ f(\boldsymbol{x}) \mid \boldsymbol{x} \in \mathbb{B}^n\ \}$$

and n is called the *size* of the problem. Remark that as $x_i = x_i^2$, representation 1 objective function f is not unique.

This $\mathcal{NP}$-hard problem (it contains as a special case the *Maximum Stable Set Problem*) is a well known combinatorial optimization problem, first because it has many practical applications (financial analysis [14], traffic message management [8], machine scheduling [1], molecular conformation [21]) and second because it is strongly related to many operations research problems (max cut problem [11], quadratic assignment problem, clique problems).

In the last years, several heuristic approaches have been developed : the first proposed by Chardaire and Sutter [20] based on a decomposition method, the second proposed by Glover, Kochenberger, Alidaee and Amini [10] based on a tabu search in association with a fast local search, the third proposed by Lodi, Allemand and Liebling [15] based on a combined approach inside a genetic paradigm, and very recently the one proposed by Katayama and Narihisa [13] is based on a simulated annealing approach.

At least three cases where the Q01P is polynomially solvable are known. The first one is the case in which all non-diagonal elements of the Q matrix are non positives [22]. The second one is when the graph associated to the objective function is series-parallel [4]. The third one is when the objective function is negative semidefinite with fixed rank [2].

2 Descent scheme and comparison criterium

2.1 Definitions and notations

We first give some general definitions we will use in the paper (can also be found in [12]). A binary vector $\boldsymbol{x} \in \mathbb{B}^n$ is called *vertex*. For $k = 1, \ldots, n$, two vertices are k-adjacent if their Hamming distance, noted d_H, is *exactly* k. A k-*neighbourhood* centered on $\boldsymbol{x}$ is defined as $N_k(\boldsymbol{x}) = \{\boldsymbol{y} \in \mathbb{B}^n | d_H(\boldsymbol{x}, \boldsymbol{y}) \leq k\}$. Vertex $\boldsymbol{x}^*$ is a k-discrete local minimum, resp. strong k-discrete local minimum, if $f(\boldsymbol{x}^*) \leq f(\boldsymbol{x})$, resp. $f(\boldsymbol{x}^*) < f(\boldsymbol{x})$, for all $\boldsymbol{x} \in N_k(\boldsymbol{x}^*)$.

Comparison operators between two elements of $\mathbb{B}^n$ ($<$, $\leq$, $=$, etc.) are component per component comparisons. For facility, we also define following three operators, applying on vertex $\boldsymbol{x}$ and indices set $I \subseteq \{1, \ldots, n\}$:

Operator	Notation	Result
flip	$\boldsymbol{x} \updownarrow I$	$x_i = 1 - x_i \quad \forall i \in I$
set	$\boldsymbol{x} \uparrow I$	$x_i = 1 \quad \forall i \in I$
reset	$\boldsymbol{x} \downarrow I$	$x_i = 0 \quad \forall i \in I$

If context is clear, we simply use notation $\boldsymbol{x} \updownarrow i$ instead of $\boldsymbol{x} \updownarrow \{i\}$. Remark that if $\updownarrow$ operator is involutive, operators $\uparrow$ and $\downarrow$ are both projective. An *improving* variable, for a given vertex, is a variable whose modification (flip, set, reset) improves the value of the objective function. Variables with value 0 are called *zero-variables* and variables with value 1 are called *one-variables.*

2.2 Descent steps

Given objective function f and vertex $\boldsymbol{x}$, we call **descent step** any application $d : \mathbb{B}^n \to \mathbb{B}^n$ with non-increasing property, *i.e.* $f(d(\boldsymbol{x})) \leq f(\boldsymbol{x})$. We present two descent steps, both based on flip operations.

Hamming-1 descent step. The *Hamming-1 descent step* is based on a steepest edge movement. Given vertex $\boldsymbol{x}$, $d(\boldsymbol{x})$ is chosen as the best improving vertex in the $N_1(\boldsymbol{x})$ neighbourhood. If more than one vertex have same value, the variable to flip is randomly chosen. This algorithm is also known as *1-opt local search.*

```
Algorithm : HAMMING1STEP(x)
    Step 1. δ* = ∞, I = ∅
    Step 2. for i = 1 to n do
                    δ = f(x ↕ i) − f(x)
        a)          if δ = δ* then I = I ∪ {i}
        b)          if δ < δ* then δ* = δ, I = {i}
    Step 3. if δ* ≠ ∞ then
                    randomly choose i* ∈ I
                    x = x ↕ i*
    Step 4. return x
```

This descent step can be generalized to $N_k(\boldsymbol{x})$, however, for computational reasons, implementations are often limited to $k = 1$ or 2 [3].

Oscillation descent step. The *constructive descent step* can be seen as a restriction of the Hamming-1 descent step in the following sense : only zero-variables can be flipped (actually set). The *destructive descent step* is similar : only one-variables can be flipped (actually reset). When iterated for at most i_{max} times, each previously defined descent step induces another descent step algorithm called *constructive phase*, resp. *destructive phase.* Given vertex $\boldsymbol{x}$, an *oscillation descent step* is simply an application of the constructive phase on $\boldsymbol{x}$, followed by the application of the destructive phase.

Algorithm : OSCILLATIONSTEP($\boldsymbol{x}, i_{max}$)

Step 1. $\boldsymbol{x}$ = CONSTRUCTIVEPHASE($\boldsymbol{x}, i_{max}$)

Step 2. $\boldsymbol{x}$ = DESTRUCTIVEPHASE($\boldsymbol{x}, i_{max}$)

Step 3. return $\boldsymbol{x}$

This descent step is more complex than the Hamming-1 descent step and does not guarantee that $d(\boldsymbol{x})$ will be in $N_k(\boldsymbol{x})$ for some $k < n$. A similar algorithm has been proposed by [9], encapsulated in a tabu approach.

2.3 Descent algorithm

Given objective function f, we call *descent algorithm* an iterative application of descent step d, starting from initial vertex $\boldsymbol{x}$, until stopping criterium S is met. The (finite) set of all generated vertices is called *descent path.*

Algorithm : DESCENTALGORITHM($\boldsymbol{x}, S, d$)

Step 1. $i = 0$, $\boldsymbol{x}^{(i)} = \boldsymbol{x}$

Step 2. while S is false

$$\boldsymbol{x}^{(i+1)} = d(\boldsymbol{x}^{(i)})$$

$$i = i + 1$$

Step 3. return $\boldsymbol{x}^{(i)}$

At this point, both *Hamming-1* descent algorithm and *oscillation* descent algorithm are well defined. We remark that constructive phase can be seen as a descent algorithm using constructive step as descent step and maximum number of iterations as stopping criterium.

2.4 Alternate criterium

A very common comparison (and stopping) criterium for Q01P heuristics with iterative scheme is the *time criterium* : TIMEMAX. The heuristic runs for a given number of seconds (maximum run-time) and comparison with other heuristics is made on the time needed to obtain the best-known solution. This approach is arbitrary mostly for computationnal reasons. First, raw implementations in low level programming languages, like C, are much faster than high-level implementations in mathematical software, like mathlab. And secondly, running time of the same heuristic, on identical computers, programming language and coding, but different operating systems may be quite different [16].

Alternative comparison criterium : Acc

For these reasons, we propose an alternate comparison and stopping criterium based on the **number of objective function evaluations**. This approach is closer to the complexity notion based on Turing machines than the notion based on time.

Given vertex $\boldsymbol{x}$, the evaluation of $f(\boldsymbol{x})$ can be done in $O(n^2)$ operations. This complexity is machine independent and generally be improved if no special structure of f is assumed. However, when *only* flip operations are involved (set or reset), using an efficient representation for objective function and current vertex can improve the complexity for evaluating $f(\boldsymbol{x} \updownarrow i)$.

Using formulation (1), for current vertex $\boldsymbol{x}$, we also store current value $f(\boldsymbol{x})$ and variations $\boldsymbol{v}(\boldsymbol{x}) = f(\boldsymbol{x} \updownarrow i) - f(\boldsymbol{x})$ for $i = 1, \dots, n$. Hence, $f(\boldsymbol{x} \updownarrow i)$ can be computed in $O(1)$ operations and updating $\boldsymbol{v}$ can be done in $O(n)$ operations. This representation is very appropriate for any single-flip descent steps (like Hamming-1 and oscillation descent steps) and has been used in [9, 15]. For detailed implementation refer to [19].

The *objective function access criterium* counts how many times n consecutive operations are executed (this can be easily done inside flip procedures) and divides the total by n, to obtain an *approximation* for the number of n^2 operations *i.e.* the number of evaluations of objective function. This number will be noted Acc and table below represents the increment of Acc depending on the operation performed.

Operation	Acc	Complexity
Evaluation of $f(\boldsymbol{x})$	1	$O(n^2)$
Evaluation of $\boldsymbol{v}(\boldsymbol{x})$	1	$O(n^2)$
Flip (set, reset) i	1/n	$O(n)$ knowing $\boldsymbol{v}$

Stopping strategy

Based on this simple Acc criterium, we use the following stopping strategy for iterative heuristics. The heuristic stops in two cases :

1. when maximum number of evaluations Acc of the objective function has been reached,
2. when best current value has not been improved for a given number of evaluation.

This approach is similar to the stopping strategy used with time or iteration limit. Note that the second condition is not sufficient, it has been proven that for some cases, flip descent algorithm leads to a descent path with length greater than a polynomial function in n [17].

3 Perturbation heuristic

We first define two useful characteristics for variables : given vertex $\boldsymbol{x}$, if variable x_i is *fixed*, resp. free, then its value cannot, resp. can, be changed by algorithms or heuristics.

3.1 Perturbation step

Given objective function f, initial vertex $\boldsymbol{x}$, parameter p representing a percent, and descent algorithm A, the *perturbation step* algorithm returns vertex $d(\boldsymbol{x})$ with properties :

a) Hamming distance $d_H(\boldsymbol{x}, d(\boldsymbol{x}))$ is greater than p precent of n,

b) $d(\boldsymbol{x})$ is a good solution as far as descent algorithm A is concerned.

Algorithm : PERTURBATIONSTEP($\boldsymbol{x}, p, A$)

Step 1. Generate $F \subset \{1, \ldots, n\}$ with $|F| \approx \frac{np}{100}$

Step 2. for each $i \in F$

$\boldsymbol{x} = \boldsymbol{x} \updownarrow i$ and fix x_i

Step 3. $\boldsymbol{x} = A(\boldsymbol{x})$

Step 4. for each $i \in F$: free x_i

Step 5. return $\boldsymbol{x}$

3.2 Perturbation heuristic

We have all necessary elements to present our heuristic. Given stopping criterium S, descent algorithms A_1 and A_2, the *perturbation heuristic* is a multistart scheme using descent algorithm A_1 as intensification algorithm and perturbation step with A_2 as diversification algorithm.

Algorithm : PERTURBATIONHEURISTIC(S, A_1, A_2)

Step 1. $\boldsymbol{x}^* = \mathbf{0}$

Step 2. repeat

Step 3. randomly choose $\boldsymbol{x} \in \mathbb{B}^n$

Step 4. for $p = 1$ to 10 step 1

Step 5. $\boldsymbol{x}$ =PERTURBATIONSTEP($\boldsymbol{x}, p, A_2$)

Step 6. $\boldsymbol{x} = A_1(\boldsymbol{x})$

Step 7. if $f(\boldsymbol{x}) < f(\boldsymbol{x}^*)$ then

$\boldsymbol{x}^* = \boldsymbol{x}$, $p = 1$

else $\boldsymbol{x} = \boldsymbol{x}^*$

Step 8. until S is satisfied

Step 9. return $\boldsymbol{x}$

Intensification algorithm A_1 must be as efficient as possible, in order to find a good solution (understand a k-discrete minimum local) : we choose A_1 =HAMMING1ALGORITHM. Stopping criterium for A_1 is satisfied when current solution has not been improved after n^2 operations (one evaluation of the objective function).

The A_2 descent algorithm, applied to perturbated vertex $\boldsymbol{x}$, has not to be as efficient as A_1. As its first purpose is to escape from local minimum, stopping criterium is typically a maximum number of iterations. We choose OSCILLATIONALGORITHM with maximum n^2 operations (one evaluation of the objective function) for stopping criterium.

4 Computational results

We present the results of the computational experiements which were performed using our perturbation heuristic. All tested instances can be found in the public OR-Library [6]. These randomly generated instances have been classified, by [7], in small ($n \leq 250$), medium ($n = 500$), large (1000) and very large (2500) size instances. Principal authors of the proposed instances are : Barahona et al. [5], Williams [23], Glover et al. [10] and Beasley [7]. If small and medium size instances been extensively explored by many authors, only [7], [18] and [13] worked on large and very large size instances.

Id	best known	Perturbation heuristic best	hit	mean	sdv	Acc mean	sdv
1	-371438	-371438	12	-371375.2	85.7	964.6	19.2
2	-354932	-354932	11	-354840.2	139.2	974.5	28.8
3	-371236	-371236	19	-371227.8	36.4	925.6	20.1
4	-370675	-370675	19	-370671.8	14.5	995.3	27.6
5	-352760	-352760	7	-352727.1	46.6	961.1	25.9
6	-359629	-359629	8	-359527.9	91.2	918.5	13.1
7	-371193	-371193	10	-371035.2	196.1	949.5	19.7
8	-351994	-351994	5	-351898.7	105.1	995.8	18.1
9	-349337	-349337	7	-349193.0	204.0	984.9	21.2
10	-351415	-351415	10	-351292.9	170.8	917.5	31.2

Table 1: Large size instances ($n = 1000$)

Experimentation. For each instance, we ran our heuristic 20 times, each time with a different randomly generated seed (for random generator). The AccMax is the only parameter of the algorithm. In order to show the performance of our heuristic, we present for each instance : the best known value obtained from benchmark [13], statistics obtained by our heuristic (best value, *hit*, mean value, standard deviation), mean and standard deviation for the Acc value. The *hit* column represents the number of times that our heuristic reached the best known value.

4.1 Small and medium size instances

For all instances with size $n \leq 250$ (small), every run of the perturbation heuristic reached the best known value with maximum Acc value of 10.

For medium size instances ($n = 500$) generated by Glover with various densities, each run of the perturbation heuristic reached the best known value with an Acc value of 10.

Same efficiency for instances of medium size generated by Beasley. At each run, the best known solution has been reached by our heuristic with Acc values between 60 and 70.

4.2 Large and very large size instances

The OR-Library also contains sets of large and very large size instances : first set has instances of dimension $n = 1000$ and second of dimension $n = 2500$. Both sets were generated by Beasley and have density 0.1 (purely quadratic representation).

Id	best known	Perturbation heuristic				Acc	
		best	hit	mean	sdv	mean	sdv
1	-1515944	-1515944	8	-1515517.1	796.2	1706.0	73.8
2	-1471392	-1471392	1	-1470776.5	394.5	1837.9	132.0
3	-1414192	-1414192	2	-1413619.9	379.8	1846.7	73.4
4	-1507701	-1507701	20	-1507701.0	0.0	1743.4	49.1
5	-1491816	-1491816	13	-1491747.9	120.5	1680.9	92.8
6	-1469162	-1469162	6	-1468928.7	315.8	1797.0	61.5
7	-1479040	-1479024	-	-1478323.8	485.0	981.3	78.8
8	-1484199	-1484199	4	-1484060.0	199.2	1766.4	95.8
9	-1482419	-1482413	-	-1482215.7	238.7	1751.3	52.4
10	-1483355	-1483355	2	-1482776.3	321.6	1920.7	75.7

Table 2: Very large size instances ($n = 2500$)

Table 1 presents results obtained for instances of dimension $n = 1000$. For each instance, the best known solution has been reached with AccMax value set to 1000.

Table 2 represents results obtained for the largest size instances. This time, AccMax has been set to 2000. We note that for instance 7 and 9, the best known solution has not been reached.

5 Conclusion

In this article, a multistart heuristic based on a perturbation scheme was presented. This perturbation heuristic was applied on small, medium, large and very large size instances, which can be found in a public library. An alternate stopping criterium based on an approximation of the number of evaluation of the objective function was also presented and applied on these instances. Using this approach, we were able, first to obtain very good results for small, medium and large size instances, and second confirm some of the best known solutions for instances of very large size ($n = 2500$). If CPU time is used as measure, our approach is competitive with the others for the former cases, while for the latter, the one proposed very recently by Katayama and Narishma [13] runs faster. We are in the process of streamlining our procedures and expect to be able to report comparable CPU performances shortly.

References

[1] G. Alidaee, G. Kochenberger, and A. Ahmadian. 0-1 quadratic programmin approach for the optimal solution of two scheduling problems. *International J. Systems Sci.*, 25:401–408, 1994.

[2] K. Allemand, K. Fukuda, Th.M. Liebling, and E. Steiner. A polynomal case of unconstrained zero-one quadratic optimization. To be published.

[3] K. Allemand and Th.M. Liebling. Perturbation heuristic for quadratic zero-one optimization. Technical report, ROSO - EPFL, 1999.

[4] F. Barahona. A solvable case of quadratic 0-1 programming. *Discrete and Applied Mathematics*, 13:23–26, 1986.

[5] F. Barahona, M. Jünger, and G. Reinelt. Experiments in quadratic 0-1 programming. *Mathematical Programming*, 44:127–137, 1989.

[6] J.E. Beasley. Or-library: Unconstrained binary quadratic programming. http://mscmga.ms.ic.ac.uk/jeb/orlib/bqpinfo.html.

[7] J.E. Beasley. Or-library: distributing test problems by electronic mail. *Journal of the Operational Research Society*, 41(11):1069–1072, 1990.

[8] G. Gallo, P.L. Hammer, and B. Simeone. Quadratic knapsack problem. *Mathematical Programming*, 12:132–149, 1980.

[9] F. Glover, G. Kochenberger, and B. Alidaee. Adaptative memory tabu search for binary quadratic programs. *MS*, 44(3):336–345, 1998.

[10] F. Glover, G. Kochenberger, B. Alidaee, and M. Amini. Tabu search with critical event memory: An enhanced application for binary quadratic programs. In *Conference of Metaheuristics*, Sophia Antipolis, June 1997.

[11] P.L. Hammer. Some network flow problems solved with pseudoboolen programming. *OR Letters*, 13:388–399, 1965.

[12] B. Kalantari. Quadratic functions with exponential number of local maxima. *OR Letters*, 5–1, 1986.

[13] K. Katayama and H. Narihisa. Performance of simulated annealing-based heuristic for the unconstrained binary quadratic programming problem. to be published.

[14] D.J. Laughunn. Quadratic binary programming. *Operations Res.*, 14:454–461, 1970.

[15] A. Lodi, K. Allemand, and Th.M. Liebling. An evolutionary heuristic for quadratic 0-1 programming. *European Journal or OR*, 119:107–115, 1999.

[16] D. Loshing. *Efficient Memory Programming.* Mc Graw Hill, 1998.

[17] G. Lueker. New results on the old k-opt algorithm for the travelling salesman problem. *Siam Comp. J.*, 28(6):1998–2029.

[18] P. Mertz and B. Freisleben. Genetic algorithms for binary quadratic programming. pages 417–424, 1999.

[19] P. Mertz and B. Freisleben. Greedy and local search heuristics for unconstrained binary quadratic programming. Technical report, Univ. Siegen, 1999.

[20] P. Chardaire P. and A. Sutter. A decomposition method for quadratic 0-1 programming. *Mathematical Programming*, 41:704–712, 1995.

[21] A.T. Philips and J.B. Rosen. A quadratic assignement formulation of the molecular conformation problem. *Journal of Global Optimization*, 5:229–241, 1994.

[22] J.C. Picard and H.D. Ratliff. Minimum cuts and related problems. *Networks*, 5:357–370, 1974.

[23] A.C. Williams. Quadratic 0-1 programming using the roof duality with computational results. Technical Report 8-85, RUTCOR, 1985.

Solving Conflicts and Sanctions: Results of an Experimental Study

Ulrike Leopold-Wildburger[1], Joerg H. Schütze[1], Alois Lafer[1], Markus Glawischnig[1], Maximilian K. P. Jung[2]

1 Department of Statistics and Operations Research
2 Department of Accounting and Auditing
Karl Franzens University Graz, Austria

The authors gratefully acknowledge several valuable suggestions from Lutz Beinsen.

We gratefully acknowledge the support of this work by the Austrian Science Foundation (FWF P13919-OEK).

Abstract

In our study we intend to gain insight into the behaviour of individuals in conflict situations which can be interpreted as sanctions. There are hardly any models of sanctions in literature which can be compared with this idea. An experiment is modelled to analyse the behaviour of individuals in a situation similar to a sequential prisoners' dilemma. Contingent decisions give us the chance to measure punishment and sanctions.
Our approach is similar to an extended model by Bolton, Brandts and Ockenfels (1997), in order to analyse reciprocity in a single framework together with the help of a questionnaire.
In our paper we concentrate on whether the attitude towards fairness coincides with the attitude towards the application of sanctions. Further on we will observe that gender and age of the subjects participating has an influence on the degree of punishment used.
Results seem to indicate that the role assigned to each participant strongly influences her/his actions towards her/his counterpart. We suppose the reason for this behaviour is that more experienced/older individuals think more about the payoff for their competitors, while less experienced/younger individuals behave significantly more selfishly.
Our objectives are to gain more insight into behaviour in dilemma situations and also seek better explanations for individual decisions. Some of the results could help to solve problems concerned with sanctions.

Keywords: Sanctions, simple dilemma games, reciprocity, value laden situations, experimental economics

1 Introduction

Most current work in experimental economics still assumes that economic agents try to maximise utility within certain limits posed by the incompleteness and uncertainty of the information available to them. An important potential area of research is to discover how choices change if there are other departures from the axioms of rational choice. For example: substituting goals of attaining specified aspiration levels (satisficing) for goals of maximisation or the question of reciprocity as a basis for action.

In our paper *reciprocity* is a key concept for analysing the choices of individuals. We understand reciprocity as *helping those who help you, and hurting those who hurt you.* (Rabin 1993, Bolton et al. 1997).

Reciprocity of punishment is a well known phenomenon which arises in the context of the problem of commons. If a decision is not respected enough, some members may be suspected of surpassing the limit. There are several ways of dealing with a suspicion. In some cases they are treated privately or in a hidden or even secret way (Ostrom, Walker and Gardner 1992). Ostmann (1994) considers a common that allows for control. Commons are said to ruin the shared resource. In order to gain more insight in those processes, laboratory experimentation can be used to produce data that is rarely available in field.

In what follows we concentrate on a somewhat different question. We take into consideration the following situation: Inspired by current political sanctions, this experiment attempts to mirror a typical situation, which is analysed within a framework of experimental economics. Our objectives are to gain more insight into behaviour in dilemma situations and also seek better explanations for individual decisions. Some of the results should help to solve problems concerned with sanctions.

In the following chapter we give an excerpt of the documentation for the experiment, namely for the so-called positive case.

2 The Experiment McCockerel

The Cover Story and the Overall Setting
The situation concerns farmers in Venezuela/South America. Fifteen farmers form a collective chicken farm in Venezuela called McCockerel.
Each farmer has a number of chickens and one cockerel. The organisation of the farm, namely keeping the chickens, buying food, running marketing and PR actions etc., is undertaken jointly.
Suddenly there is a suspicion: The cockerel belonging to Farmer A is suspected by the other 14 farmers of having a gene defect, because several abnormal chicks have been incubated. However, this could also be the result of pure chance.
There is a danger for the whole of the collective that the profit might decrease if it becomes public knowledge that the chickens could perhaps have a defect. The other 14 farmers - from now on referred to as Farmer group C - are represented by Camillo. Farmer group C suspects that Farmer A's cockerel is responsible for some defects found in several of their fledglings.

Farmer A can choose between two different strategies: He can either continue as usual, or he can undertake his own Public Relations (PR) campaign.
In other words, Farmer A can opt for A1, which means Public Relations as usual or Farmer A can also opt for A2, meaning changed Public Relations using the slogan: Farmer A's chickens from McCockerel are a good alternative! Changed Public Relations influence the quantities and therefore to a certain extent also the profit for Farmer A and the profit for the Farmer group C.
Camillo has the following options: His strategy set consists of six possibilities: {C1, C2, C3, C4, C5, C6}, whereby C1 stands for maximum separation and C6 stands for maximum co-operation, and the remaining four strategies fall in between.
Camillo has to decide on his strategy. To give a better overview, the most extreme strategies are explained as follows:
C1 means maximum separation. In this case, Camillo decides to present the chickens from his group as especially healthy, using the slogan: Farmer C's chickens are the right choice!
Sepáration has certain consequences for both groups. The consequence for Farmer A, however, is the following: Negative Public Relations decrease the demand for Farmer A's chickens and subsequently lower the profit he receives for his chickens.
C6 means maximum co-operation. In this case, Camillo decides to present the chickens from the whole group as usual, for example using the slogan: All chickens from McCockerel are great! Here, however, we have to be aware of the dilemma: Decreasing profits as a consequence of the common market! Consequence for Farmer A: Positive Public Relations increase the demand for Farmer A's chickens and subsequently the profit.

However, the profits for the chickens are not only dependent on Camillo's decisions.
As tensions exist between Camillo and Farmer A, their choices of action are taken simultaneously without knowing how the other party will act (this is a one-shot game). However, to reflect the real situation of a punishment process in which sanctions are imposed, we wanted to simulate a step by step process (i.e. Farmer A's decision is given and Camillo is asked to react by choosing his actions).
Since we would like to know each individual's decisions on behalf of both parties, we asked subjects to answer as both Farmer A and Camillo.
In an experimental study, we asked the subjects to choose strategies represented by the payoff matrix in Fig. 1.

			Camillo					
			Separating ←		PR	→	co-operating	
			C1	C2	C3	C4	C5	C6
Farmer A	a1 ☐	*Public relations as usual*	***900*** / 1650	***1100*** / 16[illegible]	***1300*** / 15[illegible]	***1500*** / 1500	***1700*** / 1450	***1900*** / 14[illegible]
	a2 ☐	*Changed public relations*	***1000*** / 1250	***1200*** / 1200	***1400*** / 1150	***1600*** / 1100	***1800*** / 1050	***2000*** / 1000

Fig. 1: Payoff matrix from the McCockerel Experiment
Payoffs for the row player Farmer A are given in italics in the upper left corner, Payoffs for the columns player Camillo are underlined and given in the lower right corner.

The subjects were asked to choose an action by checking the appropriate box for the ROW for Farmer A and afterwards the box for the appropriate COLUMN for group C.
These tasks were described as follows: "Please take on the role of Farmer A: Decide whether to proceed with Public Relations as usual or changed Public Relations. Your profit is also influenced by Camillo's choice of action. Your profit is given in bold italics in the top left corner. Camillo's profit is given in the bottom right corner. Please choose your ROW by ticking the boxes for Public Relations as usual or changed Public Relations:"
"Now change roles: Please take on the role of Camillo! Choose the course and extent of action for Camillo's Public Relations campaign. There are six alternatives. Your choice effects your profit (given in the bottom right corner). However, your profit is also influenced by Farmer A's actions (whether he chooses Public Relations as usual versus changed Public Relations). Farmer A's profit is given in italics in the top left corner."

The next decision for the participants is based on the assumption that Farmer A's strategy for Public Relations remains unchanged. Therefore the participants can choose from six strategies from six boxes above the columns to be checked.
The same task is given based on the assumption that Farmer A follows a strategy of changed Public Relations.

Afterwards the participants are asked to choose a column for the situation in which they have no knowledge of Farmer A's strategy.

Finally the subjects should say what strategy they would expect from Farmer A.

The dilemma of the sanctions consists in the following: If Farmer A is inclined to act together with the others then his Public Relations action remains unchanged. In this case his own profit will be less than if he acts alone with changed Public Relations using his slogan about the new alternative.
Camillo could also decide to act jointly with Farmer A or to act without him. Separation means declining sales results. However, it means higher payoffs for Camillo.

Special Settings
The most important hypothesis on sanctions refers to reciprocity and punishment. We used the unifying design, with the 6 column case similar to Bolton et al, offering different payoff matrices with two rows for Farmer A to choose from (PR as usual versus changed PR).
Although there was a constant reference row, the row above or below was different for the settings. So-called positive, negative and neutral settings were used:

The Degree of Punishment is measured as the difference between Camillo's choice when Farmer A decides on PR as usual and his choice when Farmer A decides on a strategy of changed PR.

Positive Setting
As introduced in the documentation above, the non-reference row consisted of lower payoffs for Camillo than the reference row.
Choosing the reference row has a negative impact on the row player's profit.

Negative Setting
The same documentation, but the Figures used were in each case 400 monetary units higher for Farmer C and 100 monetary units lower for Farmer A.
The non-reference row consisted of higher payoffs than the reference row.
Choosing the reference row has a positive impact on the row player's profit.

Free Setting / Neutral Setting
Both rows were the same: the reference row.
This was used for control reasons only (column player as dictator)
Here we used a slightly different documentation due to the identical distributions.

One import concept can be introduced by the analysis of the ratio between the profit of Camillo and the profit of Farmer A for the top and for the bottom row: The product of the ratios will referred as non weighed geometric average choice (geo. average choice) or weighed geometric average choice (geo. average choice weighed).

In the given documentation (so-called positive case) we can compute these as follows.

Geo. average choice =
square root of {(profit ratio C/A top row) * (profit ratio C/A bottom row)}

In our documentation chosen profit ratios can be further weighed with the sixth root of the product of the ratios of the profits: $\{(1650/900)*(1600/1100)*(1550/1300)*(1500/1500)*(1450/1700)*(1400/1900)\}^{1/6}$
= 1,12 (weight factor top row)
The same procedure accounts for the bottom row, where we get 0,77 (weight factor bottom row)

Example
If Camillo decides for the second column for the top row and the first column for the bottom row the geo. average choice is computed as square root of (1600/1100 * 1250/1000), which is about 1,35.

This shows, that Camillo takes in average a 35% bigger piece for himself compared to that one he leaves for Farmer A.

The geo. average choice weighed would be:
square root of {(1600/1100)/1,12 * (1250/1000)/0,77}=1,45
This enables us to compare the choices taking into account the different options in the settings.

The Questionnaire
A questionnaire was used to provide complementary information about the intentions of the subjects. For questions requiring a degree of consent or agreement, the following question set-up was used:

Sunshine increases physical well-being.

I completely agree [/] I completely disagree

The above choice indicates (position far to the left) that you agree to a great extent.

The following section explains those questions which are relevant to results presented in this paper and which do not usually form part of a standard questionnaire:

Fairness Question

During the experiment, it was important for me to distribute the available amount of money fairly

I completely agree | / | I completely disagree

Egoism Question

During the experiment, it was important for me to maximise my share of the available money

I completely agree | / | I completely disagree

Procedure

The experiments took place at the University of Graz and at Universities in Scandinavia between April 2000 and October 2000.

The participants consisted of 105 graduates and undergraduates of management studies specialising in accounting and operations research. They were recruited in different lectures with the promise of additional points for the finals and a financial compensation.

To compare the overall results in regard to the ratio of the choices we used the 104 Boston/USA cases of Bolton, Brandts and Ockenfels (1997), which were elicited not using any cover story.

Since no computer facilities were necessary, the sessions took place in a seminar room.

At the beginning of each session the participants were introduced to the experimental setting using a written manual. Parts of the manual were presented orally by the experimenter.

After the introduction, the participants had to make choices presented to them in a form. The forms were collected and analysed by the experimenter to calculate monetary payoffs.

Monetary incentives were offered to the participants: Depending on a randomly chosen question, the participant received one tenth of the profit resulting from a playoff against another participant in the opposite role. The payments varied between roughly 2.5 Euro and 12 Euro.

The questionnaires and payments were carried out anonymously using different code numbers.

The experiment required about 30 minutes per session plus around ten minutes for the anonymous payments.

3 Results

One of the main results we want to report before going into the details is the following remarkable observation: Some subjects rewarded the co operation with equal split or a similar payoff. In cases, where player A decided for changed Public Relations, however, player C reacted by choosing his strategy C1 as a form of separation too.

A sort of consistency check should be used before introducing the concept of punishment/sanctions.

Location of the game and geometric average choice
At first we investigate whether the overall setting including the location of the game has an influence on the geometric average of the choice ratios.
For this task, we use a box-plot:

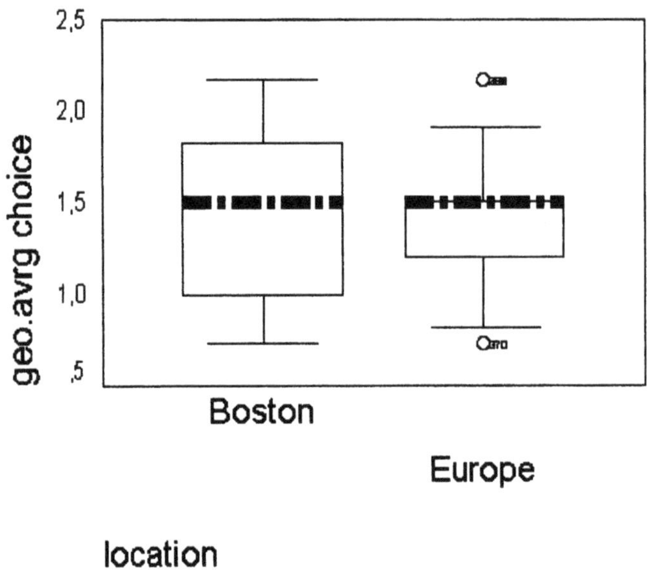

Fig. 2: Geometric average of the distributional choice

Therefore we assert:
H0: The overall setting of the game and geometric average of the choice ratios are independent of each other .
H1: The overall setting of the game and geometric average of the choice ratios are not independent of each other.
Using a U-Test we cannot reject H_0 ($Z = -1.073$, $p= 0.283$, two-tailed).

We have a closer look for the different settings:

Setting	Boston (N = 104)	Europe (N = 105)
Negative	1.76	1.77
Free	1.44	1.46
Positive	1.32	1.31

Table 1: Location, setting and geometric average choice

We conclude that in average the participants in both locations decide in a very similar way.

Sanctions and Fairness

We have in mind the obvious hypothesis that subjects differentiate their behavior according to Farmer A's conduct. Therefore we distinguish between participants who always choose the same column with a vertical movement (insistent) and participants who decide for different positions depending on the situation with a diagonal movement (severe in punishment).

In those cases in which Farmer A decides for strategy A1 subjects take advantage of the full range of choices from C1 to C6. With other words they are exhausting all opportunities of choices. If Farmer A decides for strategy A2 we expect the vast majority to choose C1, which is obviously the dominant strategy of Camillo.

Here in Fig. 3 we present the column decisions for the case of A1 (top row of the payoff matrix of Fig. 1)

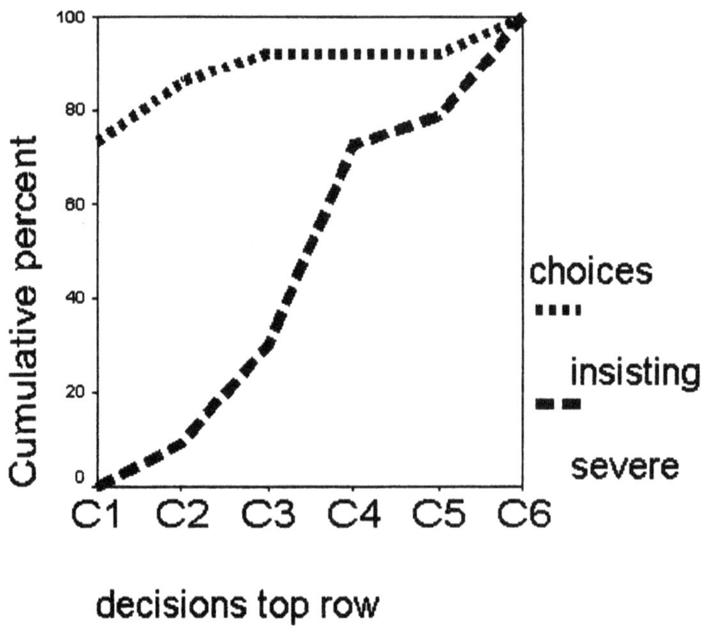

Fig. 3: Degree of punishment/sanction and choice for the top row

The lines here are obviously significantly different.
The lines support our hypothesis about punishment/sanctions: subjects who punish more severely are more inclined to choose the dominant position.

Taking game theory into account one has to compare game theoretical concepts for solving such a dilemma game situation with the actual behaviour. Therefore we state the following hypotheses:

H_0: Punishment is chosen independently of the game theoretical advice to choose the dominant strategy (sub-game perfect equilibrium point).
H_1: Punishment is not chosen independently.

	Dominant choice	Non-dominant choice
A1: top row	67.6	32.4
A2: bottom row	45.7	54.3

Table 2: Dominance in regard to different rows

For the bottom row we have to reject H_0 (Chi-square = 13.038, p = 0.000, df=1), whereas we cannot reject H_0 for the top row case (Chi-square = .771, p = 0.380, df=1).

This is obviously a clear indication that subjects significantly help Farmer A when he chooses co-operation.

Using a box-plot we visually check the impact of the fairness goal on sanctions in Fig. 3:

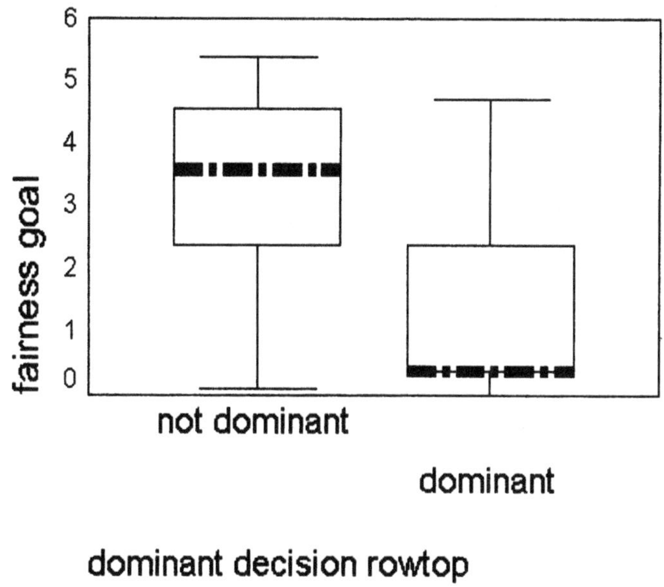

Fig. 4: Dominance and fairness

In order to compare actual decisions with the answers given in the questionnaire, we state the following hypotheses:

H_0 : Participants take the dominant position independently of their reported degree of fairness.

H_1: Participants chose their position dependently on their reported fairness

Using a U-Test we have to reject H_0 (U= - 6.144, p= 0.000, two-tailed).

We will now as well take distributional indicators into account.

Egoism and choice

In order to compare actual decisions with the answers given in the questionnaire, we state the following hypotheses:

H_0 : Participants decide their stake independently of their reported degree of egoism

H_1: Participants decide their stake dependently on their reported degree of egoism

Using a U-Test we have to reject H_0 ($U= -4.172$, $p= 0.000$, two-tailed).

We visualise this with the help of a box-plot:

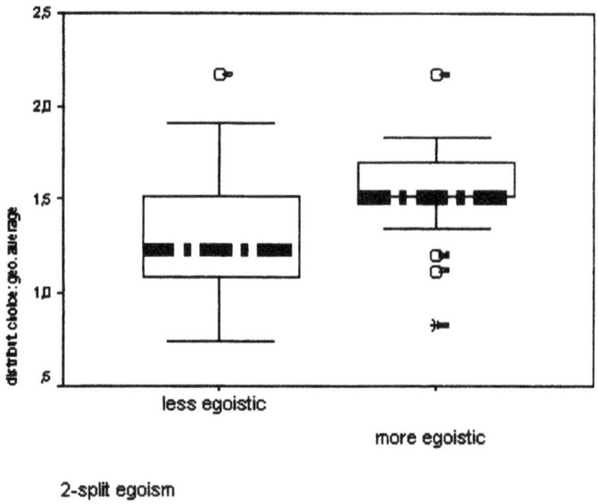

Fig. 5: Average choice and egoism over all settings

We compare the average decisions:

Setting	Geometric average choice
Less egoistic	1.24
More egoistic	1.51

Table 3: Choice compared with low and high egoism

Those individuals who report a low degree of egoism are contend with 24 % more than Farmer A gets, while those reporting a higher degree of egoism take 51 % more than what they give.

A similar result can be obtained by comparing the different settings:

Degree of egoism	Geometric average choice		
	Negative	Free	Positive
less egoistic	1.57	1.36	1.18
more egoistic	1.91	1.83	1.41

Table 4: Choice and egoism

Gender

It is often assumed that the behavior of male and female subjects is different. It is reported, for example, that males behave more strategically, whereas the behaviour of females is driven by the notion of care. Therefore we assert a strong correlation between gender and the severity of punishment. We state the following hypotheses:
H0: Punishment is independent of gender
H1: The degree of punishment is dependent on gender

According to the U-test we cannot reject H_0 ($z = -0.884$, $p = 0.377$, two-tailed).

For the preferences per setting we state the following hypotheses:

H0: The degree of punishment is independent of gender.
H1: The degree of punishment is dependent on gender.

While we cannot reject H0 for the free ($z = -1.054$, $p = 0.292$, two-tailed) and positive case ($z = -0.261$, $p = 0.794$, two-tailed) while we have reject H0 in the negative setting ($z = -2.421$, $p = 0.15$, two-tailed).

	Geometric average choice		
Gender	Negative	Free	Positive
Female	1.90	1.45	1.29
Male	1.55	1.47	1.32

Table 5: choice and gender

The negative case shows males to be content with 55 % more for themselves compared to Farmer A's stake, while females take a 90 % bigger share than what they leave for Farmer A.

Influence of age

The subjects behavior' varies with their age. Therefore we want to check whether the participants' age (elicited in the questionnaire) corresponds with their actual behaviour. This can be done by comparing their geometric average distributional choice.

For this purpose we state the following hypotheses:
H_0: Choices are independent of the age.
H_1: Punishments/sanctions are dependent on the age.
The U-test confirms that we have to reject H_0 ($z = -1.695$, $p = 0.09$, two-tailed).

We check this with the help of a box-plot:

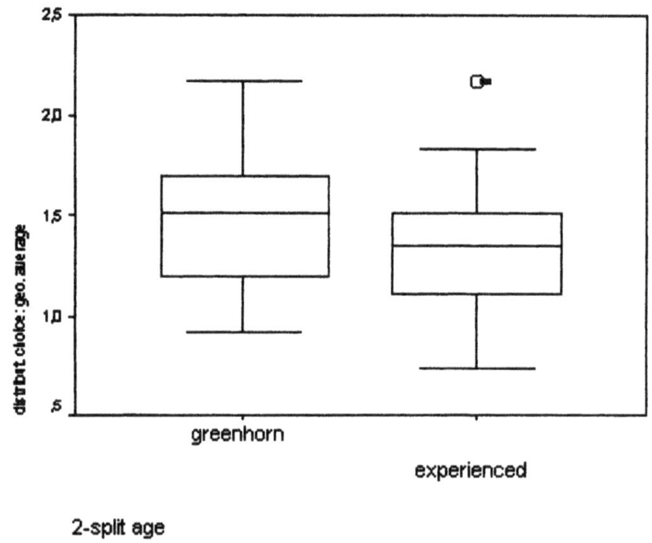

Fig. 6: Geometric average of the choice and age two-split in a box-plot

While the experienced take in average a 36 % bigger part compared to Farmer A's, the greenhorns insist on a 51 % bigger stake compared to what they leave for Farmer A.

Type	Farmer A decides "PR as usual"	Farmer A defects with "Changed PR"	Geometric Average
Greenhorns	1.25	1.83	1.51
Experienced	1.25	1.46	1.36

Table 6: Choice and age two-split: Single cases and geometric average

4 Summary

The results indicate that non-economic parameters, such as age, semester and gender have a substantial influence on decision-making.

This suggests that subjects do not act in accordance with the traditional model of the economic (wo)man referred to as the *homo oeconomicus*. The economic (wo)man would employ backward induction to solve the decision-making and would only be influenced by the economic parameters given by the payoff matrix given in the experiment.

On the other hand, the results can be interpreted using the forward induction principle. Subjects are used to employing algorithms which they have learnt from actual long-term relationships in everyday life. This is then applied in the experiment although actual long term relationships do not exist in laboratory situations. Perhaps the participants avoid sanctions in order to induce future reciprocity. Less experienced individuals think more about the payoff for their competitors, while more experienced individuals behave significantly more selfishly.

This paper shows that the attitude towards fairness coincides with the attitude towards the application of sanctions and also that gender and age influence the degree of sanctions.

It is up to you to associate the ideas in this paper with the political situation concerning Austria between February and September 2000.

References

Becker, Otwin, Kuehrer, M., Leopold-Wildburger, U., Forecasting, Encyclopaedia of Optimisation, Kluwer, Boston, 2001.(forthcoming).

Bolton, Gary E./Brandts J./Ockenfels, A.(1997) Measuring Motivations for the Reciprocal Responses: Observed in a Simple Dilemma Game, Pre-print No. 34, University Magdeburg.

Leopold-Wildburger, U. (1992a). Payoff divisions on coalition formation in a three-person characteristic function experiment. Journal of Economic Behaviour and Organisation 17, 183-93.

Leopold-Wildburger, U. (1992b). Regression analysis of co-operative payoff divisions. A contribution to experimental economics. Operations Research 91, 417-422.

Leopold-Wildburger, U. (1993). Experimental economics. In W. Diewert, K. Spremann, F. Stehling (eds.): Mathematical modelling, Heidelberg: Springer, 673-680.

Leopold-Wildburger, U., Lafer, A., Schütze, J.H. (2000) . McCockerel Solving Conflicts & Sanctions -Measuring Individual Punishment and Reciprocity in a simple value-laden Dilemma Game submitted to: EJOR

Ostmann, A. (1994), An Experimental Fishing Coop, Working Paper, University of Saarbrücken, April-1994, Saarbrücken.

Ostmann, A., Leopold-Wildburger, U. (1995). On Styles of Relating to Bargaining Partners, Albers W., Güth, W.,et al.(eds.) Understandig Strategic Interaction - Essays in Honour of Reinhard Selten, Springer, Berlin.

Ostmann, Axel, Wojtyniak, B. Beckenkamp, M. (1997): Control and Sanctions May Destroy Commons: Experimental Results and Some Microanalytical Explications. Working Paper in Game Theory and Experimental Economics 7. Department of Statistics and Mathematical Economics, University of Karlsruhe.

Ostrom, E., Walker, J. (1997). Neither Markets nor States: Linking Transformation Processes in Collective Action Arenas. In D. Mueller (ed.), Perspectives on Public Choice: A Handbook, Cambridge, Cambridge University Press, p. 35-72.

Ostrom, E., Walker, J. (1992) Ostrom, E., Covenants with and without a Sword: Self-governance is Possible. *American Political Science Review* 86, 404-17.

Roth, A. (1995), Bargaining Experiments, in: Kagel/Roth (eds.), Handbook of Experimental Economics.

Selten, R. (1998): Aspiration Adaptation Theory, Journal of Mathematical Psychology 42, 192 – 214.

Selten, R. (1999): What is Bounded Rationality, SFB Discussion Paper B-454, University of Bonn, Paper prepared for the Dahlem Conference 1999.

Selten, R. & Schuster, K. (1970). Psychologische Faktoren bei Koalitionsverhandlungen. In H.Sauermann (ed.): Beiträge zur Experimentellen Wirtschaftsforschung Vol.II.. Tübingen: Mohr 99-135.

GPSR Compliance
The European Union's (EU) General Product Safety Regulation (GPSR) is a set of rules that requires consumer products to be safe and our obligations to ensure this.

If you have any concerns about our products, you can contact us on

ProductSafety@springernature.com

In case Publisher is established outside the EU, the EU authorized representative is:

Springer Nature Customer Service Center GmbH
Europaplatz 3
69115 Heidelberg, Germany

www.ingramcontent.com/pod-product-compliance
Lightning Source LLC
Chambersburg PA
CBHW071237230926
51849CB00001B/129
* 9 7 8 3 7 9 0 8 1 3 7 3 9 *